Praise for *The Great American Ale Trail*

WINNER, SOC. OF AMERICAN TRAVEL WRITERS FOUNDATION LOWELL THOMAS TRAVEL JOURNAL.

←———•———→

"... Men and women who like their drinks simple, cold and on tap
will appreciate *The Great American Ale Trail*, in which Christian DeBenedetti
heralds 'a new golden age of American beer,' reporting state by state on the
country's best taverns and brewhouses. 'Balanced but tangy,' like the Duet beer
he tastes in a mountain town in California, this book whets a prodigious thirst."
—Liesl Schillinger, *The New York Times*, Dec. 16, 2011

"Christian DeBenedetti's book is proof that God loves us and wants us to be happy."
—Jack Hitt, author, *Bunch of Amateurs: A Search for the American Character*

"Here is joyful evidence that doomsayers who lament the dumbing-down of
America's taste are only Chicken Littles. *The Great American Ale Trail* posits that in
fact we are, right now, enjoying the Golden Age of craft beer, offering as evidence a
guide to hundreds of bars, breweries, and even barbecues around the nation that make
and/or serve the best of it. What a roadmap for taste-bud adventure! With this book in
hand, anyone who prizes good beer need never go thirsty again."
—Jane and Michael Stern, authors of *Roadfood*

"From sea to foaming sea, we've become a great Beer Hoisting Nation. And Christian
DeBenedetti is our convivial, savvy, and good-humored guide. The result of his dedicated
wanderings is a tangy compendium that's part travelogue, part practical handbook, and part
cultural history, giving us fresh perspective on the Hop Revolution that has quietly overtaken
our land, one pint at a time. Carry this book with you on your own cross-continental travels,
and bring it home stained and sour—a field manual soaked with happy memories."
—Hampton Sides, Editor-at-Large, *Outside* magazine and author of *In the Kingdom of Ice*;
Hellhound on His Trail; *Blood and Thunder*; *Ghost Soldiers*; and *Americana*.

"Some people know where they are going early on. Take Christian DeBenedetti.
He graduated college, received a fellowship and did the logical thing: He used
the fellowship to study traditional beer-making in Europe and West Africa. He was
then mentored by legendary British beer writer Michael Jackson. Now DeBenedetti
is a respected beer journalist with his first book, *The Great American Ale Trail*."
—Lynne Rossetto Kasper, host of NPR's *The Splendid Table*, Jan. 11, 2013

The
GREAT
AMERICAN
ALE TRAIL

←——————→

THE CRAFT BEER LOVER'S GUIDE
TO THE BEST WATERING HOLES IN THE NATION

←————·————→

REVISED EDITION

Christian DeBenedetti

PREFACE BY GARRETT OLIVER

RUNNING PRESS
PHILADELPHIA · LONDON

FOR MOM & CHUCK, THE "TRAVELING COMPANIONS"

© 2016 by Christian DeBenedetti

Published by Running Press, A Member of the Perseus Books Group
All rights reserved under the Pan-American and International Copyright Conventions

Printed in the United States.

Books published by Running Press are available at special discounts for bulk purchases in the United
States by corporations, institutions, and other organizations. For more information, please contact the
Special Markets Department at the Perseus Books Group, 2300 Chestnut Street, Suite 200, Philadelphia,
PA 19103, or call (800) 810-4145, ext. 5000, or e-mail special.markets@perseusbooks.com.

ISBN 978-0-7624-5969-8
Library of Congress Control Number: 2015960852
E-book ISBN 978-0-7624-4476-2

10 9 8 7 6 5 4 3 2 1
Digit on the right indicates the number of this printing

Cover design by Daniel Cantada
Book design by Amanda Richmond
Illustrations by Ryan Hayes
Edited by Jessica Fromm
Typography: Eames, Garage Gothic, and Fenway Park

Running Press Book Publishers
2300 Chestnut Street
Philadelphia, PA 19103-4371

Visit us on the web!
www.runningpress.com

CONTENTS

←———→

Preface

←———————→

WHEN THE BOARDING PASS EMERGED FROM THE WHIRRING MACHINE AT HELSINKI-VAN-taa Airport, I had to admit that I was relieved. I hadn't intended things to turn out this way, but this is what always happens, and I really should have known better. Only seven hours previously, I'd been at the pub—St. Urho's Pub, to be precise—a slightly grubby watering hole in one of the lesser-known districts of Helsinki, Finland. Finns speak a language intelligible to no one else on earth, but that has never slowed them down, especially when it comes to socializing. So now here I was, with Markku, Jussi, Kari, and a few others, telling improbable stories. I pinged my pal Matt on Facebook and told him I was drinking his beer in Helsinki. He picked up in England and pinged me back within minutes, asking how it was holding up. The beer was beautiful, and it was a fine evening—all about the ebullient company, and the company was all about the beer. St. Urho's has more than a dozen taps, all flowing with excellent beers, lovingly kept. I didn't mean to stay until 3 a.m., but that's what you do, and the reindeer pizza really *was* excellent.

I've been lucky enough to experience many evenings like this over the years. I started in the early 1980s in London, where I first fell in love with cask-conditioned British ale. I continued across Europe, racking up epic evenings in Germany, Belgium, and the Czech Republic. In those days, there was one country where great beer was not to be found, and that was the United States. I got back home from a year abroad in 1984 and found that we Americans had nothing to drink. Somehow the United States—once home to 4,000 breweries and the most exciting and varied beer culture in the world— had lost its way among the great brewing nations. Our breweries fell prey to a form of "progress" that involved removing all the flavor from one of the world's diverse and fascinating drinks. Like many future craft brewers, I started making my own beer at home—not because I wanted to *make* beer, but because I wanted to *drink* beer. Slowly but inevitably, beer took over my life, the slope became slippery, and I slid into the mash tun. I bobbed to the surface and never looked back.

Today, out of nothing, we have built everything. The United States is now the undisputed beer capital of the world, home to the most vibrant beer culture anywhere. It is difficult to overstate how unlikely this seemed twenty years ago. A newly minted craft brewer, I traveled to Europe frequently, and when I told people that I was an American brewer, the scorn was palpable. *Yes, we've heard of your American beer,* they sneered. I protested that Americans were making very flavorful beers now, but heads shook with disbelief. Slowly, however, over the late 1990s and into the 2000s, it dawned on the rest of the world that Americans had woken up to beer, and once awake we'd gotten mighty busy.

While some built breweries, others built restaurants, bars, bowling alleys, and movie theaters around great beer. Not only did we have our own beer—we had everyone else's beer, too. The complex beers of Belgium, the fruity ales of England, the malty, bracing lagers of Bavaria—all began to flow from America's taps. Great restaurants, once content with lengthy fine wine lists and dismissive gas-station beer lists, started to realize that industrial beer was an insult to their food and to their beer-savvy patrons. Today I can find the best beers of Belgium faster in a twenty-minute walk from my front door in Brooklyn than I could walking from Grande Place in Brussels.

Do you know beer places and beer people? You should, because beer brings on a sort of fellowship that wine rarely inspires. When you get off a plane and head into an American town, do you know where to find the best of everything, places where people speak your language? Frankly, despite having been all over the world, I can't say that I do. But that's okay, because we have Christian DeBenedetti to show the way. I've read many beer books, of course, but none that capture the spirit, the philosophy, the people, and the feeling of the American beer scene the way that *The Great American Ale Trail* does. This book will tell you what you really want to know—where to go, why you want to go there, how the place came to be, what kind of food they serve, what types of beers you can enjoy with it, and who's going to be sitting next to you at the bar. At the same time, you'll read the stories of men and women who turned their backs on lucrative careers, mortgaged their houses, and put everything on the line to follow their passions and build the kinds of places where they'd want to spend their time. Occasionally, just *occasionally*, until 3 a.m. So read this book, follow Christian's well-laid path, and build your own ale trail. You'll have epic evenings with good people and the world's most exciting beverage. And if you should miss your plane, don't worry. Another one will leave soon. In the meantime, there is some awfully nice beer at the airport bar.

—Garrett Oliver

Garrett Oliver is the brewmaster of the Brooklyn Brewery and the author of the award-winning book, The Brewmaster's Table. *He is also editor-in-chief of* The Oxford Companion to Beer *(2011), and has hosted more than 700 beer events in ten countries.*

Introduction

←——————→

THE MOUNTAINS AHEAD ARE BRUSHED WITH CALIFORNIA CHAPARRAL AND PIÑON JUNIPER, bathed in low angle sunlight, but I'm pulling over in the quiet little town of Alpine, California—a forty-minute drive into the Coast Range foothills outside of San Diego— to visit Alpine Brewing Company. Now the sweet, earthy smells of steeping grains and the tang of hops envelop me. It is mid-2010. There Pat McIlhenney, a former full-time fire captain with a handlebar mustache, is leading a tour of his handmade brewhouse built in an old TV-repair shop. His operation has been racking up accolades in global competitions. "I cannot make beer fast enough," he says, handing out samples.

Those beers were among the finest I've tasted anywhere: his balanced but tangy Duet is full of the fresh, citrusy flavors of Simcoe and Amarillo hops and a grainy, toasty backbone. Even back then, before his bar or taproom were ready, a stream of visitors—beer pilgrims—comes in to meet McIlhenney and buy fresh-brewed beers to go. (Today, Alpine has wide distribution in a partnership with Green Flash.) It's a scene I find again and again across the United States, in cozy beer bars and small-batch breweries, even anodyne cul-de-sacs. Where are they going next?

Ask Tim Belk. On a hazy day in the summer of 2015, he stopped by my family's farm, in Oregon, clutching a well-loved copy of this book's first edition, which was released in late 2011. With beer stains, notes in the margins, and, incredibly, fully half the destinations checked

off, that exact book had carried its owner from his home in Austin, Texas, across the nation. He'd heard about my little brewery under construction and wanted to pay a visit. If there was any moment I knew I had to update my first literary labor of love, it was then. My handheld, analog, old-school guidebook had led a beer lover on a great adventure, but now there was so much more to share. Tim, thank you again. Aside from getting the book published in the first place, that may have been my proudest moment as a beer writer yet.

But where to begin? What was true in mid-2011, when the first edition of this book went to press, is even truer today: we are living in the Golden Age of beer, and I have spent the past six years on and off traveling through America to document it. Sure, the big breweries still dominate the cooler aisle, but make no mistake: small-batch "craft" beer (a term related to a brewery's modest size and independent ownership) is roaring back. After the Great Mistake ended in 1933, only the most aggressive, consolidated companies were able to survive; beer drinkers paid the price in flavor and selection. But from the nadir of just forty-four breweries by the end of the 1970s, there are now more than 4,000 from Anchorage to the Big Apple, Kona to Kentucky, surpassing the national brewery count of 125 years ago.

Styles and flavor profiles are cross-pollinating like a botanist's fever dream. Innovation, flavor, choice: all are almost infinite at this stage. Ambitious new breweries are bursting forth like forest mushrooms after a good rain. Since that book first hit the shelves, in late 2011, well over 2,000 new small breweries have opened, and likely as many beer bars, bottle shops, and growler stations. That's more than ever even existed up to 2011—encompassing the craft beer's entire, frenetic, three decade–long rise—from the late 1970s on. To size up this frothy tsunami another way, that's roughly two new breweries per day.

Not even the drinker wild with curiosity, endless free time, and a bottomless travel budget can keep up. Whole brewery districts have formed in cities where the idea of craft beer was alien just a few years ago. Garage-based startups founded in 2010 are buying whole city blocks and winning World Beer Cup medals. A beer bar and tasting menu restaurant in Brooklyn open for a couple of years has a Michelin star—a level of prestige never seen before in beer cuisine. Every day I get a dozen stories in an e-mail news alert based on the phrase "new brewery." The number of options and flavor dimensions and travel possibilities within craft beer have gone completely kaleidoscopic.

There's a simple reason for this: good beer is part of a good life. The late British beer writer Michael Jackson once said, "You wouldn't walk into a restaurant and order 'a plate of food,' so why would you do the same with your beer?" Craft beer is about originality, flavor, and complexity derived from the many malts, hop varieties, yeast strains, water sources, and even oak barrels a brewer can use, no matter where they live.

It's a beautiful sight, even though we all know not all will survive. Few breweries have closed since late 2011, but a few that shall not be named have been swallowed by huge corporations. Why? Isn't good beer worth exploring regardless of ownership? I argue that when it comes to beer, company size and local ownership are relevant. The dreamers who doggedly pursued the art and craft of brewing for years, to get us where we are now, are the heroes of this book, not corporations with $100 million war chests. *The Great American Ale Trail* is a road map of intentional communities and the roads in between, a chart of the ties that bind beer lovers to their favorite places. Some of those now-corporate owned breweries that were featured in volume one were solid, even great, for their time. And I congratulate them on striking it rich. But I won't be writing about many of them in this new edition. This document of the craft beer adventure unfolding is all about the small axes still chipping away, batch by adventurous batch, at the robot-powered factories that continue to churn out—millions of flavorless gallons at a time—90 percent of America's beer.

Like the first edition, this book wanders from region to region, from the forests of the Pacific Northwest where I grew up all the way to the mangroves and palm trees of Florida, where a terrific beer scene is gathering force. In 2015 alone something like fourteen breweries opened in L.A. County. It's a tidal wave of beer. I've traveled as much as I could since the book first came out. What I have found out there is nothing short of amazing. The craft beer revolution has spread to every state, every large city, and to zip codes where, just a couple of years ago, the only beer you could buy came in thirty-six-packs.

Even Portland, Oregon, with about ninety to date, continues to welcome new outposts. And thus, in this primer, there are many more breweries included, but,

no matter what, naysayers will have a field day. What about X, and why hasn't he included Y, Z, and the other 300 flavors of the moment? Readers, hear my plea. Please do not glance in these pages and declare your glass half-full. To cover all the breweries in America, you'd be reading a twenty-volume collection—which would be pointless (and quickly outdated).

Instead, raise a glass to our beery good fortune. The breweries and beer bars included in these pages were selected for outstanding beer, first and foremost, and for breaking trail in areas where craft beer was once unheard of. Many have won recognition at the World Beer Cup and Great American Beer Festival (GABF) and have a tap handle or three in the most discerning beer bars. Others have taken their ambitions into the barrel, dedicating entire operations to the art of aging beer in oak casks, once a niche, experimental side of beer. As for those cut from volume one, some simply closed, sold out to faceless corporate owners—removing some of the appeal, for a small-town guy like myself—or never really evolved. Others were still good but simply had to be cut to make space for the dozens of worthy new destinations I include—almost 150 new spots. Was it easy? Not on your life. It's agonizing to choose between great beer scenes. But with almost 500 places to whet your thirst, I hope you'll crack the book and say, "Wow, what a great selection. Where to start?"

A wonderful thing happens when you travel with beer in mind: the world opens up in a more friendly way. During my travels, I met hundreds of dedicated, inspiring American brewers, barkeeps, chefs, and beer lovers, every one in love with the art and science of brewing. There's a bit of luck and joy in all this, but there's also a lot of hard work. So wander and bring a map, too: in this book, spots are organized in clusters, generally speaking, but not always. And talk to people: in every single one of the places in this book, you're going to meet pilgrims hitting the road for the love of beer. You're not likely to meet warmer and more friendly people. And along the way, I hope *The Great American Ale Trail* will help posit a new definition of craft beer: The growing love of artisan-made brews isn't because beer is becoming more like wine. It's becoming more beer-like.

Think of this humble offering as a heartfelt, if necessarily nonencyclopedic,

roadmap of inspiration. If you've been to many, or even half of these, toast that, too. Then hand off the book, dog-eared and beer-stained, to another beer lover. Celebrate the abundance of this unique era by reading, sharing, and exploring, making your own ale trails, tasting your own way to a deeper understanding of and appreciation for the alchemy of malt, hops, yeast, and pure water. Brewing goes back to our Founding Fathers, and eons earlier, when Sumerians recorded beer batches as prayers in clay tablets. We're tapping into something ancient, something necessary. To the lucky ones who know, it makes perfect sense. And I hope that with this book, you'll begin your own search. The only question is: Where to go first?

—Christian DeBenedetti
Newberg, Oregon
December, 2015

The PACIFIC NORTHWEST and ALASKA

OREGON

THANKS TO A BAND OF BOLD BREWING PIONEERS STARTING IN THE LATE 1970S AND early '80s, the entire state is blessed with hoppy wonders, with Portland as its shining beer capital. Today, there are no less than 90 breweries and counting in and around the small city of 600,000 known to many as Beervana. Some say it's the rain driving drinkers indoors; others point to the tough, timber-country ingenuity and independent spirit ingrained in the gene pool. Either way, craft beer is so popular throughout the state, you can pick up an artisan brew at the gas station.

The history of this good-beer revolution is well documented, but suffice it to say that Portland embraced craft beer early, becoming the brewing epicenter of the Northwest—and arguably the entire United States and even the world—by being both aggressively provincial and always innovative. With access to top-quality grain and regionally grown hops (and relatively inexpensive real estate), brewers thrived amid a population that loves to drink beer as much as it loves to climb, ski, surf, roast fair-trade coffee, build exotic bikes (and ride them around naked—why not?), and forage for mushrooms. It didn't hurt that in the 1970s and '80s the Oregon wine country emerged as a world-class destination amid the stirrings of Oregon's gourmet-inclined Slow Food movement. Throughout the state, from tiny upstarts to established regional and national brands like Widmer, there's no town too small for an excellent brewpub these days. With snowy peaks, smart cities, and verdant forests, what other excuse do you need to visit?

ITINERARIES

1-DAY
Portland: The Commons, Cascade Brewing Barrel House, Bailey's, Gigantic, Higgins

3-DAY
Portland plus wine country and the Columbia Gorge: one-day itinerary plus Wolves & People, Breakside, Belmont Station, Double Mountain, Full Sail, Logsdon, Edgefield

7-DAY
One- and three-day itinerary plus Fort George, Buoy, Deschutes, and Ale Apothecary

Portland

APEX

1216 SE Division St. • Portland, OR
97202 • (503) 273-9227
apexbar.com • Established: 2010

SCENE & STORY

Built in a small industrial garage-like space by former New Belgium Brewing sales representative Jesse McCann, Apex is a squeaky-clean beer bar, which perfectly captures the lifestyle of Portlanders circa 2015: single-speed bike parked out front, barrel-aged Belgian ale in hand. Smoking? Never—that's so last year. Table service? Nope, stretch those legs. (Dogs, kids, and credit cards are also ixnayed.) But lest the scene sound too doctrinaire, it's ideal on a sunny day when you can bike there (you can even borrow a lock from the bar's own stash), grab a taco from the little place next door (no food is sold at the bar), and maybe shoot some pinball. Easy does it, except for the (often) blaring heavy metal.

PHILOSOPHY

Serious about beer—intense, even, but not joyless. "I've been told I keep my beer too cold," says McCann, speaking of scolds, with a wry chuckle. But there are beers that are simply better cold—ice-cold—especially when it's ninety-five degrees in the shade (rare in Portland, but not unheard of). So, thank heavens for one little nod to an older, less uptight mode of beer drinking: amid the list of esoteric brews is a lone "Cheap, Cold" Hamm's can for $2.50—a nice, if ironic, touch.

KEY BEER

McCann brings in bonafide rarities and displays an impressive forty-two-tap selection on a flat-screen TV over the bar, so simply peruse the fast-changing list, try some samples, and engage the beer experts at work behind the bar. There are beers here no other bar in Portland can even think about getting, like Moonlight's Working for Tips, a garnet-colored 5.5% ABV ale spiced with redwood tips instead of hops that's only seldom spotted outside of the Bay Area.

HORSE BRASS PUB

4534 SE Belmont St. • Portland, OR
97215 • (503) 232-2202
horsebrass.com • Established: 1976

SCENE & STORY

It was with heavy but grateful hearts that thousands of fans (present company included) turned out for the wake to honor Horse Brass founder Don Younger in January of 2011 when he died at age sixty-nine from complications related to being a wise, hard-drinking old buzzard. To hear the gray-bearded, long-haired, raspy-voiced Don tell it between puffs on his ever-present smoke, he woke up one day smarting from a big night of beer (and whiskey, which he loved dearly) and discovered he had bought the bar with his brother, Bill, the late Bill Younger.

What happened next helped make Portland the great beer town it is. Bringing in scores of rare and hard-to-find beers, and championing the first efforts of the brewers in town, the Youngers' Horse Brass became one of the most famous and respected beer bars in the land. When Don drove a gray '72 Rolls around town, he did it in a T-shirt. And there was something else about Don: without fanfare, he loaned or simply gave money to a number of earnest young Portlanders trying to get a leg up in beer, in life—Duane Sorenson, founder of Portland's famous Stumptown Coffee Roasters, for one—and never made a fuss about it.

PHILOSOPHY

Generous and communal. The motto of the Horse Brass ("If it were any more authentic, you'd need a passport. . . .") is apt, because it looks as if it were airlifted stick by stone out of old London. But Don also loved to say something a bit cryptic, too, something worth considering only with a beer in hand. "It's not about the beer. It's about the beer," he'd say, and then order you another round—on the house.

KEY BEER

There are fifty taps and seventy-five bottled selections, but before you drink anything else, order the always-on Younger's Special Bitter (YSB), named for Bill, who died first, and raise a toast to the Youngers.

THE COMMONS BREWERY

630 SE Belmont St. • Portland, OR 97214 • commonsbrewery.com
Established: 2011

SCENE & STORY

In 2010, soft-spoken local founder Mike Wright, with almost clairvoyant business sense, decided to expand his garage-based Beetje (meaning "small," in Flemish) 1bbl nanobrewery into a 7bbl system based on a quiet street in southeast Portland. In 2011, Germany-trained, Oregon-native brewery Sean Burke joined the team, and with their superb, Belgian-inflected beers and strong word of mouth, that 700 percent size increase soon proved insufficient. By the middle of 2015, Wright and Co. moved into a stunning, 100-year-old industrial building with massive beams and rafters overhead, and added a 15bbl system and several new fermenters. But all this growth, paradoxically, has seemed, to outsiders at least, unhurried. In the airy, sun-lit taproom with exposed brick and shining, but not showy bar, beer lovers feast on creations like Biere Royale (a yogurt-fermented sour ale with currants) and Myrtle (a citrusy, mimosa-like farmhouse ale) that have won the hearts of beer lovers and judges over and over again. Local cheese impresario (*fromager*, if we're being fancy) Steve Jones installed a kiosk for small cheese plates, an ideal companion to the Commons' Belgium and France-inspired farmhouse-style beers. No visitor to Portland should miss it. And with the "House of Sour" Cascade Barrel House, and multitap, beer-garden blessed Green Dragon pub up the street, the southeast Belmont area of Portland is fast becoming a world-class brewery district.

DETOUR ➡ OREGON BREWERS FESTIVAL

Summer is the ultimate season here, and no weekend says it better than the one known locally as "brewfest"—the OBF, or Oregon Brewers Festival, around the end of July—when upward of 80,000 revelers gather in the city's sprawling Tom McCall Waterfront Park under massive, beer-filled open-air tents, and, every ten minutes or so, spontaneously start cheering like fans at the Super Bowl, glasses held high. 2015 marked the festival's twenty-eighth year.

Chalk the good cheer up to the setting: With the city and its Willamette River as a backdrop, some 100 breweries from around the country show up to pour their latest. Guest brewers are flown in from Denmark and New Zealand. Live bands jam on stages as local-fave restaurants like Horn of Africa proffer healthy, spicy, beer-friendly fare. Trading wooden nickel tokens for tastes, imbibers mingle good-naturedly, old friends reunite, and, as the sun goes down, those cheers grow longer and louder, and, well, a heck of a lot more infectious. When the kegs run dry—*sic transit gloria mundi*—downtown taprooms fill with beer lovers celebrating the bounty until the wee hours. Go early in the day; lines for the buzziest brands form immediately. And keep an eye out for growing, but cozier Portland summer events like the Portland Fruit Beer Fest, which pack a punch in a much smaller format. (oregonbrewfest.com)

SOUR POWER 101
INSIDE THE ART OF SOUR, BARREL-AGED BEERS

To speak beer-ese in Portland, or just about anywhere else these days, you've got to know what makes sour beers pop the way they do. Simply put, they're usually made by fermenting beer with a complex grain bill (for long, slow, layered fermentations) with Lactobacillus and/or other superactive, benign bacteria and wild yeasts, and aging them. This can happen in stainless steel and it can happen in oak barrels that once contained wine, port, sherry, absinthe, rum, whiskey, or bourbon, occasionally with fruits and other flavorings added. After a period of, say, three months to three years, the acidified brews are blended with one another in a stainless-steel tank to taste, at which point fresh fruit additions or brewers' sugars are occasionally added again. Lastly, they're kegged or bottled like Champagne, often with a cork and wire cage. Executed well, these acid-forward ales echo the heft of certain big wines (meaty tannic reds, bright whites, and tawny old ports), and pair well with rich foods like cheese, charcuterie, and pork belly. One look at the beer lists in Portland's top restaurants confirms: sour is the new black.

PHILOSOPHY

Gather around beer is the Commons' mantra, officially. Unofficially, one employee tells me, the modus operandi is "kick ass quietly." They do it well. In a sea of new breweries competing for attention with aggressively hopped beers and thumping heavy metal in the taprooms, the Commons stands out for its methodical, thoughtful, and above all excellency-minded approach.

KEY BEER

Urban Farmhouse, a spicy, classic saison, put the Commons on the map (and pulled down medals including a prestigious World Beer Cup bronze). It's delicious, with a balanced, grassy, peppery bite. Also look for Flemish Kiss, a GABF silver medal–winning Brett pale ale, which has a fruity funkiness made for soft cheeses. Then work your way through their ever-changing list of tart and wild ales, esoteric lagers, and other farmhouse-inspired rarities.

BELMONT STATION

4500 SE Stark St. • Portland, OR
97215 • (503) 232-8538
belmont-station.com • Established: 1997

SCENE & STORY

Founded by Carl Singmaster and the late, legendary publican Don Younger of the Horse Brass in that bar's tiny adjacent alleyway in southeast Portland, Belmont Station was an idea far ahead of its time. With thousands of imported beers, glassware, and other beer-related gifts, it was a hit with locals who would wander in after a pint and perhaps a chat with the irascible, inimitable owner Don Younger, who died in 2011. (Disclosure: By the good graces of Younger, I worked at Belmont Station briefly in its earliest days, helping ship beer, something the place no longer does. I was enormously grateful for the gig.) Since then, the shop has moved a block north to Stark Street and has expanded to include its own bar with 20 taps, 1,200-plus bottles stored behind UV-filtered light, regular tastings, and brewmaster appearances. They even hold their own festival in July: Puckerfest is a weeklong celebration of sour beer.

PHILOSOPHY

Know thy beer. Belmont Station's employees know a ton about beer and are glad to share their wisdom, sans attitude.

KEY BEER

The best beer is the one you taste fresh off one of the twenty taps as you wander the aisles, which is a lot of fun. Simply put, the selection here is incredible: up to date, varied, well cared for, and organized.

UPRIGHT BREWING CO.

240 N. Broadway, Ste. 2 • Portland, OR
97227 • (503) 735-5337
uprightbrewing.com • Established: 2009

SCENE & STORY

You know you're in a serious craft beer town when NBA fans cram into your subterranean taproom for every home game and sip barrel-aged beers before heading to the stadium. Alex Ganum's Upright Brewing Company is located a few paces from the Rose Garden arena, home of the Portland Trail Blazers. Ganum moved to Portland (he's from Michigan originally) for culinary school but fell in love with the beer scene instead. After an internship at the celebrated Brewery Ommegang in Cooperstown, New York, he drew up plans for Upright, and these days his beers are all over town, and his brewing capacity is maxed out.

Still, the brewery (named for Charles Mingus's stringed instrument) remains low-key, with just six wall-mounted taps, a couple of picnic tables, and barrel racks of aging ales to admire as you sip away. Be sure to check out the open steel fermenters behind glass. The five year-round beers are Four (4.5% ABV; light, wheaty, and lightly sour), Five (5.5% ABV and markedly hoppier), Six (spicy and caramel tinged at 6.7% ABV), Seven (8% ABV and floral, aromatic), and the delicious, draft-only Engleberg Pils (5.5% ABV). My advice: order a tasting tray and try every one.

PHILOSOPHY

Ganum's beers exhibit the spice and earthiness of styles Portland brewers haven't explored much until recent years: Belgian saison, bière de garde, and other, sometimes wild barrel-aged experiments resulting in funky, sour, earthy ales. But rather than simply mimicking Low Country classics, Ganum is also stretching out with experiments that place these beers firmly in Oregon soil.

KEY BEER

Upright's April seasonal is Gose (5.2% ABV), based on a near-extinct German style developed in Leipzig, which incorporates salt and ground coriander seeds. The result is an unfiltered wheat beer with a cloudy yellow color and appealingly tart, dry finish. That beer put Ganum on the podium at the 2010 World Beer Cup in Chicago. On the other end the spectrum: several excellent stouts and strong ales, from an award-winning oyster stout to the excellent Billy the Mountain, a fulsome, 9.1% ABV old ale partially aged with *Brettanomyces* (wild yeast), or "brett," wafting aromas of oak, wine, and leather.

BREAKSIDE BREWERY

820 NE Dekum St. • Portland, OR 97211
(503) 719-6475 • breakside.com
Established: 2010

5821 SE International Way
Milwaukie, OR 97222 • (503) 342-6309
breakside.com • Established: 2012

SCENE & STORY

Breakside might as well change their name to "breakneck," as in "breakneck speed." Their rapid-fire approach has been nothing short of remarkable: what started as a 3.5bbl brewpub in the quiet northeast Portland neighborhood of Woodlawn has expanded to include a second, production-focused brewery and twenty-four-tap tasting room (in another location, in southeast Portland's Milwaukie neighborhood), hundreds of beer releases, reams of press, and stacks of medals. The brewpub continues to thrive and the production brewery is up to 20,000 barrels per year. In other words, what might have gone off the rails in less assured hands has evolved into a super-accomplished company. This is arguably Portland's strongest all-around—yet still approachably small—brewery. Lazing on the front patio of the original brewpub on a sunny evening with a passion fruit-infused Berliner weisse, seared wasabi tuna sandwich, and sweet potato fries makes all kinds of sense.

PHILOSOPHY

The logo is a lawn chair, but the MO is overachiever. When, in 2014, Harvard grad and brewmaster Ben Edmunds collected a gold for American Style IPA (in a field of over three hundred entrants), the proof was served up in tangy, near-perfect balance. He'd entered Portland's competitive, world-class beer scene with training at the prestigious Siebel Institute and Doemens Academy in Munich, but with no prior professional experience. Not a bad first few years on the job.

KEY BEER

Breakside's award-winning IPA is a ubiquitous offering in many local taprooms, and even Trader Joe's sells the affordable twenty-two-ounce bottles. It's become a welcome staple. But don't neglect some of Edmunds's more unusual beers, from sour and barrel-aged numbers to the much-loved Salted Caramel Stout, a rich and chocolaty collaboration with Jacobsen's Salt, an innovative sea salt company based on the Oregon Coast.

GIGANTIC BREWING CO.

5224 SE 26th Ave. • Portland, OR 97202
(503) 208-3416 • giganticbrewing.com
Established: 2012

SCENE & STORY

Gigantic is the brainchild of talented local brewers Van Havig and Ben Love. With a 15bbl brewery housed in a quiet industrial section of southeast Portland, this delicious oxymoron of a brewery is anything but huge—except when it comes to flavor. Havig, once a PhD candidate in economics, spent sixteen years with chain brewers Rock Bottom in their downtown Portland location, gaining notoriety by producing beers outpacing the larger chain's reputation, and, as he would cheerfully assent, running off at the mouth at industry conventions. Love, formerly of Pelican (on the coast) and the first head brewer of Portland's Hopworks, plays cheerful yin to Havig's yang, and together, the duo seems to do no wrong, cranking out batch after unique batch with a sure hand (and terrific, pop-art-influenced labels). Among the beers they've gained notice for in a few short years: everything from delicate, hoppy grisette to tawny Russian imperial stouts (the cleverly named "Most Premium"), and an impressive variety in between, many with names rising above the usual stonerish pablum. It's a refreshing approach. And the beer is very good, too.

Gigantic isn't in the center of downtown Portland, but a trip to the taproom offers a clean, well-lit affair with red and gray highlights, soccer games on flat-screens (especially when the Portland Timbers are playing), and outdoor seating made for sunny afternoons (dogs are also welcome). The site was launched with a "Champagne Lounge" as well, which really means you can order a good bottle of champers or a split of prosecco (but none by the glass). It's simply more vintage dry wit from the brewers who brought the world "Geezers Need Excitement," "Whole in the Head," and "the Most Interesting Beer in the World." Well played, lads.

PHILOSOPHY

Try anything once. Gigantic has only one year-round beer: IPA, and a very good one at that. But every other beer is a one-off. This is by turns satisfying (when, as usual, the beers are excellent), and sad (when you realize it could be your last). But the recipes are posted online, so ambitious home brewers can try their hands at resurrecting the flavors.

KEY BEER

Obviously, the IPA, brewed with ample amounts of Cascade, Centennial, Crystal, and Simcoe, is the brewery's standard. What will they brew next on any given day is anybody's guess.

CASCADE BREWING BARREL HOUSE

939 SE Belmont • Portland, OR 97214
(503) 265-8603
cascadebrewingbarrelhouse.com
Established: 2010

SCENE & STORY

Pucker up, Portland. To the truly devoted beer geeks, tart, barrel-aged beers are the next IPAs, and brewer Ron Gansberg—a veteran of the wine industry and residencies with both BridgePort Brewery and Portland Brewing Company—is Stumptown's resident chief sourpuss. His award-winning wine-, whiskey-, and port-barrel-aged Belgian-style brews crackle with acidic notes and woody tannins that blur stylistic lines (and go nicely with cheese).

In the summer of 2010, Gansberg opened this 6,000-square-foot facility with barrel-aging rooms and sixteen taps, including at least two directly from the barrels. It was the country's first bar dedicated to sour beers, which begged the question: In the land of hops, wouldn't an IPA bar make more sense? Not so fast. Despite a basic food menu (so far) the bar is normally busy if not packed.

PHILOSOPHY

"Bring your A game," says Gansberg. "If a beer isn't really making a statement, then it's really hardly worth our time to brew."

KEY BEER

Cascade Apricot (usually around 8.5% ABV) is a crisp, tart ale that goes through sixteen months of lactic fermentation and then spends four months resting on Washington State apricots in French oak wine barrels. Cascade has a huge lineup of beers, but this is consistently my favorite.

HAIR OF THE DOG BREWING CO.

61 SE Yamhill St. • Portland, OR 97214
(503) 232-6585 • hairofthedog.com
Established: 1993

SCENE & STORY

Once housed in a pub-less, ramshackle warehouse space in deep southeast Portland, the venerable Hair of the Dog operation has a new home in the friendly inner southeast industrial district, a chic mixed-use area of start-ups, farm-to-table eateries, and loft spaces in converted meatpacking and produce warehouses. There, founder Alan Sprints and family have set up shop in an airy space brightly painted in hues of teal, gray, and green around a polished eight-tap central bar. Off to the right side of the room is a little open kitchen where Sprints (a trained chef) himself does a lot of the cooking, like a recent dish of beer-braised beef served with whole grain mustard and spring greens.

PHILOSOPHY

Innovative and community-minded, Sprints was among the first brewers in the country to adopt the use of bourbon and whiskey barrels to age his beers, some of which are variations of long-forgotten styles like adambier, a strong aged ale from Dortmund, Germany. Sprints got the idea from legendary Portland beer writer Fred Eckhardt, who happily scored the first bottle. (RIP, Fred. Portland will always miss you.)

KEY BEER

Sprints made his name with Adam and Fred (named for the late Eckhardt) and other big, boozy brews numbered for the purpose of cellaring; vintage bottles are available at the taproom (batch #1 of Adam, seventy-five dollars for twelve ounces). But today his Blue Dot double IPA is setting a lot of tongues (or tails?) wagging. It's 7% ABV with waves of sweet, grapefruity hops and a crackingly dry, bitter finish.

Germany, touring the city's famed kölsch producers and hanging out in atmospheric bierstubes during college. Back in the states, he attended brewing school through the Vermont-based American Brewers Guild, and then honed his skills in a Eugene brewpub and Portland's Laurelwood Public House. Ettinger opened his kid- and bike-friendly brewpub in southeast Portland (often called simply HUB), using organic grains and innovative green-brewing practices like biodiesel to fuel the kettles, eco-friendly building materials, and both CO_2 and heat recycling. Recently, Ettinger has embarked on a fairly extensive barrel program at the brewery, opened a new bar in northeast Portland (Bikebar, summer 2011), and continues to sponsor a hugely popular party, Biketoberfest, at the brewery in September.

HOPWORKS URBAN BREWERY

2944 SE Powell Blvd. • Portland, OR
97202 • (503) 232-4677
hopworksbeer.com • Established: 2007

SCENE & STORY

San Francisco native Christian Ettinger found his beer inspiration in Cologne,

PHILOSOPHY

Ettinger keeps it simple. "Any [one] can throw a wall of ingredients at something and come up with a bold flavor, and some people will like it. I love simplicity. If it isn't simple, skip it." Recent collaborations with Bitburger in Germany and a planned housing development on the site of the Powell Blvd. location show Ettinger's considerable ambitions.

KEY BEER

An homage to the birthplace of the pilsner style, the ample but not heavy Czech-style HUB Lager (5.1% ABV). "It's the most rewarding beer to make," says Ettinger, "because it's so simple and so stark. There's little body to hide behind; there's no formidable hop character to hide behind. That beer has to be made perfectly every time." So far, so good.

SARAVEZA BOTTLE SHOP & PASTY TAVERN

1004 N. Killingsworth St. • Portland, OR 97217 • (503) 206-4252
saraveza.com • Established: 2008

SCENE & STORY

With the exception of one ill-fated USFL (United States Football League) team, the Portland Breakers, Portland has never had anything approaching professional American football to cheer about (the MLS Timbers, on the other hand, are a different story). So it is incredibly refreshing to walk into Wisconsin native Sarah Pederson's northeast Portland shrine to the Green Bay Packers and beers of every era. Overhead, check out the vintage signage and bottle cap murals as intricate as any ancient Roman mosaic—and settle in for some down-to-earth conversation, or take in a gridiron game on TV. Before you head out, take a little shopping spree through the 250-plus international beers in cool, old green vintage coolers. Saraveza—a play on Pederson's name and on the Spanish word *cerveza*, for beer—has nine beers on tap, homemade soups, and those made-from-scratch pasties—try the Nater, a delicious blend of braised beef, potato, carrot, rutabaga, and onion. It doesn't matter if you're not into rushing stats and field goal attempts; you're just here to soak up some good, old-fashioned, unironic midwestern hospitality.

PHILOSOPHY

Pederson has assembled the best bar staff in Portland, helpful and open-minded, a major selling point in the occasionally too-cool-for-school city of "Beervana." Brewers and purists might cringe at the thought, but certain bartenders here are experienced and confident enough to hand you a blend of tap beers of different origins and profiles. Want a little more zing and hops in your malty Belgian tripel? Done. Lately

Saraveza has been hosting excellent little festivals, like the Peche Fest and Farmhouse Fest, which have boasted insanely good selections—and no lines whatsoever. Call it a well-kept secret.

KEY BEER

The beer list is superb: up-to-the-second, heavily local on draft and Low Countries–focused in the coolers. Look for complex, handmade beers from Block 15, in Corvallis, Portland's Upright, McMinnville's Heater Allen, Hood River's Logsdon, and Boneyard in Bend. Or, to go Saraveza native, don't be afraid to order the pride of Milwaukee, Wisconsin, an icy-cold mug of Hamm's (4.7% ABV).

BAILEY'S TAPROOM AND THE UPPER LIP

213 SW Broadway • Portland, OR
97205 • (503) 295-1004
baileystaproom.com; theupperlip.net
Established: 2007

SCENE & STORY

Unlike hilly Seattle, Portland's downtown is wonderfully walkable, with airy park blocks leading from the river nearly to the West Hills and Forest Park (a must for city dwellers in need of a quick urban escape). Located within walking distance to the iconic Powell's Books and several of Portland's better boutique hotels, Bailey's

Taproom has high glass windows and a streamlined, almost minimalist interior, keeping the focus on craft beer. There are twenty taps and ninety-nine bottled selections (bringing a certain song to mind), all specializing in Oregon's diverse craft beers, with occasional forays outside the borders into California and Washington, and cask tappings on Mondays. During the week and on sunny afternoons there's a constant crowd of beer lovers, but it's seldom slammed to the point of "nope, let's bail." With lots of small festivals throughout the year, it's one of downtown's best beer bars. The stylish, quiet, speakeasy-style sister "Bailey's Upper Lip" bar around the corner at 720 NW Ankeny Street may be open—check with bartenders—where you'll find a world-class smaller selection of draft and bottled beers, cocktails, plus shuffleboard (and a peaceful spot overlooking Broadway).

PHILOSOPHY

Efficient. While there's no food, the owner of Bailey's struck up a genius deal with Santeria, the excellent Mexican restaurant across the street adjoining the venerated Mary's Club (Portland's oldest strip joint). Simply call up to order (menus are kept behind the bar), and Santeria will deliver the goods directly to your table (try the tinga with anything).

KEY BEER

Downstairs, check what's just been tapped. Maybe it's Silver Moon Bridge

Creek Pilsner, from Bend (4.7% ABV), the ideal companion to some spicy Mexican food. On a recent visit to the Upper Lip, I scored a pair of bottles of Rayon Vert, a rare Belgian-style pale ale from Green Flash that was last packaged in twelve-ounce bottles in 2012. With its Brettanomyces kick and bottle-conditioning, the beer had held up amazingly. And at six dollars, it was an incredible bargain.

HIGGINS RESTAURANT & BAR

1239 SW Broadway • Portland, OR 97205
(503) 222-9070 • higginsportland.com
Established: 1994

SCENE & STORY

Located just off the leafy park blocks in downtown Portland, Higgins is a restau-

GET FRESH *with your* ALES

Every fall in the Pacific Northwest, America's cradle of hops production (now on par with Germany), ripened hops' tall, leafy trellises begin to sag with the weight of millions of flowers. On the best back roads, the air in Oregon's Willamette (it's "Will-am-ett," not "William-et," dammit) is redolent with the grapefruity smell of the delicate pinecone-like flowers, which are soon picked, dried, and packaged. But not all hops make it to the temperature-controlled storehouses where they're monitored to avoid spontaneous combustion (true!). Some are hauled off the trellises and added directly into unfermented beers in nearby breweries, creating a fresh—and fleeting—genre of beer, interchangeably referred to as fresh-hopped or wet-hopped. Brewers in the south of England have long called them harvest ales, always an excuse for a roaring party. (Portland's first big fresh hop festival kicked off in 2010.)

How it works: Working with growers, brewers time their arrival to a farm to coincide with a batch of beer nearing the boil stage. Then they race back and plunge the flower cones directly into what's called the whirlpool step. In the best years, this translates into pure brewing magic, with floral aromas that hit your nose within milliseconds of cracking a finished beer open.

The only drawback to fresh hop ales? Now you see them, now you don't. Brewed only in the fall, these beers don't age or travel well. What's more, they tend to drain from kegs faster than Keystone Light at a tailgater. Fresh hop ales are catching on around the country, but Oregon leads the pack. Look for them from Laurelwood, Deschutes, and Gigantic on tap (and sometimes bottled, like Deschutes' Hop Trip).

Whatever you do, don't miss the freshest beers of the year.

rant in two parts: one, a white tablecloth dining room with an open kitchen; two, a warm and inviting beer café/bar with a solid list of Belgian and craft beers and mouthwatering food. How do a fresh saison beer and a warm tart of leeks, oyster mushrooms, and cave-aged Gruyère served with hazelnut and fennel salad sound?

James Beard Award–winning chef Greg Higgins and Co. will cook your socks off. You could head there after a concert, or an art opening at the Portland Art Museum a couple of blocks away. You don't need a reservation to walk into the bar on a random night, and you're likely to meet a local brewmaster refreshing at the bar, talking shop with the knowledgeable—and ultracourteous—staff.

PHILOSOPHY

As ambitious and eco-minded as they come. Higgins is an ardent champion of local purveyors, and that includes brewers, of course. Long before it was fashionable, Higgins worked with Hair of the Dog brewer Alan Sprints on a beer made with organic kabocha squash (4.5% ABV and called Greg), and promoted a series of elegant beer and brewmaster dinners with the likes of Pike Brewing Company.

KEY BEER

Beer steward Jason Button looks after the ten-tap, 100-bottle list, packed with unusual domestic and European choices. But sometimes an easy local sipper is the

way to go. "Come summer, with sweet corn and peppers coming in, we like to steam clams in kölsch," he says. "Double Mountain in Hood River makes a nice one. So: steamed clams, sweet corn, peppers, and a kölsch for yourself. Always hits the spot."

Wine Country: The Willamette Valley

WOLVES & PEOPLE FARMHOUSE BREWERY

30203 NE Benjamin Rd. • Newberg, OR 97132 • (503) 487-6873
wolvesandpeople.com • Established: 2014

SCENE & STORY

Admittedly, I'm biased. Wolves & People is my own brewery, which, over the course of a long, drudging year of construction, I built on the farm where I grew up. I started dreaming about this brewery during my freshman year of college at Whitman, in Walla Walla, oh-so-many years ago. A good friend who lived across the hall taught me to brew. One crisp, hoppy taste of Abe's Ale told me he knew what he was talking about. And with a single stir of my own kettle, I was hooked. I could write a book about my path from that dusty section lounge to the present day, and maybe will someday. With help from former Jester King head brewer Jordan Keeper, who spent a year working on site, the brewery was constructed from October 2014 to the fall of 2015.

Wolves & People, located down a quiet country road in the Oregon wine country next to a hazelnut orchard, is housed in my family's 100-year-old white barn, gently restored and converted to brewing starting in the summer of 2014. The mission was to build a true farmhouse brewery, with nods to Belgian traditions and new-era techniques, and to share the results on site in a tasting room with visitors (and bottle the rest). The farm supplies many ingredients used in beers, from heirloom plums to Douglas fir and cedar tips, herbs, and other fruits. Inside, visitors encounter a copper-clad 7bbl system (formerly used by Heater Allen Brewing Co.), exposed wood beams (which, in the late '60s, came out of my late father's meat packing plant in Portland's industrial inner southeast), rows of oak barrels, and a mill room I built with help from a dear, former teacher friend (and current neighbor) from salvaged barn windows and stained hemlock. There are several tasting areas inside the barn, and as of this writing, plans for outdoor seating under shade, alongside the old filbert trees.

If it's open, wander upstairs to the loft and admire the *Soulboat*, an art installation first hung from the rafters in 1994. Built by an acclaimed Washington, D.C., artist, *Soulboat* was formerly displayed in the Smithsonian, then joined a traveling tour. When it reached Portland, Larry Kirkland, its creator, and my mother, Ellen, were chatting at a party. Kirkland needed a home for his massive mobile-like piece; she offered up the barn's beautiful loft, and soon the barn had its most long-term, most mystical inhabitant.

PHILOSOPHY

"Wolves & People" is the name of a nighttime game of tag I played with my older brothers and cousins on the farm growing up. And it relates to hops (*humulus lupulus*, Latin for "wolf among weeds"). As a lover of saisons and wild ales as long as I have been legally allowed to drink, my passion is for those styles above all. With the fruit and nuts we grow on the farm itself, I aim to brew vivid, food-friendly beers that truly express a sense of place. The yeast we use in the brewery came from a wild strain I propagated off an old Italian plum tree in our field. The soft, pristine water comes from our own farm's well, tapping the Parrett Mountain aquifer directly below our farm. Our grain comes from the Northwest, especially Mecca Grade, an heirloom barley farmer in eastern Oregon. And our hops come from nearby family farms like Crosby and Annen (along with a few pounds off our place, too).

KEY BEER

Sebastian, our signature saison, is named for Sebastian Brutscher, the Bavarian immigrant who was the first non-native settler on Springbrook Farm's land, around 1850, and who gave Newberg its name (he was born in Neuberg am Danau, in Bavaria). Brutscher, a woodsman and later both the postmaster and schools' superintendent of the area, grew oats, wheat, and hops here (among other crops), so all those ingredients are in our signature saison. A blend of young- and barrel-aged, brett-kissed saison, dry-hopped and carefully bottle-conditioned, Sebastian aims for an earthy, grassy, slightly tart character, dry finish, and a rich meringue-like head. And if we have any imperial stout aged on estate filberts, we'll gladly share that, too.

HEATER ALLEN BREWING

907 NE 10th Ave., McMinnville, OR 97128 • (503) 472-4898 • heaterallen.com
Established: 2007

SCENE & STORY

As IPAs multiplied around him, Oregon native Rick Allen, a mild-mannered home brewer living in the heart of Oregon's pinot noir country, eyed the negative space. Perhaps his previous career as an investment banker had taught him to look for what was missing as much, if not more, than what was piling up. In an era of unprecedented hoppiness in beer—the first massive, pungent American-style and Double-IPAs were being imitated across the state, indeed, the nation—but instead of walking that path, he looked to Bavaria, where balance is the ultimate pursuit. In 2007, excellent craft-brewed pilsner was still fairly rare. He decided to go pro and name his brewery by joining his wife's maiden name, shared with a famed early pioneer to the area, Benjamin Heater, and his own. Labels would be clean, clear, and direct. The mission was clear: to brew exceptional handcrafted lager beer.

After countless home-brew batches, including fourteen pilsners in a row, in 2007 he was ready to ramp up his favorite—a crisp, flowery number—on a handsome, used, copper-clad 7bbl system housed in a small warehouse next to a winery in McMinnville, Oregon's quiet granary district. He decorated the tasting room with empty grain sacks from Weyermann, the celebrated Bavarian maltsters. Tasting room hours were limited at best. But slowly, Allen's detail-oriented, no-nonsense approach, and bright, grainy, substantial pilsner, achieved nothing less than cult status. Not long after launching, Heater Allen Pils, 200-gallon batch by 200-gallon batch, eventually earned the top spot in

RateBeer's entire pilsner category. As of this writing, the tasting room is open on the second Saturday of every month from 12 to 5 p.m., and by appointment.

Since 2009, Allen's daughter, Lisa, who has a background in winemaking, has taken on more and more brewing, and the cheerful Allens recently completed an expansion, doubling the brewing capacity and entering the California market in the process.

PHILOSOPHY

Think straightforward, clean, fresh superb German- and Czech-style lagers, with perhaps a touch more hops than the Old Country.

KEY BEER

The Allens have created more than a dozen beers, but three take top billing: the Pils, a Vienna lager called Coastal, and a super schwarzbier. By all means start with the Pils (4.9% ABV) and work your way through the offerings.

DETOUR ➡ THE SIDEWAYS OF BEER

McMinnville is the beating heart of Oregon's vaunted pinot noir country, scarcely a drop of cheap merlot in sight. But brew tanks are increasingly standing tall, too. Touring Mac (as locals call it) on foot offers another fine, spacious, newish brewpub, Grain Station (grainstation.com), a few steps away from Heater Allen. Visitors can also raise a well-made glass on the patio at Golden Valley (a brewpub popular since the mid-1990s); later, go deep into more esoteric styles with the Bitter Monk's focused list of Belgian and American wild ales (thebittermonk.com). It's the best Oregon beer bar outside of Portland, these days. Night cap on the roof deck—then sleep it off—at McMenamins' historic Hotel Oregon (mcmenamins. com/HotelOregon); revive at Community Plate, a chic, airy breakfast and espresso sanctuary that could have been airlifted out of Portland (communityplate.com).

Corvallis

BLOCK 15 BREWERY & RESTAURANT

300 SW Jefferson Ave. • Corvallis, OR
97333 • (541) 758-2077 • block15.com
Established: 2008

SCENE & STORY

Housed in the historic corner building that used to be the *Gazette-Times* newspaper office, Block 15's name comes from its address (or block number) from the early days of Corvallis. It's a small brewery, relatively speaking, but it holds a lot of significance locally as a popular watering hole, with fourteen taps (seven rotating), two floors, and room for about 120 imbibers. There's an appealing menu of fare like house-smoked pork shoulder, burgers, and crispy fries. It's also a rallying point for the fermentation science majors at Oregon State University, who get their own dedicated tap to showcase experimental brews. Suddenly, Corvallis has a bigger beer scene. "We're in our own little island," says brewer and co-owner Nick Arsner, "but we've got a great little beer culture growing here in Corvallis."

PHILOSOPHY

Nonconformist. Given that Corvallis is something of a conservative town, with endless acres of corn, hops, and locals in big pickup trucks, Arsner's cutting a different track. "I love the art in barrel aging and mixed fermentations rather than kicking out IPA," he says. There's even a little coolship in the cellar. It was among the first in the country just a few years ago.

KEY BEER

Pappy's Dark, brewed with six different Belgian and British malts and aged in nine- and ten-year-old bourbon barrels, is a velvety, deep, and rich beer with flavors of bourbon, caramel, and woody vanilla (10% ABV). And ask what other saisons, sours, and other experiments are in the works.

Enterprise

TERMINAL GRAVITY BREWING CO.

803 SE School St. • Enterprise, OR
97828 • (541) 426-0158
terminalgravitybrewing.com
Established: 1998

SCENE & STORY

East of the Cascades, dense Douglas fir forests yield to rolling hills of wheat, with narrow ribbon roads connecting small towns like Enterprise (population: 1,000). After a series of brewing jobs big and small, brothers-in-law Steve Carper and Dean Duquette moved back there to launch their own operation, Terminal Gravity (a brewing term for the end of fermentation). In 2014, new owners (and an expanded team) took over, polishing up the website and adding staff and new beers to the lineup. This is pristine Wallowa County mountain country, spitting distance from Kokanee salmon-filled Wallowa Lake, one of America's only true glacial lakes, and the Hells Canyon recreation area, a major adventure-travel hub. And what's a spin through the great outdoors without a beer to cap off the journey?

PHILOSOPHY

"Middle of Nowhere . . . Center of the Universe." This little brewery is a treasure, a quaint yellow-painted, Craftsman-style cottage with a few tables and stools inside and three acres of grounds outside where travelers meet to drink beer on the porch, play volleyball, and toss horseshoes— then stand around a roaring bonfire: the definition of summer itself.

KEY BEER

Terminal Gravity IPA, the tangy and ultrabitter bottle-conditioned beer that made this tiny brewpub regionally famous (6.8% ABV).

Eugene

NINKASI BREWING CO.

272 Van Buren St. • Eugene, OR 97402
(541) 344-2739 • ninkasibrewing.com
Established: 2006

SCENE & STORY

Back in 1994 the irrepressible Jamie Floyd was just slinging hobby home brew for University of Oregon parties. After graduation he considered academia but scored a gig manning the kettles at Steelhead Brewery in Eugene instead. Now Floyd and Co. have a staff of several dozen, and a 100,000-barrel-capacity brewhouse, not to mention a rabid fan base. In part by harnessing the power of community involvement through the arts and social networks (the company boasts a massive Facebook presence) and guerrilla marketing (at night, for example, with the Ninkasi logo "Bat Signal" spotlight), the firm has solidified its place in Oregon's beerscape. There have been, in just nine years, four major expansions. Next up, the world?

How about outer space? In what was a PR gambit of interstellar proportions, in 2013 the team set up what they called the Ninkasi Space Program (NSP), with one goal: "send brewer's yeast to space, return it to Earth, and use it to brew delicious craft beer." It took two launches, but the project succeeded in getting a yeast sample into orbit, which, once recovered back on terra firma, was used to brew Ground Control, an Imperial Stout brewed with Oregon hazelnuts, star anise, and cocoa nibs.

Ninkasi's tasting room and outdoor patio features year-round beers, seasonals, and occasional limited specialty releases on tap, and big summer block parties are guaranteed. And there's a limited menu of large soft brewery-dough pretzels, pasties, and soup.

PHILOSOPHY

"We make beer-geek- [approved] beer, but we don't make beer for beer geeks," says Floyd. "We encourage everybody [to drink beer], not just the supernerdy 1 percent."

KEY BEER

The intensely bitter and tangy Total Domination IPA (6.7% ABV) is one of the top-selling twenty-two-ounce beers in the state, but they've been accomplishing amazing things with lagers lately, even pulling down a coveted GABF gold medal for Pravda, a sparkling Bohemian pilsner, in 2013.

AGRARIAN ALES

31115 Crossroads Ln. W. • Eugene, OR 97408 • (541) 632-3803 • agales.com
Established: 2012

SCENE & STORY

Built on a bucolic seventeen-acre farm plot in a converted dairy barn just north of Eugene, Agrarian is one of the most authentic farmhouse breweries in the nation. Starting in 2002, Nate and Ben Tilley (brothers whose parents established it as Crossroads, an organic farm, in 1985) began tending hops, reviving a practice from the farm and area going back over a century. Today they grow eight varieties of Northwest hops plus two Old World varieties, and operate a small, heartfelt brewpub with a busy weekend scene, live music, yoga and lecture sessions, barn dances, and other programs. Without any discernible hype, Agrarian has become one of Oregon's best beer destinations, especially on warm summer nights, an authentic farmhouse brewery in every sense of the word.

PHILOSOPHY

Even by the most stringent DIY standards, the fact that head brewer Tobias Schock and Co. use only estate-grown hops makes them a real rarity. Few breweries can pull it off, because hop farming is time-consuming, labor-intensive, resources-intensive work (especially in the busy beer season of late summer and early fall). All ingredients are sourced locally, and the crew sells excess hops in the farmers market. The result here is an appealing mix of hop-forward farmhouse ales, with forays into fiery and experimental terrain using farm herbs, honey, peppers and other crops. With an organic certification in process (no small task), Agrarian is an idealistic operation to stay the least.

KEY BEER

In late fall, look for Harvest Belgene, a dry-hopped Belgian-style saison (5.5% ABV) brewed with organic pilsner malt and a blend of two farmhouse yeasts. The nugget and crystal hops add potent, but not overpowering, herbal notes. And Field Beer, a "farmhand session beer" of 4%, is more or less a standby.

Troutdale

MCMENAMIN'S EDGEFIELD

2126 SW Halsey St. • Troutdale, OR
97060 • (503) 669-8610
mcmenamins.com • Established: 1991

SCENE & STORY

For those who live in the Northwest, the McMenamin Brothers' quirky empire of fifty-nine (and counting) inns and brewpubs in artistically converted old churches, schools, theaters, utility buildings—even a lighthouse—are everyday neighbors, seldom spoken of with much passion anymore. It's all too easy to forget that the Dead Head brothers Brian and Mike were right there at the start of things, though, with the Widmers and Ponzis of BridgePort in lobbying the Oregon state legislature to legalize brewpubs.

The fact is that after years of mediocrity the beer and food and service are much improved. And most—if not all—of their loving, Age of Aquarius–inspired restorations, earnest local history murals, and other psychedelia-tinged whims will stand the test of time. The bars might serve only McMenamins' beer, but the quirks and design are worth celebrating. Edgefield, a sprawling seventy-four-acre Works Progress Administration compound built in 1911 just outside of Portland—is the jewel in the crown, with a 100-room inn, brewery, distillery, winery, movie theater, multiple bars, concert stage, and rambling grounds complete with gardens and a par-3 golf course. (And a resident glassblower, naturally.) A summer concert series has gone from good to great lately, with musical guests along the likes of Wilco, Steely Dan, and local heroes the Decembrists. Show or not, on a warm summer night, you can't do much better than strolling around the grounds with a beer in hand, ducking into the cigar-friendly Little Red Shed, a tiny, candlelit, ten-seat hideaway built in the farm's former incinerator, now covered with creeper vines.

PHILOSOPHY

"Welcome to the Kingdom of Fun."

KEY BEER

On a hot day, the raspberry sweet-tart 4.4% ABV Ruby does the trick, getting plenty of zing from forty-two pounds of berries in every small batch.

Hood River

PFRIEM FAMILY BREWERS

707 Portway Ave., Ste. 101
Hood River, OR 97031 • (541) 321-0490
pfriembeer.com • Established: 2012

SCENE & STORY

Hood River, an adrenaline junkie–filled ski and river town about forty-five minutes east of Portland, has become a real hub of craft brewing, with Full Sail, Logsdon, and Double Mountain breaking trail. In 2012, locals eagerly embraced cofounder/brewmaster Josh Pfriem's brewpub, dubbed pFriem with internal capitalization, perhaps to help beer lovers pronounce (and easily recall) its name. By mid-2014, the brewery was really cranking, with fifty different beers released and an annual output of 4,000 barrels. By the middle of 2015, pFriem had gained a solid retail presence in the region, thanks in no small measure to clean, elegant branding. The brewpub, located a short walk from Columbia's wind-swept riverfront (which, on any tolerable afternoon, is teeming with board sailors), is an excellent stop, especially on a sunny afternoon post-waterfall hike or Mt. Hood ski. Be prepared for a wait to get inside the airy modern brewpub, attractively appointed with exposed beams, cool, old barrel-hoop chandeliers, polished cement floors, and, helpfully for some, a kids' corner. There's an ambitious menu, but it's classics like the burger and mac 'n' cheese with bacon that truly standout.

PHILOSOPHY

Pfriem is a garrulous, exacting brewer, and the releases are, across the board, very clean and sometimes adventurous, such as in the case of a recent, well-made Flanders blonde, which spends 18 months aging in oak.

KEY BEER

Like an amped-up dubbel, Belgian strong dark ales are all about grain-given flavors of plum, toffee, and raisin. They're also a bit higher in alcohol and tend toward a peppery tang and dryness, ideally, balancing those richer, sweet notes. Pfriem's is arguably their most complete offering yet, with fulsome waves of malty flavor. It's a superb example of the style.

DOUBLE MOUNTAIN BREWERY & TAPROOM

8 4th St., No. 204 • Hood River, OR
97031 • (541) 387-0042
doublemountainbrewery.com
Established: 2007

SCENE & STORY

After hiking waterfalls in the Columbia Gorge you're going to have a wicked appetite, so get yourself to Double Mountain to set things right with a fresh pint and tasty pizza. Named for a local viewpoint where you can see both Mt. Hood and Mt. Adams (two of the many impressive Cascade Range peaks), the family-friendly brewpub was founded by Full Sail brewery alumni Matt Swihart and Charlie Deveraux, who met working in production and began a series of tactical brainstorms masquerading as long nights of drinking. Pinned with demand immediately after opening, the Double Mountain pub is close to Full Sail and Hood River's main drag, with a cool sage-green interior, living room couches, offbeat local artworks, and the odd live band. A recent expansion added much needed table space for beer, pizza, and music.

PHILOSOPHY

Hop lovers to the hilt, the Double Mountain team goes for huge additions of whole flower hops and minimal handling of the beer, for a powerful but not overly aggressive character, followed by long conditioning rests and no filtration.

KEY BEER

The 6.5% ABV India Red Ale ("I.R.A."), a scarlet, malty beast with the hop profile of an IPA, is a good match for the piquant pepperoni pizza. Or take a pull off the Vaporizer, a dry, golden-hued pale ale with pilsner malt and Challenger hops, grown in Washington's Yakima Valley (6% ABV). Recently, cherry-driven sours such as Tahoma, Devil's Kriek, and Rainier Kriek are gaining many ardent fans.

FULL SAIL BREWERY & TASTING ROOM & PUB

506 Columbia St. • Hood River, OR 97031
(541) 386-2247 • fullsailbrewing.com
Established: 1987

SCENE & STORY

Early settlers here braved Hood River's wind-tunnel conditions, and the fruit orchards they established thrived and made it famous. Fast-forward 200 years: today, the quaint Columbia River–side town of 6,500 located an hour east of Portland still boasts the same majestic views of Mt. Hood and fertile fruit trees. But thanks to that steady wind, it's now regarded as one of the world's top destinations for windsurfing and kiteboarding. Since 1987 it's been a beer town, too, home to the once-tiny, now huge Full Sail, where you can drink a beer and watch the speeding sails embroider the waves. (This is preferable to attempting actual windsurfing, which, for most of us, becomes an infinite wipeout.)

PHILOSOPHY

Progressive and green-minded. In 1999 Full Sail became 100 percent employee-owned, and employees work four ten-hour days to save resources (and make the most of powder days up on Mt. Hood and winds on the Columbia, no doubt). In 2015 those employees decided to sell a controlling stake to Encore Consumer Capital, a San Francisco-based private equity group.

KEY BEER

If you're visiting in the fall (a beautiful season to be in the area), look for the fresh hop ales—there's often two or three on at a time, made with huge quantities of just-picked hop flowers. "To get a comparable extract out of the hop (compared to the dried version), you have to use about five times the amount, and when you add that much more, you get more of a green, chlorophyll, leaf, and vegetative matter flavor," says former Full Sail brewmaster John Harris, who has made many in his day (and check out his latest creations at Ecliptic, in northeast Portland). The rest of the year, try Full Sail Amber, the company's flagship and Oregon's first craft beer in bottles, which came out in 1989 and won a gold at GABF the same year. It's 5.5% ABV and on the sweet and malty side, with a light touch of Mt. Hood and Cascade hops.

DETOUR → FACE FALLS FIRST: OREGON'S WATERFALL-FILLED COLUMBIA GORGE

The Columbia Gorge—a short drive east from Portland on highway I-84 toward Hood River—is braided with postcard cataracts that lure masses. Multnomah Falls, at 620 feet, is the nation's second-highest waterfall after Yosemite. Hike 800 feet up to stroll past the more serene Wiesendanger and Ecola Falls, invisible from ground level. Marginally tougher to reach (but far lesser known) is Oneonta Gorge, a gloamy slot canyon lined with neon-bright lichens accessed by fording a log-jam (one that, thankfully, discourages the faint of heart) merely a quarter of a mile away. (oregon.com/hiking)

SCENE & STORY

Plenty of American brewers these days claim to brew "farmhouse" ales (meaning the refreshing, yeast-driven beer that was traditionally brewed in the Belgian and French countryside for local consumption) but there's just one problem: no farmhouse. Not so for Oregon's Dave Logsdon, who was the founding brewmaster of Full Sail, and went on to found Wyeast Laboratories, a hugely successful wholesale and retail yeast company for the wine and beer industries. With a former partner, experienced brewer Charles Porter, Logsdon opened the brewery on his family's beautiful working farm outside of Hood River, complete with a big red barn (where the kettles, tanks, and barrels currently live), pets, horses, and highland cattle, in 2011. Unfortunately, the farmhouse setting is no longer open to beer pilgrims. Following lengthy debates with county zoning officials, Logsdon opened the tasting room in Hood River proper in 2015. It was a period of change for the young company. In late 2015 head brewer Charles Porter decamped to begin his own (to be announced, as of this writing) brewery, and Logsdon sold the company but stayed aboard to help guide the brand. Plans to move or alter production, as of fall 2015, were unclear.

PHILOSOPHY

Purist. "How do you make a farmhouse beer if you're not in a farmhouse? That's a really important part of the definition for me," says Logsdon, who grows his own schaerbeekse kriek (cherry) trees imported from an orchard in East Flanders to use in barrel-aged beers. The ingredients are all certified organic. With his wood-aged beers, he's going for a smidge less sourness than some of the more intense Belgian ales: "I try to create a lot of maltiness to carry the acidity but also to keep the acid in check, so it makes it a nice drinking beer—tart and thirst quenching at the same time."

KEY BEER

Seizoen Bretta (8% ABV), a traditional malty, yeasty saison with an addition of Brettanomyces adding fruity notes, acidity, and woody, earthy, almost leathery flavors.

The Oregon Coast

DE GARDE BREWING

6000 Blimp Blvd. • Tillamook, OR 97141
(503) 815-1635 • degardebrewing.com
Established: 2013

SCENE & STORY

The Oregon coast is a mix of sublime geology and charming towns (Manzanita, Cannon Beach) and, well, a few less-than-charming towns. But with five rivers converging in Tillamook Bay—primo steelhead and salmon habitat—there's some rare air there. Former Pelican brewer Trevor Rogers and his wife, Lindsey Hamacher, are making the most of it, relying, they say, on airborne yeasts for their primary fermentation. It's been an art form in Belgium for centuries, but here in the United States, the art of spontaneous fermentation is just beginning to catch on. From Maine (Allagash) to the Texas Hill Country (Jester King) and even Tulsa, Oklahoma (Prairie), some very daring brewers are exposing their unfermented beer to air (while held in a shallow cistern called a coolship) in hopes that the naturally occurring wild yeast aloft will result in pleasing tastes (instead of face-contorting acids and other off-flavors). Until recently, no one would have suspected Tillamook, Oregon, to be on the list of successful zip codes for the method, but De Garde has done well,

fast becoming a collector favorite. While the brewery keeps its coolship indoors in a windowless room, and also has used plenty of lab-grown yeast (as is standard in breweries worldwide), any successful reliance on spontaneous fermentation earns bragging rights.

While it started as a garage project, today De Garde occupies a larger industrial space near a famous old hangar from World War II, which housed airships used by U.S. military to hunt Japanese submarines along the coast. There are five sour beers on draft for four dollars per twelve ounces, and the mostly out-of-town clientele often stocks up on bottles to go. Bottle releases are crowded affairs (check newsletters and social media).

PHILOSOPHY

Relying on a coolship is a game of Russian roulette, but when it works, the result is truly special. Think about good homemade sourdough, which succeeds by similar metrics. De Garde is using a lot of local Oregon fruit, too (including pinot noir), making for an array of brews that run the gamut from the merely tart and angular to extremely sour and vividly colored.

KEY BEER

The best known product is Bu Weisse, a 2.3% Berliner weisse that really pops with tart and lemony notes. But look for any of the dozens of variations on saison, fruited sour, and other wild ales they're doing, with everything from cranberry to nectarine to apricot, blackberry, and peach added. What you'll find when you arrive depends on the brewery's many fans that beat you to the beach.

Astoria

FORT GEORGE BREWERY & PUBLIC HOUSE

1483 Duane St. • Astoria, OR 97103
(503) 325-7468 • fortgeorgebrewery.com
Established: 2007

SCENE & STORY

Astoria, positioned at the mouth of the Columbia River as the Oregon Coast's northernmost town, began as an outgrowth of Fort Clatsop, the settlement established by Lewis and Clark upon reaching the Pacific. For years, Astoria was a roughneck port—in the 1920s it was deemed the most dangerous town in America because so many unsuspecting tavern-goers were shanghaied onto fishing vessels never to be seen again. Today, the town is still a bit gritty, a mosaic of nineteenth-century canneries, warehouses, and craftsman homes but with an indie-rock appeal. Visitors should check into the eighteen-room Commodore Hotel, which was renovated a few years back with a Wes Anderson–like attention to detail; Plus, it's walking distance to Fort George Brewery.

Brewery founders Jack Harris and Chris Nemlowill, too, have a near-obsessive attention to detail, and took over the derelict Fort George building they'd first toured in late 2005, which was built on the site of the city's old fort and a healthy spring. After opening in 2007 to steady crowds, the duo arranged to buy the whole block with help from a city loan. The twelve-tap brewpub is classic Northwest, with heavy exposed beams and big windows looking out to the streets. Order up a fresh beer and some house-made sausages or perfectly ungreasy fish and chips, and you'll taste the wisdom of their plans.

PHILOSOPHY

Classic local brewpub, with big ambitions (hence a new canning line added in 2011). And they love their stouts: February is always "stout month" featuring their own stouts on tap and a bunch of guest handles, concluding with a stout-and-oyster pairing dinner.

KEY BEER

Vortex IPA (7.7% ABV), served right out of a mason jar, honors the original brewhouse, which was transported through a tornado en route to Oregon from the Midwest. Now available in sixteen-ounce cans, it's a juicy twister of lemon, grasshops, and sweet, fruity graininess.

DETOUR →

THE GOOD BEER COAST:
THE BEST BEER AND SEAFOOD ON THE OREGON SHORE

No trip to the Oregon coast would be complete without a serious seafood and beer fest, and there's no more classically Oregonian place to do it than Jetty Fishery, a ramshackle seafood shack and campground on Nehalem Bay just north of Rockaway Beach on Highway 101 (800-821-7697; crab from nine dollars per pound). If you've got the time, rent a boat and go out with some crabbing pots to get your own haul (seventy-five dollars for two hours, up to five people), then have the guys at the pier clean and cook it on the spot while you swig post-expedition brews. Short on time? There's plenty precaught grub, too. Grab a sixer, some hot sauce, and paper napkins from inside the little store, then sidle up to the old yellow picnic tables outside by the water's edge and a fire pit while you wait for fresh-as-fresh-gets grilled oysters, steamed clams, and mussels, or Dungeness crab boiled in Nehalem Bay seawater. Word to the wise: try to go on a midweek afternoon. Weekends get crowded and crazy, especially when the owners fire up their 10,000-watt karaoke system for locals, RVers, and assorted campground yahoos.

After Jetty Fishery, you've got options. To the south, look for Yachats Brewing, housed with a picturesque farm store and headed up by former Logsdon brewer Charlie Van Meter, who makes a range of well-crafted beers from extra pale ale to saisons and stouts (yachatsbrewing.com). Or head north up to Manzanita, nine miles north on Highway 101, a 564-person town that used to be just a blip on the map. Perhaps because of this anonymity, Manzanita has started to draw in creative types, just as Big Sur, California did back in its heyday, and it's got a peaceful, progressive vibe. Down on the main drag of Laneda Avenue, pop into the relaxed San Dune Pub (sandunepub.com) and sip a juicy, intense Inversion IPA from Deschutes with an oyster po'boy and warm up by the fireplace.

North of Manzanita, 101 unwinds like a wire, bending around headlands and plunging into cathedrals of Sitka spruce and Douglas fir. Empty beaches emerge unexpectedly, the most striking of which is at Oswald West State Park (503-368-3575). The sandy stretch has become famous for its protected break, and you're likely to see some surfers braving the frigid waters. The short wooded path down to the beach is worth the trouble, without question.

After a day of crabbing, surf scoping, and beach walking, you'll be ready for some sea-borne comfort food again before long. And if Manzanita is Oregon's Big Sur, then

Cannon Beach, ten miles north, is its Carmel, a stretch of Cape Cod–style homes with not a chain store in sight. Best bet: perfectly icy G&Ts on the patio at the Driftwood (541-988-4384), or beers at Bill's Tavern & Brewhouse (503-436-2202), a sunny and cheerful spot with bright murals on the walls and a good, pet-friendly patio. Wind up your afternoon with some fresh, flaky, beer-battered halibut fish and chips and a pint of fresh-brewed beach beer, like the Duck Dive Pale Ale (4.8% ABV). Mission complete.

Bend & Central Oregon

THE ALE APOTHECARY

61517 River Rd. • Bend, OR 97701
the.ale.apothecary.com • thealeapothecary
@gmail.com • Established: 2011

SCENE & STORY

Brewer Paul Arney, descendant of an apothecary, left his position after six years as R&D/head brewpub chief of the legendary Deschutes Brewery to start his bold, 500-square-foot, wilderness-based brewery that remains one of the nation's most unusual. Instead of stainless steel, Arney brews in open oak barrels, harnessing wild yeast aloft in the woods. He's even employed a hollowed-out spruce tree that was hauled through the woods on horseback, in homage to the Norwegian tradition of mashing in with a *kuurna*, or hollowed juniper tree lined with juniper branches. Every beer is a statement of his purist ideals and wild creativity from grain to glass. His brewery has always been an appointment-only affair, but now that he's got a tasting room coming together in Bend proper, it could be somewhat easier to spot the mystic at work.

PHILOSOPHY

"My beer-brewing philosophy is the same as my life philosophy, I suppose," Arney told me. "I feel our contemporary culture pushes us to a 'destination' or to fulfill specific goals—retirement, consumerism. I brew beer in the manner that I try to live my life; to push back against this force and focus instead on the mystery of the experience. . . . As long as people are curious about the unknown, our beer should have no problem finding a market."

KEY BEER

The vinous, 9.8% ABV Sahalie wild ale is a revelation. With intriguing layers of earthy, angular flavors derived from wild yeasts and a full year of barrel aging in oak, as well as from a month of dry-hopping (in the barrel!), it's a beer of remarkable intensity of flavor, with flavors and aromas recalling lime, grass, and apricot. Amazing stuff.

DESCHUTES BREWERY

1044 NW Bond St. • Bend, OR 97701
(541) 382-9242 • deschutesbrewery.com
Established: 1988

SCENE & STORY

Making their debut in 1988 at Gary Fish's little Bond Street brewpub in Bend, the beers were good—really good. There was—and still is—something ideally calibrated about Deschutes' juicy, quaffable Mirror Pond Pale Ale. Is it the prismatic Cascade hops, perfectly applied? Jubelale, a malty and warming winter seasonal, was also an instant smash hit in bottles (the first Deschutes beer packaged in glass). It seemed the brewery would never be big enough for demand.

Today, Deschutes has also opened an upscale little brewpub in Portland's swank Pearl District—often packed and playing host to a summer street fair and high-profile cooking events. Its former head brewer, Veronica Vega, a serious cyclocross racer turned brewer, was just named assistant brewmaster of the entire company. The production brewery, in a massive industrial building on Simpson Avenue, offers free, forty-five-minute walking tours with four samples on the house. They've expanded the little old Bond Street pub, too (ask about changes when you're there). From ski-bum hangout to industry heavyweight the company is currently ranked around seventh in the United States for sales volume.

PHILOSOPHY

Success hasn't come at the expense of quality. The more states that pick up the beer (some thirty at this stage), the more brewers seem free to experiment on the side with barrel-aged stouts like the Abyss and sours like the Dissident, a Flanders-style oud bruin aged in oak barrels with cherries, both of which are excellent.

KEY BEER

Deschutes has pulled off some exceptional Belgian styles like the Dissident, but their area of domination is truly in the British-style ales, IPAs, porters, and stouts. Black Butte Porter deserves a victory lap. It's a little-known fact that Guinness Extra Stout debuted under the brand Extra Superior Porter and remained so for forty-one years, a stronger, darker version of the dark-hued London-born drink. Today the style has taken on many forms of its own around the world, from purist English versions to hefty Baltic variations and even American riffs that incorporate peppers and sour notes. In Deschutes' formula, tangy Northwest hops come to the fore with finesse, balancing its cocoa, coffee, and toffee notes from its blend of roasted malts. And, at 5.5% ABV, it's a touch lighter than the old Extra Superior.

DETOUR → THE BEND ALE TRAIL

Various locations, Bend, Oregon • BendAleTrail.com

Deschutes may rule the roost in terms of sheer size, but there's something about that high desert air, with no less than twenty-eight established breweries in and around the city of Bend (population: 82,000). Deschutes former head brewer Larry Sidor helms the innovation-minded Crux Fermentation Project (cruxfermentation. com), opened in 2012, with a solid menu (and crowds) to match. GoodLife (good-lifebrewing.com) and Worthy (worthybrewing.com) are large production breweries canning up cleanly made, summer session-worthy brews like the latter's Easy Day kölsch. Silver Moon (silvermoonbrewing.com) has regular live music and makes a tasty pilsner, among others; Bend Brewing Co. offers great Berliner weisse these days (bendbrewingco.com). The once-scrappy-but-now-big-dog Boneyard excels with IPAs like the aromatic, 6.55% ABV RPM (boneyardbeer.com). Stay at McMenamin's Old St. Francis School, a brewpub and hotel built in an old school, or the stylishly renovated Lodge at Suttle Lake, outside of Sisters (thelodgeatsuttlelake.com).

BEST *of the* REST: OREGON

BUOY BEER CO.

1 8th St. • Astoria, OR 97103 • (503) 325-4540 • buoybeer.com

Buoy's motto is "Where the Unstoppable Meets the Unyielding," a memorable koan for the river it overlooks: the mighty Columbia, sliding west, perhaps five miles from the Pacific. This 2014 newcomer (built in a ninety-year-old cannery along Astoria's historic boardwalk) has a handsome split timber and steel-appointed taproom from which you'll gaze out at sea lions, barges, the occasional tall wooden ship as you sip well-made Czech-style pilsner, IPA, and cream ale. Bonus: an impressive menu—try the fried oysters with jalapeño jam and goat cheese. Buoy's perfect throwback logos and clever, cool tap handles simply deepen the vibe of coastal cool.

PELICAN PUB & BREWERY

33180 Cape Kiwanda Dr. • Pacific City, OR 97135 • (503) 965-7007 ourlittlebeachtown.com/pelican

Pelican, founded in 1995, began a $1.4 million expansion in 2013 into downtown Tillamook with a shiny, new restaurant and production brewery (and planned brewpub in Cannon Beach). But to find out what made it famous, hit the original location in Pacific City overlooking Cape Kiwanda, a stunning seaside monolith, at sunset. Actually, get there at least an hour before sunset, because you'll definitely wait for a beachside seat. Their Kiwanda Cream Ale is an unfussy, 5.1% ABV Oregon favorite.

BARLEY BROWN'S PUB & BREWERY

2190 Main St. • Baker City, OR 97814 • (541) 523-4266 • barleybrownsbeer.com

From Portland, the trip to Baker City (population: 9,800), nestled between the Elkhorn and Wallowa Mountains, with the Powder River wending through town, is not a quick one (5 hours/300 miles). But it pays off with some truly great beer. Founded in 1998, Barley Brown's sailed under the radar for years. Now they have dozens of decorated beers, with a growing presence throughout the region. Look for the crisp, floral Hand Truck pale ale and work your way up through their decorated IPAs and stouts.

THE HOP & VINE

1914 N. Killingsworth St. • Portland, OR 97217 • (503) 954-3322 • thehopandvine.com

A quiet, cool little combo bistro and bottle shop with connoisseur-friendly taste but no attitude. Expect terrific food and an ever-changing tap list with a little extra focus on esoteric wild and sour ales. Events in the light-dappled back patio area have included memorable beer brunches with the likes of the Rare Barrel, Sante Adairius, and Almanac of San Francisco, and Zwanze Day, the annual global toast to Cantillon, Brussels, Belgium's, most celebrated lambic brewery.

EX NOVO BREWING CO.

2326 N. Flint Ave. • Portland, OR 97227 • (503) 894-8251 • exnovobrew.com

In 2014, local engineer and home brewer Joel Gregory founded perhaps the nation's first nonprofit brewpub in a big, old 1940s warehouse with soaring wooden trusses and the sort of lived-in, weathered wood and clean, steel details that have defined the modern brewpub movement. What elicited a few eye-rolls soon proved to be more than an earnest publicity grab, with well-crafted beers (I like the Damon Stoutamire, named for former Portland Trailblazer and local hero Damon Stoudamire) and a solid menu of food offerings, including "bacon for the table," eight dollars, ("because we can, and you should").

ECLIPTIC BREWING CO.

825 N. Cook St. • Portland, OR 97227 • (503) 265-8002 • eclipticbrewing.com

Ecliptic is an ambitious northeast Portland brewpub restaurant with a star at the helm—and stars in its eyes, named for the astronomers' term for the Earth's path around the sun. This is a spacious brewpub with diverse beers and very good food. It's no surprise to see it reach high: founder and head brewer John Harris, a jolly deadhead who always seems to have a grin, started his career with McMenamins and moved to Deschutes (where he created the recipes for some of the nation's best-selling and most decorated craft beers, including Mirror Pond Pale Ale). He spent the next 20 years as brewmaster at Full Sail before founding Ecliptic.

BAERLIC BREWING CO.

2235 SE 11th Ave. • Portland, OR 97214 • (503) 477-9418 • baerlicbrewing.com

In a city literally jammed with breweries, it would be all too easy to overlook Baerlic, a quiet spot on a leafy street in Southeast with no food, video games, few crowds, and no hype. Don't make that mistake. What you'll find is very good beer in a squeaky clean environment that is simultaneously pristine and cozy at the same time. Try whatever's on, especially Primeval, a 6.8% ABV American Brown Ale, falling somewhere delicious and chocolaty on the spectrum between IPA and India Black Ale.

OCCIDENTAL BREWING CO.

6635 N. Baltimore Ave. • Portland, OR 97203 • (503) 719-7102 • occidentalbrewing.com

Like Heater Allen out in wine country, Occidental is oriented toward sturdy Germanic traditions of the Old Word, with outstanding hefeweizen, kölsch, and altbier (a German-style of ale conditioned at cooler temperatures, made famous in Dusseldorf) and all in gorgeously simple, colorful, throwback cans. Located out in St. John's, once a standalone city northeast of the Rose City that was formally annexed into Portland in 1915, making a trip here affords not only the great beers at the brewpub but also nearby views of the magnificent, Gothic-style St. John's Bridge (2,000 feet wide), plus funky dive bars (Slim's) and quirky shops on the old main street, under perpetual pressure from gentrification. See it before the less-cool locals sell out.

FALLING SKY BREWING HOUSE & GASTROPUB

1334 Oak Alley • Eugene, OR 97401 • (541) 505-7096 • fallingskybrewing.com

With a home-brew store around the corner and the much-loved Pour House delicatessen opened in 2013 (on Blair Boulevard, about half a mile away), Falling Sky is quickly becoming one of Eugene's most beloved craft beer businesses. All three locations are worth visiting, but it's the sunny, spacious brewpub on Oak Alley that seems to brighten even the darkest Oregon afternoon. It's got vaulted, white-painted wood ceilings and a handsome, polished copper brewhouse behind tall barn-glass windows, making it a perfect place for a fresh pint with old friends.

THE VICTORY BAR

2509 SE 37th Ave. • Portland, OR 97202 • (503) 236-8755 • thevictorybar.com

A diminutive but perfectly thought-out beer bar out in neighborhoody Southeast, Victory (established in 2007) has six taps and sixty bottled selections from Oregon and around the world. Food options go the tapas route, from soup to clams, burgers, and some very tasty spaetzle. A recent gem on tap: the funky, bready, and sour Moinette Brune (8.5% ABV) from Belgium.

THE BIER STEIN BOTTLESHOP & PUB

345 East 11th Ave. • Eugene, OR 97401 • (541) 485-BIER • thebierstein.com

A central meeting place for Eugene beer fanatics since 2005, the Bier Stein has ten taps and over 1,000 bottled selections from all over the world and a small menu of salads, sandwiches, and soups. Owners Chip Hardy and his wife, Kristina Measells, cultivate close relationships with breweries and distributors to get specialty bottles and drafts. The only thing you won't find? B.M.C. (Bud, Miller, Coors) and 40 oz'ers.

CHATOE ROGUE

3590 Wigrich Rd. • Independence, OR 97351 • (503) 838-9813 • rogue.com

Independence, Oregon, was once known as the Hop Capital of the World, and the land there is still embroidered with huge stands of trellised hops supplying brewers in Oregon and beyond. Chatoe Rogue is essentially a compound in Independence consisting of forty-two acres of proprietary hops surrounded by cherry and filbert orchards; a 100-year-old, five-bedroom farmhouse available for rent as accommodation; and a small tasting room containing Rogue's Farmstead Nano-Brewery operation.

THREE CREEKS BREWING CO.

721 Desperado Ct. • Sisters, OR 97759 • (541) 549-1963 • threecreeksbrewing.com

If your trip to Bend from Portland takes you through Detroit Lake on the Santiam Highway, a.k.a. Highway 20—and it should, as it's an incredibly pretty drive in good weather—you'll pass through the historic town of Sisters (population: 1,700). Just south of Sisters, this big, comfortable log cabin–like brewpub opened in 2008 amid a stand of Ponderosa pines. A combination family restaurant, beer bar, and brewery, it's worth seeing. Try the 5.8% ABV Firestorm Red if Rudolph's Imperial Red (8.6% ABV) isn't on.

WASHINGTON

SIP ON THIS: WITHOUT WASHINGTON'S CRAFT BEER REVOLUTION, STARBUCKS COFFEE MIGHT never have gotten off the ground (read on to see why). The fact is, Washington's beer history goes all the way back to the 1850s, but it's the last couple of decades that tell the most about this beautiful and diverse state's beer potential and how it's now a part of daily life for many living here. With a gold mine of hops from the Yakima Valley (the country's biggest hop-growing area and second-largest in the world, after southern Germany), this was fertile ground for Red Hook, the first microbrewery to make a major impact in the early 1980s. In converting beer drinkers from the classic (if under-flavored) Northwest beers like Rainier and Hamm's, newcomers like Red Hook, Pike, Hales, and later pathbreakers like Holy Mountain have carved out quite a legacy. Now Seattle is a genuinely great beer bar town, and new breweries are popping up all around the state. So what if it rains all the time?

ITINERARIES

1-DAY Holy Mountain, Beveridge Place Pub, Naked City, The Masonry

3-DAY One-day itinerary plus Parkway Tavern, Brouwer's Café, Pike Brewing, Latona Pub

7-DAY One- and three-day itineraries plus Chuckanut, Diamond Knot, and Walking Man

Seattle

HOLY MOUNTAIN

1421 Elliott Ave. W. • Seattle, WA 98119
holymountainbrewing.com
Established: 2015

SCENE & STORY

For a time, Seattle seemed to lag behind Portland and San Francisco's zeitgeisty progress, where so many new breweries were nailing all the latest styles. No longer. Holy Mountain is one of several new breweries that have changed the game in the Emerald City. Nestled in an industrial building along busy Eliott Ave., just west of Seattle's Queen Anne neighborhood, Holy Mountain debuted to hearty local acclaim in early 2015. With a focus on innovative styles (and no IPA), they debuted with beers including Brettanomyces-kissed saisons, Belgian strong ales, and a lager aged in rye whiskey barrels. The taproom is, like Tørst, in Brooklyn, New York, a study in understatement, with swaths of clean white tile, polished cement floors, stark chalk boards and warm, weathered wood. It's the epitome, in late 2015, of brewhouse chic, but the brand doesn't come off as humorless hipster. They are truly serious about making excellent beer. The sky's the limit for these holy mountaineers.

PHILOSOPHY

Small batch, one-off, wild-yeast influenced, distinctive beers presented in minimalist packaging (think: thin black fonts and contours on white or beige labels). The names are as much tongue-in-cheek Tarot card ("Astral Projection") as Game of Thrones ("River of Ash"), all in good fun.

KEY BEER

Kiln & Cone is Holy Mountain's "house" pale ale; previous batches have been hopped with catty Nelson Sauvin and passion-fruity Galaxy hops, but look, too, for the Goat, a hazy-gold saison brewed with four grains, ample hops, and three months of aging time in a huge oak *foudre* with a secret strain of Brettanomyces. It's got the funk and tang of traditional farmhouse ales from the motherland, Belgium.

BEVERIDGE PLACE PUB

6413 California Ave. SW • Seattle, WA 98136 • (206) 932-9906
beveridgeplacepub.com
Established: 2003

SCENE & STORY

If for nothing else, step inside this west Seattle landmark beer haunt (on the corner of California and SW Beveridge Place, hence the name) to check out the eleven-foot-high, twenty-foot-wide back bar, a turn-of-the-twentieth-century showpiece salvaged from a defunct Kent, Washington, tavern called the Buzz Inn. At first, its three mirrored archways and gorgeous carvings were stained a deep brown (thanks to a century of cigarette smoke), but after three months spent cleaning the patina, a sumptuous cherry-stained tiger maple was revealed. A local metalsmith provided a custom tap tower and today the thirty-six-tap, 150-plus selection of bottles draws a steady crowd of locals.

PHILOSOPHY

Owner Gary Sink was inspired by a trip to the British Isles; the bar exudes community with couches, books, darts, a few (but not too many) TVs, well-maintained pool tables, and retro video games— Tron, anyone?

KEY BEER

The list focuses on Washington crafts and international bottles, with casks frequently. Look for the orange-hued Manny's Pale Ale (5.4% ABV) from Georgetown Brewery, which is slightly sweet and honey-ish, but balanced with fresh, floral hops. Or kick the hops up a notch with Bale Breaker Topcutter IPA, brewed on a working Yakima Valley hop farm (6.8% ABV), which massive waves of Citra, Simcoe, Mosaic, and other tangy hops.

BIG TIME BREWERY & ALEHOUSE

4133 University Way NE • Seattle, WA 98105 • (206) 545-4509
bigtimebrewery.com • Established: 1988

SCENE & STORY

Smack in the middle of "the Ave" in the U District (University of Washington) in Seattle, Big Time is more relaxed-but-thirsty grad student than college-frosh-getting-sloshed. With its faded wood walls and shuffleboard, it's a sure bet in the area for good beers and a good bite (try the pizzas).

PHILOSOPHY

These guys are big-time hopheads. There are up to four house IPAs on tap at any given time, with dozens of recipes in the brewer's logs.

KEY BEER

Old Sol is beer of the wheat wine style, which is something like an English-style barley wine but made with a majority of wheat, giving the beer some softness on the palate. Released on the summer solstice each year, it's spicy and fulsome at 10% ABV, but disappears all too quickly, like summer in the Pacific Northwest.

BROUWER'S CAFÉ

400 North 35th St. • Seattle, WA 98103
(206) 267-2437
brouwerscafe.blogspot.com
Established: 2005

SCENE & STORY

Owners Matt Bonney and Matt Van De Berghe have created a beer fortress of sorts, with a dark and somewhat castle-like interior featuring a parlor-level balcony curling around the main bar floor and some heavy chandeliers. The sixty-four taps and 300-plus bottled selections are stored with care and served in beer-specific glassware, but it's the policy of using a new piece of serving tube for every new beer on tap that shows how far Brouwer's goes to present craft beer at its best. The food is hearty, stick-to-your-ribs fare like croquettes, mussels, and a spicy lamb burger with fries (and go for a side of roasted garlic to take your taste buds even deeper).

PHILOSOPHY

You know you're in a Belgian beer shrine when you're greeted by a heraldic metal lion symbolizing Belgium and the Netherlands on the door, while inside there's a replica of the *Manneken-Pis*, a Brussels sculpture of a boy playfully taking a wiz that has come to symbolize the carefree joie de vivre of Belgian café culture.

KEY BEER

Orchard White, a 5.7% ABV witbier (unfiltered wheat-based beer doped with coriander and other spices) from Orange County, CA's, cult-fave the Bruery, is light on the tongue, with hints of dry apple flavor. It would make a good start before heading into bigger beers and barley wines, which are a specialty here.

Crunch Time

Local potato chip guru Tim Kennedy introduced Tim's Cascade Style Potato Chips—the ultimate beer snack—in 1986, giving them a signature crunchiness that may be audible from space. With their classic old-timey, red-and-white bag, they're easy to spot, too, but even easier to eat in embarrassing quantities. Don't pass them up when you're in the area, especially the sea salt and vinegar or jalapeño flavors, and wasabi for the brave. (timschips.com)

COLLINS PUB

526 2nd Ave. • Seattle, WA 98104
(206) 623-1016 • thecollinspub.com
Established: 2003

SCENE & STORY

Downtown Seattle's Pioneer Square area can sometimes feel like a drab warehouse district, even a bit sketchy at night. Thankfully, the Collins Pub, fourth-generation local Seth Howard's craft beer shrine in the historic five-story brick

Collins Building, is a welcome oasis, especially on weekends when the work-week happy hour crowds have dispersed and it's warm enough to take a seat on the enclosed sidewalk patio. There are twenty taps and more than sixty-five bottles, and amid the exposed brick dating to the 1890s, hardwood details, a heavy hanging mirror flanked by hand-blown glass-and-metal sconces, cozy booths, and way-above-average pub fare, it's easy to see an evening or afternoon disappear in a hurry. Carnivores must try the lamb chops or hand-formed Collins Burger with Oregon Tillamook cheddar cheese. The fresh ling cod fish and chips, fried with a Chuckanut pilsner beer batter, is a strong option, too. For the best service, sit at the bar, and be sure to come long before the 2 a.m.-posted closing time; it often closes much, much earlier, around 11 p.m.

PHILOSOPHY

Affordable gastropub meets private beer bar.

KEY BEER

The local and PacNW beer list shines, or go for a rarity from far away, such as Dogfish Head's Palo Santo Marron (12% ABV), a rich stout aged in Paraguayan wood related to frankincense, crude-oil black, and milkshake creamy.

ELYSIAN BREWING CO.

1221 E. Pike St. • Seattle, WA 98122
(206) 860-1920 • elysianbrewing.com
Established: 1996

SCENE & STORY

The original Elysian location on Capitol Hill represents the paradigmatic brew-pub—exposed beams, polished cement floors, high industrial ceilings, and walls lined with gleaming brewing tanks in a ninety-year-old converted warehouse. (There are three other newer locations: Elysian Fields, a large brewpub in the Stadium District, Elysian BAR, Tangle-town, a smaller location in South Green Lake, and Elysian Airport Way, a production brewery in Georgetown.) Behind all the beer was celebrated founding brewer Dick Cantwell, born in Germany and raised in the United States, who led the Seattle firm to scores of awards with massive array of styles brewed with sure-handed skill. Elysian made headlines around the United States in 2015 when it was scooped up by Anheuser-Busch, a merger that Cantwell—and scores of PacNW beer fanatics—just couldn't swallow. Cantwell resigned soon after. Howls of purists' protests don't stop mega-million-dollar deals, of course, so consider your feelings about David vs. Goliath if you waltz into one of these brewpubs. It's been bought and sold to the highest bidder. The beer, of course, is still very good.

PHILOSOPHY

Collaborative. In 2008 Elysian began an exchange program of sorts ("collabeerations") with New Belgium Brewery, for which brewhouses, knowledge, and manpower are exchanged in order to keep things fresh and innovative. The program resulted in the Trip Series of experimental beers like a Black Belgo IPA and a juniper-infused ale.

KEY BEER

Like Boston Lager, the Wise ESB (a reference to the goddess Athena, and Elysian's first beer) shows a lot of malty backbone, a grain-given sturdiness that's typical for the style. Alas, ESBs also occasionally suffer from a cloying, fruit-like sweetness. Not so with the Wise: Its drier profile makes it far more quaffable in high volumes, which, frankly, has its own intrinsic wisdom. Even better, there's an overlay of mellow spiciness derived from three different kinds of tangy Northwest hops, making it perfect for fall's cool nights (5.9% ABV).

HALE'S ALES

4301 Leary Way NW • Seattle, WA 98107
(206) 706-1544 • halesbrewery.com
Established: 1983

SCENE & STORY

Like many Americans, Mike Hale tasted his first old-world craft beer in college while traveling abroad, and studied its curious properties with a deep and abiding conviction. About ten years later, still searching for the flavor and fired up by stories about Jack McAuliffe's efforts down at New Albion in California, he relocated to southern England in 1982, volunteered at Gale's Brewery and Guinness, and within a year of returning home to the Seattle area, he'd founded Hale's Ales.

The new little brewery was immediately hit with demand. After a few expansions in different locations over the years he settled on the current 17,000-square-foot location between Fremont and Ballard (in an old hose manufacturing plant) and opened a brewpub and beer garden to go with his new bigger brewhouse. It's got a wide-open feel with views directly into the operations area, complete with mirrors angled for views into the open fermenters.

PHILOSOPHY

"The main thing is to keep the main thing the main thing," Hale says, speaking about quality brewing practices. And to keep things running smooth with his accounts across the Pacific Northwest, Hale also restored a beautiful red double-decker bus and outfitted it with a draft bar, hot water, bathrooms, and plush club seating. Don't be surprised if you see him, Red Baron–style in the cockpit, the engine juddering away and the passengers raising toasts. It's a beautiful sight, but alas, not one he can legally open to members of the public. It must be used for "educational purposes" only. Isn't school great?

KEY BEER

Hale's 5.2% ABV Pale American Ale set a new standard in the Northwest when it was released, but it's the smooth, sessionable Cream Ale; grassy, grainy kölsch; and recent spate of double IPAs like Supergoose (7.5% ABV) that are the ones to try.

LATONA PUB

6423 Latona Ave. NE • Seattle, WA 98115
(206) 525-2238 • pubs.com/Latona.html
Established: 1987

SCENE & STORY

With its corner spot and high, wide windows, the Latona looks inviting from the outside, but it's the warm service, approachable clientele, and healthy but hearty pub fare (served on classic Fiestaware plates) that really set this beer bar apart. The menu reaches for a culinary grace note or two without grasping, and the beers (ten on tap, thirty bottled) are fresh thanks to quick rotations and a steady, curious clientele.

PHILOSOPHY

Reverential. "The beer brewed in our own backyard is created by some of the most talented, creative people in the world," write the owners on the website for the Latona and their two other Seattle pubs, Hopvine and Fiddler's Inn. "At our pubs, we want to present to you the closest thing to what the brewers create. We take care of the beer we pour."

KEY BEER

With its light-bodied notes of coffee and bitter chocolate, Big Time Brewery's Coal Creek Porter (4.5% ABV) would go nicely with the green chile chicken quesadillas.

NAKED CITY BREWERY & TAPHOUSE

8564 Greenwood Ave. N. • Seattle, WA 98103 • (206) 838-6299
nakedcitybrewing.com • Established: 2009

SCENE & STORY

Owners Don Webb and Donald Averill were home brewers with a common dream of opening their own breweries when they met and joined forces. Webb is a major film buff, hence the noirish theme running through the signage and art in the place; Naked City came out in 1948 based on the iconic book of New York real-life crime photos of the same name by Arthur Fellig, a.k.a. Weegee, in 1945 (check out the big framed movie poster for it in the taphouse). In filmmaking terms, Webb and Averill were thinking in big-budget 70mm Technicolor; in the end, budget constraints were more along the lines of an indie production, though hardly Spartan. They installed a 3.5-barrel system (about 100 gallons) and a twenty-four-tap bar, curated a vegan-friendly menu with sandwiches and starters like white truffle pâté and landjäger, a dried German sausage. It's a simple, smart arrangement.

PHILOSOPHY

Respect greatness, in beer or film form. Instead of reality shows and sports, the TVs show iconic old films; the taps are dedicated to craft beers made in small batches.

KEY BEER

Local and regional breweries like Chuckanut and Schooner Exact dominate the list; try Naked City's the Big Lebrewski, a 12% ABV Imperial Stout with blockbuster levels of roasted malt.

THE PIKE PUB & BREWERY

1415 1st Ave. • Seattle, WA 98101
(206) 622-6044 • pikebrewing.com
Established: 1989

SCENE & STORY

Located in the Pike Place Market area,

the pub is a multilevel, brightly painted beer lover's warren of three bars chockablock with a truly impressive collection of breweriana. The story this collection tells is the story of Charles and Rose Ann Finkel, who founded Pike after helping launch the American craft beer scene through Merchant Du Vin, a gourmet food, wine, and beer importing company they created in 1978. Through that pathbreaking firm, the Finkels introduced American palates to extraordinary beers never before tasted on these shores, including such iconic brands as Orval and Rochefort of Belgium, Samuel Smith's of Yorkshire, England, and Ayinger of Bavaria, Germany, all of which are considered classics of European brewing traditions.

Along the way, Finkel emerged as a talented graphic artist, designing beer labels for U.S. markets and eventually several books about beer and design. The Finkels opened Pike, their dream brewery, in 1989, and quickly accrued a trove of brewing industry medals and thirsty accounts. By 1997 they sold the brewery and import company to an unnamed investor, but after realizing they longed to be back in the beer fold, bought the brewery back in 2006.

PHILOSOPHY

The warm and charming Finkels are both conservationists and foodies, involved with Salone del Gusto (the biannual Slow Food convention in Turin, Italy), and they're ambitiously ramping up both the beer and food options in their brew-pub accordingly.

KEY BEER

While Pike's excellent Pale, IPA, XXXXX Stout, and Kilt Lifter Scotch Ale made the company famous, newer releases such as Pike Dry Wit are gaining notice from the likes of legendary Chez Panisse chef, Alice Waters. It's a wit, or unfiltered, Belgian-style white beer spiced with Nugget and Cascade hops, dried orange peel, coriander, chamomile, and organic lavender (5% ABV). In June 2014, Pike Brewing released Locale Skagit Valley Alba pale ale, with hops from Yakima, grains from Skagit and Whitman counties, and Pike Brewing's own yeast.

Woodinville

RED HOOK BREWERY & FORECASTERS PUBLIC HOUSE

14300 NE 145th St. • Woodinville, WA 98072 • (425) 483-3232 • redhook.com
Established: 1981

SCENE & STORY

Red Hook is one of the cornerstones in the church of Pacific Northwest craft brewing, but there was little hope things would go as well as they have. Founders Paul Shipman and Gordon Bowker started out inauspiciously with a Belgian ale brewed in a converted transmission shop in Seattle's Ballard neighborhood. Locals dubbed it "banana beer" and fewer than 1000bbl sold in year one. But Blackhook Porter and Ballard Bitter, released in 1983 and 1984, respectively, changed them from laughing-stock to growing concern, and in 1987 the ESB (Extra Special Bitter) became a clarion call to beer drinkers around the region. Bowker went on to found a little coffee shop called Starbucks, and today the brewery is a huge national brand with three plants and national distribution through Anheuser-Busch, an arrangement that irks many industry watchers and fills others with envy. In 2014 the brand ballooned to over 250,000 barrels per year, a 68% jump from the previous year.

The Woodinville operation is a big draw for Seattleites and area beer lovers for the al fresco movies and concerts, five-dollar tours of the brewery, and a bite in the brewpub (warning: hit-or-miss food; slow service). The best way to visit is on bike. Each year the Haul Ash Tour de Brew commemorates the 1980 eruption of Mount St. Helens. It's a round-trip ride from the brewery in Woodinville to Seattle's Fremont neighborhood along the verdant Burke-Gilman Trail.

PHILOSOPHY

Loosely? "Ya sure, ya betcha," as the Ballard Bitter labels once read in homage to the area's Scandinavian roots. These are clean, malt-forward beers taking off on British styles (mostly) with admirable fresh Pacific Northwest hop character.

KEY BEER

Just as good as it was back in '87—if perhaps cleaner and more consistent today—the 5.5% ABV Redhook ESB is a throwback to the English Extra Special Bitters, redolent of toasted malt with a pleasant sweetness and the tang of four hop additions. In 2009, the beer took a gold at the Great American Beer Festival, proving it's a still a benchmark beer decades after the first batch, no matter who's doing the brewing.

Tacoma

PARKWAY TAVERN

313 N. I St. • Tacoma, WA 98403
(253) 383-8748 • No website
Established: 1936

SCENE & STORY

Sometimes little old bars open since the 1930s with no website translate as: cool spot/bad beer. Not so with the Parkway. Its home of Tacoma (located down I-5 a bit between Seattle and Olympia) has a proud beer history, with no fewer than eight breweries up and running between 1888 and Prohibition. Built upon the restoration of lawful beer drinking in what appears to be a converted old shingled house in a quiet residential neighborhood, the Parkway Tavern is a retro gem with a beer list very much of the moment.

As for the bar itself, I'm sure you've heard those stories that begin "there used to be a beat-up old drop ceiling in here. We pulled it down and found this . . ." Which, when you look up, turns out to be acres of gorgeous stained wood. That's the Parkway's thirty-plus tap front room, with mahogany paneling, cherry wood tables, and polished bar. There's also a working fireplace and a game room of sorts in the back where guests play pool, darts, shuffleboard, and pinball (yes!). And don't leave without a visit to the Zebra Room. You'll know it when you see it.

PHILOSOPHY

There's an old bar sign that reads "the liver is evil . . . it must be punished," but with the excellent beers on tap here, you're hardly taking hard knocks. There are multiple festivals and tasting events here year-round for barrel-aged beers, barley wines, and IPAs.

KEY BEER

This would be the perfect place for the roasty but unpunishing Moylan's Dragoons

Dry Irish Stout (5% ABV), or perhaps a fresh Russian River tap, as they're frequent.

Bellingham

CHUCKANUT BREWERY & KITCHEN

601 W. Holly St. • Bellingham, WA 98225
(360) 752-3377
chuckanutbreweryandkitchen.com
Established: 2008

SCENE & STORY

Founder Will Kemper tells the story of walking into the old Rainier brewery (now shuttered) in Seattle to ask the brewmaster how he might get started in the trade. The brewer told him he'd have to have been born into it. Wrong answer. Kemper armed himself with the top degrees in brewing (which would lead to eventual teaching appointments in California and London) before going on to found the influential Thomas Kemper brewery (a venture which was later sold to Pyramid). He became a globetrotting consultant, setting up or running scores of breweries in Mexico, Europe, and in Turkey before making his most recent move, to Bellingham, where he set up this technically advanced brewery with

an off-kilter name. Today the little seventy-five-seat Chuckanut brewery (built in a converted waterfront warehouse) is a sunny affair with six rotating taps, buttery walls, and a gleaming, fully automated brewhouse. Kemper's latest venture was honored with best brewer and small brewpub of the year in 2009 at the Great American Beer Festival, which just goes to show you can't keep a good brewer down. In 2015, the company announced plans for a larger brewery at the Port of Skagit, near the Skagit airport.

PHILOSOPHY

Clean, controlled, and mostly true to established styles, Kemper's operation is one of a variety executed with a true perfectionist's eye for detail. There's an open kitchen with a wood-burning oven for preparing pizzas and tasty, healthy food to pair with his beers.

KEY BEER

Try the pale golden kölsch, with a refreshingly light, herbal, hay-like taste and crisp finish (5% ABV), which won a gold in 2015 at the GABF. They also took a gold in 2014 for their Chuckanut Dunkel.

DETOUR ➡ THE ULTIMATE ALE SAIL

Schooner Zodiac • 1221 Harris Ave., PNB 2 • Bellingham, WA 98225 • (206) 719-7622 • schoonerzodiac.com

Washington's Puget Sound is known for roving pods of killer whales and soaring bald eagles, craggy remote islets with sleepy sea lions, bobbing otters, barking harbor seals, and the occasional humpback. It's also home to a handful of breweries accessible by sea. What better way to tour them than on a majestic 127-foot topsail schooner built in 1924? The Schooner Zodiac will occasionally set sail from Bellingham on multi-day tours with steaming breweries in the looking-glass every day, including but not limited to stops at Snoqualmie Brewery & Taproom, Chuckanut Brewery & Kitchen, and Port Townsend Brewing Company. In between brewery tours, the skilled onboard chef keeps your belly full, fueling afternoon kayak excursions among forested islets and sessions spent learning the ropes, hauling sheets and lines, and generally earning a bit of ale (dispensed freely when the anchor's down). At last, it's time to home brew some "Schooner Rat IPA" under the stars with noted Northwest brewers—if you've got the energy to stay awake.

DIAMOND KNOT

621-A Front St. • Mukilteo, WA 98275
(425) 355-4488 • diamondknot.com
Established: 1994

SCENE & STORY

The merchant ship Diamond Knot sank in 1947 a quarter mile from Port Angeles in 135 feet of water carrying precious cargo: an estimated 5.7 million cans of choice Alaskan canned salmon. Insurers said it was a lost cause, but crewmen and locals jury-rigged a vacuum system to hoover the edibles out of the ocean, and the successful mission came to symbolize local, er, can-do spirit. When home brew buddies and coworkers at Boeing Bob Mophet and the late Brian Sollenburger decided to launch a self-distributing brewing company without quitting their day jobs, they were discouraged, too. But they channeled the fabled can-rescue operation, took over a converted transit building garage that once housed a pub, and started brewing big beers with boatloads of Northwest hops in every batch. Just fifteen years later, the business has grown to include this location, a gloriously funky spot with sawdust on the floors and crowds of locals, a second brewpub, and a third establishment, a beer bar.

PHILOSOPHY

Where there's a will, there's a way.

KEY BEER

The big, burly, and pungent Diamond Knot IPA put these Boeing cabin boys on a downwind. Look for dry-hopped versions with Simcoe, and the Shipwreck XXXIPA, an Imperial IPA with a leviathan's bite.

Stevenson

WALKING MAN BREWING CO.

240 SW First St. • Stevenson, WA 98648
(509) 427-5520 • walkingmanbeer.com
Established: 2000

SCENE & STORY

Just across the river from the Oregon beer-blessed town of Hood River in the scenic Columbia Gorge, this small-town brewpub has a bevy of tanks shoehorned into a back room, twelve taps, lots of wood paneling, and a collection of bottle openers on a vertical wood beam next to the cash register. The pub fare is heavy on pizzas, and the patio is great in the summer, with live music in a grassy little garden area. In homage to the legendary Sasquatch, there's an ambulatory theme to most of the beers (Jaywalker; Old Stumblefoot; Pale Strider). And there's just something to love about a place where the bathrooms are themed "Readers" and "Dreamers."

PHILOSOPHY

Big beers with big feet. Higher-than-usual alcohol and hopping rates define most of the Walking Man beers, which vary in drinkability. The brewery also hosts the Sasquatch Legacy Project, a yearly charity brew by recipients of the Glen Hay Falconer Scholarship named in honor of the late influential Oregon brewer.

KEY BEER

Knuckle Dragger, an American Pale Ale of 6.5% ABV, is a malty, hoppy citrus bomb that would send Big Foot into naptime in no time.

BEST *of the* REST: WASHINGTON

THE MASONRY

20 Roy St. • Seattle, WA 98109 • (206) 453-4375 • themasonryseattle.com

Launched in August 2013, the Masonry is affable founder Matt Storm's wood-fired, charred crust Neopolitan pizza oasis, with fourteen well-chosen taps (plus wine and cider, too). It's one of Uptown Seattle's most popular spots thanks to that pizza—and frequent brewery dinners with the likes of Anchorage Brewing Co., Jolly Pumpkin, and Belgian cult favorite De Struise, plus an outstanding annual farmhouse beer fest.

THE PINE BOX

1600 Melrose Ave. • Seattle, WA 98122 • (206) 588-0375 • pineboxbar.com

Opening in 2012 with more than thirty beers on tap, founder Ian Roberts (a veteran of Seattle Beer Week and Brouwer's Café) brought Capitol Hill a thoroughly modern beer hall, albeit one constructed in a former mortuary with lots of hardwood and leaded glass. The creative food list gets high marks, and the list is peppered with new-school faves like Almanac, St. Petersburg, Florida's surging Green Bench, and Seattle's own Black Raven. Mondays are often dedicated to sour beer, a nice touch.

BLACK RAVEN BREWING CO.

14679 NE 95th St. • Redmond, WA 98052 • (425) 881-3020 • blackravenbrewing.com

Opened in 2009, Black Raven is a production-minded brewery (read: no restaurant inside) that has marched confidently into the Seattle and Washington beer scenes over the past five years. With a 15bbl system and an ambitious barrel-aging program (using bourbon, rye, red, white, and cognac barrels), Black Raven has a huge following these days, thanks to beers like Trickster IPA, as well as Pour les Oiseaux, a viognier barrel-aged saison, and Splinters, a 10.8% ABV Scotch Ale. Wednesday is cask night, allowing brewers to present their latest one-offs and experiments.

FREMONT BREWING

1050 N. 34th St. • Seattle, WA 98103 • (206) 420-2407 • fremontbrewing.com

An oasis in Fremont, an industrial/artist enclave, this eco-minded brewery and beer garden (founded in 2009) is a must-hit sunny day stop when visiting Seattle. Founder Matt Lincecum and his team take a classic approach, focusing mainly on sessionable pale ales and IPAs like Interurban, but plenty of bigger and even sour beers have graced the taps. The addition of a canning line threw fat on the fire; crowds are common, but don't let it keep you from a visit.

THE BURGUNDIAN

2253 N. 56th St. • Seattle, WA 98103 • (206) 420-8943 • burgundianbar.com

Matt Bonney, owner of Bottleworks (a bottle shop in Wallingford that offers over 950 mostly Belgian bottles) and the famed Brouwer's Café (sixty-four taps), opened Burgundian in early 2012, in Tangletown. On offer: a solid array of acclaimed beers, plus cocktails, and a comfort-food menu of much-loved chicken and waffles, biscuits and gravy, and fluffy egg dishes served all day long.

THE BEER JUNCTION

4511 California Ave. SW • Seattle, WA 98116 • (206) 938-2337 • thebeerjunction.com

Every city needs a great bottle shop. This is one of Seattle's top stops. Opened in 2010 and moved to this new, busy, central west Seattle location in early 2012, you'll find 1,300-plus beers, sixteen rotating taps, and a good variety of beer-related gifts. The goods are well organized, the service is good, and there's even a small parking lot. Just don't expect to have the place to yourself when you arrive.

REUBEN'S BREWS

5010 14th Ave. NW • Seattle WA 98107 • (206) 784-2859 • reubensbrews.com

This Ballard taproom is the new outpost for much-loved local home brewer turned pro Adam Robbings, who, with his family, has gone from strength to strength since opening in the summer of 2012. Sample up to twenty-four house brews on tap. Start with the award-winning cream ale and work your way through a huge variety of beer styles, from strong porter to IPA and a highly-ranked gose.

STOUP BREWING

1108 NW 52nd St. • Seattle, WA 98107 • (206) 457-5524 • stoupbrewing.com

Also in Ballard, this airy little spot (founded by a trio of science majors, named for old English drinking vessels, and launched in 2013) is best enjoyed on a rare sunny afternoon. Sample a variety of styles very much in the Pacific Northwest mold, from IPA to Robust Porter, which took a prestigious silver in the World Beer Cup in 2014, and refuel at food carts parked out front.

THE STUMBLING MONK

1635 E. Olive Way • Seattle, WA 98122 • (206) 860-0916 • No website

This tiny little corner beer bar on Capitol Hill has twelve taps and fifty bottled selections, and better yet, no loud music or TVs. Nor is there a menu of food (unless you count potato chips as food), but you can order in. In classic dive bar fashion, you come here for board games like Scrabble, Connect Four, and Battleship. It gets cramped and sweaty. But this is a dive bar that also happens to boast a great list of beers, from the exotic sours of Portland's Cascade Barrel House to Belgium's iconic pale ale with Brettanomyces, Orval (6.2% ABV).

ÜBER TAVERN

7517 Aurora Ave. N. • Seattle, WA 98103 • (206) 782-2337 • uberbier.com

There's a reason locals talk of the Über warp—time disappears when you step in the door. Opened in 2006 with seventeen taps and 150 bottled brews (heavy on the Belgians and upstart regionals like Black Raven and Beer Valley, of Ontario, Oregon), this idyllic little Green Lake–area beer bar is neither dive nor stuffy, beer-snob perch, with cool neon signage outside and a rapidly rotated beer list within its cobalt-blue walls (and I have to mention the gas-flame fireplace table). Look for Anacortes Brewery's Locomotive Breath, a bold, barrel-black Imperial Stout (8.5% ABV).

BOUNDARY BAY BREWERY & BISTRO

1107 Railroad Ave. • Bellingham, WA 98225 • (360) 647-5593 • bbaybrewery.com

Bellingham, the college-y "City of Subdued Excitement," got quite a bit more buzz in 1995 when this standout brewpub came to be. With twelve taps, nine bottles, and two casks at any given time (plus a hearty menu of burgers, beer-barbecued pork, smoked salmon chowder, mac 'n' cheese, and fish tacos) this large, brick, neighborly hangout located on Railroad Avenue has done well thanks to beers like Inside Passage Ale (an IPA of 6.4% ABV) and the outdoor patio and lawn beer garden, hosting live music and spontaneous hula-hoop contests. Recent chef-driven beer dinners and the Galbraith Mountains series of single hop brews have been heartily embraced.

EVERYBODY'S BREWING

151 E. Jewett Blvd. • White Salmon, WA 98672 • (509) 637-2774 • everybodysbrewing.com

Established in 2009 with sixteen taps (up to nine of their own), Everybody's has a twenty-six-foot-long handcrafted bar, long wooden banquet tables, and idyllic views of Mount Hood across the Columbia Gorge in Oregon. Remember, you're in hop country, so order the Country Boy IPA (6.2% ABV) and head out to the porch. Recent projects include the "Tiny Tank" series brews with new-school hops like Mosaic and Citra.

THE NORTH FORK BREWERY, PIZZERIA, BEER SHRINE & WEDDING CHAPEL

6186 Mt. Baker Hwy. • Deming, WA 98244 • (360) 599-2337 •northforkbrewery.com

True to its name, this funky spot (established in 1997) along the Mount Baker Highway about thirty minutes from Bellingham has a whole lot of love going on for one place. With just five taps from a tiny little 3.5bbl system, it may look a little like Navin R. Johnson's family home from *The Jerk*, but that's exactly while you'll want to make drive. Where else can you hang out in a log house with ninety years' worth of beer bric-a-brac, drink nano-brewed beer (try the 11% ABV 1000 barley wine to steady those nerves), eat pizza pie, and get hitched?

IDAHO

IDAHO, LIKE OH-SO-MANY OTHER STATES IN THE UNITED STATES, USED TO HAVE PRECIOUS few good beer spots. The beer lists were predictable. No longer. From 2011 to 2013 the state's barrel output fully doubled to over 40,000bbl. Specialty styles and experimentation are taking hold. Now the whole state, especially Boise, is booming with over fifty breweries in 2015, a near $200 million industry. And with new-era taprooms opening up, the state's overall selection is growing by the minute. The scenery is spectacular, especially in summer. Make a beer-based road trip through "the gem state" and you'll unearth a trove of hoppy emeralds.

Coeur d'Alene

CRAFTED TAPHOUSE & KITCHEN

523 Sherman Ave. • Coeur d'Alene, ID
83814 • (208) 292-4813
craftedtaphouse.com • Established: 2014

SCENE & STORY

Flanked by a pair of ski hills (Schweitzer and Silver Mountain), northern Idaho's Coeur d'Alene, named for the Coeur d'Alene Indians, is a very, very pretty spot. Overlooking the vast Lake Coeur d'Alene, the city has really boomed in recent years. The city is surrounded by mountainous country filled with lakes and campgrounds. All that activity stokes a discerning local crowd, and with its industrial-chic interior, airy patio, ambitious gastropub menu, and supercosmopolitan beer list, local Rob Berger's beer-focused spot has made a mark in a short time. The burgers are a big draw. And they are big themselves. If you're not into the huge two-hander style, consider the manageable "#42," made with local ground beef, cambozola cheese, roasted garlic-bacon jam, arugula, and a house-baked bun.

PHILOSOPHY

This is a spacious (3,000-square-foot) modern beer lover's spot, with fifty taps and bright modern aesthetics that wouldn't feel out of place in, say, suburban Los Angeles. In the summer, with its Mediterranean climate, this makes a lot of sense. Grab a spot outside, and let the knowledgeable servers guide you into some serious beer and good food. Just to remind you it's a very small town, the big draw Friday nights is turtle races—featuring actual turtles—treading across a huge white disc.

KEY BEER

The list is filled with some pretty hard-to-find brews, but it's the local and regional specialties that get top billing, like No-Li, out of Spokane, Washington.

Victor

GRAND TETON BREWING CO.

430 Old Jackson Hwy. • Victor, ID 83455
(208) 787-9000 • grandtetonbrewing.com
Established: 1988

SCENE & STORY

Grand Teton Brewing Company was actually founded seventeen miles away from Victor, in Wilson, Wyoming, as Otto Brothers' Brewing in 1988, by Charlie and Ernie Otto. It was the first modern microbrewery in the state, and represented the first malt beverage production

permit in Wyoming in thirty-five years. Eventually changing their name and relocating to beautiful Victor in 2000, the brothers have embarked on a few interesting firsts.

One, they claim to have reintroduced the sixty-four-ounce growler into modern use after an offhand comment by their father, who recalled using lidded tin pails in Germany to transport beer. And more recently, they created an all-Idaho beer, using only ingredients grown or sourced from within the state. The uncommon Zeus and Bravo hops were grown in southwest Idaho, the barley was grown and malted in the southeast, and the water came from a spring in the Tetons. If you're anywhere near Victor and the Grand Tetons, you can get a taste of this brew (no food, though) at their quaint little taproom seven days a week.

PHILOSOPHY

Progressive. The brewery has worked with fifty charities in the area, and the beers keep getting more innovative with each batch.

KEY BEER

There are five year-round beers, including the flagship, Bitch Creek Extra Special Brown (6% ABV), which has nutty, cocoa-like flavors mingling with a lightly hoppy finish. But look for the Cellar Reserve brews, like a recent imperial pilsner, Persephone (8.75% ABV).

BEST *of the* REST: IDAHO

CLOUD 9 BREWING

1750 W. State St. • Boise, ID 83702 • (208) 336-0681 • cloud9brewery.com

Opened in 2014 in Boise's North End by locals Maggie and Jake Lake, Cloud 9 is an ambitious nanobrewery with a little four barrel system, based on eco-minded sourcing (read: certified organic ingredients in the brewhouse and kitchen). With eight on draft and rotating specialties, several beers are gaining fans around Boise and beyond. Try the smooth and cocoa-like 9 Grain Porter (6.9% ABV).

SLATE CREEK BREWING

1710 N. 4th St., Ste. 115 • Coeur d'Alene, ID 83814 • (208) 664-7727 • slatecreekbrewing.com

A new local favorite opened in 2014 by outdoorsy brothers Jason and Ryan Wing, Slate Creek is named for one of their favorite fishing and boating spots deep in the forest, a tributary of the St. Joe River in Northern Idaho. On the wall: a huge elk head, from a bull Ryan stalked. Try the Norse Nectar juniper pale ale (5.7% ABV), a cross of Finnish sahti (the Wings are Scandinavian by heritage) and American pale ale brewed with juniper and rye malt.

SELKIRK ABBEY

6180 E. Seltice Way • Post Falls, ID 83854 • (208) 292-4901 • selkirkabbey.com

Even in late 2015, it's still fairly surprising when an American craft brewery hews exclusively to Belgian brewing modes. It's even more surprising to find such a brewery in a somewhat remote stretch of northern Idaho. Selkirk Abbey, founded in 2013 between Coeur d'Alene and Spokane in Post Falls (population: 29,000) has a cozy, abbey-themed taproom. Start with a low-ABV saison and work up through the amber, spicy Infidel Belgian IPA to much bigger beers like 12°, a well-made Belgian strong dark (9.8% ABV).

PAYETTE BREWING CO.

111 W. 33rd St. • Boise, ID 83714 • (208) 344-0011 • payettebrewing.com

Named for a historical French trapper, Payette was founded in 2010 by local former Boeing engineer turned Siebel Institute grad Mike Francis in Boise, quickly capturing the attention of the local beer scene with a range of solid brews (and good food trucks for sustenance). Francis and Co. were soon cranking out over 10,000bbls a year on a 15bbl system—a huge output for the size—much of it in the form of Outlaw IPA in cans. Another brewery pulled trademark rank, so it will be renamed, but Francis isn't slowing down. In mid-2015 the crew broke ground on a new, $4.5 million, 30,000-square-foot facility with production brewery and tasting room to open in 2016.

BITTERCREEK ALEHOUSE

246 N. 8th St. • Boise, ID 83702 • (208) 429-6340 • justeatlocal.com/bittercreek

Opened in 1996, this Boise standby is plushed out with dark woods and leather and stocked with thirty-nine taps from Idaho, Oregon, Washington, Montana, Colorado, and California (and a small selection of regional bottled beers). They rotate the tap list daily, throwing a cask on the bar on occasion, and the pub grub ranges from sandwiches and burgers to fish and- chips, Alaskan salmon, Idaho pork chops, and a barbecue plate. Look for the Terminal Gravity Breakfast Porter (5.7% ABV), especially if you're in the place for your first meal of the day.

LAUGHING DOG BREWING

55 Emerald Industrial Park Rd. • Ponderay, ID 83852 • (208) 263-9222 • laughingdogbrewing.com

A very dog-friendly brewery with very hoppy beers, Laughing Dog is a chilled-out, hometown, family kind of place. Established in 2005, production is north of 4,500bbls, and the tasting room has twelve taps, with a few goodies stashed away. Look for Dogzilla (6.9% ABV), considered one of the earliest India Black Ales (a.k.a. Black IPA), brewed with Simcoe and Cascade hops, pale and Munich malts, and black barley.

ALASKA

LIFE IN ALASKA HAS NEVER BEEN EASY, BUT BEER HELPS, ESPECIALLY IF YOU DON'T have to import it. Stoked by home brewers who could make beer affordable by brewing it at home rather than paying for cost-prohibitive beer shipments, the craft beer scene in Alaska is hitting a rolling boil. While Alaska's capital, Juneau, has the state's oldest bar and first craft brewery, Anchorage is pulling its weight in the beer department with a slew of high-quality brewpubs, beer bars, and the annual Great Alaska Beer & Barley Wine Festival, held in the icy depths of mid-January. *But isn't it cold at that time of year?* Yes. It's bleakly, face-numbingly, eye-frostingly cold, though locals walk around in Windbreakers and wonder aloud how warm it seems. *But it gets dark so early.* Yes, all the more reason to make hay while the sun shines and then go drink delicious beer. No matter how you approach it, a beer trip to Alaska will be a great adventure.

Anchorage

Fact is, the winter weather in Anchorage doesn't stop locals from gathering, much less going mountain biking (with snow tires!) along the water with views of Mount McKinley (elevation: 20,320 feet) or even across a frozen lake, with the soaring Chugach peaks behind town. Nor does the drop in the mercury stop brewers from showing up with their best stuff—high-strength, cellar-worthy barley wines are popular up here—especially during the festival. A midwinter visit to Anchorage is all about the camaraderie of the state's growing brewing scene: for the annual Great Alaska Beer & Barley Wine Festival, over fifty breweries band together, including twenty-plus operating in Alaska—and about 2,000 locals a night don their finest going-out-on-the-town clothes, making it fun and unexpected—kind of like mountain biking in January.

ANCHORAGE BREWING CO.
148 W. 91st St. • Anchorage, AK 99515
(907) 677-2739 • Established: 2011
anchoragebrewingcompany.com

SCENE & STORY

Alaska's most remarkable modern brewery is the vision of soft-spoken Gabe Fletcher, formerly the head brewer at Anchorage's Midnight Sun. Fletcher launched his brand in 2011 with the help of another Anchorage brewer, Sleeping Lady Brewing Company, from whom he sourced wort and gravity-flowed it into his own cellar space below the building for fermentation and aging. The results were nothing short of spectacular, and Fletcher recently moved his entire operation into a massive 8,000-square-foot facility near the intersection of 92nd Avenue and King Street (word to the wise: bring your mapping-enabled phone or GPS unit). There he's amassed a truly amazing collection of French oak barrels and *foudres* (huge upright oak fermenters), and other casks for aging, during which time beers accrue interesting acidic angles, tannins, and vanillin from the wine-soaked wood. After a period of time, he blends, then bottles the Belgian-style brews according to the *méthode champenoise*. It's a simple, immaculately clean operation with a modest-size tasting room, long wood tables, and garage doors. Outside, plans call for fire pits. For all those who can't make the trip to Anchorage, Fletcher's beers became only the third brewery on American soil to be distributed by the Shelton Brothers, America's most adventurous importers of specialty, small batch, and farmhouse ales from around the world.

PHILOSOPHY

Flanders on the Klondike. This is innovative, Belgian-style brewing in the heart of wild Alaska—as unexpected as they come. Recently Fletcher has launched the Culmination Festival, a small but ultraprestigious gathering of American and European brewers that use hops, wood, and wild yeast to memorable effect.

DETOUR → WINTER WARMER

The Great Alaskan Beer & Barley Wine Festival, started in 2005, is held every January, traditionally in downtown Anchorage's Egan Convention Center. Brewers compete for medals and bragging rights in the Barley Wine category and mingle with about 2,000 fans a night. Do as the locals do and hang out in the Alaska section of the fest, where just about every single commercial brewery in Alaska has a booth with fresh beer. There's a Connoisseur Session on the final afternoon, for which the brewers present beers they used to hide under the tables. Highly recommended for tried-and-true craft beer lovers. (auroraproductions.net/beer-barley.html)

Collaborations and guest brewer visits have included the likes of Jolly Pumpkin (resulting in Clementina, a clementine, yuzu, and lime peel brew dosed with pink Himalayan salt and coriander), as well as Vermont's Hill Farmstead, and the global icon of sour beer, Cantillon.

KEY BEER

Fletcher debuted at the 2011 Great Alaskan Beer & Barley Wine Festival with Anticipation, a superb double IPA (9% ABV), though it was more a test run (not barrel-aged in the cellar), and began releasing his main line of six distinct beers in 2011. These included the intriguing Love Buzz Saison, brewed with rose hips, peppercorns, and fresh orange peels, then dry-hopped in the pinot noir barrel with Citra hops, and bottled with a cork-and-cage, in the manner of traditional Belgian beers. But let's face it: if you made it there, you're trying everything in sight.

HUMPY'S GREAT ALASKAN ALEHOUSE

610 W. 6th Ave. • Anchorage, AK 99501
(907) 276-2337 • humpys.com
Established: 1994

SCENE & STORY

The twin sister to Humpy's in Hawaii, Humpy's is a serious beer bar, but is by no means pretentious. It's named for pink salmon, a species also known as humpback salmon because the spines of the males eventually bend (developing a hump) from the effort of chasing females upstream and back to their birthplace every summer. And it's consistently busy, especially in the summer, when cruise ships bring hordes of tourists in and out of ancient fjords, so there's really no time for attitude here.

It's a casual place inside, with padded booths, an octagonal bar, and a back patio for king crab feasts when in season. Founder Billy Opinsky is thoughtful and polished, and stands somewhat apart in the land of unironic trucker hats and foot-long beards with his passing resemblance to a young Al Gore. Deeply involved with Alaska's nascent craft beer scene from its early days, he has stocked the bar with fifty-five taps and fifteen bottled selections, with about half of the tap row consisting of beers from the state. The bar is known for good live musical performances from local and touring acoustic acts, and for unusual beer-tasting events during the big festival in January.

PHILOSOPHY

For beer lovers, by beer lovers. This is a classic good beer spot with no extraneous frills.

KEY BEER

Ask what's freshest and taste tap beer to make sure lines are clean—a regrettable recent issue here. A dependable tap is Midnight Sun's coppery Sockeye Red IPA (5.7% ABV), with a powerful, fragrant, and spicy hop character.

MEET ME *on the* BEER FRONTIER

THE GREAT NORTHERN BREWERS CLUB AND BREWERS GUILD OF ALASKA ANNUAL MEETING

For a small group of Alaskans, there's an eagerly anticipated event that takes place each year at the Snow Goose Brewing Company's early 1960s ballroom. Amid giant tapestries hung from the wood-paneled walls (polar bear, grizzlies, a unicorn), the Great Northern Brewers Club—a statewide organization founded in 1980 that appears to consist partly of fur trappers, Woodstock time-travelers, and Carhartt-clad loggers—calls itself to order, and simultaneously hosts the Brewers Guild of Alaska for its only meeting of the year.

This is a beer thing, of course, so it's not exactly solemn. The 100 or so home-brew club members—some of whom were said to have bush-planed in from the interior—bring potluck dishes of chili (and one labeled simply "moose") and coolers with beer, and gather around in circles of folding chairs.

I crashed the 2011 meeting, during which Jim "Dr. Fermento" Roberts (head of the state brewers' guild, a separate entity, and a local beer authority for the Anchorage Press and the California-based *Celebrator Beer News*) took the little stage in a plaid shirt, khakis, and a pair of spectacles to read Important Announcements, which he unfurled like a scroll to the floor. It was a warm welcome to just about everyone in the room, including two "Beerdrinkers of the Year" (a contest held each year at Wynkoop Brewing Company in Denver), representatives of most of the Alaska-based breweries, and the keynote speaker, Sierra Nevada's Ken Grossman. Dr. Fermento wound it up five minutes later with the admonition "Drink responsibly; throw up strategically—make it count," which provoked a laugh because Fermento seems about as wild as a ceramics teacher.

The introductions complete, Fermento passed around a Victoria's Secret shopping bag; this was to collect donations for an injured community member. Next was Ken Grossman's absorbing I-was-a-home-brewer-too talk; you could have heard a pin drop. For the rest of the night, Grossman, Alaskan Brewing Company founder and Guild "Lead Berserker" Geoff Larson, Fermento and others mingled as a few Big Lebowski–era John Goodman types in hunting vests and trucker hats discussed delicate brewing experiments gone amok in one breath, and tropical illness and Thailand's phallic shrines the next.

Things were just warming up when the band took the stage. Clad in a Hawaiian shirt, Tom Dalldorf, publisher of the *Celebrator*, gamely led his Rolling Boil Blues Band in a rendition of "Home Brew," to the tune of Clapton's "Hand Jive." As I wandered around and sampled beers of varying ambition—from good IPA to stout and then one pilsner that tasted, well, a little like cat pee smells—I got the sense that if it weren't for this club, there would be no surging Alaskan brewing industry today (and thus no Guild), and that certain Alaskan citizens might never venture out of their snowbound cabins in the dead of winter, if not for the chance to toast each other's hard work—and share some of that tasty moose.

MIDNIGHT SUN BREWING CO.

8111 Dimond Hook Dr. • Anchorage, AK 99507 • (907) 344-1179 midnightsunbrewing.com • Established: 1995

SCENE & STORY

Under the watch of brewer Gabe Fletcher for twelve years, Midnight Sun emerged as Alaska's most innovative brewery, and built a strong reputation in the Pacific Northwest for big, interesting beers. New brewer Ben Johnson has a tough act to follow, but he's got plenty of training and a huge standing army of dedicated fans. And with a new brewhouse and "the Loft"—an upstairs area with some fifteen to twenty taps, sleek metal tables and chairs, and polished cement floors—MSBC remains a top draw for beer travelers (and locals) every day of the week from 11 a.m. to 8 p.m. (Note: Alaska state law forbids breweries without certain licenses from staying open past 8 p.m. or serving individuals more than thirty-six ounces, but package and growler sales help take care of that wrinkle.) Call for detailed directions or a map, as the brewery can be tricky to find. Once a month it's First Firkin Friday, for which they feature a local artist and—you guessed it—tap a fresh firkin, a traditionally English bar-top, forty-one-liter cask of beer.

Beers with Years

Aged-beers might sound like a lark, but it's not only wine and whiskey that can benefit from a bit of cellar time. Good beer is universally drinkable the minute it leaves a brewery, but, like a good dry-aged steak, time can add new layers of complexity to brews with a higher alcohol content— roughly two and a half times stronger than your average supermarket lagers. (They don't improve with time, hence their "drink by" dates. Chug away.) There's an array of styles that lay down well, including imperial stouts, English-style barley wines, Belgian lambics and other sours, as well as barrel-aged and other strong beers. Alcohol by volume generally needs to be in the area of 9 to 10 percent to give the beer any chance of improvement, and the cork or cap should be in good shape to avoid oxidation, which gives beer a wet cardboard taste. Beers with Brettanomyces can continue to change in the bottle as the voracious single-cell organisms metabolize every last molecule they can find. Ultraviolet light must be avoided to spare a beer from the skunk effect, a more serious problem with green or clear bottles (as opposed to brown ones, which filter UV light). With the exception of sour-style beers, which often have little hop character, the process of aging mellows bitterness and aroma while deepening and accentuating malt characteristics, often drying out the last fermentable sugars and sometimes adding an acidic, vinous note that can pair well with desserts or certain rich poultry and beef dishes. Aging beers simply requires patience, the proper setting (a cool, dark place), and an open mind.

PHILOSOPHY

"We make a lot of crazy stuff," says Midnight Sun owner Mark Staples. "We always try to avoid what everybody else is doing; we didn't brew an amber for like ten years because Alaskan Amber dominated this market. Every brewer that works for me started on the bottling line and washing kegs. Not one of them is some fancy brewer from some school. As a result, our beers are a little bit unique. We just brew what we feel like brewing."

KEY BEER

There are ten year-round offerings, including the flagship Sockeye Red IPA (5.7% ABV), four seasonals, five special edition beers, and several other one-offs and collaborations to try. Try the clove-y, creamy, Belgian-style dark Monk's Mistress and Arctic Devil, a nutty, warming, complex barley wine (typically around 13% ABV) that has cleaned up at the Great Alaskan beer festival for years.

GLACIER BREWHOUSE

737 West 5th Ave., No. 110 Anchorage, AK
99501 • (907) 274-2739
glacierbrewhouse.com • Established: 1997

SCENE & STORY

Glacier BrewHouse enjoys a superb location downtown and seems disconcertingly like just another high-end brewpub chain at first glance. But tastes of the beers (especially stronger styles, including eisbocks and barley wines, head brewer Kevin Burton's passion) prove you're in a special place. There's an expansive menu of good food here, and a huge array of beers available, from clean interpretations of classic styles like IPA and stout, to wilder, bigger beers fermented in "the wall of wood," Burton's basement stash of fifty wine, bourbon, and other oak casks from around the world. A couple of yearly highlights are Burton's Twelve Days of Barley Wine, leading right up into the Christmas holiday, with a different pair of aged barley wines on offer in the brewpub each day, and the Beer Train, a 100-mile train trip along the Turnagain Airm from Anchorage to Portage aboard an Alaska Railroad locomotive loaded with good beer.

PHILOSOPHY

Ambition is its own reward. "You're always striving for that perfect one," says Burton.

KEY BEER

Big Woody, an annual vintage-dated barley wine release. Using pricy English floor–malted barley and aged in various oak barrels including Jim Beam and Napa Valley wine barrels for a minimum of a year, it's intensely malty with notes of vanilla, wood, cherry, and toffee, and usually about 11% ABV.

Juneau and Region

For a town that cannot be accessed by road—to get to Juneau, the state capital of Alaska, you must fly or arrive by boat—there have been a lot of firsts here. The state's first big gold strike, in 1880, was close by. About a century later, the state struck gold again, in say, drinkable form. In 1986, Geoff and Marci Larson founded Alaskan Brewing Company—Alaska's first brewery since Prohibition—in Juneau.

In all seriousness, consider a midwinter visit, not only to coordinate with the Great Alaska Beer & Barley Wine Festival in Anchorage, held in mid-January, but also to get a sense of the authentic character—and characters—of the place. The millions of cruise ship passengers trundling ashore all summer long to gawk at glaciers and buy a plastic king crab refrigerator magnet have no idea what local dwellers are really made of. It's in the winter you discover that even mild-mannered locals like Donovan Neal—comptroller of Alaskan Brewing Company—moonlight as alpine guides, leading winter climbs (and ski descents!) of Cascade volcanoes. You see the Larsons (of Alaska Brewing Company fame) and their neighbors up near the Eaglecrest ski area on Douglas Island, just across the channel, with huskies and malamutes volunteer training for catastrophic avalanche victim recovery. The sheer 3,576-foot face of Mount Juneau looms immediately behind town; a 1962 slide took out seventeen houses. *National Geographic* later pronounced it the city with the highest avalanche danger in America.

You won't miss the sun and you sure won't miss the crowds. And you've got incredible powder to ski; a mid-January weekday run to the excellent Eaglecrest ski area (a twenty-minute drive) can mean lift lines in the single digits—as in you and a buddy. And most of all, you've got great fresh beer to drink in atmospheric old bars like the Alaskan bar (since 1913). Gold rush, indeed.

THE ALASKAN BREWING CO.

5429 Shaune Dr. • Juneau, AK 99801
(907) 780-5866 • alaskanbeer.com
Established: 1986

SCENE & STORY

Geoff and Marcy Larson met while bouncing around in various national parks jobs in the late 1970s. "I was hitch-hiking across the country during a summer off college and ran out of money in Montana," recalls Geoff, who was previously more stably based in Maryland. He met Marcy, a Florida native with a photojournalism degree, while both were working in Glacier National Park, where the two embarked on a "summer romance gone really wild," recalls Marcy. By 1981, they were living in the Klondike State, dreaming full-time about opening a brewery for the locals, who seemed interested in high-quality imported brews but had no local options. A big Anchorage-based German brewery built during the pipeline years called Prinz Brau had gone under in the late 1970s; the Larsons felt they could succeed with something more, well, Alaskan.

They decided to go for it. With "no experience and no money of our own, nothing whatsoever" as Marcy recalls, and after thirteen stressful months of raising loans from various friends, family, and locals, the Alaskan Brewing Company became the sixty-seventh operating brewery in the United States and the only one in Alaska. It was 1986. The early days were rocky; Alaska's economy was in the tank, and skeptics said they'd soon go under.

Not so fast. In 1988, Alaskan won the consumer preference poll at the GABF, and sales were rocketing. Today it's the twelfth-largest craft brewery out of some 4,000 in the country (and still employee- and local investor-owned), manufacturing over 100,000bbl per year for seventeen states. The first brew (now the flagship) was their Amber, based on a 1907 purchase order for altbier ingredients a local collector had preserved from a long lost area brewery—smooth and full of caramel malt goodness, with a

DETOUR ➜ KA'S BEST LATE NIGHT SHACK: PEL'MENI

2 Marine Way • Juneau, AK 99801 • (907) 463-2630

Who needs a menu? At Pel'meni, a hole-in-the-wall Russian café in the classic old blue Merchants Wharf building down by the water, there are really only two choices—beef or potato (you want both). When you walk in, it's just five little tables, a small counter, and a wall of vinyl records with an old record player spinning tunes (recent cut: Sérgio Mendes and Brasil '66's "Agua de Beber"). What you get for a few dollars is a Styrofoam box of piping hot, tortelloni-like Russian dumplings called pelmeni. Once steamed, they're zipped around in a hot pan with butter and served with a dash of vinegar, cumin powder, fresh cilantro, a dollop of sour cream, and Sriracha sauce. There may never be a better late-night snack. And thankfully, it's open after the bars close. (Juneau authorities: Please never, ever tear down the Wharf building or close this effortlessly perfect place.)

compelling, if faint, noble hop spiciness.

Today the brewery offers five year-round beers, including the Amber and two seasonals (Summer Ale, a superb kölsch-style brew, and Winter Ale, spiced with spruce tips, after the brewing methods used by Captain Cook to combat scurvy among his crew). All of them are made from water out of Juneau's glacier-fed aquifers. The tasting room is a charming affair, with free tours, nine taps, and cool old photos and memorabilia from the early days—all of it thanks to one hot, dusty summer gone wild in Montana.

PHILOSOPHY

High quality, eco-friendly, and unpretentious. "You have to make the best beer you possibly can for a whole variety of reasons," says Geoff. The brewhouse utilizes a number of sustainable practices, such as the country's first CO_2 recovery system (which has become more common these days), a mash filter press (a system common in Belgium which reduces water and grain consumption without compromising beer quality), and a spent-grain dryer to prepare brewery by-products for shipping down to farms to use as feed in the lower forty-eight.

KEY BEER

Alaskan's 6.5% ABV Smoked Porter, introduced in 1988, is a rauchbier, or traditional German "smoke" beer, made by smoking brewers' malt over alder wood branches, which is done by hand in small batches in Juneau. True to its name, it's got all the spice and char of a campfire, with appealing cocoa and chocolaty notes. Alaskan's is one of the first brewed successfully outside of Germany, and is one of the winningest—if not the winningest—beers ever at the GABF.

THE ISLAND PUB

1102 2nd St. • Douglas, AK 88824
(907) 364-1595 • theislandpub.com
Established: 2005

SCENE & STORY

Across the Gastineau Channel from Juneau lies Douglas Island, a seventy-seven-square-mile tidal isle with a sandy beach made of mine tailings. It's the home of the long disused Treadwell mine, largest in the world in its day, and the vastly underrated Eaglecrest ski area, which has 1,400 feet of vertical (40 percent of it expert) served by four double chairs. But perhaps best of all, it's home to the Island Pub, the ultimate après-ski pizzeria. With open seating, large picture windows, and a sleek square center bar area, it's surprisingly contemporary, but entirely inviting. Built in what was once "Mike's Place," a quaint former dance hall dating to the 1930s, it's updated now, but make sure to stroll around and look at the historic photos of patrons sashaying over the wood floors.

PHILOSOPHY

Quintessentially local. Six of the pizzas on the menu are the handiwork of area residents who competed for the honor of having their own pizzas on the menu for an entire year.

KEY BEER

There are nine taps and twenty-five bottled selections, including the local treats, of course. The Sitka spruce-tip-spiced, 6.4% ABV Winter Ale from Alaskan, when in season, makes a great match for meaty, zesty pizza.

Haines and Region

HAINES BREWING CO.

Main St. at 4th Ave. • Haines, AK 99827
(907) 766-3823 • hainesbrewing.com
Established: 1999

SCENE & STORY

Fans of Paul Wheeler's beer used to traipse through tidal bogs and dense forest to try his beers at his house. Then starting in 1999, the bright-eyed brewer—who sports a beard that would have made Walt Whitman jealous—has been operating a little 3.5bbl brewery in another out-of-the-way location—inside a quaint Old West general store building on the "Dalton City" set for the movie White Fang, a

short seaplane or ferry trip from Juneau. In 2015 Wheeler and his partner Jeanne Kitayama opened a new brewery and tap-room on main street in Haines, greatly expanding visitor capacity (forty-nine plus a beer garden outside).

PHILOSOPHY

Big, brawny, frontier beer, brewed with no apologies for a dedicated local audience.

KEY BEER

Wheeler's beers are excellent, especially Dalton Trail Pale Ale, and the DMMDI IPA (Devil Made Me Do It IPA; 6.66% ABV), Black Fang Stout (9% ABV), and Captain Cook's Spruce Tip Ale, an homage to Cook's method of brewing without hops—as well as to Wheeler's former job as a forester.

Healy-Denali National Park

49TH STATE BREWING CO.

Mile 248.4 Parks Hwy. • Healy, AK 99743
(907) 683-2739 • 49statebrewing.com
Established: 2010

SCENE & STORY

Seattle-based chef David McCarthy was planning to open a restaurant in Chicago

when a motorcycle trip to Alaska changed quite literally everything. He ended up in Denali National Park, and took a job flipping hot cakes at popular restaurant for extra cash. There he met local former whitewater guide Jason Motyka, and the pair hatched a vision for something bigger in Healy, zero miles north of the entrance to the Denali National Park. A grocery and liquor store came first. Then a pizzeria with a good beer list. Soon it was time go big on brewing. McCarthy enrolled in the Siebel Institute in Chicago, where he met brewer Jay Bullen, who would become 49th State's first head brewer. In their first year, they only produced a scant twenty-seven barrels, but demand surged. With a new 15bbl system and a bottling line, there's no question that motorcycle trip was a good idea.

Alaska draws some hearty types, to be sure. It also draws the inexperienced. When the movie *Into the Wild* came out in 2007, documenting Christopher McCandless's ill-fated walk twenty miles into the mosquito-infested woods, people started trekking out to his doleful death spot in alarming numbers, getting seriously hurt and even dying in the process (i.e., while trying to ford the Teklanika River). This is, obviously, stupidity, and to help combat it, 49th State scored the actual bus used as a prop in the movie and parked it outside. But that's just the icing on the cake. Go during the right time of year (April to October), and enjoy a huge array of excellent, award-winning beers, weekly all-you-can-eat pig roasts (twenty-two dollars), sustainably raised food, and live music.

PHILOSOPHY

Exploratory. Because this is a seasonal brewery closed during the winter months, McCarthy and Bullen travel like crazy during the off-months, touring dozens of breweries in Europe and around the United States. The result: ever-expanding beer knowledge in the brewhouse. To make the most of that time away, they lay down beers for what they call the "Hibernation Series," which lager away as they crisscross the ancient homelands of beer.

KEY BEER

The Smoked Märzen, an amber homage to the rauchbier tradition of Bamberg, took gold in the smoked beer category at the 2015 GABF. Try anything in the Hibernation Series as well, like the recent Seward's Folly Imperial Stout (11% ABV).

BEST *of the* REST: ALASKA

THE ALASKAN HOTEL BAR

167 S. Franklin St. • Juneau, AK 99801 • (907) 586-1000 • thealaskanhotel.com

Built in 1913, this is the bar where you go to "drink with an Alaskan at the Alaskan." But it's not the tourist trap one might imagine from that old chestnut of a phrase, nor from the spindly Victorian-era balustrade, weathered felt-pattern wallpaper, or corny, wrought-iron park lantern next to the parlor stairs. Instead, local rabble and well-heeled citizenry alike gather around the old antique bar without going all Wyatt Earp, to name one former carouser in town. They're bobbing heads to an acoustic ballad courtesy of the open mike and drinking the lemony, coriander-kissed Blanche de Chambly, a 5% ABV witbier on tap from Quebec. How gunslinger is that?

THE HANGAR ON THE WHARF

2 Marine Way, No. 106 • Juneau, AK 99801 • (907) 586-5018 • hangaronthewharf.com

With its location convenient to the Merchants Wharf building, the bright, clean, and crisply run Hangar (opened in 1996) is a beloved local watering hole and tourist favorite. It's got an airplane and seaplane theme thanks to the building's 1940s tenant, Alaska Coastal Airlines, but isn't kitschy. Overlooking the channel with huge glass windows and outdoor seating, it makes an ideal spot for an afternoon beer and bite as the seaplanes buzz in and out and the ships dock. There are some twenty taps and seventy bottled beers, and a solid menu of sandwiches, wraps, and fresh local seafood dishes.

THE BEAR TOOTH GRILL & BEAR TOOTH THEATER PUB

1230 W. 27th Ave. • Anchorage, AK 99503 • (907) 276-4200 • beartoothgrill.net

The Bear Tooth compound combines a sleek, remodeled concert and film venue (featuring headline acts from the Lower 48 like Ghostland Observatory, and both first run and 3-D movies) and a cool, little glass-and-brick enclosed bar and eatery. The brews are standard but far from disappointing: try the hazy orange Fairweather IPA, 6.1% ABV and strongly redolent of graham crackers and grapefruit.

DENALI BREWING CO.
& TWISTER CREEK RESTAURANT

13605 E. Main St. • Talkeetna, AK 99676 • (907) 733-2536 • denalibrewingcompany.com

The southern gateway to Denali National Park, little Talkeetna (population: 960) is both a stopover for climbers headed to Mount McKinley and a destination on its own for its excellent fishing and whitewater rafting. Denali Brewing Co. doubled capacity every year since 2009 on the strength of beers like their light, silky, black, and roasty Chiuli Stout. There could be no better place to drink it than on the sunny patio of the log cabin–style Twister Creek restaurant. Now the brewery has two locations, with a separate brewery, and canning line (with two new beers going into cans in 2016), making it the second-largest brewer in the state. One cool, recent project: the brewery asked fans to deliver fresh, hand-picked Alaskan high bush cranberries for the winter Wassail, paying four dollars per pound.

SILVER GULCH BREWING & BOTTLING CO.

2195 Old Steese Hwy. N. • Fairbanks, AK 99712-1023 • (907) 452-2739 • silvergulch.com

Built in the historic mining town of Fox in 1998 Silver Gulch is one of the largest breweries in Alaska and as of 2011 the farthest north. The corrugated metal exterior gives the look of a farm facility, but the interior is spacious and cleanly furnished with lots of dark wood tables, chairs, and booths. In addition to the brewpub's own ten taps there are around 100 to 125 international beers available in bottles, including a surprisingly deep collection of rare British, German, and Belgian beers. It's hugely popular with locals so make a reservation ahead of time to secure a spot; try the 5.8% ABV Coldfoot Pilsner, a hybrid of German and Czech-styles.

CHAIR 5

171 Linblad Ave. • Girdwood, AK 99587 • (907) 783-2500 • chairfive.com

The Aleyeska Resort, opened in 1954, is a classic experts' ski area with a reputation for steep terrain and flinty locals. And Chair 5, established in 1983, is Girdwood's après-ski beer playground, with twenty taps and forty-nine bottles of Alaskan and other Lower 48 specialty beers from Deschutes to Sierra Nevada, Midnight Sun, and Kona.

CALIFORNIA

and

HAWAII

CALIFORNIA

IT'S GOSPEL AMONG CRAFT BEER FANS THAT MODERN AMERICAN MICROBREWING WAS BORN in Sonoma County at John "Jack" McAuliffe's New Albion Brewing Company in 1976. That ragtag operation didn't last long, but McAuliffe's English-style ales, some with whole peppers in the bottle, did leave a gigantic impression on locals like Ken Grossman, who was on his way to starting what would become Sierra Nevada. And that was almost ten years after Fritz Maytag, another ambitious beer lover, took over the foundering Anchor and began to burnish that old company's shine.

Today, what is happening throughout the state is nothing short of revolutionary: Like Napa's wine boom in the 1970s, and Sonoma's in the 1980s, there are now pockets of brewing innovation dotting the entire state. From airy coastal beer gardens in San Diego to chic gastropubs in San Francisco and barnlike wine country hideouts in the North—and even throughout Los Angeles—the entire freewheeling, sun-bleached state has good beer to discover. There are nearly 400 breweries in California, far too many to take in on a single trip. That shouldn't stop you from trying. Maybe it's the sunshine, or the sea, or the good vibes from the Golden State's surfer days and beatnik nights, but California has always been an inspiring place to travel and, now more than ever, it's one of the world's finest places to drink delectable craft-brewed beer.

ITINERARIES

1-DAY (San Francisco) Magnolia, the Trappist, Church Key, Social Kitchen, Cellarmaker, Toronado

3-DAY (NorCal) One-day itinerary plus Zeitgeist, Russian River, Sante Adairius, Anderson Valley

7-DAY (Statewide) Three-day itinerary plus the Bruery, Stone, the Lost Abbey, Alpine, Pizza Port, Modern Times

San Francisco and the Bay Area

MAGNOLIA BREWING CO.

1938 Haight St. • San Francisco, CA
94117 • (415) 864-7468
magnoliapub.com • Established: 1997

SCENE & STORY

Some places just get it right. Magnolia, on the corner of Haight and Masonic, is one of them, and should be your first stop in the Haight, for brunch and a breakfast beer. The carefully aged patina of the place (faded paint, antiquely sconces, padded black leather booths) exudes cool, but the menu is generous. Start with the crispy pork belly served with baked beans, fried shallots, and a poached egg—it makes the ideal base for a beer tasting. Owner and founding brewer David McLean's recipes manage to be inventive, fresh, flavorful, and artfully balanced, qualities that can be elusive in the anything-goes world of today's craft beer scene. Now he's got Smokestack, a Dogpatch brewery and barbecue joint (see next entry); don't miss that either.

PHILOSOPHY

Quirky and classic. Freshness is paramount, and the servers know how to recommend beers to pair with Magnolia's seasonal, market-driven menu.

KEY BEER

Kalifornia Kölsch (4.8% ABV), Dave McLean's take on the northern German classic style, all bright, golden hues and lip-smacking finish. It's the ultimate breakfast beer, as light and bright on the tongue as a good mimosa. McLean serves it in the proper glass, called a stange, or "rod," a slim fifth of a liter (6.8 ounces) that is only 0.04 inches thick, akin to the heft of a champagne flute, easy (and soon empty) in the hand.

SMOKESTACK

2505 3rd St. • San Francisco, CA 94107
(415) 864-7468 • magnoliasmokestack.com
Established: 2014

SCENE & STORY

Dogpatch is a sleepy industrial area between the Bay and Potrero Hill in San Francisco. So when local hero and die-hard deadhead Dave McLean (founder of Magnolia Brewery) announced he would be launching this excellent barbecue and brewery outpost in a former can factory around 2012, word traveled fast. But starting a brewery takes a lot of time. After almost two years of buildout and unavoidable delays, McLean's much anticipated Smokestack (and Magnolia's new 30bbl system, adjacent to the bar) opened in the late spring of 2014.

It was worth the wait. With long, distressed wood tables made of salvaged black acacia, painted wood floors, plus accents of iron, cement, copper, and a wide wood and marble bar, Smokestack (named for the Grateful Dead song, "Smokestack Lightning") is as pretty as it is packed. Inside, the aromas of whiskey, brewing, and woodsmoke wrap guests in a big bear hug. In short, Smokestack is a hybrid meat counter and high-end craft beer and craft cocktail bar with a lot of happy people inside. What else do you need, really?

PHILOSOPHY

"Nondenominational" barbecue means just what it sounds like: instead of hewing to traditions from, say, Kansas City or North Carolina, the barbecue flavors roam the globe. And the beer? "Think simpler, flavorful, well-made beers that aren't going to burn out your palate," says McLean.

KEY BEER

McLean has always been an adherent to brewing lighter, sessionable English styles and cask beers, and Smokestack presents them well. So you'll find the popular Kalifornia Kölsch here, Proving Ground IPA, which stands up well to rich cuts, and new beers in constant rotation.

MIKKELLER BAR

34 Mason St. • San Francisco, CA 94102
415) 984-0279 • mikkellerbar.com
Established: 2013

SCENE & STORY

Danish twin brothers and gypsy brewers Mikkel Borg Bergsø and Jeppe Jarnit Bjergsø, have, in short order, created two of the most distinctive beer brands in the world. Having both been serious runners growing up in Denmark, they're famously competitive, and seldom seen together. It's a dizzying diagram: Mikkel's brand, dubbed Mikkeller and based in Denmark, is brewed mainly in Belgium by De Proef, a venerated test brewery. Jeppe's beer brand, four years younger, is brewed in Charleston, South Carolina by Westbrook Brewery, and named, with maximum cheek, Evil Twin. Now each is building a mini empire of his own around the world in the form of cafés and restaurants and other collaborations, each more ambitious than the last.

When Mikkel announced San Francisco would be the home of his first American bar, beer geeks, especially on the West Coast, were jazzed. Mikkeller beers have become cult objects, with pop art–like labeling and high-ranking flavor profiles among the beeriest cognoscenti. Mikkeller Bar, which took over a former nightclub spot in the Tenderloin, is a supersized version of Mikkel's original Copenhagen outpost. It's roomy, with eighty seats, Keith Haring-esque murals by his label artist Keith Shore adorning the walls. Forty silvery taps shine above a thirty-seat, four-sided bar in the middle of the room. Staff is ultrafriendly and knowledgeable, and sidling up to the bar is a guarantee of meeting some of the most die-hard beer fanatics in the world. Did I mention the food? It's terrific, too, elevated but not deconstructed or fussy. News in 2015 that Mikkeller is partnering with AleSmith in the latter's San Diego facility only underscored the Dane's love for (and success with) the West Coast beer scene.

PHILOSOPHY

Mikkel started out with four beers served only in the bar, and the list is heavily focused on Belgian, Dutch, and American brands that are pushing the stylistic envelope, yet with a few nods to classic styles such as pilsner. Downstairs, Mikkel (and partner Chuck Stilphen of the Trappist) built what they call the Tivoli Sour Room, a thirty-seat "secret" bar dedicated only to sour beers, from Mikkeller and many other brewers of the tart styles increasingly found taprooms across the country.

KEY BEER

Of course you should order some Mikkeller beers like the 5% ABV Tenderloin Pale Ale, and go from there. Expect a great list from the likes of Beachwood BBQ, Brasserie de la Senne, To-Øl, and

Allagash, and other specialties.

THE CHURCH KEY

1402 Grant Ave. • San Francisco, CA 94133 • (415) 986-3511 • No website
Established: 2009

SCENE & STORY

A sly, little space in North Beach with exposed brick, understated décor (retro wallpaper inside; no sign outside except the symbol of an old key), and a quiet loft upstairs, the Church Key draws a cool crowd, and its beer menu is one of the smartest in San Francisco. Beer hunters will find rarities they're after, such as Firestone Walker's Oaktoberfest, a barrel-aged märzen-style beer (a clean, coppery German style of lager). The bartenders are knowledgeable, but not obnoxiously so, and the music (by DJ, on vinyl) hits the right notes. Should hunger arrive, as it always does, you can order some tasty meat pies, or there's a great pizzeria down the block (Golden Boy Pizza; 542 Green St.; 415-982-9738) and the Church Key owners don't mind if you bring it in and eat right there.

PHILOSOPHY

Call it the David Bowie of beer bars. This is the place to find genre-benders that push the envelope in terms of stylistic interpretation, defying easy categorization. And it's stylishly understated, an elusive quality in beer bars.

KEY BEER

Two dollars gets you a "mystery beer," but this is usually a can of bland American lager. Better with your pizza would be the ultrarare hybrid-style Belgian IPA called XX Bitter from Brasserie De Ranke (6.2% ABV), which has a melony roundness but finishes dry and bitter, with an herbal afterglow.

TORONADO
547 Haight St. • San Francisco, CA 94117
(415) 863-2276 • toronado.com
Established: 1986

SCENE & STORY

Farther down the Haight into the Fillmore, Toronado abides. It's been open for over twenty years, and has the dust and clutter to show for it, but what's more important is behind the bar. Or behind the antlers, tap handles, and other ephemera . . . somewhere. Despite its tiny size, you're not likely to find many better beer lists (including rarities and aged beers) anywhere in California. It's one of those bars that emit a tractor beam for serious beer lovers, and, one day, they find it. Some never seem to leave, growing long beards and huddling over their barley wine with contented grins. True, certain

bartenders ignore you if you ask for the wrong beer, or one that just blew. And the crowds, during special cask nights and tastings, resemble a rugby scrum. But in the end it's worth it. Beer lovers the world over know Toronado, and to visit it is to enter into a kind of covenant with them. Recently affiliated bars Toronado San Diego and Toronado Seattle have joined the brotherhood, too.

PHILOSOPHY

Drink big or go home. All the great northern, central, and Southern Californian beer makers are represented here, with special focus on barley wines and other high-alcohol styles. Order with authority.

KEY BEER

From January to April at least, look for Almanac's Valencia Gold, a tasty, 8.5% ABV Golden Ale brewed with—you guessed it—valencia oranges and orange blossom honey. And there's always a good fresh IPA on tap from Alpine, Stone, Green Flash, or other Cali hophead mainstays.

ANCHOR BREWING CO.
1705 Mariposa St. • San Francisco, CA 9410
(415) 863-8350 • anchorbrewing.com
Established: 1896

SCENE & STORY

Founded as Anchor in 1896, this is a shrine

for any self-respecting beer pilgrim for one reason: the brewhouse. It's a thing of beauty, all gleaming copper kettles and creamy tile work; to tour the facility and see the brewers working in their white work suits (in the unhippified fashion of traditional German brewers) is to see a true classic in action. Facing closure after a string of half-interested owners from the end of Prohibition to 1965, this brewery found new life in the hands of a young Stanford graduate named Fritz Maytag (great-great-grandson of the man who founded the Maytag appliance company), who bought it in 1965 and helped kick-start the American craft beer revolution. Anchor is famous, of course, for Anchor Steam Beer, a kind of ale-lager hybrid also known as California Common. There's no steam used in the brewing process; the word refers to the hissing sound old wooden kegs used to make when aging.

Maytag developed several beers before selling the company in 2010, including Old Foghorn, a viscous, almost brandy-like barley wine; a Christmas ale with a secret yearly changing recipe; and a light, brightly spiced summer wheat beer, among others. He also added a microdistillery, with housemade gin and rye whisky, and tirelessly publicized America's craft brewing revolution. It's one of the best brewery tours in America, and it's not to be missed.

PHILOSOPHY

Old-world sophistication with quiet, unpretentious skill. But let's not forget the impact of international financiers. The new owners, the entrepreneurs who created Skyy Vodka, have been doing Anchor's heritage justice, and introduced some excellent new beers in recent years. In 2013, they announced plans to add a 212,000-square-foot brewery at Pier 48 with production and distribution facilities, a restaurant, museum, educational center, and other attractions.

KEY BEER

Liberty Ale (6% ABV) was first brewed in 1975 to commemorate the ride of Paul Revere. It has a Champagne-like dryness and aromatic, crisp finish that goes well with local foods like Dungeness crab and sourdough bread.

LA TRAPPE CAFÉ

800 Greenwich St. • San Francisco, CA 94133 • (415) 440-8727
latrappecafe.com • Established: 2007

SCENE & STORY

Amid the tacky red sauce joints of North Beach, there's a salve for the soul at the corner of Mason and Greenwich: a broad list of good Belgian ales and an array of classic Belgian dishes, like moules à la bière and well-made waterzooi, a seafood stew made of manila clams, mussels, and shrimp served over a piece of grilled sea bass. Skip the blah upstairs and immediately head to the subterranean bowels for nineteen taps of beer and a 250-plus bottle menu, the best possible antidote to Fisherman's Wharf tourist overload. It's also right on the Powell cable car line; hop on for an escape up into Chinatown or up over the hill toward Market Street and the Ferry Building, and some of San Francisco's best beer bars and breweries.

PHILOSOPHY

La Trappe proclaims a zero-tolerance for the plastic kegs some bars and breweries have been using for convenience, believing them to have adverse effects on beer.

KEY BEER

On draft, North Coast La Merle (7.9% ABV) is an underrated Californian take on the Belgian style of saison. The Fort Bragg brewer's version is wheaty and hazy gold with a lemony, slightly herbal kick.

fences, and a vista of a highway overpass. On entering, it is normal for most to feel somewhat apprehensive. Then you scan the beer list of more than forty taps, pick out something inordinately good and cheap, and amble outside on a vast patio with picnic-style tables lined up in the gravel. On warm nights the garden fills up with lanky bike messengers, big-bearded musicians, and energetic beer fanatics taking advantage of the reasonable prices and cheap burgers and dogs off the grill.

PHILOSOPHY

Officially, it's "Warm Beer and Cold Women," but it's not all really so bad. Don't take photos, though, of anyone or anything but your own friends. You can get the boot for that.

KEY BEER

Moonlight Death & Taxes Black Beer—inevitably.

ZEITGEIST

199 Valencia at Dubose • San Francisco, CA 94103 • (415) 255-7505 • zeitgeistsf.com
Established: 1986

21ST AMENDMENT

563 2nd St. • San Francisco, CA 94107
(415) 369-0900 • 21st-amendment.com
Established: 2000

←——————————→

San Leandro Location: 2010 Williams St.
San Leandro, CA 94577 • (510) 595-2111

SCENE & STORY

Zeitgeist is a biker-style dive bar with decaying, red-shingled walls, razor wire

SCENE & STORY

It would be too easy to dismiss this brewery on the basis that they make a popular canned beer infused with watermelon and used to contract brew all their beer (in general, this means using excess capacity in other companies' breweries to save money, rather than brew and ship from a single location). But free-wheeling founders Nico Freccia and Shaun O'Sullivan—who met in a brewing class at UC Davis—are producing a whole range of great beers in cans, and their huge, loft-like brewpub and beer garden complex in San Francisco's South Park area (south of Market Street, a couple of blocks from the San Francisco Giants Stadium) is the kind of place anyone would feel at home drinking. When, after three years and untold millions of dollars in investment, they opened their 95,000-square-foot, state-of-the-art San Leandro location near the Oakland airport in 2015, the beer world raised a collective glass. Found in and around the huge facility: a vast tasting room, beer garden, as well as a (planned, at time of press) restaurant, "floating bars" and a treehouse bar overlooking the production floor. Well done, guys.

PHILOSOPHY

Freedom to brew. Named for the constitutional amendment that abolished Prohibition, 21st Amendment embodies good-natured fun, and the cans (their only packaging) have inspired names and label art.

KEY BEER

21st Amendment Back in Black IPA combines the evergreen pine of ample hops with the dark cocoa and coffee flavors (and onyx hue) of darkly roasted barley. Also known as Cascadian Dark Ale and Black IPA, this style—India Black Ale—is the latest brewing to be recognized by the Association of Brewers, and in 2010, 21st Amendment released the first year-round version available in cans, their chosen packaging. It's got all the vintage attitude of AC/DC's Bon Scott in his prime, but not so much bite you can't have more than one. And don't miss Bitter American, their 4.4% ABV sipper. It's delicious stuff.

THE ALEMBIC BAR

1725 Haight St. • San Francisco, CA 94117
(415) 666-0822 • alembicbar.com
Established: 2007

SCENE & STORY

The Alembic isn't a beer bar per se, but it is the brainchild of Magnolia's David McLean, so it has a considered list and the décor—a warm, dark, enveloping interior and exposed-bulb lighting—to go with it. San Franciscans have come to expect nothing less from the hirsute Deadhead turned craft beer lover. The Alembic has ten taps and thirty bottled selections, many hard-to-find Belgians, and high-end gastropub fare like sweetbreads, duck kebabs, and foie gras. In 2015 McLean and Co. were expanding seating and adding a number of other guest amenities.

PHILOSOPHY

Neo-nineteenth-century urban chic meets locavore food and drink.

KEY BEER

Beer cocktails have been around for a long time now, but recently have been getting more attention. Most interesting for beer lovers here is a pair of cocktails using beer: the Vice Grip, a mixture of coffee-flavored rum liqueur and red wine topped with foam made from Marin Brewing Company's Point Reyes Porter, a smooth, rich brew; or the tart-sweet Pale Horse, made with cachaça, lemon, and caramelized pale ale syrup.

hand-ground sausage, braised pork belly and beef cheek, and suggested menu pairings from the twenty-four-tap, 180 bottle list, with a special stash of vintage beers stored in a temperature-controlled cellar (twenty-five to sixty dollars and up, depending on size and year).

PHILOSOPHY

Seasonality is everything: the small, producer-driven beer list morphs with the calendar, just like the heirloom fruits and vegetables.

KEY BEER

Burning Oak Lager, a German-style black lager of 5.2% ABV from Linden Street Brewery in Oakland, is nearly opaque, with notes of char and smoke mingled with a faint sweetness and light spicy hops.

THE MONK'S KETTLE

3141 16th St. • San Francisco, CA 94103
(415) 865-9523 • monkskettle.com
Established: 2007

THE TRAPPIST

460 8th St. • Oakland, CA 94607
(510) 238-8900 • thetrappist.com
Established: 2007

SCENE & STORY

Monk's has something of the classic beer bar feel—dark woods, low light, sparkling clean glassware—but the menu is tuned in to the "delights and prejudices" of ambitious farm-to-table cooking more than most (to borrow a phrase from the title of one of James Beard's classic books). Expect house-cured ham and

SCENE & STORY

Sometimes the best bars are in the most unlikely places. Just a short hop east across the bay on the BART train delivers you right down the block from the Trappist. Despite the somewhat forlorn downtown Oakland location, it's the kind of bar you'd plan a vacation around.

You'll feel it when you walk through the "front bar" door and enter a narrow space with exposed brick, gorgeous dark wood trim, white-and-black tile floors, and vintage lighting. Then you consider the twenty-eight rotating taps, with another 100 to 130 bottled selections. Once you have a beer in hand, it's time to wander back past barrels on end (ersatz tables), the stained-glass doors leading to the bathrooms, and into the warmly lit "back bar," with deep green trim, wainscoted ceiling, and a lovely old bar of its own. Back in front there's a line of smiling faces at the bar, and perhaps a great California band's song playing—the rootsy anthem "Home" by Edward Sharpe and the Magnetic Zeros on a recent visit—and you realize this is exactly where you want to be.

PHILOSOPHY

Belgian beer, speakeasy style. They opened a second location in the nice Rockridge neighborhood of Oakland in 2013: a specialty beer café and bottleshop, with nine taps and ninety-nine bottles of beer on the wall. And lately their annual Sour/Bitter festival has been gaining steam.

KEY BEER

Moonlight's Reality Czeck, a 4.8% ABV pilsner. It may not be Belgian style but is very rare and very good, like this bar.

THE RARE BARREL

940 Parker St. • Berkeley, CA 94710
(510) 984-6585 • therarebarrel.com
Established: 2013

SCENE & STORY

Without a doubt one of the most talked about entrants into the West Coast beer scene in recent years, the Rare Barrel is all-sour blending operation based in a warehouse in Berkeley, where brewmaster and blender Jay Goodwin (formerly of the Bruery) and his business partner (and former roommate) Alex Wallash ferment, age, blend, and bottle some of the best sour beers in the United States. Inside, more than 850 barrels are meticulously arranged around a stand of shining tanks. Goodwin sources the wort—or unfermented beer—from four base styles of pale, gold, red, and dark brewed locally by breweries with extra production capacity. After the liquid is trucked to the headquarters, the beer is primary fermented in steel, then racked to oak barrels with wild yeast and cultures, like *Brettanomyces* (wild yeast), or "brett," and Lactobacillus, aged, sometimes with fruit and other adjuncts, and later bottled. The process can take from several months to a year or more. It's not an easy way to make beer, but the results speak for themselves. Patience is a virtue.

PHILOSOPHY

All sour, all the time, in balance. It's no

easy task. "You need to match the acids and flavors of two things that grow themselves—yeast and fruit," Goodwin told me. "It's like trying to raise two kids who get along perfectly."

KEY BEER

Attendees of the 2014 World Beer Cup in Denver gasped in proud and envious amazement as the Rare Barrel's very first release— the funky, raspberry-kissed Ensorcelled— was named a gold medalist in American-style sour ale category. About seven months later they took gold again in the same category, this time at the 2014 Great American Beer Festival with Cosmic Dust, a sparkling, faintly rosy sour golden ale with hibiscus. Hit the tasting room on the weekend to see what's pouring, but bottles to go are almost always sold out.

A BEER WITH
BRIAN HUNT, MOONLIGHT BREWING COMPANY

3350 Coffey Ln., Suite A • Santa Rosa, CA 95403 • moonlightbrewing.com
(707) 528-2537 • Open Saturdays 2-7 p.m.

In the fall of 2009, almost as soon as I'd arrived in the Bay Area, I began hearing about a man named Brian Hunt of Sonoma County's Moonlight Brewery in the hushed, reverential tones normally reserved for exiled Tibetan leaders. He doesn't allow visitors. He's like a mad scientist. He brews the best beer in the whole Bay Area. He's really cranky. No one visits Brian Hunt.

The last statement is basically true. But because I had some help from my friend Sean Paxton, a.k.a. the Home Brew Chef, I had the chance to meet the man behind Death & Taxes, a silky 5% ABV black lager on tap in San Francisco's best beer bars. And while I don't recommend driving up his dirt road outside the hamlet of Windsor unless he's expecting you, he's not the crank some had made him out to be.

No indeed. What I found at Moonlight was sort of everything and nothing I'd been expecting, a crucible of California's future brewing ingenuity and a potent symbol of its roots. His brewery, founded in 1992, is tiny, packed improbably to the ceiling of a former tractor barn. Steel tanks called grundies precariously crowd around the kettles and tables strewn with tools and parts.

And in the middle of it all, Hunt—a graduate of UC Davis's fermentation science master's degree program and a self-described dropout from the industrial brewing world—holds court on his creations with a combination of pride and prejudice (toward those who would classify his beers in rigid styles, mainly). He's Moonlight's only full-time employee, and brews about 1,000 barrels per year, available in only about seventy-five locations around the Bay Area, which he personally keeps supplied. In any case, we tried his whole repertoire, retiring to a set of Adirondack chairs near some anemic-looking hop trellises. Lambs baa'd in the distance. This was a farm brewery if there ever was one. Hunt's beers were a revelation: some rock solid classic, others wildly inventive, nearly all delicious.

What Hunt is trying to do, in his own cantankerous way, is shake things up. He bristles at the notion his beers can be classified into set styles, scoffing at what he considers hidebound conventions of acceptable brewing norms. He's the guy who stands up during brewing conferences of industry types and asks the probing questions everyone's thinking but doesn't quite have the guts to ask.

First came the jet-black Death & Taxes, which is as light as an American canned lager like Budweiser but vastly more flavorful, bursting with tangy hops and roasted malts. Then we moved on to a spicy, clean Reality Czech and bready Lunatic Lager, another black lager called Bony Fingers, and an IPA-like offering, Twist of Fate California Style Bitter.

But with the next beers Hunt veered into terra incognita. Hunt is doing something few brewers in America would ever consider: making completely unhopped beers, to test the possibilities of using other plants to spice and balance flavors. It's a bit like attempting to make gin without juniper, but to the fifty-four-year-old provocateur, such rules mean nothing. We tasted his Artemis, an ale spiced with mugwort, bee balm, and wild bergamot that tasted a bit like pencil wood (in a good way). Working for Tips, an ale spiced with redwood needles, was one of those beers you don't forget—ever—and its garnet color had me mesmerized.

By that point I was beginning to believe what I'd heard in all those San Francisco beer bars. We finished with what Hunt called a "Norwegian farmhouse beer" by the name of Uncle Fudd, named for a song lyric Johnny Cash made famous ("The Tennessee Stud"). It's ale made with rye grain and branches of the Thuja tree, a cousin of Western Red Cedar. The result? At that hour of the day, after tasting about a dozen of Hunt's concoctions, my palate was fairly shot. But there was something intangible in that beer, like the others, something compelling, if radically unfamiliar. Maybe, as Hunt might say, it's just moonlight. Who knows what he'll come up with next? This is brewing as alchemy. Hunt's mystic approach, otherworldly skill, and mischievous persona give Moonlight an inescapable aura. Look for it.

Wine Country

ANDERSON VALLEY BREWING CO.

17700 Hwy. 253 • Boonville, CA 95415
(707) 895-2337 • avbc.com
Established: 1987

SCENE & STORY

By all means if you get the chance, "jape" on down to the verdant farm-country town of Boonville to enjoy one of America's most distinctive breweries. Jape? Yep. That's the word for "drive" in Boontling, the folk language of this old farming community, said to have been developed by isolated farmers in the area's early sheep and hop fields. Few use the dialect now, but you might be able to find some locals to teach some choice phrases over some bahl hornin ("good drinking") at Anderson Valley Brewing. The partially solar-powered brewery itself is a down-to-earth affair, quaint and unpretentious, located on a farm with its own well, livestock, tasting room, and eighteen-hole Frisbee golf course. But inside the brewery are some of the most beautiful brewing kettles in the United States, polished to a mirror finish, and tours are a popular primer for the twelve-tap tasting room. In 2011 the brewery celebrated the fifteenth annual Legendary Boonville Beer Fest (held at the Mendocino County Fairgrounds), with over fifty California breweries and thousands of thirsty fans.

PHILOSOPHY

Traditional, unpasteurized brewing using well water rich in bicarbonates, pristine practices in the brewhouse, and a sense of humor everywhere outside it.

KEY BEER

With the soaring ascent of IPAs and Belgian-style beers over the last few years, an uncommon but essential beer style has slipped off the radar: the humble amber. This is too bad. Unpasteurized and never sterile-filtered, AVBC's flagship Amber (5.8% ABV and brewed under the watchful eye of respected industry veteran Fal Allen) has a lively kick and caramel-kissed smoothness, not to mention a glowing garnet color that's as attractive as the copper kettles inside the brewery. Also don't miss the mahogany-hued Brother David's Double, a rich and malty Belgian-style ale melding cavalcades of malt flavor with a bracing 9% ABV, and if they have any, the recent, innovative Blood Orange Gose, a salty, citrusy treat.

RUSSIAN RIVER BREWING CO.

725 4th St. • Santa Rosa, CA 95404
(707) 545-2337 • russianriverbrewing.com
Established: 1997

SCENE & STORY

The little brewpub in downtown Santa Rosa where Russian River sells its beers directly and a vast menu of Italian-American pub grub isn't long on atmosphere, and you can't tour the brewery (for now at least), but it is still a top stop for beer travelers in wine country. There are fifteen beers on tap, eight bottles to go, occasional live music performances and other beer-related events, and dependable crowds on weekend nights. Lunch time and Sundays are quieter; order the fifteen-dollar sampler immediately to taste everything.

PHILOSOPHY

Belgian beers and a laid-back West Coast attitude.

KEY BEER

Tart, fruit-enhanced Belgian-style beers run the gamut from offering a nice, mild, back-of-the-tongue zing to the sort of full-on, face-contorting shock human taste buds seem designed to avoid. Supplication (7% ABV) is complex, woody, tart, and fleetingly sweet, infused with the juice of whole sour cherries while aging in pinot noir barrels. It's one of those beers referred to as a "life-changer."

LAGUNITAS TAPROOM & BEER SANCTUARY

1280 N. McDowell Blvd. • Petaluma, CA 94954 • (707) 769-4495 • lagunitas.com
Established: 1993

SCENE & STORY

Suddenly, Lagunitas is everywhere. In 2011, the makers of some of America's cleanest-tasting and most distinctive pilsner and IPA announced $9.5 million plans to quadruple capacity to around 600,000bbl/yr, putting them in the league of Boston Beer Company (Sam Adams), Sierra Nevada, and Goose Island. In the meantime, for the last two years their headquarters on the outskirts of sleepy Petaluma has turned into a circus—literally.

For the "Beer Circus," a series of raucous parties now held at the Petaluma fairgrounds, the fun-loving owners have gone more Burning Man than Bozo, with crazed-looking stilt-walkers, burlesque, the "R-Rated Marching Band," and a bondage demonstration for good measure (all fairly tame, actually, and the beer garden is understated and quite stylish). Should you miss the big top (the

DETOUR ➡ THE RUSSIAN (RIVER) REVOLUTION

If there is one brewery that defines the changing American craft beer land-scape of post-2000, it is Russian River, led by the affable Vinnie Cilurzo and a lineup stretching the parameters of American tastes for beer. The son of winemaker parents, Cilurzo could have his own winery by now, a patch of heaven near Temecula, California, where he worked in the cellar during harvests as a boy. "Pretty much all I've done in life is fermentation," he says. But it wasn't winemaking that got him excited during his college years. It was brewing beer.

By 1997 Cilurzo had brewed enough in his free time to score a job running Korbel Champagne Cellars' fledgling beer division, Russian River. But soon Korbel, like so many other Johnny-come-latelies, facing a looming industry-wide downturn, planned to drop the line. Cilurzo decided to buy the division out, firm in the belief that beers like Blind Pig, a 6.5% ABV Double IPA he'd come up with in 1994—the nation's first such concoction—would find its fans. "We didn't do any market research," he claims. "We just believed passion would carry us through." Cilurzo scraped up investors and reopened Russian River in 2004. Good move: Soon the craft beer market had returned to double-digit growth and Cilurzo was dominating prestigious tastings. Today fans of his most sought-after beer, Pliny the Younger (a resinous double IPA of 11% ABV, brewed once a year) line up—quite literally by the hundreds, for days—to take home a few bottles before it's gone.

Aside from Pliny, most of Cilurzo's beers are fermented in French oak barrels for up to two years. They're fermented using wild yeasts and bacteria (that give the beer funky flavors more commonly found in rare cheeses), then wire- and cork-topped to create an ironclad seal for vigorous natural carbonation in the bottle.

And they're incredibly rich, complex, and drinkable. But this mad scientist approach—he adds volatile bacteria like Lactobacillus and Pediococcus to certain creations—has its risks. Brettanomyces, the wild yeast strain with a leathery, earthy-sour profile used in certain Russian River beers and some of Cilurzo's Belgian inspirations, can run amok, altering fermenters, pumps, and hoses for good, and must be carefully quarantined. "It's like playing with fire," Cilurzo says. "You know how a dog can sniff out a person who's afraid? With Brett, bugs, and critters, if you're afraid of it, it's going to bite."

parties always sell out in advance), visit for a brewery tour and then beers on a warm night under the stars with live music (roots, rock, and reggae, of course, offered about five nights a week during the warmer months). And with the Bay Area, redwood forests, and the Point Reyes National Sea Shore within easy reach, Lagunitas makes a great place to cap off an idyllic Golden State adventure. Brewery walking tours are free Wednesday through Friday at 3 and 5 p.m.

PHILOSOPHY

Hippietarian with a great sense of humor. Amid the Great Recession of 2010 and 2011 their contribution to gross national happiness was a protest beer called Wilco Tango Foxtrot, or WTF for short, "a malty, robust, jobless recovery ale." Back in 2005, founder Tony Magee (a sometime reggae band member) was hit with a potentially ruinous one-year license suspension for an employee caught smoking some of California's largest cash crop on-site during a sponsored "420" party (the cops were undercover for weeks). On appeal, the sentence was cut to three weeks, and Lagunitas used the ban time to install a massive new bottling line.

Their dues to society paid, they later dared the regulators to approve a new beer called Undercover Investigation Shut-Down Ale, printed with some choice antiestablishment Benjamin Franklin verbiage and pointed mockery of the agents who had been unable to get anyone to sell them any pot—it was, naturally, always offered for free. But recently, "free" has not been the buzzword at Lagunitas, which in 2015 announced some fairly stunning news, given their antiauthoritarian bent: in a groundbreaking $500 million deal, Heineken took ownership of half the company. With the suits involved, will the clever circus continue, or turn into a global Cirque-du-So-What?

KEY BEER

Lagunitas Pils Czech-Style Pilsner (6.2% ABV) is great, now almost standard, go-to beer suited for all occasions. And it may have a goofy name, but their Sonoma Farmhouse Hop Stoopid Ale (8% ABV) is a serious beer in the Double IPA style (a.k.a. Imperial IPA), with cavalcades of tangy West Coast hops "for those mornings when you have to cut right to the chase."

Chico

SIERRA NEVADA BREWING CO.

1075 E. 20th St. • Chico, CA 95928
(530) 893-3520 • sierranevada.com
Established: 1980

SCENE & STORY

These days Sierra Nevada's beers are

easy to find, but not long ago, out in the fertile farm country of the northeastern Sacramento Valley in Chico, home brewer Ken Grossman—on an obsessive quest for the perfect pale ale—was the only one drinking them. While roasting his grains at home, jury-rigging brewing equipment out of fish tanks and washer-dryers (for an ill-fated experimental malting operation), and squeaking out rent as a bike shop repairman, he dreamed of bigger things: real brewing kettles, the copper kind. He had a long way to go and little money. In 1976 he opened a home-brew store "to feed my hobby, really," Grossman recalls.

Grossman doggedly kept home brewing, keeping meticulous notes, dreaming big. Inspired by Anchor and New Albion, he wrote a business plan with a partner in 1978, then hit up the banks, who weren't the least bit interested. To get started, "I spent all my savings, all my business partner's savings, and the savings bonds my grandfather had given me for school," Grossman recalls. Finally, with the help of family and friends, Sierra Nevada (named after the mountain range), brewed its first batch, a stout; the first pale came a few days later. (A dozen batches went down the drain until he arrived at a brew he was happy with.) And with his young daughter in the passenger seat, Grossman delivered the first pallet of Sierra Nevada beer from the back of a beat-up one-ton '57 Chevy pickup.

The pale ale he labored so long to get right struck a chord, and today, the piney, balanced brew is widely imitated, and one of the two best-selling craft beers in the United States, next to Samuel Adams Boston Lager. Grossman, who was sixty-one in the end of 2015, got those gleaming copper kettles, to say the least. The brewery has gone from strength to strength, and now has a massive state-of-the-art brewery near Asheville, North Carolina. What's more, Sierra Nevada Pale Ale now comes in cans.

In the brewery, tours take in lovely trompe l'oeil murals in the brewhouse from a glassy elevated platform and other marvels no other American brewery can boast, like one of the largest private solar arrays in the country, utilizing heliotropic cells. There is nothing unconsidered, dusty, or out of place; the scope is awe-inspiring, and the rows of 25,000-gallon conditioning tanks lined up in majestic symmetry are a sight to behold.

Today, the operations take up fifty acres, with estate-grown hops and a thirty-five-acre barley field. The taproom and restaurant has its own organic herb and vegetable garden the size of a Walmart. The brewery's own cows are fed partly on healthful spent grain from the brewing process, and the restaurant and taproom cook over almond wood fires. The bright and comfortable eatery is full of art nouveau stylings, stained glass, and brilliant copper trim work. And no matter what beer you try, from the lightest Summerfest lager to the Estate line (using all ingredients from the property) and high-octane barley wines and collaboration beers, the beers are all superbly crafted (try the too-often overlooked Porter, for example). After a bite, visitors can catch concerts in the state-of-the-art concert venue, or catch a ride on a kooky (but highly enjoyable) pedal-powered, stereo-equipped rolling tap-mobile. It's a brewmaster's dream come true.

Of a company that does all this for its fans without spending a dime on shameless TV advertising, there's little left to say but "Thanks. What are you brewing next?"

PHILOSOPHY

Pioneering, eco-conscious, and consistently delicious, Sierra Nevada's beers are made with fanatical attention to detail and a generous, family-driven spirit.

KEY BEER

The beer that changed *everything* is Sierra Nevada Pale Ale. It's still brewed with whole Magnum, Perle, and pungent Cascade hop flowers, giving it a satisfying bite and grassy, floral nose. It's easy to forget that it's bottle-conditioned, meaning each individual bottle is carbonated by means of tiny additions of yeast and brewer's sugar—an insanely difficult thing to pull off on such a large scale. And as mentioned, it's now in cans. Brewers like to debate whether or not you can taste a difference.

Central Coast

FIRESTONE WALKER BREWERY

1400 Ramada Dr. • Paso Robles, CA 93446 • (805) 238-2556
firestonebeer.com • Established: 1996

SCENE & STORY

Run by former Marine Corps captain Adam Firestone and his brother-in-law, British expat David Walker (a former high-tech entrepreneur), Firestone is located in somewhat of a flavorless industrial area just outside town. There is a good-size tasting room and gift shop with dark wooden tables, but the most interesting action is amid the fifty-barrel brewhouse and its extensive barrel program; you'll want a tour. There's also a restaurant in Buellton (near Santa Barbara) with high-end fare and fresh Firestone beers.

PHILOSOPHY

Experimental yet restrained. The brewery uses a variation on something called the Burton Union System, a Rube Goldberg contraption developed by the British that links oak barrels with a yeast-collecting network of troughs, resulting in extraordinarily soft, smooth beer. Marston's, in England's Burton-on-Trent, is the classic example of a brewery making beer in this fashion, and explains it all by means of a three-hour tour. You won't need quite that much time at Firestone Walker, and the beer at the end is more interesting across the board.

KEY BEER

The pale ale ("31") has been around so long it's almost retro. But don't pass it up. Big beers like Sucaba really get beer geeks fired up these days. This spring seasonal release, a bourbon barrel-aged barley wine, all caramelized brown sugar, dark chocolate, tobacco, and dark cherry notes, as rich and smooth as a mousse, ideal to pair with strong cheese. And I'd be remiss without mentioning a new cult classic, Pivo Hoppy Pils, a formerly festival-only favorite that the brewers wisely scaled up for bottles and cans. Pivo (Czech for "beer") has a grand, fluffy head, dry, crisp finish, and lush aromas of bergamot and lemongrass from additions of German Saphir hops. At the 2015 Great American Beer Festival, Pivo Pils and DBA (Double Barrel Ale) each earned gold medals in their respective categories for the third time, including three in a row for Pivo since its inception in 2013. Not bad.

FIRESTONE WALKER BARRELWORKS

620 McMurray Rd. • Buellton, CA 93427
(805) 350-7385 • firestonebeer.com
Established: 2013

SCENE & STORY

From their iconic Pale 31 to DBA, Wookey Jack, and Pivo Hoppy Pils, Firestone Walker is in a class of its own (and the awards committees definitely agree). I asked Matt Brynildson—the brewmaster in charge of every one of them—to shed some light on what it's like being an American brewer today. "It's very nice to simply be the nation leading the cause for better beer after so many years of being the 'light lager nation.' I don't know exactly where it is going, but I do know that we are collectively tuning back into better food and better health through our food. Craft beer fits into that movement, and the people behind it are as passionate as any artisanal producer can be about their trade."

One direction it's all going, for sure, is into the sour spectrum—food-friendly beers made by means of benign bacteria additions (often added in oak barrels) which create depth, complexity, and tartness, a process that's far from simple. In 2012, Firestone Walker opened Barrelworks, its own standalone sour beer operation, in Buellton, about an hour and twenty minutes south from the original brewery, just off 101. Head blender (and original Firestone Walker brewer) Jeffers Richardson took some time to describe the project. "We are learning. This style of beer is hard to make, to control, to manage, and it takes time. Some are fermented spontaneously, some in barrels; all use a menagerie of wild yeast and bacteria to complete the fermentation process." What you'll find when you visit is pretty spectacular: a huge swath of barrels, stacked neatly beneath high ceilings and huge wrought-iron chandeliers. The tasting room itself is a small affair nestled between the barrels and restaurant. All the rare and barrel-aged beers Firestone Walker makes are available in three-ounce pours, but note, there could be few bottles to go.

PHILOSOPHY

"Whether it is hoppy beer or sour beer, balance and drinkability are always the keys," Brynildson told me. "With our wild beer program, we focus on using tart, sour flavors to enhance the experience. Beers with acid help to 'lift' heavy or fatty food. Acid creates depth. These beers should drink like wine. But the acid shouldn't lead, it should support the rest of the beer."

KEY BEER

"Agrestic is a sour beer based on our original flagship beer, Double Barrel Ale, or DBA," says Richardson. To hear him describe it attests to the massive effort involved. "[It] begins its journey as DBA then continues on through a 'chrysalis' process involving 87 percent French and 13 percent American Oak barrels, and our proprietary collection of microflora. To blend, we selected beer matured eight to twenty-four months in barrels . . . toasted oak and lemon pith swirl on the nose and palate, followed by an amazing harmony of vanilla, coconut, Earl Grey tea, and spice. The finish is crisp, with a mouth-watering acidity and chewy tannins." There you have it.

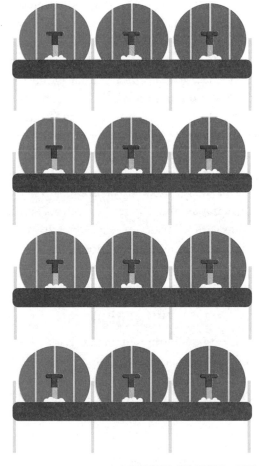

SANTE ADAIRIUS RUSTIC ALES

103 Kennedy Dr. • Capitola, CA 95010
(831) 462-1227 • rusticales.com
Established: 2012

SCENE & STORY

Adair Paterno and her business partner Tim Clifford, like many other beer pioneers, perceived a need for good, innovative beers exactly where they lived, and set out to make it happen. Paterno, a lawyer by day, and Clifford were (and still are) supercommitted beer geeks with a passion for tart, funky saisons and hop-forward IPAs. In 2011, the duo started gathering old dairy tanks and whatever they could make work in a small space in Capitola. Opening on Memorial Day 2012, they were immediately slammed. An early draw was bottle sharing nights. Paterno and Clifford had perfectly divined the area's thirst for good, hoppy, fresh beers as well as sours made with a variety of carefully cultivated microorganisms: bottle dregs, in other words, that they used and reused and grew and trained into a delicious house culture.

PHILOSOPHY

In a wide-ranging interview with Good Beer Hunting, a website out of Chicago, the charming and upbeat Paterno reflected on the brewery's mission. "We want to add to the tradition of saison making. But first and foremost, we are a home brewers' brewery. We have a piece of equipment from Lipton that we turned into a kettle and we have a bunch of used dairy tanks hanging around." It's an approach, you might say, that is more about beer drinking than it is about the shiny, ever-expanding industry and commerce of beer. "We really don't need all of our beers to be 'shelf stable.'" Paterno says. "I'm not packaging a clean, hoppy beer that needs to be consistent three months down the line when someone buys it at a liquor store. We do brew those beer styles, too, but those beers are getting tapped and enjoyed and then they are gone in about two weeks."

KEY BEER

Vanilla Joe is a an occasional, taproom-only version of their Joe Chavez porter infused with coffee and vanilla beans overnight in a home-brew keg. Also look for Cask 200, a tart, complex saison aged in a 660 gallon wine *foudre*. But the best known brew is West Ashley, a delicious, tart saison aged in wine barrels with California apricots (7.3% ABV).

Los Angeles and Surrounding Areas

Until recently L.A. (like New York), was a craft beer Mojave Desert. But thanks to the arrival of several craft breweries plus some beer-savvy chefs, a nascent beer culture is changing the entire timbre of the L.A. food-and-drink scene. Angelenos (like Portlanders, Denverites, and even New Yorkers before them) have embraced craft beers, all the better when made with locally foraged ingredients like so many snap peas, heirloom pork bellies, or pinot noirs. Instead of the coolly manufactured glam of, say, Spago, a more communal, unshaven, nose-to-tail chic is all the rage now. Food carts have gone upscale; local coffee roasters and farmers' markets are multiplying. And yet, there are still relatively few local breweries—so far. In a city with 9.8 million people (compared to, say, Portland, Oregon, which has 675,000 people and around ninety breweries), it's only a matter of time before Tinseltown gets the beer bug in an even bigger way.

THREE WEAVERS

1031 W. Manchester Blvd
Inglewood, CA 90301 • (310) 400-5830
threeweavers.la • Established: 2013

SCENE & STORY

L.A.'s beer scene leaped forward with Three Weavers. Founder Lynne Weaver (whose three daughters are the "three weavers") chose an industrial section of Inglewood not far from LAX and fought for the right to brew in an area where residents weren't in favor of more alcohol vendors. But Weaver had the chance to tell her story and convince local officials to give her a chance, and she succeeded. It's a good thing. They were poised for success early on. Weaver's head brewer Alexandra Nowell had parlayed a paid internship at Sierra Nevada into a cellar job at Drake's, then helmed the kettles at Kinetic Brewing Company, where she won a pair of medals at GABF. The interior is clean, stylish, and colorful. It wasn't long before Three Weavers was one of L.A.'s most talked-about brands, with glowing coverage in the *Los Angeles Times*, Eater.com, and others. In October 2015, *LA Weekly* named it L.A.'s best new brewery.

PHILOSOPHY

Officially, "It's more than beer. It's community." Three Weavers marches to the beat of an altruistic drum, with a chorus of communal sentiments, from unity to fairness and equality. It's a true improvement to L.A.'s often plastic-y social fabric. And the fact that it at least began as an all-female business (and it may well still be!) is commendable in a sea of arriviste craft breweries staffed by self-serving "dudebros."

KEY BEER

Deep Roots ESB emerged as an early flagship, but it's the one-offs and experiments that have really soared, like Cambria's Seafarer Kölsch, a grapefruit-accented triumph that was a personal favorite at in the Farm-to-Table "Paired" event at the 2015 GABF.

BEACHWOOD BBQ AND BREWING; BEACHWOOD BLENDERY

210 E. 3rd St. • Long Beach, CA 90802
(562) 436-4020 • beachwoodbbq.com
Established: 2006

⟷

Seal Beach: 131 Main St. • Seal Beach, CA
90740 • (562) 493-4500

SCENE & STORY

With two locations and a new, massive, 1000-barrel blendery project (next to the Long Beach location), you're coming here for baby back ribs, brisket, fried green tomatoes, hush puppies, and coleslaw—and beer, of course. Long Beach is the larger, more popular location. With roll-up doors opening into downtown Long Beach, mini outdoor beer garden, and thirty taps of super well-made beers (as well as guest taps), you'll have to take your time running through the list. Know this though: the beers running through the lines are well cared for. Founder Gabe Gordon is not only famous for beer and barbecue, he's become well known for something jokingly referred to as the "Flux Capacitor," a wall of valves that can control keg pressure and the gas mix therein (still with me?), ensuring the beer is never flat or foamy. What sounds like a lark is a smart concept that several other breweries and beer bars have employed (with Gordon's help), like Tørst in Brooklyn (see page 303), and Crooked Stave, in Denver.

PHILOSOPHY

Ambitious barbecue and beer, what's not to like? The barbecue hews to North Carolina style, marinated and dry-rubbed pork, with sauces on the side (and subtly discouraged). The beer is excellent across the board, and you've got to love the most off-kilter names (Pablo Escobeer; Hef Leppard).

KEY BEER

While the blendery is "on an undoubtedly geeky quest to create American-style lambics" (so just see what they have available in any location when you arrive), my pick for barbecue is Amalgamator IPA, a tangy, citrusy, dry American-style IPA very much in the West Coast tradition. It's great with spicy fare like ribs and pulled pork.

LAUREL TAVERN

11938 Ventura Blvd. • Studio City, CA 91614 • (818) 506-0777 • laureltavern.net
Established: 2008

SCENE & STORY

With its simple black façade, hardwood floors, exposed brick walls, pressed tin details, and L-shaped bar, this San Fernando Valley bar looks almost too perfect—like a movie set instead of a real, live, breathing beer bar. But it's definitely the real deal. With funky sky-blue metal stools along the bar, Edison lighting, and an artful food menu, there's little not to like. The short but sweet menu is based around beer-friendly foods like prosciutto and burrata, chorizo fondue, roast marrowbones, a bratwurst plate, and a famed burger with white cheddar, arugula, and caramelized onions. As for the beers (sixteen on tap, no bottles), most are California taps, with a pair or three for East Coast treats like Allagash and Dogfish Head. Word to the wise: Avoid weekend nights, or come in very early to get in position for the best people watching.

PHILOSOPHY

Craft beer gets its SAG card.

KEY BEER

Craftsman Heavenly Hefeweizen for starters (4.7 % ABV), which has the lively spice and ample heft of authentic German hefeweizen. "I think it's completely misunderstood in America," says Craftsman brewer Mark Jilg, citing Widmer and Pyramid brewing companies by example, whose hefeweizens are markedly less spicy. "We're going for a dry, crisp beer, with a clovey, banana-like estery palate. And we encourage people to lose the lemon slice."

TONY'S DARTS AWAY

1710 W. Magnolia Blvd. • Burbank, CA 91506 • (818) 253-1710 • tonysda.com
Established: 2010

SCENE & STORY

This dive bar reborn as an eco-friendly, full-on craft beer palace has forty taps of hard-to-find beers and a no-bottle, no-can policy—the conservation ethic runs deep. The main menu item is gourmet sausages (with extensive vegan options, too); beers are organized into IPA and "Not IPA." Both categories are filled with exceptional beers from the likes of Stone, Alpine, AleSmith, Bear Republic, and Russian River. In 2011, founder and owner Tony Yanow organized the "colLAboration" series of pop-up beer gardens around L.A. with Verdugo and the Surly Goat's Ryan Sweeney, among others, bringing craft beer to the streets of Los Angeles. A new classic bar—and likely, a new tradition—was born.

PHILOSOPHY

"All Craft, All Draught, All California."

KEY BEER

Stone's Smoked Chipotle Porter (6% ABV), which is sable black and laced with spicy, rich notes of pepper and smoke.

THE SURLY GOAT

7929 Santa Monica Blvd. • West Hollywood, CA 90046 • (323) 650-4628 surlygoat.com • Established: 2010

SCENE & STORY

When you tire of dodging the beautiful people who cram the streets of Hollywood, sipping beer under the mounted head of a mountain goat named Gus starts to sounds a whole heck of a lot better. Luckily, this nearly unmarked beer bar has a sweet rotating list, solicitous bartenders, leather seating, and a couple of old arcade games and a foosball table to keep things on the lighter side. There are even a few screens with a rotation of retro movies (*Star Wars, Ferris Bueller's Day Off*); if you get hungry, you can bring in food from the barbecue place next door, to name one very close option. There are twenty-seven taps and

a cask beer, with genuinely rare bottles to choose from as well (ask for the leather-bound list). This is a spin-off of local beer maven Ryan Sweeney, who opened Verdugo Bar and helped propel Los Angeles's interest in craft beer into what it is today: a genuine movement.

PHILOSOPHY

Not particularly surly, really. Just remember the usual Friday and Saturday night caveat—you might have to wait to get in.

KEY BEER

This is a great spot to try some of the latest creations from new-school California brewers like Bagby, Ladyface Ale Companie, and Societe.

VERDUGO BAR

3408 Verdugo Rd. • Los Angeles,
CA 90065 • (323) 257-3408
verdugobar.com • Established: 2008

SCENE & STORY

A complete renovation of a 1930s bar known for being quite sketchy—in a neighborhood that still is, so heads up—the Verdugo Bar has no windows and just a simple old glass, black-lettered sign light reading "cocktails." It's not much to look at, but then you walk inside to its serpentine, dimly lit bar, low couches, DJ in a booth, and epic beer list. There's a California-centric twenty-two-tap row, eighty-five bottles, and one cask to choose from, all served at the proper temperature and in the right glass, never sloshed on the bar. Thanks to L.A. craft beer scene maker Ryan Sweeney, a Certified Cicerone (one step down from beer's equivalent to Master of Wine), things are looking even better already.

Once you've got your beer, step outside to the patio and picnic table area. On the best weekend afternoons at 3 p.m., you'll find a "patio session" in progress: As the DJ spins, a chilled-out crowd lounges in the sun enjoying some of the city's best gourmet food carts like the famous Grill 'Em All (burgers) and Danky's Döners (kebabs and sandwiches).

PHILOSOPHY

Beer, booze, and beats.

KEY BEER

Look for Tropical & Juicy IPA from Hop Concept, the all-hoppy brews offshoot line by Lost Abbey. And go on Mondays. If you do, you keep the glass your beer came in.

BLUE PALMS BREWHOUSE

6124 Hollywood Blvd. • Los Angeles,
CA 90028 • (323) 464-2337
bluepalmsbrewhouse.com
Established: 2008

SCENE & STORY

While Hollywood these days is full of reality show losers, tourists, and plastic surgeons, it's not all bad. Eight blocks from the Walk of Fame and adjacent to the historic Henry Fonda Theater is one of the city's best beer bars, with a strong, constantly rotating, and California tap list of twenty-four (plus ninety bottles and a cask), a tradition for brewmaster appearances and beer dinners, and a good and none-too-pricey food menu. It's got Prohibition-era terrazzo floors, high ceilings in ruddy red, wide wooden beams, oversize mirrors, and some living palms, giving it a nice touch of Old Hollywood ambiance.

PHILOSOPHY

Retro look, today's beer.

KEY BEER

Sudwerk Lager, a German helles-style beer from Davis, California, is a solid starting point—light, grassy, grainy, and bright on the tongue but not without a malty backbone (4.9% ABV).

EAGLE ROCK BREWERY

3065 Roswell St. • Los Angeles, CA 90065 • (323) 257-7866 eaglerockbrewery.com • Established: 2009

SCENE & STORY

Jeremy Raub, a former film music editor, and his father, Steve, an ex-Navy man and dedicated home brewer who taught his son to brew, overcame a mountain of red tape delays in order to get their 15bbl brewhouse open in 2009, making it the first brewery in Los Angeles proper in some sixty years. Its ultraclean, organized taproom has been busy ever since, giving tours on Sundays from 12 to 6 p.m. As at Verdugo, food trucks are often on hand to provide the sustenance.

PHILOSOPHY

"Beer for the People" is the slogan, and the Raubs play with a neo-revolutionary theme in beer names like Manifesto and Solidarity. The beers are technically vegan (in avoiding fining, or clarifying, agents from animal products), and run the gamut of styles, from English mild to American wild, with some experimental ingredients (rose petals).

KEY BEER

Solidarity Dark Mild (3.8% ABV) is a light, chocolaty, grainy-tasting British session beer, meaning it's low in alcohol and meant for sustained periods of beer drinking without intoxication.

Orange County

THE BRUERY

717 Dunn Way • Placentia, CA 92870 714) 996-6258 • bruery.com Established: 2008

SCENE & STORY

A few years ago, Patrick Rue was reluctantly headed for a law career, but the trouble was, beer brewing was the only thing that held his attention. With his nose buried in a home brewing book his wife bought from a ninety-nine-cent bookstore, Rue was soon blowing off homework to craft dozens, even hundreds of batches. "I'd brew almost every weekend and during the week when I was 'studying,'" Rue recalls. In other words, he was preparing for a different kind of bar.

After taking a massive leap of faith

with family and personal investments, one of the more successful American breweries of the last two decades was born. Rue and head brewer Tyler King hew mainly to Belgian brewing traditions, which, generally speaking, tend to produce beers that are spicier, more intensely flavored, and higher in alcohol content than their American counterparts, and often bear the tannins and acids from wood barrels and wild yeasts. They're wild, but often delicious and food friendly. The hype surrounding the beers has been surprisingly loud, cranking up even higher after a dominant showing in the 2010 World Beer Cup in two hotly contested categories with sixty-eight runners up in all.

Visitors to the brewery in Placentia encounter a bland exterior (with a taco truck if you're lucky), but inside, there's a brighter space, with yellow and sage walls and a nice little tasting bar area next to fermenters and stacks of oak barrels. This is also the site of beer release parties, like one in October 2009 he might prefer to forget. The plan was to release 2,400 bottles of an onyx-black, 19.5% ABV, bourbon-barrel-aged stout called Black Tuesday, and 700 people showed up to buy it, causing a minor melee when supplies ran out, which left about seventy-five people empty-handed. "It was insane," Rue recalls. "We heard some people flew in to get it. It's almost embarrassing." The 2010 event was a somewhat smoother affair, only crashing the website. Such scenes are now, remarkably common around the country when reserve beers are released. By late 2015, Rue and Co. planned to open Bruery Terreux, a separate, sour- and barrel-aging and blending business designed to isolate wild beers from the rest of production and capture the zeitgeist rush for sour and wild ales.

PHILOSOPHY

Unorthodox. Since its inception, the Bruery has released beers conjured out of such ingredients as Thai basil, pasilla chiles, and purple mangosteen, some of the concoctions only dimly recognizable as beers to the layperson. To make his award-winning Autumn Maple, Rue roasts yams on a barbecue until they are soft and sugary, then smashes them up and adds them to a mash tun, the brewer's tank used to extract fermentable sugars that normally come entirely from grain.

KEY BEER

Orchard White and Black Tuesday have made the biggest splashes, but try the Humulus Lager to really shock your expectations. It's a superstrong lager (in the bock territory, at 7.2% ABV), aromatically hopped like an IPA.

A BEER WITH
MARK JILG, CRAFTSMAN BREWING COMPANY

1260 Lincoln Ave., No. 800 • Pasadena, CA 91105 • craftsmanbrewing.com

←——————→

Pasadena's Mark Jilg is as likely to expound on the paradox of being an artisan brewer in the middle of Tinseltown as he is to offer an impromptu lecture on the tendency of hops to spontaneously combust (true story). About fifteen years ago, Jilg left his job as an analyst for NASA's Jet Propulsion Laboratory to make beer instead, founding Craftsman in 1995. Today, his tiny brewery, in an unassuming industrial park about forty miles from Disneyland, produces beers that are defiantly pushing the outer limits, too, with Valencia orange rind, Cabernet grapes, white sage, and Brettanomyces. "There are a lot of people that are focused on food culture here, savoring wine and so on. But they haven't considered beer, so when they taste something like mine, it blows their mind," he told me.

His best-selling beer reflects craft brewing's return to America's pre-Prohibition beer landscape: 1903 is a 5.9% ABV lager using a proportion of corn in the mash (as lagers of that era did, adding body and a certain corn flakes–like flavor profile), bittered with Nugget hops and finished with late additions of Mt. Hood to add a nice, delicate hop presentation and aroma.

Jilg doesn't have a taproom or take visitors—it's basically a one-man show in a 2,500-square-foot space—so look for the beer on tap at good L.A. beer bars like Laurel Tavern and Lucky Baldwin's in Pasadena. Maximiliano, in Highland Park, has become a semi-official Craftsman tasting room. Jilg hasn't started bottling, but if he does, the whole operation ought to blast off. His delivery van may be a green 1946 M-15 Studebaker, but the beer is next generation.

Farther South

SMOG CITY BREWING

1901 Del Amo Blvd. • Torrance, CA 90501
(310) 320-7664
smogcitybrewing.com • Established: 2013

SCENE & STORY

For some reason there's a Rob Lowe portrait hidden somewhere in the taproom at Smog City, an unexpected gag for what is essentially a straightforward venture built in a huge, conventional warehouse space. "We always wanted a place that felt like you were in the brewery, so that's what people get," says Jonathan Porter, founder. Expect "tanks, barrels, chalkboards, knowledgeable staff and great beer." Porter, who started home brewing in 2003 and attended the American Brewers Guild in 2006, then started as a keg washer at BJ's in Brea, CA. After a stint as head brewer at Tustin Brewing Co. in Orange County, CA, he set out to build his own place with his partner Laurie Porter and opened Smog City up in May of 2013.

PHILOSOPHY

"Balanced beer is the best beer" says founder and head brewer Jonathan Porter. "Whether light and crisp, super hoppy, or loaded with coffee, our beer is all about balance. We love to make all styles of beer and so visitors to our taproom find a lot

of pilot batches, fruited saisons, and IPAs that don't leave the brewery."

KEY BEER

In 2015 Smog City pulled down a silver GABF medal for their Kumquat Saison, and look for barrel-aged, wild, and other sour beers in development in late 2015.

PORT BREWING CO. / THE LOST ABBEY

155 Mata Way, No. 104 • San Marcos, CA 92069 • (800) 918-6816
lostabbey.com • Established: 2006

SCENE & STORY

Port Brewing Company and its Belgian-beer-influenced Lost Abbey line of beers are produced under the watchful eye of award-winning brewer Tomme Arthur, founding brewer of Pizza Port, and one of the first American craft brewers to employ barrel aging. The operation is based in an industrial space on the northern perimeter of San Diego County (one that used to house Stone, which outgrew the space and moved a few miles down the road).

One of San Diego county's biggest beer traveler draws, Lost Abbey (as most refer to it now) has a spacious tasting room stacked high with oak barrels and kegs on end with grain or brewers' sugar sacks for cushions at the forty-two-foot bar. In its first six years, Lost Abbey won over 100 medals and awards in the competitive craft brewing world and become a real draw for travelers who come to taste, trade stories, and leave with rare bottles in tow. On the weekend there are free, informal guided tours, but the main thing to do is sample here. There are twenty taps at all times with at least sixteen different beers available to take out in bottles. The scene here has real energy and buzz. "It's like Sonoma County in the late 1970s," says former tasting room manager Sage Osterfeld. Lost Abbey opened another location in Cardiff in 2015.

PHILOSOPHY

Belgian-style beers with cork-and-wire cage and a medieval theme running through the label art and brew names.

KEY BEER

Ask for Duck Duck Gooze, a wild yeast beer of 5.5% ABV made of a blend from young and older barrel-aged ales. But it's extremely rare, so you might have better luck with Bourbon Barrel Aged Angel's Share, a beer on the other, less acidic, but no less interesting end of the flavor spectrum (12% ABV). In distillers' parlance, the "angel's share" is the proportion of precious spirit lost to evaporation in the barrel. This barrel-aged brew marries the woody, vanilla-laced smokiness of a classic sipping bourbon to a rich, port-like beer.

PIZZA PORT SOLANA BEACH

135 N. Highway 101 • Solana Beach, CA 92075 • (858) 481-7332
pizzaport.com • Established: 1987

SCENE & STORY

There are now three other Pizza Port locations (San Clemente, Carlsbad, and Ocean Beach), but this one—founded by siblings Vince "Vinny" and Gina Marsaglia, who sold its first beer in 1992—is the original, smallest, and to many, the best. Located in an unassuming stretch of the Pacific Coast Highway with the beach close enough to smell but not see, Pizza Port combines two very elemental things: great pizza and great beer. The inside is cozy and cheerful, and if you sit to the right of the tap row, you can look down into the sunken brewing area to watch the action unfold.

PHILOSOPHY

Pizza and beer, good times are near.

KEY BEER

The rich, dark, and coppery Sharkbite Red (6% ABV) is the big seller here—it goes well with spicy pizza dishes—but try the seasonal as well.

STONE BREWING CO. AND WORLD BISTRO

1999 Citracado Pkwy. • Escondido, CA 92029 • (760) 471-4999 • stonebrew.com; stoneworldbistro.com • Established: 1996

SCENE & STORY

Founded in San Marcos, Stone moved to its present location in 2006, and it's more or less a Disneyland for beer lovers. First they built a sprawling eco-friendly compound, complete with a natural-boulder-tunnel-like entrance, an acre of gardens, and a huge roof solar array, cutting the power usage considerably. Then there's a chic, glassy, 12,000-square-foot restaurant looking out on the gardens and a patio of reclaimed bricks (with side and outdoor bars, for overflow).

The eatery has a central U-shaped bar area with thirty-two drafts and 120 bottles from Stone and other excellent domestic and international craft breweries. It's all laid out around an island of boulders and bamboo growing from a bed of river rocks in the center of the room, which has nice old weathered wood tables for a counterpoint. The menu is long, using only local and organic vegetables and breads, hormone-free and natural meats. The spicy duck tacos, made with chile de árbol and the brewery's Levitation Ale-infused barbecue sauce, will require quantities of cold beer close at hand—they're fiery.

PHILOSOPHY

Righteous. Brewing-wise the beers are always well put together, if on the intense side (with notable exceptions), and sometimes great. For the most part, Stone Brewing's "extreme" beers are like standard ales in overdrive, with a side dish of attitude. (These are the fellows who brought the beer-drinking public "Arrogant Bastard" ale, after all.) Steve Wagner, Stone's brewmaster, has spent years creating radical riffs on traditional styles: aggressively hopped ales fermented to a high alcohol percentage, usually around 7% ABV but sometimes nearly double that. But getting customers soused isn't the point; the point is creating complex layers of flavor through long, robust fermentations with a rich mix of grains and huge amounts of resiny, fresh, green hops. With a new brewery recently opened in Berlin, Germany, Stone is taking this bombastic approach around the world. Will Germans embrace it, or merely American tourists? Time will tell.

KEY BEER

Until Levitation Ale came along, the unspoken rule on Stone brews was this: Don't drink them before dusk unless you have time for a nap. These beers are tasty; they're also tranquilizing. Like any beer from Stone, Levitation is loaded with grainy, fruity malt flavors and topped off with a sturdy dose of fragrant hops. At 4.4% ABV, though, it's easy-going.

Southern California and San Diego County

That an American city often associated with surfing and skateboarding should turn out to be one of the country's top craft beer destinations comes as a surprise to many. But it's absolutely true: There are more than fifty top-tier brewing companies in the entire region now, and dozens of excellent beer bars. From crisp, refreshing lagers to pungent IPAs, funky Belgian ales, and even porters and stouts smoked with chipotle and other peppers, the brewers' bold creativity stems from the area's lack of brewing history. There are no expectations to live up to and no pressure to follow traditions.

MODERN TIMES FLAVORDOME

3000 Upas St. • San Diego, CA 92104
(619) 269-5222 • moderntimesbeer.com
Established: 2013

MODERN TIMES BEER—LOMALAND FERMENTORIUM

3725 Greenwood St • San Diego, CA 92110
(619) 546-9694

SCENE & STORY

Battle-tested PR handler Jacob McKean learned a thing or two about buzz and big beers at his former workplace Stone Brewing Co. under Greg Koch, one of the brashest and most polarizing figures in the industry. So it was no surprise in April of 2013 that McKean's Kickstarter campaign to launch his own brand pulled in $20,000—in a single day (the final tally was over $65,000, the highest ever hauled in for a brewery at the time, though that is but a tiny fraction of the costs required of any start-up brewery over a barrel or two in size). Nonetheless: most impressive.

The timing was ideal for a new business in the booming San Diego market, and McKean brought a lot of fresh, and frankly un-Stone-ish, ideas to the bar:

a website popping with bright, retro yet design-forward cans and crowd-sourced recipes that were exactly *au courant*. A public consultation with Michael Tonsmeire (a.k.a. the Mad Fermentationist, a brilliant home brewing blogger in the midst of writing a now benchmark book called American Sour Beer), it was, in sum, a masterclass in humble yet confident promotion, but McKean's project was based on a pro team of brewers that quickly established Modern Times as a brand worth reckoning. Once the Lomaland taproom was built—complete with a young local artist's mural depicting pop star Michael Jackson and his pet chimpanzee made out of over 10,000 Post-it notes—the die was cast: Modern Times was a big story. Is the mural pure pop art, or earnest homage? Clever riff on the weird nature of celebrity, or deeply ironic nod to the beer world's heroic Michael Jackson, the late British author of sixteen celebrated books on beer and whisky? All of the above, if you ask me.

In the Lomaland location you'll find a bright space with sixteen-tap bar (and that mural). The Upas Street location is a cozier affair with newsprint walls, a book-themed tap row, and lampshades hanging upside down from the ceiling, allusions to McKean's six years as a freelance writer.

PHILOSOPHY

Having already announced a huge expansion and a packaging hall (plus a surging coffee line and distribution through Costco), McKean and Co. have already created a brand beyond beer based, in his words, "on aroma-driven, complex, flavorful, sessionish beers. We often brew hybrid styles, combining the features we like from established categories to create new, Island-Of-Doctor-Moreau-style mash-ups." In other words, think: thoughtful, stylish beers calibrated for maximum conversation.

KEY BEER

Fortunate Islands is a 5% ABV hybrid wheat beer and IPA, with Citra and Amarillo hops for days, as the kids say. But there are also four seasonals and monthly releases showcasing the range of this up-to-the-minute brewery.

SOCIETE BREWING

8262 Clairemont Mesa Blvd.
San Diego, CA 92111 • (858) 598-5409
societebrewing.com • Established: 2012

SCENE & STORY

Doug Constantiner was working as a young investment banker—set for life, likely. But there was something nagging at him: brewing beer. Starting with a cheap kit, he'd been bitten by the bug. Besotted with the process, yet lacking experience, he bailed on the banking job in NYC and enrolled in Siebel classes, then decamped to San Diego where he eventually scored a job at Green Flash. Next thing he knew, he was working in one of San Diego's most revered new breweries.

Cofounder Travis Smith, meanwhile, had been soaking up wisdom from two Jedis in the industry, Vinnie Cilurzo of Russian River and Brian Hunt at Moonlight, outside of Santa Rosa, California. Eventually Constantiner and Smith would each end up in LA working the Bruery, where, over beers, they hatched plans and made their own move back to San Diego—a bit late to the party, but there's always room for great new project. Their first beers met with a lot of encouragement, to say the least. Chad Jakobson of Denver's Crooked Stave Artisan Beer Project was an early fan. "It was phenomenal, so flavorful," Jakobsen told me. "They're going to do Belgian-styles, they're going to do barrel-aged beers—and I'll be really excited to try those—but their IPA was off the hook." Visit their cozy, wood-paneled tasting room and see what he meant.

PHILOSOPHY

Societe divides their beer families four ways: Out west (read: IPA, IIPA), Old World (Belgian pale ales; saison; golden strongs), Stygian (referencing the Underworld's River Styx, i.e., dark and intense), and Feral, for sour and wild brews.

KEY BEER

The Pupil, a fragrant American Style IPA, is on the boozy side at 7.8% ABV, wafting tropical notes of guava and mango-like aromas. It's a popular San Diego beer these days, but is just one of many they're doing well.

GREEN FLASH BREWING CO. (CELLAR 3)

6550 Mira Mesa Blvd. • San Diego, CA 92121 • (858) 622-0085
greenflashbrew.com • Established: 2002

SCENE & STORY

In the tradition of other San Diego County breweries, Green Flash could not have launched in a more flavorless location, an industrial warehouse space inside a business park off the highway. No matter—even if the walls were adorned with little more than dry-erase boards, the beers were anything but bland, and it was busy every weekend. Crazy busy. Now the brewing facility has moved to the Mira Mesa location while the original became a vast wood cellar operation (Cellar 1 and Cellar 2). Meanwhile, nearby, Green Flash opened a new barrel aging location ("Cellar 3"), set up for visitors who gawk at over 8,000 oak casks, several *foudres*, and a cork-and-cage bottling line. Standing around tasting amid the tanks and casks in either location, it's easy to chat and mingle with other beer lovers who have made the trek.

PHILOSOPHY

Hoptopian. The best-known beers of Green Flash are by turns pungent, dank, grassy, piney, and bitter. If that's your thing, this is your place. Lately though, the brewery has been doing a number of Belgian-style beers, including Bière De L'Amitié, a 9.5% ABV collaboration strong pale ale with Brasserie St. Feuillien in southwestern Belgium.

KEY BEER

West Coast IPA gets most of the love, but the fiery Hop Head Red (6% ABV), a copper-hued amber dry-hopped with Amarillo, is a fun beer to drink and would go well with pepperoni pizza. And look for Le Freak, an American-Belgo-style ale which took gold at GABF 2015. From Cellar 3, it's all about Silva Stout, a 10% ABV bourbon barrel-aged imperial stout with serious heft.

WHITE LABS

9495 Candida St. • San Diego, CA
92126 • (858) 693-3441 • whitelabs.com
Established: 2012

SCENE & STORY

Drinking in a brewery is one thing, but drinking in a world famous lab where yeasts are cultivated for the world's top brewers? That's taking it to an entirely new level. With thirty-five taps, up to three casks at a time, and chic design elements made of glass beakers and test tubes, the super clean and cool White Labs showcases different yeasts in every beer style, an incredibly educational—and tasty—experience. After a tour through the incredibly high-tech facility, you hit the taproom for beers brewed on site. This is a must visit on any beer lover's trip to San Diego.

PHILOSOPHY

Yeast is king. In the early 1990s, founder Chris White was a busy home brewer and lab technician while earning his PhD at UC San Diego. Some of his fellow home brewer buddies went on to found a little (heh) company called Ballast Point. White wanted his own brewery, too, but he also (brilliantly) saw the need for professional yeast services and lab work. With a $5,000 loan from his parents, White launched White Labs Pure Yeast and Fermentation. Today, thousands of breweries, distilleries and wineries rely on White for lab-cultured yeast. The lab also banks yeast samples for breweries needing analysis of house and spontaneous or wild strains.

KEY BEER

Well, what's your favorite yeast strain? That line might have earned taproom laughs a few years ago, but in today's beer-nerd paradise, one can ask and get an informed answer. The most interesting thing about White Labs is trying different beers made with the same strain, illustrating the massive impact yeast has on beer flavor.

ALESMITH BREWING CO.

9368 Cabot Dr. • San Diego, CA 92126
(858) 549-9888 • alesmith.com
Established: 1995

SCENE & STORY

AleSmith, one of San Diego's early breakout successes—400 medals and counting!—has stayed small as others in the area (i.e., Stone) have grown at an incredible rate. But founder Peter Zien is content to keep production where it is (around 1,000bbl per year), so the little brewery and taproom remain almost a homespun affair, little more than a rectangular room in an industrial park with a walk-in cooler and the brewing tanks off to the side. This is a good thing; beer is the sole focus, and it's no less of a draw for beer travelers (Saturdays get busy). No matter when you seek it out, though, you're likely to meet fellow beer lovers there, who, having trekked from across the country, or even from abroad, are eager try every last beer on offer. There are free tours on the last Saturday of each month; call ahead. A new tasting room is planned, along with a facility partnership project with Mikkeller. AleSmith estimates it will jump from producing 25,000 barrels to 40,000 next year.

PHILOSOPHY

"Hand Forged" is the MO officially, and it fits nicely with AleSmith, a small, solid operation with consistently high quality in American interpretations of British and Belgian styles, primarily.

KEY BEER

Speedway Stout, at 12% ABV, is already a huge beer, carbon black and dense with coffee, chocolate, and roasted malt flavors. The barrel-aged version takes it to 11, with even deeper notes of vanilla, oak, espresso, and caramel, having lived in wood for a full year.

BALLAST POINT BREWING CO./ HOMEBREW MART

5401 Linda Vista Rd., Ste. 406
San Diego, CA 92110 • (619) 295-2337
ballastpoint.com • Established: 1996

SCENE & STORY

Ballast Point Brewing Company, ranked as the top small brewery in the country in 2010, started with a home brewer's dream. True story: Jack White opened his little home brew shop in 1992, and soon a community of home brewers eager to try his beers helped him think even bigger. By 1996, White was ready to install a 15bbl brewhouse, and Ballast Point was born. Today there's several Ballast Point locations, but Homebrew Mart retains the charm (and the original brewing equipment, still in use) of the early days in San Diego's beer revolution.

Brewmaster (and vice president) Colby Chandler leads a team that's playing around with barrel aging, Belgian-style sour beers, and wild yeasts. These vinous ales overlaid with hints of oak and brandy are blended on site, with production so small-scale that most of these beers are rarely seen outside of San Diego County. Try the full Ballast Point line in the back of the store at the little tasting bar, with the barrel projects available on occasion. It's the best-kept secret for finding—and sharing—beer knowledge in San Diego.

PHILOSOPHY

Beer creates community. And good beer is worth good money people should be able to share, too. In 2015 Ballast Point also announced an I.P.O. for a mere $173 million, then was acquired in the end of the year by Constellation brands for $1 billion. That's billion, with a B. And it's business as usual in the craft beer world of this era.

KEY BEER

Ask about the barrel-aging projects. Or try the flowery, tangerine-y double dry-hopped Sculpin IPA (7% ABV), which offers an aromatic blast of citrus and flowers. A new version called Grapefruit Sculpin (with grapefruit juice added) was a huge hit in the summer of 2015 on the West Coast.

HAMILTON'S TAVERN

1521 30th St. • San Diego, CA 92192
(619) 238-5460 • hamiltonstavern.com
Established: 2006

SCENE & STORY

Almost end to end, San Diego's 30th Street has turned into a craft beer lover's avenue in recent years, with Hamilton's anchoring the quiet, residential southern reaches near the southeast corner of Balboa Park. Formerly a dive bar known as Sparky's, and site of the oldest liquor license in San Diego (first listed around seventy-five years ago), Hamilton's is the brainchild of owner Scot Blair, who cleaned it out, hung the ceiling with a wild collection of tap handles, and added a sandwich and burger café next door. There are twenty-eight taps, 150 bottled options, and two casks on all times, with a strong focus on California specialties like Russian River, AleSmith, and Firestone Walker, and a few especially interesting choices from small European brewers.

PHILOSOPHY

Come on in. Hamilton's is a friendly neighborhood bar with a superb beer list and great food next door. Herman Hamilton, a teetotaling elderly U.S. Marine who lives in the neighborhood and for whom the bar was named, despite having no taste for drink, is said to have spent a fair amount of time visiting and telling stories with the bearded Blair and his friends, who keep the bar hopping—but seldom slammed to the point of annoyance.

KEY BEER

Brasserie Ellezelloise's Quintine Blonde, an 8% ABV Belgian strong pale ale on the sweet side, with honey, bread, and herbal notes. And on a recent visit, I scored a rare bottle of Logsdon Peche 'n Brett, a tart treat to share with old pals.

TORONADO

4026 30ᵗʰ St. • San Diego, CA 92104
(619) 282-0456 • toronadosd.com
Established: 2008

SCENE & STORY

Cleaner and less cluttered than its parent bar in San Francisco, Toronado San Diego is about one thing, and one thing only: craft beer. A small, narrowish bar in North Park, it has a world-class selection of taps emanating from a metal-plated wall in the corner. The beer list skews toward SoCal brewers like AleSmith, Lost Abbey, Pizza Port, Alpine, and Green Flash, with some Belgian left

fielders like De Landtsheer for good measure. The goods are routinely fresh and served in the right glass by someone who knows what they're talking about, and there's a nice little patio out back should crowds get to be a bit much for the stools and small high tables. Every time I walk in, it seems I run into someone interesting from the beer world. No matter what, it's worth a trip for anyone looking for a great selection in a relaxed atmosphere.

PHILOSOPHY

Unpretentious excellence. While it can surely happen, attitude is not generally served up at Toronado. It's just a great place to have a beer, try something new, and meet or make friends.

KEY BEER

Alpine's California Uncommon (5.7% ABV), Pat McIlhenney's version of "steam" beer, the sort of lager beer fermented at warmer temperatures that Anchor made famous. It's got a wallop of hop character and a soft, caramel malt base for harmony.

Alpine

ALPINE BEER CO.

2351 Alpine Blvd. • Alpine, CA 91901
(619) 445-2337 • alpinebeerco.com
Established: 1999

SCENE & STORY

From downtown San Diego, it's about a forty-minute drive into the Coast Range foothills on Interstate 8 toward Yuma, Arizona, to get to Alpine Brewing Company, where Pat McIlhenney, a former full-time fire captain, and his son Shawn built their own little corner of heaven: a small-production brewery and barbecue café in an old TV-repair shop, with copper-sided kettles running a few times a week. Or at least, that's how it was supposed to be. Now, thanks to the fast-spreading fame of their IPAs in particular, they're brewing and bottling practically dawn till dusk, adding fermentation tanks and a cold storage room and a barbecue café next door to boot. All of it was built by hand. It seems to be working. "I cannot make beer fast enough," said the elder McIlhenney. His twelve tap and eight bottled brews achieved cult status, heightened by their rarity—and a slew of laurels, like a gold in 2010 in American-style strong pale ales for O'Brien's IPA, beating fifty-eight other contenders. Until recently, you had to drive up to Alpine or—at the very least—find a great beer bar in San Diego County to drink the good stuff. In 2014 it was announced Alpine and Green Flash were merging operations, a development that means one thing: lots more fresh Alpine beer.

PHILOSOPHY

The McIlhenneys keep it simple: "Drink Alpine Beer or Go to Bed!"

KEY BEER

Duet IPA (7% ABV), full of the fresh, floral flavors of Simcoe and Amarillo hops, two once fairly rare varieties.

BEST *of the* REST: CALIFORNIA

CITY BEER STORE

1168 Folsom St., No. 101 • San Francisco, CA 94103 • (415) 503-1033 • citybeerstore.com

In this little SoMa bottle and draft emporium (inspired by wine shops and organized by style rather than brand) visitors sip fresh, ultrarare domestic and imported craft beers and snack on artisan cheese plates and freshly baked breads. There are six taps for growlers and more than 300 bottled beers to mix and match. Opened in 2006, it has become a key gathering place for San Francisco craft beer fanatics.

BEER REVOLUTION

464 3rd St. • Oakland, CA 94607 • (510) 452-2337 • beer-revolution.com

This combination bottle shop and craft beer bar opened in 2010 and became an anchor of east Bay Area drinking culture, despite its humble location and pallid fluorescent lighting. All 500 selections are available to take home—or pop open right here for a mere dollar. Then there are forty-seven drafts to choose from and a sunny patio for al fresco tastings. Add in correct glassware for every beer, appearances by notable brewers, and afternoon barbecues, and you have all the ingredients for a serious craft beer party.

SOCIAL KITCHEN & BREWERY

1326 9th Ave. • San Francisco, CA 94122 • (415) 681-0330 • SocialKitchenandBrewery.com

Located a short walk from Golden Gate Park, this brewpub opened in 2010 is a SF beer brunch must. What you find inside is a narrow yet roomy (as in, tall) brewpub with eighteen taps and a long bar inviting you to sit down and start tasting. With a gold medal for Mr. Kite's Pale Ale in the Classic English Pale Ale category at the Great American Beer Festival, 2015, head brewer Kim Sturdivant cemented his already stellar reputation. And the food is terrific. Try the braised brisket hash if they have it on, and a craft michelada. You'll be all set.

CELLARMAKER BREWING

1150 Howard St. • San Francisco, CA 94103 • (415) 863-3940 • cellarmakerbrewing.com

Connor Casey and Tim Sciascia are brewing well-made, hop-forward ales with every-thing from South African Southern Passion to New Zealand Riwaka hops. Beers tend to be one-offs, but look for brews like Saison Francisco, aged in sauvignon blanc barrels with peaches and pluots, and Tiny Dankster (5.8% ABV), brewed with heaps of Mosaic, Citra, and Nelson hops.

TRIPLE ROCK BREWERY & ALEHOUSE

1920 Shattuck Ave. • Berkeley, CA 94704 • (510) 843-4677 • triplerock.com

A pilgrimage to Triple Rock is a trip into American craft brewing's earliest days: When it opened in 1986 after a lengthy battle with town officials (who feared a fac-tory), it became just the fifth brewpub in the United States. Today it's the only of those five still owned by the founders. The Triple Rock is just as welcoming as ever, though with far better beer and a full menu. Try the Dragon's Mike Brown Ale (6.5% ABV) with toffee, smoke, and floral notes that work well together.

FAT ANGEL FOOD & LIBATION

1740 O'Farrell St. • San Francisco, CA 94115 • 415-525-3013 • fatangelsf.com

This is your (note: tiny) spot to hit before a show at the historic Fillmore, which is right around the corner. The late afternoon is perfect timing for a seat outside. There's an ambitious wine and cocktail program, but you're there for the nine taps of draft and 100-plus bottle list, packed with obscure Belgians, sours, farmhouse ales, and rarities like the Evil Twin/Sante Adairius mashup Joey Pepper Belgian pale ale.

HEALTHY SPIRITS

1042 Clement St. • San Francisco, CA 94118 • (415) 682-4260
healthy-spirits.blogspot.com • 2299 15th St. • San Francisco CA 94114 • (415) 255-0610

Simply put: this is a beer bottle shop with a huge selection, especially favoring Bel-gium and cultish American craft beers, as well as a bourbon and Middle Eastern foods (i.e., great hummus). Spotted recently: Prairie Artisan Ales, Cascade, Grimm (Brooklyn, NY), Anchorage, and Dieu du Ciel! out of Montreal, Canada.

HOPMONK TAVERN

230 Petaluma Ave. • Sebastopol, CA 95472 • (707) 829-7300 • hopmonk.com

Built in a gorgeous, old, stone barnlike structure and lined with 100-year-old salvaged Douglas fir floors, this spacious brewpub (established in 2008) features house ales among the sixteen taps and 100 bottled selections including a swath of Russian River, Sierra Nevada, and Anderson Valley beers. The menu features beer-focused cuisine, such as charcuterie plates, cider-braised salmon, and hot beer sausage. If you haven't found it yet, this is the place to try Russian River's superb Temptation, a 7.25% ABV blonde ale aged in Chardonnay barrels with a touch of Brettanomyces yeast. They also have a location in Novato and one in Sonoma.

BEAR REPUBLIC

345 Healdsburg Ave. • Healdsburg, CA 95448 • (707) 433-2337 • bearrepublic.com

Racer 5 is an American-style IPA of 7% ABV that, over the past few years, has likely zoomed into the best beer bars in America based on its incredibly floral aroma alone. It's a reliably delicious beer, top in its class at the 2009 GABF, and now produced in a much bigger brewery nearby that isn't open to the public. But the family-owned brewpub where it was born—decorated with memorabilia of auto racing—shows off what founder and head brewer Richard Norgrove has in the engine next, including one-offs in the original brewhouse.

FIGUEROA MTN. BREWING CO.

45 Industrial Way • Buellton, CA 93427 • (805) 694-2252, ext. 110 • figmtnbrew.com

With multiple, additional locations from Malibu all the way up to San Luis Obispo, this Santa Barbara County mainstay founded in 2010 in Buellton has horseshoes, fire pits, bean bag toss, and hordes of local fans. In recent years "Fig Mountain" as some call it has racked up a crazy number of medals at GABF and even the World Beer Cup. There's an array of lighter kölsch and summery wheat beers in every spot, but don't miss the malty Danish Red Lager (5.5% ABV) and robust Davy Brown (6% ABV), both super clean beers brewed to traditional styles.

LIBERTINE BREWING CO.

1234 Broad St. • San Luis Obispo, CA 93401 • (805) 548-2337 • libertinebrewing.com

Founded in 2012, Libertine grew from a funky, little brewpub on Morro Bay into a 9,000-square-foot facility with a brewery, tasting room, restaurant, and coffee shop in downtown San Luis Obispo. Inside: a small copper-clad brewhouse surrounded by oak barrels, where founder/brewer Tyler Clark oversees production of a range of experimental brews like a recent saison hopped with obscure hops called Lemon Drop and Boadicia. You'll get a dollar off your pour if you show up with your own vinyl records; spin some tunes while watching Clark and the brewers wield every artisanal method you can think of: super heated volcanic rocks, a coolship (see page 265), and wood-barrel aging.

WAYPOINT PUBLIC

3794 30th St. • San Diego, CA 92104 • (619) 255-8778 • waypointpublic.com

Opened in 2013 with former *Top Chef* contestant Amanda Baumgarten at the stove, this spacious, bright, and stylish gastropub was a great addition to an already amazing beer lovers' neighborhood: North Park. Baumgarten moved on, but the restaurant hasn't really missed a step, with a huge variety of comfort foods and sought-after CA beers from the likes of Almanac, Noble Ale Works, Alpine, and Societe. Cofounder Brian Jensen also owns the terrific Bottlecraft shops in San Diego's North Park and Little Italy neighborhoods (make sure to check them out when in the area).

BAGBY BEER COMPANY

601 S. Coast Hwy. • Oceanside, CA 92054 • (760) 270-9075 • bagbybeer.com

With the motto of "World-class beer, simple food done well, inviting hospitality," industry veteran Jeff Bagby moved into an 8,500-square-foot brewery and spare lot in 2012. The former Pizza Port Ocean Beach brewer had racked up so many awards it was only a matter of time before he stepped out on his own. The Oceanside brewpub is clean, modern, and open, with pale varnished woods, shiny gray-brown tiles, and chartreuse walls, and multiple outdoor patios. Try whatever's fresh, especially pale Belgian style blondes like the crisp, 4.4% Yvanke, and snack on yellowtail crudo and local pork belly, just for starters.

HAWAII

BACK IN THE LATE-1960S "TINY BUBBLES" ERA OF DON HO—AND THE LAST DAYS OF SURFING pioneer Duke Kahanamoku—the Hawaiian Islands' beloved beer was an inexpensive industrial lager called Primo, which lacked much flavor but dated all the way back to 1898. The nostalgic brand withered away over the next couple of decades as corporate owners (Schlitz, then Stroh, then Pabst) moved production to the mainland and scrimped on glass and ingredients, choices that won't ever spur much of a luau.

These days, craft beer is surfing its own wave in the islands, brewing the freshest, best beer they can for the breezy beaches of the fiftieth state. Beer bars, beer blogs, and bottle shops—the trifecta of businesses that complement great local breweries—are popping up all over the place. Even the restaurants are getting into it. Town, in the hip Kaimuki neighborhood of Honolulu on Oahu is doing great business with local brewers. On Maui, in Lahaina at Mala Ocean Tavern, you can drink world-class Jolly Pumpkin sour beer overlooking the ocean. On and on it goes, like waves off a nice point break. There are even breweries popping up on Kauai, the Garden Isle I visit every winter. It's not at all easy to brew in paradise—there are no malt houses or large hop suppliers, for starters—but that's not keeping craft beer from finding a home, their taprooms full, and their kegs running dry.

MAUI BREWING CO.

605 Lipoa Pkwy. • Kihei, Maui, HI 96753
(808) 213-3002 • mauibrewingco.com
Established: 2005

Kahana Gateway Center • 4405
Honoapiilani Hwy., No. 217 • Lahaina, HI
96761 • Established: 2009

SCENE & STORY

What's paradise without incredible beer? Exactly. When you tire of nearby Kaanapali Beach (if such a thing is possible), take a break from tiki drinks and head for a taste of the best beer in the islands. Known by its unmista.k.a.ble cans (especially the retro hula girl on Bikini Blonde Lager), Maui Brewing is the only microbrewery on Maui; in many ways it could be the natural heir to Primo, only with a far better beer, but the focus is more on quality than quantity. Founded by the outgoing Garrett Marrero and Melanie Oxley, Maui Brewing Company is nevertheless finding a bigger audience with each batch, having made 400 barrels by the end of year one—and 11,000 a year later in 2010. A major expansion completed in 2015 moved the brewery from Lahaina to Kihei.

There's a tasting room at the new brewery location, but the newer brewpub—a sleek, modern space with high ceilings and large U-shaped bar island—is a little more accommodating, open every day of the week from 11 a.m. to midnight. The pub serves Maui's three year-round beers, all of them good: Bikini Blonde, Big Swell IPA, and the award-winning CoCoNut PorTeR—a far better beer than it sounds. Then there are ten more taps of brewpub-only and experimental offerings, a small number of which make their way to the Left Coast on occasion. Marrero, from San Diego originally, features guest taps like Stone alongside his own brews. Recently, Marrero's experiments included a collaboration brew with Pizza Port and brown ale made with a famous local ingredient: the sweet Maui onion.

He sees it as part and parcel of a holistic, back-to-the-land lifestyle. "In these days of mass production of sub par, unnatural products, we need to get some attention back on knowing where your food and drink comes from," says Marrero. "It is sad to see local farms across the country closing at an alarming rate when they really are the backbone of fresh, local, organic, and natural food products. It's also fun to see people's faces when you say 'Hey, try my Maui Onion Beer,' and they look at you almost cross-eyed: 'Onion in beer? Weird . . . I have to try that!'"

PHILOSOPHY

Marrero preaches a mantra of environmental responsibility and stewardship, supplying local farmers with spent grain, growing hops at a local farm and in Lahaina (which will help reduce the impact of shipping hops from the mainland), making bio-diesel from kitchen by-products in the pub, and using photovoltaic panels to capture solar energy. "Hawaii is generally associated with tropical fruits, nuts, and flowers, and we try to draw from what the 'āina ('land') provides to make innovative and fun beers," says Garrero. "We take traditional, sometime old-world styles, and give them new life or dimension by adding these agricultural products to the brew."

KEY BEER

While it sounds like it might taste like Coppertone, Maui's CoCoNut PorTeR, at 5.7% ABV, is actually a silky, slightly sweet delight, a blend of coffee and cocoa flavors mingled with hand-toasted coconut and a dash of spicy hops to balance it all out. Drink it in a sunny place—preferably Maui.

Big Island & Oahu

KONA BREWING CO.

75-5629 Kuakini Hwy. • Kona, HI 96740
(808) 334-2739 • konabrewingco.com
Established: 1994

KOKO MARINA CENTER

7192 Kalaniana'ole Hwy. • Honolulu,
HI 96825 • (808) 394-5662
konabrewingco.com • Established: 2003

SCENE & STORY

Established in 1994 by father-and-son team Cameron Healy and Spoon Khalsa, Kona Brewing Company is now the thirteenth-largest craft brewery in the United States and owned by the Craft Brewers Alliance, which includes Red Hook of Seattle, Widmer of Portland, Oregon, and Chicago's Goose Island. Kona's head brewer moved on as of summer 2011; most of the company's beers sold on the U.S. mainland are contract brewed in New Hampshire and Portland, Oregon, and distributed by Anheuser-Busch. The brewpub in Kona, built on-site a few years later, brews 2,000bbl a year for locals; the Honolulu location is a bar and eatery. Beer travelers can count on a fresh and relaxing beer in the Kona location with its verdant patio and menu of hand-tossed pizzas, sandwiches, salads, and pupu plates (appetizers). Free tours are also offered, and there's a cool little growler station for beer to go. The larger Koko Marina spot in Honolulu overlooks a placid bay of boats tied up to the piers and has a spacious indoor taproom. But not even peaceful Hawaii is immune from the clamor of constant expansion. In 2015 Kona announced that it will invest approximately $15 million to expand with a new state-of-the-art, 30,000-square-foot brewery bringing the total output to 100,000 barrels per year, and a $1 million renovation to the Koko Marina location.

PHILOSOPHY

Easy in the islands.

KEY BEER

Da Grind Buzz Kona Coffee Imperial Stout (8.5% ABV) is a winter seasonal brewed in Kona that's made with coffee beans grown, harvested, and roasted in nearby Holualoa. It's as aromatic as a freshly iced espresso but creamier on the tongue and black as ancient lava.

BEST *of the* REST: HAWAII

HUMPY'S BIG ISLAND ALEHOUSE

75-5815 Alii Dr. • Kailua-Kona, HI 96740 • (808) 324-2337 • humpys.com

Sister bar to craft beer maven Billy Opinksy's famous Humpy's Great Alaskan Alehouse in Anchorage, Alaska, Humpy's opened in 1994 right across the street from the water, overlooking a couple of slender palms and the Pacific. There's ample outdoor seating, a sports-bar-like interior, and a vast menu.

BIG ISLAND BREWHAUS

64-1066 Mamalahoa Hwy. • Waimea, HI 96743 • (808) 887-1717 • bigislandbrewhaus.com

A fast-growing and wildly popular brewery started by brewmaster Tom Kerns, Big Island Brewhaus is producing award-winning brews like Overboard IPA, White Mountain Porter, and Golden Sabbath, a Belgian-style ale brewed with Hawaiian honey.

REAL: A GASTROPUB

Marukai Market Place, 1020 Auahi St. • Honolulu, HI 96814 • (808) 596-2526 • realgastropub.com

Troy Terorotua, former beer buyer of Whole Foods Kahala (on Oahu) packs in a growing cadre of beer geeks nightly with one of the best beer menus I've seen—anywhere, and not just in the islands. Every single server has the level one Cicerone Certification, and the food is very tasty (try the beer-braised brisket poutine). With an annual beer fest launched in July and a venture planned in 2015 for the up-and-coming Kaimuki neighborhood, Terorotua is helping shape Honolulu's beer scene.

HONOLULU BEERWORKS

328 Cooke St. • Honolulu, HI 96813 • (808) 589-BEER • honolulubeerworks.com

Recycled wooden walls, weathered benches, and cabinets greet you at this super attractive brewpub near downtown and Waikiki. By sponsoring night markets and the Honolulu brewers fest among other events, Honolulu Beerworks is playing a vital role in the ever growing scene. The flagship beer is a saison, Pia Mahi'ai (farmer's beer), a tribute to the farmers of Hawaii brewed with locally grown oranges, tangerines, lemons, limes, lemongrass, and Big Island honey.

COLORADO
MONTANA
and the
ROCKY
MOUNTAINS

COLORADO

ASK ANY BEER LOVER TO NAME THE BEST BEER STATE AND CITY IN AMERICA, AND, DEPENDING on their zip code, you'll soon be besieged with per capita statistics and other "inside baseball" minutiae, a puffed-chest conversation brewers and industry watchers refer to as "the arms race." The fact is, there's room for more than one Super Power on Craft Beer Planet. But with 100 new breweries statewide since this book first came out, Colorado and Denver make a very strong case.

From the leafy streets and sunny taprooms of Fort Collins to the cavernous barrel-aging rooms in Boulder, sleek gastropubs in downtown Denver, and wood-stove-warmed, log-cabin-like Rocky Mountain brewpubs, there are scores of beer-friendly spots and some of the country's most scenic drives between them. Denver alone merits a stop in this state: the mile-high city is home to the Denver Beer Fest, a ten-day annual craft beer festival culminating in the Great American Beer Festival (GABF), the world's largest mass beer tasting (for number of beers on offer—more than 2,000) and America's largest beer festival of any kind. Denver is also the home of Colorado governor and brewmaster-in-chief John Hickenlooper, a cofounder of Wynkoop Brewing Co. No beer lover should miss making a good long visit, especially during the Denver Beer Fest and GABF, to see—and taste—what all the fuss is about. After visiting Denver, Boulder, and Fort Collins, head west into the Rockies and then south to Durango, a 450-Mile epic of 11,000-foot passes, atmospheric taprooms, and thirst-stoking outdoor options.

ITINERARIES

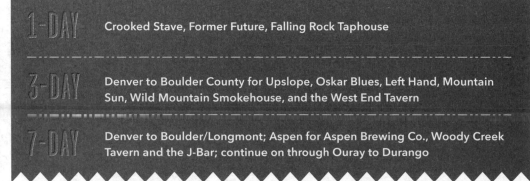

1-DAY Crooked Stave, Former Future, Falling Rock Taphouse

3-DAY Denver to Boulder County for Upslope, Oskar Blues, Left Hand, Mountain Sun, Wild Mountain Smokehouse, and the West End Tavern

7-DAY Denver to Boulder/Longmont; Aspen for Aspen Brewing Co., Woody Creek Tavern and the J-Bar; continue on through Ouray to Durango

Denver

CROOKED STAVE ARTISAN BEER PROJECT

3350 Brighton Blvd. • Denver, CO 80216
(720) 550-8860 • crookedstave.com
Established: 2011

SCENE & STORY

Over the past few years, one of the most talked-about stories in craft beer—and not just Colorado—has been the founding and success of Crooked Stave Artisan Beer Project. Founder Chad Yakobson wrote a dissertation on *Brettanomyces* yeast (wild yeast), or "brett," while studying brewing science at Scotland's Heriot-Watt University, then returned to the States, opened Crooked Stave in 2010 (after stints at Odell at Funkwerks), and, in short order, helped spark a firestorm of American wild ales. There were several well established brewers across the United States making sour and wild ales with Brettanomyces and bacteria, but Yakobson's timing (and beer) was impeccable. He also had a smart start-up model, brewing and procuring wort (unfermented beer) with local breweries which had excess production capacity, and transferring the liquid to his own warehouse for fermentation, aging, blending, and bottling—a *garagiste* of beer. (Anchorage Brewing Co. and the Rare Barrel are two successful brewers who started similarly.)

Yakobson's success caught the Denver beer scene off guard. Within a year he was serving his sour beers beyond Denver, even to revered Belgian lambic guru Jean Van Roy of Cantillon at a now-legendary beer festival in Worcester, MA, in the early summer of 2012, which gathered over 100 European brewers and a smattering of Americans for a sort of global artisanal beer summit. Then, in late 2012, shut out of the Great American Beer Festival, he organized a sort of stray-dogs party called What the Funk?! with scores of other upstart American brewers focused on sour, wild, and farmhouse ales. It was a smash (and is now an annual party).

As of this writing, Crooked Stave's tasting room was inside the Source, a stunning artisanal wares collective with a baker, two restaurants, wine shop, and other modern specialties (a designer hotel with a rooftop beer garden is on the way). Last time I saw Yakobson, at a beer event in Florida, he was ablaze with plans for a massively expanded cellar at the production warehouse a couple of miles from the Source, including a new twenty-five hectoliter brewhouse, ten 50hl fermenters, 300 wine and spirits barrels, and twenty-two *foudres*—massive French oak fermenters—ranging from 60hl to 120hl (read: wow). "We're looking to grow the taproom and bring an additional one back to the original brewery space. We now have over 12,000 square feet of production space," Yakobson said.

PHILOSOPHY

Yakobson calls himself a hophead with a serious penchant for sour beer, and Crooked Stave's lineup fits this disposition. Think 100 percent Brettanomyces beers, saisons, sours, and other whimsies, all barrel-aged.

KEY BEER

The dry-hopped, tropical-tasting Hop Savant series is brett-fermented and then barrel-aged and soured-up pale ale showcasing new school hops like Galaxy and Citra. "Wild Wild Brett," an early experiment of all-brett beers based on the color spectrum is now a part of the Crooked Stave lore, too. Wild Wild Brett Yellow was a sour beer flavored with the following menagerie: turmeric, mango, East Indian spices (garam masala: ginger, coriander, green and black cardamom, Tellicherry peppercorns, nutmeg, date mace, Ceylon cinnamon, Jamaican allspice, Madagascar clove, and Szechuan peppercorns.

PROST BREWING COMPANY

2540 19th St. • Denver, CO 80211
(303) 729-1175 • prostbrewing.com
Established: 2012

SCENE & STORY

If you're a self-respecting beer fanatic, you'll make it to Denver. If you're a full-on, dyed-in-the-wool beer acolyte like myself, you're going during GABF. And one of the most beloved traditions of that weekend (along with late nights at the Falling Rock Tap House, and Star Bar) is an afternoon at Prost, which, in stark contrast to Crooked Stave and other breweries focused on barrel-aged sour and wild beers, is 100 percent committed to clean, German-style beers served up deliciously fresh. And what beers they are. It's a short cab ride (or a long walk) from downtown, but a late-afternoon visit to Prost for a couple of steins of hef, helles, or what have you is just about as relaxing as doing the real thing in Germany. No matter what you do, make sure to get a look at the shiny, copper brewhouse itself. Prost reports it's a "Ziemann GmbH, built in 1963, formerly installed at Bucher Bräu in the German city of Grafenau and used there until 1984. In 1984 it was overhauled and sold to Brauerei-Gasthof Hümmer of Breitengüßbach, Germany, a village in the Franconian region of Bavaria." In other words, it's the real thing.

PHILOSOPHY

German beer styles, expertly crafted. You drink it at long wooden tables, with the sun streaming in. What else matters?

KEY BEER

Keller-Pils, a golden, unfiltered, bready-soft *zwickelbier* of 4.6% ABV with crisp noble hops flavor, took gold at the 2013 GABF. One taste and you'll know why.

FORMER FUTURE BREWING CO.

1290 S. Broadway • Denver, CO 80210
(720) 441-4253 • embracegoodtaste.com
Established: 2014

SCENE & STORY

James was a high school science teacher with a microbiology background. Sarah was a marketing major who worked in customer service, pursuing a graduate degree in counseling. The duo fell in love with beer while taking a New Belgium tour (true story) and decided shortly after their wedding that they would open their own space. How's *that* for romantic? The brewery, a long narrow space with lots of white and wood, provides a simultaneously warm, cozy, rustic, and industrial feeling. The bar itself is made of an old, shiny, rivet-covered 1950s Cessna airplane wing, and the lights above the bar are fabricated from old runway cones. Pendants throughout the taproom are made from barrel rings.

PHILOSOPHY

Think about the term "former future." To me, it sounds a lot like an alternate path not taken—like the paths both Sarah and James Howat were on. In keeping with that spirit, "we like to produce beers that take people by surprise," Sarah told me. "Sure, you might be drinking a por-

DETOUR ➡ HIKE FOR YOUR HOPS

Beers Made By Walking is a long-running collaboration project helmed by Portlander Eric Steen. The concept is simple: Steen and his cohorts invite brewers and beer fans on hikes both in the wild and across urban areas to forage for ingredients (from sagebrush to shagbark hickory and everything in between) and talk about beer. The brewers later brew with these ingredients, and, over time, the collaborations multiply, yielding enough beer for truly interesting parties across the country. The beers, understandably, veer into esoteric territory, often deliciously. In 2015, Denver's Crooked Stave Artisan Beer Project brewed a saison with Colorado white sage, Colorado chanterelles, dill, and rosemary salt. Or how about Scratch brewing's stein beer, brewed with pink granite rocks heated in white oak embers and added to the boil, which was bittered with shortleaf pine, cedar, coreopsis blossoms, wild quinine, and hops? Learn more and sign up for a hike at BeersMadeBy Walking.com.

ter, but it's a salted caramel porter, and it tends to make people say, 'Wow.' We focus on balanced, approachable, yet *different* beers—everything from pale ales to German doppelbocks to Belgian tripels to Berliner weisse and those English porters."

KEY BEER

Aside from the salted caramel porter? Ask about their award-winning Black Project line, 100 percent spontaneous and wild beers which never see any lab-cultured yeast. On the contrary, the Howats hoist an ersatz coolship on the roof and let Denver's night air do some magic. "We want to educate our customer, to connect with our customer, and most of all, sow them with the beauty and intricacies that can come from true wild fermentation under knowledgeable care," says Sarah.

THE GREAT AMERICAN BEER FESTIVAL

September or October, annually
Colorado Convention Center • 700 14th St.
(near intersection of Colfax and Speer Blvds.)
Denver, CO 80202 • (303) 447-0816
greatamericanbeerfestival.com

SCENE & STORY

What do you get when you take 50,000 beer lovers, 500 breweries, over 2,000 of their latest creations, and mash them all together for three sunny fall days in Denver? The Great American Beer Festival is what you get. What started over thirty years ago with just a few friends from small breweries and about forty on the list is today the mother of all beer festivals.

It's also a significant event for the brewers that submit beers for judging, culminating in the all-important Saturday morning medal announcements that generate roars of approval and surprise. The atmosphere is nothing if not raucous at times—crowds can get boisterous, loud, drunk, and (alas) even sick, but it's unforgettable to weave through the seemingly endless aisles of smiling brewers, servers, and beer fanatics celebrating the mighty abundance of it all. Wacky costumes? Yep. Silent disco? Definitely a hot spot. It can be a bit dizzying at first, but after a few tastes, the entire thing seems like the smartest festival ever created, as long as you pace yourself.

"If you've never been to the beer festival before," says GABF founder Charlie Papazian, "it's very important to remember that it's not a sprint, it's not a marathon—it's a 100-mile run. Or, actually, a 2,200-beer run." The savvy taster arrives early for the earliest session and comes with a plan, having studied the layout of the exhibitor hall, which is organized geographically beneath a massive banner of the late British beer writer Michael Jackson, a.k.a the Beer Hunter, whose thoughtful gaze should inspire considered sampling. And yet, without fail, a few minutes into any of the sessions (ticket holders should carefully study the hours, which are posted online and supplied at sign-in), all plans for quiet discovery seem to go out the window as the biggest assemblage of beer in the world works its magic on the crowd.

Still, especially at the first session, brewers are on hand dispensing beer from behind the taps. The key strategy, beyond that of all-important moderation, is to coordinate meals and hydration throughout the festival to avoid overdoing it, and to pick a hotel that's close to the convention center so you can recharge your batteries easily for sideshows or the after-session pub crawls to Wynkoop, the Falling Rock Taphouse, Euclid Hall, and others, where many of the brewers themselves gather to catch up.

PHILOSOPHY

From end-to-end, GABF is a celebration of everything that craft beer has achieved in the United States—the vibrancy, the variety, the quality, the fun, and ambition behind it all. It's impossible not to come away awed at what America's small breweries have achieved, and with a broad smile on your face.

KEY BEER

They're all key.

WYNKOOP BREWING CO.

1634 18th St. • Denver, CO 80202
(303) 297-2700 • wynkoop.com
Established: 1988

SCENE & STORY

The Wynkoop (as it's sometimes known) is a vast, three-story bar with acres of pool tables on the second floor and an inviting downstairs bar area. The place holds a special place in Colorado beer history: Colorado governor (and former Denver mayor) John Hickenlooper was part of the vanguard that made it Colorado's first brewpub.

Housed in a massive brick fortress known as the J. S. Brown Mercantile Building (built in 1899), Wynkoop has preserved many vestiges of an earlier time without devolving into a kitschy tourist trap, which easily could have happened. It's the home of monthly poetry and science enthusiast meetups (known as "Café Scientifique"), comedy and burlesque shows, beer dinners, and the Beer Drinker of the Year contest, which is far more serious than it sounds. This is a very nice place to meet some local beer lovers, or simply enjoy a beer and catch a game.

PHILOSOPHY

Wynkoop feels traditional, local, and a bit roadhouse-esque inside, utterly western. The owners have long taken great pains to reduce their carbon footprint. It's a no-frills, friendly operation, with malt-forward beers that are generally well made and quite sessionable.

KEY BEER

Railyard Ale, at 5.2% ABV, is a straightforward, copper-hued session beer somewhat similar in flavor to an Oktoberfest or märzen-style beer, but with a more fruity finish that takes it in another direction. Like many Rocky Mountain brews, it's more on the slightly sweet, malty side, good for extended pool games. Hopheads will want to try Mile Hi-P.A., an American IPA, and Mister Fister, a Double IPA (also known as IIPA), both of which are well-made, big, brassy beers with ample but not too much bitterness.

A BEER WITH
CHARLIE PAPAZIAN

Not many brewers are asked for their autograph. But not many brewers have résumés like Charlie Papazian's: The University of Virginia–trained, former nuclear engineer heads up the Brewers Association (an industry group representing some 4,000 American craft breweries), launched the Great American Beer Festival (GABF) in 1981 and *Zymurgy* magazine, and authored the home brewers' bible, *The Complete Joy of Home Brewing*, in 1984 (now sailing beyond twenty-five printings, three editions, 1.2 million copies). He's been permanently elevated to beer demigod, a signer of autographs, a coveted snapshot.

Papazian, for all the hype going on, in, and around what he's helped create, has a quiet, humble, and considerate air, is rather slight of build, and possesses the slightly fuzzy features and gentle diction of a rabbi. As he speaks about the Colorado scene, he's struck with what seems like genuine wonderment, a wide smile always on his face. He wouldn't look out of place in a cassock, but he's wearing a simple cotton dress shirt. "When I first came here in 1972, there was no beer scene other than the Coors brewery," he recalled in 2010. "It all started back in 1978 with the Boulder Beer Company. They were one of the first ten microbreweries in the United States, the first in Colorado."

SCENE & STORY

Call it the craft brew Valhalla. The designated after-GABF victory hall for hordes of visiting brewers and their fans, "the Falling Rock" as most simply call it, is among the most respected (and most visited) beer bars anywhere. Within walking distance from Coors Field and the convention center, it's ideally located in LoDo (Lower Denver). From the spacious outdoor patio to the massive tap row of hard-to-find crafts from the United States and abroad (seventy-five handles, give or take), to the deep bottle list of rarities (200-plus, I'm guessing), and pool-table-equipped, college-party-esque basement,

It didn't exactly take off like wildfire. "Things were slow to start," says Papazian. "But then a guy named John Hickenlooper, then-mayor of Denver, changed a law to permit brewpubs in Colorado. After that law changed, [Hickenlooper] started the Wynkoop brewery down here in Denver, and the success of that place really opened up people's eyes to what beer could be, what beer culture could be, and what the beer community could be. At the time the whole concept of beer other than light lager was a long conversation with every beer drinker. And not every beer drinker was willing to try something new."

Today Denver's beer scene is indeed enviable. "The community is tight, they help each other out," says Papazian. "And I would guess that half of the 3,400 volunteers at the GABF are avid home brewers. It's that home brew community. We started back in the 1970s, one batch at a time, making friends. That's what got things going. And we're still on a roll. And if you're involved, the next friend you make here could be a brewer, too, and the start of another community. There could be double the number of breweries here that we have already."

Looking back on all the good he's done for Colorado beer, Papazian remains humble—and deeply honored. "A lot of people come up to me at the festival and say they wouldn't be here if they hadn't read my book five years ago, or twenty years ago, and it's cool to meet people that are so satisfied with their jobs. It makes me feel like I've made a difference in people's lives. I've been blessed with many things, and that's one of them. They're thankful for something I shared with them, and they're trying to share it back with handshakes and a smile—and a beer!"

it can be a lot to take in at once. Locals sometimes line the bar and get first dibs, but once you make yourself at home, the experience can measure up to a slice of craft beer heaven. There are over 2,000 empty bottles decorating the walls, some comfy leather couches, one or two giant screens, forests of tap handles arrayed in endless rows, gloriously dilapidated bathrooms, and a pervasive sense that the world would be a much better place if we all could simply set aside our differences and try an amazing brew from some far away corner of the world.

PHILOSOPHY

As officially stated, it's "No Crap on Tap," and the list generally feels well curated, with a wide geographical and stylistic selection on offer, from mellow session beers to the most cultish, extreme, sour, smoked, and otherwise funked-out brews in the world, like the 8% ABV Pliny the Elder, of California's Russian River.

KEY BEER

Certain imported beers seem to show better in the bottle than on tap, so, agitated crowds notwithstanding, ask for a few samples before you take the plunge, or at the least, what's freshest. Staffers sometimes announce a "Blue Light Special" style, which means that something rare and tasty is about to start pouring, so listen up. A recent winning choice: Boulevard Tank 7 Saison, out of Kansas City.

EUCLID HALL BAR & KITCHEN

1317 14th St. • Denver, CO 80202
(303) 595-4255 • euclidhall.com
Established: 2010

SCENE & STORY

In bringing her new restaurant Euclid Hall to Denver's tourist and foodie district, Larimer Square, noted Denver chef Jennifer Jasinski has also brought craft beer directly into the heart of the city's food scene. Craft beer lovers laud this development, as surely other restaurants in the area will need to step up their approach. Once home to a Masonic lodge, the Colorado Women's Relief Corps, and a high-end brothel, among other organizations, the centrally located, two-story building is both a bit dramatic and immediately welcoming. Upon entry, one is greeted with a chalkboard overflowing with mouth-watering ideas. There, Jasinski's open kitchen feeds the cozy downstairs while a wide staircase leads upstairs to more gastropub tavern tables.

Upstairs or down, the hand-cranked sausages, poutines, and schnitzels shine, and the pickle assortment is a must-order: one pickle is infused with hops. Mustards are also hand-ground and house cured, and you can't throw a napkin without hitting some sort of high-low riff like the gourmet corndog or chicken-and-waffle plate. For the beer-obsessed, there are PEI

A BEER WITH
CHRIS BLACK, PROPRIETOR, FALLING ROCK TAPHOUSE

———————◆———————

When it comes to craft beer in Denver, Falling Rock owner Chris Black is both king and court jester. The taphouse is a monument, he says, to his friends who love beer as much as he does. He seems to feel like he was born for the job. "When I was in high school I went away to Europe for five weeks and found out what beer was supposed to taste like, at least for that time," he says. "And when I was in college, at the University of Texas in Austin, there was a very early beer bar there called Maggie May's. I ended up hanging out there so much they gave me a job," he recalls. After a postcollege stint for an importer and several more years of tending bar, working in breweries, beer bars, and for distributors large and small, he borrowed money from his father to open the Falling Rock, starting the work in 1996.

"My goal was to make this one of the top beer bars in the United States within five years, and the best way to do that was to tell all the beer journalists who come here from all over the world every year for the beer festival who have no place to go. So that's what we did. We built a place for everybody. I built my own favorite place to hang out." It wasn't an overnight success. "We were very cash poor, but we did everything ourselves and it didn't really matter. As this area has grown, and we got a baseball team that started winning, the business has really grown, and the Great American Beer Festival has been a huge part of it. Here we are thirteen years later. I'm seeing all my friends every year, welcoming them into my place to have a good time," he says. "The highest compliment is when someone brings their mom in. If it's cool enough for your mom, and you like hanging out here, too, I think it's kind of an okay place, right?"

The endeavor has been fruitful, to be sure, but its success, Black says, comes at a price: "The hardest thing about this job is this week," he says of the Great American Beer Festival every fall, when Falling Rock bursts at the seams every day. "Physically and mentally, it's completely exhausting. I average five hours of sleep for over two weeks. It's a double-edged sword." Black, who wears a goatee and a contented grin, indulges in the odd cigar, and takes great pleasure in a good bottle of red wine when the workday is done, brief though the respite may be.

mussels steamed in tripel, beer-battered cod, and an ice cream dessert made with stout. It's a fun menu and environment, both resolutely urban and yet down to earth (a credit to the unpretentious staff), and it's often very, very busy. One of the axioms of Euclidean geometry is that the whole is greater than the sum of its parts, which is a fitting assessment of Euclid Hall itself. Its food menu or beer list are both excellent on their own, but taken together, you have something approaching ideal.

PHILOSOPHY

The motto is "Crafted. Not Cranked Out." The canned and bottled beer list is divided into somewhat kooky categories (arithmetic, algebra, geometry, trigonometry, calculus, quantum mechanics) meant to relate to complexity of flavor, but there's no extra credit for only drinking from the complicated end of the spectrum.

KEY BEER

Make sure you eyeball the "Very Special Brews" list, though be prepared for some sticker shock. On a recent visit, Port Brewing Company's Older Viscosity, an American Strong Ale, was going for $36.95 for a 375-milliliter bottle. On the standard can and bottle list, Del Norte's Mañana Amber Lager is a solid, food-friendly choice (way up in the "easy" arithmetic section, a bit unkindly, as it happens—it's not easy to make). And Durango's Steamworks makes the draught house beer, Euclidean Pale Ale (5.5% ABV).

DETOUR ➡ RIVER NORTH DISTRICT

Denver's most concentrated hotbed of year-round beer is the mostly walkable industrial area known as the River North Art District ("RiNo"), and it should not be missed. Look for Beryl's Beer Co., focused on barrel-aged beers (3120 Blake St.; berylsbeerco.com); Black Shirt Brewing Co., focused on saisons, rye beers, and double IPA (3719 Walnut St.; blackshirtbrewingco.com); Crooked Stave Artisan Beer Project (see page 137; 3350 Brighton Blvd.; crookedstave.com); Epic Brewing Co., the Salt Lake City-based company known for big-hearted styles (3001 Walnut St.; epicbrewing.com); Great Divide Brewing Co.,which built a massive production brewery and tasting room (3403 Brighton Blvd.); Our Mutual Friend, which roasts its own grains and focuses on everything from pale ale to gose and wood barrel–aged sours (2810 Larimer St.; omfbeer.com); and Ratio Beerworks, with a big, light-filled, design-driven taproom and experimental styles (2920 Larimer St.; ratiobeerworks.com).

Boulder

AVERY BREWING CO.

4910 Nautilus Ct. • Boulder, CO 80301
(303) 440-4324 • averybrewing.com
Established: 1993

SCENE & STORY

Avery started in a bland industrial park, outgrew it, and, after twenty-two years in the same location, moved into spectacular new digs in nearby Gunbarrel in 2015. Adam Avery, who started the brewery with his chemist father, is among the best known of Colorado brewers. His beers have always been big in malt and hops. The new $30 million facility, on 5.6 acres of land, is a showpiece with a 86bbl German brewhouse, elevated catwalks over the production floor and a gorgeous restaurant managed by culinary pros presenting a menu of local meats, cheeses, produce, barbecue, poutine, and other stomach-lining whimsies like nachos with pork belly.

PHILOSOPHY

Avery's public pledge is to make "big, artful beers" and brew with "utter disregard for what the market demands," while searching out fans with "equally eccentric palates." Judging from their jump from small-time roots to national distribution, it seems to be a useful set of guiding principles.

KEY BEER

Keeping pace with the popularity and possibilities of barrel aging, there are several high-acid beers, too, aged in oak, which are sporadically released in miniscule quantities. Easier to find and diabolically strong at 15.1% ABV, Mephistopheles offers a taste of the awesome power that a beer can unleash—but be careful, you may not be able to feel your taste buds for an hour. This cinder black brew is rich and roasty with flavors of coffee and rum-soaked black cherries, with a velvety smoothness that lures you back sip after sip. It's hell to brew no doubt, but heaven to drink.

BOULDER BEER CO.

2880 Wilderness Pl. • Boulder, CO 80301
(303) 444-8448 • boulderbeer.com
Established: 1979

SCENE & STORY

Opened with a homemade, one-barrel system (thirty-one gallons) by two University of Colorado physics professors, David Hummer and Randolph "Stick" Ware, in a goat-shed outside of town, BBC became the first microbrewery in Colorado and was among the first to open nationally— they were granted the forty-third license to brew beer in the United States. The two friends even consulted the Coors family, who, according to Ware, called them "crazy." Early supporters included famed beer writers Michael Jackson and Fred Eckhardt, who were joined by a nascent groundswell of beer drinkers ready for sweeping change in the beer aisle. While Hummer and Ware ceded financial control of the brewery to the Rock Bottom chain in 1990, the Boulder beer scene had been well launched, and their brewpub became an institution.

With the Flatiron Mountains rising behind Wilderness Square, the brewpub taproom is a popular spot, with free tours of the brewery offered daily. Should they be full, you can settle for the view of the bottling line from the taproom.

PHILOSOPHY

While the policy of offering a generous sample of beer with a tour of the brewery speaks to the overall relaxed feel of BBC, the company works ceaselessly to keep up with the ever evolving tastes of the American beer lover.

KEY BEER

The piney, copper-hued Hazed Session Ale (5% ABV) is all about Nugget, Willamette, Crystal, and Centennial hops.

THE KITCHEN AND THE KITCHEN UPSTAIRS

1039 Pearl St. • Boulder, CO 80302
(303) 544-5973 • thekitchencafe.com
Established: 2005

SCENE & STORY

A farm-to-table restaurant catering to Boulder's most discerning foodies, there's always something cooking at the Kitchen seven days a week, from classes to winemaker and brewer dinners, to "community hours" that offer discounted dining and other gastro-pursuits.

Chef-owner Hugo Matheson expanded his busy restaurant in 2005 to include the "Upstairs," a candlelit and fireplace-warmed wine bar area above the restaurant with a deep wine cellar. Soon after, then-bar manager Ray Decker overhauled the beer list, giving it star treatment and including a number of vintage and rare beers. Beer is served with care here and food pairings are readily suggested. It's one of Boulder's most assured restaurants, with knowledgeable, attentive service. It also commands higher prices than some craft beer lovers will be accustomed to paying. But with award-winning chefs at the stove, it's a refreshing change from the usual pub grub, and perhaps the ultimate way to cap off a trip to GABF in Denver.

PHILOSOPHY

Sunset magazine dubbed it "the West's Greenest Restaurant" in 2008, praising Chef Matheson's fare and eco-friendly approach. And a superb, international beer list complements the cuisine, with special attention to Belgian ales and American pathbreakers like Jolly Pumpkin.

KEY BEER

Ask a server to recommend beers with your meal, as all the menus and lists change constantly. A reddish, Belgian-style farmhouse ale like Jolly Pumpkin's La Roja (which I recently sampled here) or a barrel-aged beer from Norway's HaandBryggeriet or Belgium's Drie Fonteinen would complement many of the Kitchen's richer dishes.

WEST END TAVERN

926 Pearl St. • Boulder, CO 80302
(303) 444-3535 • thewestendtavern.com
Established: 1987

SCENE & STORY

Boulder has become a craft brew capital with Avery, Oskar Blues, and Upslope breweries, just to name a few. But there's a deep craft brew passion in select bars as well. At the multilevel West End Tavern, owner Dave Query brings a touch of down-home Southern soul to upscale Boulder, with a vast tap list heavy on local brews and a great bourbon list to boot. The upstairs taproom is airy and modern, with metal tables and chairs and sight lines out to the sky, but it's the rotating tap list filled with craft rarities and two outdoor decks that really draw in the locals, especially the beer brewers themselves, like Upslope's cofounder Matt Cutter, who I met on a random evening there sipping beer.

PHILOSOPHY

There's no telling what will be on tap at the West End, because the list is constantly changing, but expect to see local and West Coast beers heavily represented.

KEY BEER

Look for regional specialties like Avery's Dugana IIPA (8.5% ABV), a big, floral, resinous brew, in addition to West Coast cult beers from Russian River, Lagunitas, Stone, and Port.

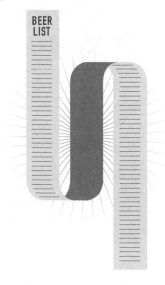

THE MOUNTAIN SUN

1535 Pearl St. • Boulder, CO 80302
(303) 546-0886 • mountainsunpub.com
Established: 1993

THE SOUTHERN SUN

627 S. Broadway • Boulder, CO 80305
(303) 543-0886 • mountainsunpub.com
Established: 2002

SCENE & STORY

A relaxing Boulder standby, the Mountain Sun expanded by popular demand with a second brewpub, the Southern Sun, in 2002. (There's also a related pub in Denver, the Vine Street Pub.) None other than GABF founder Charlie Papazian is a fan of the trio, especially the Southern Sun location, which has Flatiron mountain views. "It's a cool beer scene," he says. "It's all about the beer and a place to meet friends—smaller and more intimate [than the Mountain Sun]. It gets crowded so get there early."

PHILOSOPHY

"There will never be televisions at our pubs because we want our guests to meet and discuss the world in which we live or simply to play Scrabble," reads the company's website. There you have it.

KEY BEER

Mountain Sun and Southern Sun have won numerous medals for their beers, with the hop bomb of an India Pale Ale

known as FYIPA (about 7.5% ABV) gaining the most recent notice.

Fort Collins

NEW BELGIUM BREWING CO.

500 Linden St. • Fort Collins, CO 80524
(970) 221-0524 • newbelgium.com
Established: 1991

SCENE & STORY

Maker of the craft brew smash Fat Tire Ale, New Belgium is the largest craft brewery in Fort Collins and the third-largest in the United States. In spring 2016, they launched a second location in Asheville, North Carolina, and it's essentially a household name, at this point. As the story goes, Jeff Lebesch started the brewery with his then-wife (and current company CEO), Kim Jordan, after discovering the incredible array of beers lovingly and idiosyncratically produced in Belgium while touring that country on his mountain bike in 1989. No visit to Colorado would be complete without a tour here (it's popular, so plan to reserve two to three weeks ahead). Follow it with beers in the airy, sleek taproom, dubbed the "Liquid Center"—revamped in 2015 to include an outdoor beer garden and space for more visitors.

While the nave-like brewing hall feels like a cathedral, with creamy, colorful tile work around the bases of the kettles, the beating heart of this operation is in an unassuming corner of a storage warehouse behind the taproom, where rows of massive *foudres* stand in a tower of amber-hued wood and iron bands. There, New Belgium ages ales into vinous liquids for later blending, some exuding aromas that are the products of alcoholic compounds called esters. Though fruit is not always present, the beers aged in this way can exhibit aromas of pineapple and tangerine, as well as chewy red wine-like tannins, and a flavor like sour cherries.

New Belgium has been a pioneer in introducing Americans to the Belgian styles called Flanders Red and Oud Bruin ("Old Brown") of which the crowning example is generally thought to be Belgium's Rodenbach Grand Cru, reddish ale aged in huge oak vats and later blended with younger beer to round out the acidic flavors created by prolonged exposure to wood. New Belgium's Belgian head brewer, Peter Bouckaert, worked for Rodenbach for years, and he's considered a true master of barrel aging. This is not how all New Belgium beer is brewed, but it's how the best and most interesting ones are matured, sometimes with additional fruits in the tanks.

PHILOSOPHY

Outside magazine has named the employee-owned company one of the "Best Places to Work" in the United States, and it's easy to see why. There's a sense of institutionally mandated fun here: The Tour de Fat is an annual bike festival celebrating zero-emissions commuting, with a concert on a solar-powered stage and beer served in compostable cups. There's a company climbing wall and foosball table, a slide from the second to first floors, and even an on-site dirt bike track. All employees earn a new cruiser bike after one year at the company; after four more they're taken to Belgium to follow in the founder's footsteps.

KEY BEER

Fat Tire Amber Ale, a biscuity-tasting brew of light to medium body, made New Belgium a national player, but the company's more adventurous, smaller release concoctions, such as La Folie, New Belgium's version of Rodenbach, are the ones to seek out. Now marketed through the brewery's Lips of Faith line, La Folie is a landmark, polarizing beer—it's uncompromisingly tart, with a bracing flavor profile that can sucker-punch the unprepared. But to the initiated, it's nothing short of nectar.

DETOUR → THE BIG ONE: ANHEUSER-BUSCH

2351 Busch Dr. • Fort Collins, CO 80524-9400 • (970) 221-0922 • budweiser.com

A tour of Anheuser-Busch's plant in Fort Collins is a stop I unironically recommend for all craft beer lovers. *Blasphemy*, you say? Not at all. In fact, for any lover of beer, this is a stop worth making for one simple reason: perspective. Touring this maze of robots churning out millions upon millions of identical beers is a look at beer making's outer technological frontier. Take the "Brewmaster's" tour (twenty-five dollars) and you'll see massive brewing kettles that look like something out of *Star Wars*. You'll gape at a canning line churning out Bud Light at a rate of *thirty-three cans per second*. Brewers are technical people by nature, and there are many who speak of factories like this with a begrudging reverence. They might not want to make beer the same way, but the sheer mechanical ingenuity is something to behold, even if the end result is akin to "wet air" as the famous 1987 *Atlantic* article, "A Glass of Handmade," by William Least Heat-Moon memorably attested.

And yet wandering through the futuristic forest of stainless tanks, myriad pipes, conveyor belts, and grated stairways you'll taste something quite remarkable: unfiltered Bud Light. Yes, it's made of 40 percent rice. Hop character: nada. But after the so-called beechwood aging (it's real wood, I can at least tell you that much), and before filtration and pasteurization has rent the last of any remaining flaws asunder, Bud Light has an appealing flavor, surprisingly full bodied and slightly sweet. It's a treat to try beer at this stage of the process. Germans and Czechs have been releasing beers in this state for eons, calling them by various names including *kellerbier, zwickelbier*, and, in the case of the fabled Mahr's brewery of Bamberg, Germany, *ungespundet hefetrüb*. For the record, I suggested that the manager pitch a commercial version of unfiltered Bud to her superiors. (I can see the commercials now.) But I'm not holding my breath. We don't really need another ersatz-craft beer from corporate bean counters. But with Bud Light Golden Wheat a national brand, maybe Bud "Kellerbier" doesn't sound so crazy, after all.

SCENE & STORY

Odell was the second craft brewery to open in Colorado (after Boulder Brewing Company), starting with a little five-barrel brewery in a 1915 grain elevator. Early on, founders Doug Odell, Wynne, and Corkie Odell maintained a draught-only focus while struggling to keep up with demand. So they added a bottling line in 1996, which effectively supercharged the marketplace for their beer. Flash-forward to 2015, and the brewery is currently making about 100,000 brewers' barrels (or bbl; one barrel equals thirty-one U.S. gallons) of beer, sold throughout the middle of the country in eleven states and counting. A canning line came on in 2015, too.

With live music every Wednesday, the sunny taproom (and outdoor patio) is one of the most popular destinations for beer lovers in Fort Collins. Best of all, success hasn't spoiled the makers of the popular Scottish ale called 90 Schilling. There's a warm, family-friendly feel to the place, which makes more sense when one learns that in all, there are five married couples (some of whom met here) who work together at the brewery. Which is a sizable chunk of the staff. It might be the happiest place in America.

PHILOSOPHY

Fortunately, the original five-barrel system remains in use for special one-offs, in which the beers depart from standard English ales and head into parts unknown, but not unappreciated. One such recent brew was Angry Robin, an English strong ale aged in merlot barrels and spiked with a dash of Brettanomyces bacteria, giving it a barnyardy kick. And I got to brew a one-off fresh hop ale on it with Odell brewer Brent Cordle, resulting in PUBlisher, a tasty American pale ale (if we do say so ourselves).

KEY BEER

Every fall, Odell releases a one-off beer aged in American oak barrels, echoing the Old World techniques over at New Belgium, though on a much smaller scale. Woodcut Nos. 1, 2, and 3 were all variations on the theme of strong ale aged in oak, which adds layers of vanilla-like woodiness to the brews. No. 4 was a strong amber lager. On and on the variations have continued. These beers are beautifully labeled and corked in 750-milliliter bottles, and may be available in limited quantities at the taproom. Otherwise, try any other barrel-aged "pilot system" beers, such as the earthy, acidic—and interesting—Brett Porter. These are brewed on the original 5bbl (about 350 gallons) system that started it all.

Longmont Area

LEFT HAND BREWING COMPANY

1265 Boston Ave. • Longmont, CO 80025
(303) 772-0258 • lefthandbrewing.com
Established: 1993

SCENE & STORY

Housed in an old meatpacking plant in an industrial area of Longmont, Left Hand has slowly grown from a raggedy upstart into a world-class small brewery. It all began when head brewer Eric Wallace, who had traveled around the world tasting beers while in the Air Force, joined forces with his college friend Dick Doore, who was a home brewer. In the first year, the guys took home a gold medal at the Great American Beer Festival. They grew in a sustainable fashion, and eventually morphed into what is now a laid-back—but not lazy—brewing company. "It's kind of an after-work place," says Wallace. "We get engineers from all these tech companies and biotechs around here, bicyclists, arborists, and painters."

Originally called Indian Peaks Brewery, for a nearby mountain range, Wallace and Doore's brewery was forced to change names after a branding dispute with another company. They settled on Left Hand, after an Arapahoe word ("Niwot"), which was the name of a chief who over-wintered nearby on the banks of the St. Vrain River. And then there's a more, shall we say, colorful connection: Curtis Green, the early sausage maker tenant of the building, lost his right arm in the grinder one day.

In the weeks leading up to the brewery's twentieth anniversary, the St. Vrain River swelled in what was deemed a 500-year flood, which nearly destroyed the brewery (and caused tens of millions of dollars in damage to area homes and businesses). It was a terribly close call, and Left Hand stepped forward, donating $60,000 of relief funds to the community, which still (understandably) speaks of the events in sorrowful tones.

PHILOSOPHY

Left Hand isn't trying to outgun other companies in the IPA arms race—they're not heavy-handed with the hops. "Our brewing approach is all about balance," says Wallace. "When we started, we were brewing beers that we wanted, that we weren't really finding out there in the marketplace. We're still out there exploring flavors and styles that we like. Overwhelmingly, we'll always fall back to balance. In the end, is it drinkable? Does it have complexity, depth? And that balance? It's all about the flavor."

Nitro—meaning the service of beer blended with nitrogen, giving it a creamy mouthfeel—is also big with these guys. They launched a nitro beer line at the

Great American Beer Festival in 2011, including the exceedingly popular Milk Stout Nitro, and since 2014 they've hosted a Nitro Fest, an event dedicated to nitrogenated beer, Colorado art, and food.

KEY BEER

Left Hand Polestar Pils. In the push to brew ever stronger, stranger beers, the subtle pilsner often gets neglected. That's too bad, because a great pilsner is a thing of beauty—an alcoholic beverage that is somehow more refreshing than a glass of ice water on a Death Valley afternoon. Like the best American versions, Polestar also stands out for its perfect use of hops; it's brewed with three varieties, which together lend a powdery floral aroma. While it's only occasionally available, Left Hand Smokejumper Imperial Porter is also worth seeking out. Next to your dog, a smoked beer (made with wood- or peat-fire smoked malt) may be the ultimate fireside companion. Left Hand's is a briny, coffee-black 9.2% ABV beast of a beer that calls to mind bacon. Even better, Wallace and Co. donate proceeds from this rare, hand-smoked seasonal to a scholarship fund for the children of smokejumpers killed in action.

Return of the Can

There was a time when only cheap beer came in cans. . . . Even so, the aluminum can, introduced to this country's beer drinking public in 1935, became iconic—even if the beer it contained was often unremarkable. Quality notwithstanding, the *cssffft* sound that issued forth upon opening each new can was a harbinger of good things, especially on a hot summer day.

But today the humble can is new and improved and experiencing a renaissance: Since the release of Dale's Pale Ale in a can in 2002, hundreds of American microbrewers have started packaging their finest stuff in aluminum. There are even mobile canning lines available to small breweries who lack the expensive gear. Thanks to special linings, there's no interaction whatsoever between the metal and liquid; there's less "head space" between the top of the can and the brew, meaning, less beer-spoiling oxygen remains in contact with the beer. What's more, cans offer benefits that bottles don't: Harmful UV light rays are blocked, sparing the beer from the dreaded "skunk" effect (avoid green and clear beer bottles when you can; brown glass blocks more UV rays). Today, hundreds of American craft brewers have adopted cans. They're easier to carry (especially on camping trips), less likely to break and cut someone, and more quickly cooled. Crack one open as soon as you can.

OSKAR BLUES HOMEMADE LIQUIDS & SOLIDS

1555 S. Hover Rd. • Longmont, CO 80501
(303) 485-9400 • oskarblues.com
Established: 2009

SCENE & STORY

Think: bayou-on-the-front-range, equal parts shiny taproom, soul food smorgasbord, and juke joint blues bar. The smell of applewood smoke greets you before you reach the door; that's thanks to the "Midnight Toker," an in-house smoker used for slow-smoked North Carolina–style barbecue pork, spare ribs, beer-can chicken, salmon, and turkey. Inside, there's a mouth-watering display of shrimp and other shellfish, scores of interesting pieces of folk art from the Deep South, and good music, including live blues, alt country, rockabilly, and bluegrass five nights a week. "We made a commitment early on that we were going to do good music," says founder Dale Katechis of the atmosphere. "We weren't just going to book $200 'Mustang Sally' bands." There's even a line of Oskar Blues hot sauces, based on five different beers. Try the Ten FIDY Imperial Stout version, made with the world's hottest pepper Bhut Jolokia, or "ghost chile," if you dare.

PHILOSOPHY

A rising tide lifts all ships. This Oskar Blues location features scores of guest taps from other Colorado and American brewers, making the forty-three-tap pub a great place for a Colorado beer tasting.

KEY BEER

The clean and crisp Mama's Little Yella Pils, at 5.3% ABV, makes a great quencher for spicy ribs and other dishes they do so well here. But don't miss other OB rarities like Smoke on the Water, a lightly smoked, 7% ABV winter warmer.

OSKAR BLUES TASTY WEASEL TAPROOM

1800 Pike Rd. Unit B • Longmont, CO 80501
(303) 776-1914 • oskarblues.com
Established: 2009

SCENE & STORY

The Tasty Weasel is a cozy little taproom within the massive Oskar Blues brewing facility, a behemoth headed north of 150,000bbl annual capacity (plus a new Brevard, North Carolina location producing 85,000bbl per year). Expect an industrial yet intimate setting (corrugated metal walls, funky art) popular with beer fanatics and locals, an up-close view of massive, beer-filled fermenters, cool music on the hi-fi, British-style casks called firkins, and oak-aged beer tappings on Tuesday and Friday nights.

PHILOSOPHY

No risk, no reward. "I grew up in the restaurant business and I always had a dream of opening my own restaurant, and Lyons seemed to be about the riskiest place to do it," recalls founder Dale Katechis. "When I moved there it was Mayberry in the mountains." That roll-the-dice business model has proved a savvy strategy, but the results have presented challenges of their own. "It's just 100 percent growth year after year," he says of the entire operation. "The job now is holding onto the culture and the soul and why we started doing it, and in business sometimes that's hard." The Tasty Weasel—and for Katechis, commuting between parts of the factory on a BMX bike—is part of that quest to maintain that fun-loving culture at the heart of Oskar Blues.

KEY BEER

This would be the place to sample the successful 10.5% ABV Ten Fidy, a roasty, fulsome Russian Imperial Stout, or better yet, the oak barrel–aged Ten Fidy, which is quite rare. The wood imparts rich notes of vanilla and caramel.

Lyons

OSKAR BLUES GRILL & BREW

303 Main St. • Lyons, CO 80540
(303) 823-6685 • oskarblues.com
Established: 1997

SCENE & STORY

The old mining town of Lyons, (population: 1,500), sits at the confluence of the St. Vrain North and St. Vrain South Creeks, just about twenty miles from Rocky Mountain National Park. Surrounded by reddish sandstone peaks, it's an outdoor lover's paradise, and it's also known for an amazing music scene, with the annual Rockygrass Bluegrass Festival held every summer and regularly drawing such luminaries as David Grisman and Tony Rice. The Grill & Brew is the town's social hub, with its Southern-themed, forty-five-tap bar, dining room, and outdoor patio overlooking the little brewhouse building and a barn that has been converted for special events and parties. On a good summery night the patio is the place to be, sipping some fresh craft beer in the breeze.

PHILOSOPHY

"We're all hopheads," says Eric Huber, head brewer at the Lyons location. "We do love classical styles, we do love a lot of what the other guys are doing, but it's about what we want to drink ourselves. We've got a clientele who loves what we've been doing, and we've been training them to drink the hoppy beers we've been drinking for years. The best way to find out if it's a great batch is put it on and see what the local boys think."

KEY BEER

Dale's Pale Ale, 6.5 % ABV. Initially laughed off, Katechis's delicate craft beer packaged in aluminum cans was an unlikely success. For one, Katechis didn't live in Portland or Seattle, where craft is king. He lived in the Deep South. "In 1989 or 1990, there were not too many home brewers in Auburn, Alabama," he says. "Actually, I knew of one—and that was me." He had developed a recipe for Dale's Pale Ale, an extremely hoppy beer, almost IPA-like, outside of the style guideline of a pale ale, which evolved with his first-hired brewers. And the rest, as they say, is history.

North Boulder

UPSLOPE BREWING COMPANY

1501 Lee Hill Rd., No. 20 • Boulder, CO 80304 • (720) 379-7528
upslopebrewing.com • Established: 2008

←——————————→

Flatiron Park: 1898 S. Flatiron Court Boulder, CO 80301 • (303) 396-1898
Established: 2013

SCENE & STORY

In a generic North Boulder strip mall on Lee Hill Road, some enterprising, beer loving, home brewing friends built a booming business. The taproom is decorated with photos of the brewery's fans drinking Upslope brews in the wilds of Colorado and beyond. The founders themselves, a garrulous bunch, are quick to recount close scrapes from the early days, coping with limited space, little money, harsh winter temperatures, and other setbacks. But like the Flatiron Mountain images that decorate their cans, things went straight up for Upslope. In 2013, Upslope opened its second location in Flatiron Park, a 27,000-square-foot brewery complete with a 2,300-square-foot taproom, and announced plans for a 11,000-square-foot Boulder location and barrel-aging facility soon after, as well.

PHILOSOPHY

Upslope's MO is simple. Great craft brews should be canned and ready to rock at a moment's notice. "We're all about drinking our beer, not just in a pub, but on the side of a mountain," says assistant brewer Alex Violette. "It's a completely different experience. Take it rafting with you. Get out there and have fun with it, you know?" Better yet, it's easier to leave no trace with canned beer: crush up the cans and pack them out. The approach also makes sense from a business standpoint. The same amount of beer weighs about 40 percent less in the can than in a bottle, and stacks more efficiently in a truck, making it a more energy-efficient product going out of the brewery, as well.

KEY BEER

Upslope's beers are firmly in the middle of the typical Colorado beer lover's palate, with big, malty, hop-accented beers that finish clean. Their marquee beer is Upslope Pale Ale (5.8% ABV). "It's brewed in the tradition of American-style pale ale except for one different aspect: we use Patagonian hops," says Violette. "They add a little bit more of an earthy-spicy flavor to our pale ale. It's also a very approachable beer, not over-the-top hopped. It's something that's really easy to drink on a warm summer day."

High Rocky Mountains and Beyond

CASEY BREWING & BLENDING

3421 Grand Ave. • Glenwood Springs, CO 81601 • (970) 230-9691
caseybrewing.com • Established: 2013

SCENE & STORY

In life, blending is a good thing. Just think: Root beer floats. Neapolitan ice cream. Troy Casey knows a thing or two about blending. Casey earned a reputation as an expert on sour ales aged in oak and blended in the ancient (and ultra-time-consuming) Belgian tradition while he worked for AC Golden, the MillerCoors–owned beer incubator in Golden, Colorado. Casey left AC Golden in the end of 2013 on good terms with his big brewery colleagues, ready to forge a path of his own.

In his new venture, Casey Brewing & Blending overlooking the Roaring Fork river canyon in Glenwood Springs, Colorado, Casey is focusing on sour ales aged on local fruits. "We're getting flavors that you can't get anywhere else," Casey told me. "It's the freshest fruit flavor in a beer and is a form of fruit preservation. When you're picking fruit at its peak and putting it in a beer, the fruit doesn't age. Six months from now, you can open a cherry beer and have those flavors. Depending on when the grape harvest is, we might try to use some grapes. We're having fun with beer."

It's a stark departure from his former days inside the industrial AC Golden. And it comes as a bit of a surprise. "I never had dreams of opening my own brewery," Casey told me. "I was very excited to be a company man for Miller-Coors because large companies are interesting—they have a lot of moving parts. But things shifted in the industry and I realized that it wasn't the future I wanted." Lucky for us.

PHILOSOPHY

"When I drink a German pilsner, I'm usually bored by it only because I know a lot about how that beer is made," Casey says. "For me, making these Belgian styles, it's still a mystery—I don't know what's happening. There's a symbiotic relationships in a barrel that's unlike anything else. No matter how much you look at the science, you'll never understand. I made these beers and I can't tell you exactly why they taste that way. Another brewer could do the same thing I did and they'd make a completely different beer. It's all about the climate, the temperature, the type of barrel, the humidity you have.

That's why it's really fun."

KEY BEER

Casey has two core brands, 100 percent fermented and aged in oak—the Saison and a Belgian-style sour which comes in variations with local raspberries, cherries, plums, peaches, and other fruits. "I'm very proud of my Saison," Casey says. "It's 5.5% ABV; it's very dry and pleasantly tart. It has a really interesting naval orange taste that I've never tasted in a beer before. I don't believe it could be any better if it was made with ingredients from anywhere else. It's very important to use what you have available. I don't think of it as limiting. I use that as a challenge to make something that no one else can make."

WILD MOUNTAIN SMOKEHOUSE & BREWERY

70 E. First St. • Nederland, CO 80466
(303) 258-9453 • wildmountainsb.com
Established: 2007

SCENE & STORY

About seventeen miles west and 3,000 feet higher in elevation than Boulder, tiny Nederland—an old Ute Indian trading post turned silver mining town (population: 1,700)—is home to a lot of hippies, mountain bikers, and "the Frozen Dead Guy," a.k.a. Bredo Morstoel, a Norwegian whose body has been kept at -60°F by the townspeople for more than twenty years (long story), making him something like a bizzaro town father. It's also home to a reasonably priced little beer and barbecue getaway very much worth a drive out of Boulder.

With well-made beers, a mountain view from the back patio, and high marks for soul food (especially the hardwood-smoked ribs and wings, and the sweet potato fries), Nederland's little brewery would be worth visiting on its own accord, but there's still another reason people flock there, in late summer: NedFest, a three-day roots music festival that has welcomed such iconic artists as the mandolinist David Grisman, Cajun jammer Dr. John, and "newgrass" aces Yonder Mountain String Band.

PHILOSOPHY

Beer and barbecue go together like peanut butter and jelly, right? This is a restaurant dedicated to the relatively simple mission of making great beer for great barbecue and vice versa.

KEY BEER

There are always four house brews on tap; try the Brewski Sampler (samples of four draughts and a guest tap) to see what's freshest. The house brew Otis Pale Ale has been a standby, and the bottle list has included selections from Russian River, Lost Abbey, Stone, and Left Hand.

BRECKENRIDGE BREWERY & PUB

600 S. Main St. • Breckenridge, CO 80424
(970) 453-1550 • breckbrew.com
Established: 1990

SCENE & STORY

"Breck" was founded beneath a soaring peak which would later become one of the top ski areas in North America, with steep, exposed, sought-after black diamond runs like the Lake Chutes. Runs like those were the first love of local Richard Squire, who, when not skiing, was home brewing. As the state's craft beer industry fired up, Squire saw his chance and took it; today Breckenridge beers are available in more than twenty-five states. The original location of the Breckenridge family of brewpubs (an aggressive brewpub expansion strategy was scaled back in the late 1990s), this spacious brewpub has mustard yellow and deep red walls, with metal railings and plenty of space, giving it a modern feel. The hearty fare, if nothing too adventurous, is just right for après-ski. Score an outside table with a view of the peak (and those Lake Chutes), and the picture is nearly complete. There's a twelve-acre, 85,000-square-foot production brewery in Littleton now, and five other restaurants affiliated with the brand, which to some dismay, was sold to AB InBev in December 2015 for an undisclosed but surely mountainous sum.

PHILOSOPHY

Squire's dream: ski all day and drink great beer every night. That about covers it, doesn't it?

KEY BEER

The 7.85% ABV Extra ESB, part of the small batch series, deftly blends a roasted and slightly sweet caramel character with astringent hops. Expect to see many new barrel-aged and large format releases in coming years.

ASPEN BREWING CO.

304 E. Hopkins Ave. • Aspen, CO 81611
(970) 920-2739 • aspenbrewing.com
Established: 2008

SCENE & STORY

Two friends not long out of college opened Aspen Brewing Co. in a cluttered old architect's studio, decorating the place with hand-carved tap handles, Tibetan prayer flags, maps, and other bric-a-brac. Former Keystone Light drinkers, the roommates had discovered the incredible spectrum of flavors in craft brews on tap while going to school in Boulder. They started home brewing, and, being regulars in Aspen, dreamed they could bring the movement back to Aspen, local craft brewing pioneer Flying Dog having long departed to Denver, then Maryland. The optimism was well founded: their first batches blew out in a matter of days, a scenario they clearly still regard in awe.

The duo moved quickly to auger into Aspen's social fabric, contributing to charities, bringing in new brewers, and scouting property for the next level—they were already thinking bigger. Today, the crew has graduated to a shiny taproom closer to Main Street, and to the well-heeled tourists that flock to Aspen practically year-round, while production has expanded to a warehouse out near the airport.

PHILOSOPHY

Stewards of the land, with a hearty thirst for beer. "We're not just punks out of college," says Duncan Clauss, one half of the founding team. The Aspen crew was one of the first three breweries, alongside New Belgium and Odell, to sign on to the Clean Water Act with Environment Colorado and the U.S. Environmental Protection Agency.

KEY BEER

The big, juicy, American-style India pale ale known as Independence Pass (7% ABV) is a grassy, floral blast of Cascade, Palisade, Columbus, and Simcoe hops, with a foundation of sturdy malt.

DETOUR ➡ CRAFT BEER, GONZO STYLE: THE WOODY CREEK TAVERN

2858 Upper River Rd. • Woody Creek, CO 81656 • (970) 923-4585 • woodycreektavern.com

The saying "Good people drink good beer" might not be the best-known line from Hunter S. Thompson, whose seminal work, *Fear And Loathing in Las Vegas,* scorched the pants off the literary world in 1972, but it is—obviously—one of his best. And, although traveling in the usual manner of Dr. Gonzo (bat-eyed high with a trunk full of drugs, firearms, dynamite, and rats, to be deposited on some politician's front lawn), is not even remotely recommended, it *is* a good idea to visit the writer's two most famous old haunts, one in glitzy Aspen, and one right outside it in a dustier spot.

Start at J-Bar, a Victorian gem with a marble floor and tin ceiling in the lobby of the Hotel Jerome in Aspen proper. This watering hole started hydrating silver miners in 1889 and later became the preferred liquid-rations stop for 10th Mountain Division soldiers-in-training during World War II. Thompson used the place as his headquarters for his campaign for sheriff in 1970, running on his "freak power ticket" with a pledge to regulate illicit drug sales, replace the city streets with dirt, and, more than anything else, as he would later write, prevent "greedheads, land-rapers and other human jackals from capitalizing on the name Aspen." (He lost by only 400 votes.) For years after, Thompson was a regular here, stopping by after the post office to eat, drink, and read his mail, generally making less of a scene than on the drunken night when he duct-taped fellow partier Bill Murray to a chair and pushed him into the hotel pool, nearly drowning him. The first of Thompson's two memorials was held here after his death in 2005; behind the bar today, there's a print of the poster Thompson and artist Tom Benton created for the sheriff's campaign with its iconic double-thumbed fist clenching a peyote. On tap, look for locally brewed Aspen Brewing Co; for dinner, there's a good half-pound burger for fourteen dollars. Good enough for government work, as they say, even if you're not running for sheriff with a head full of high-grade smoke.

Thompson loved the area outside of town, too, which he first visited in 1961. While Aspen itself was (and still is) full of private jets and Hollywood types, Thompson's chosen corner of the woods, Woody Creek, was and is a lot grittier. "He could walk naked on the porch of his mountain house, take a leak off the porch into a blue toilet bowl with a palm tree growing out of it, and squeeze off a few .44 slugs at some gongs mounted on the hillside. He could chew mescaline and turn the stereo up to 100 decibels without pissing off the neighbors," writes Paul Perry in his book, *Fear and Loathing: The Strange and Terrible Saga of Hunter S. Thompson.* Fans of the writer (who coined another personal favorite, "When the going gets weird, the weird turn pro") will deeply enjoy making this pilgrimage, deeper into Gonzo territory.

The Woody Creek Tavern, founded in 1980 by theoretical physicist, spark-plug fortune heir, and longtime HST neighbor George Stranahan, resides up a curling canyon road about eight miles outside the town of Woody Creek. There's not much to see besides; as a local bumper sticker puts it, Woody Creek consists of "a bump, two dips, and a rumble strip." No matter; not only is this celebrated dive Thompson's most celebrated watering hole (and a shrine with innumerable photos and tributes adorning its walls), it's also a business intertwined with Colorado craft beer history and even a thread of statewide politics.

Stranahan, a tireless entrepreneur, opened Aspen's first new brewery in a century in 1991, naming it the Flying Dog after a piece of folk art he'd seen on a wild-haired trek to the Baltoro Glacier in Pakistan. By 1994, the business was booming, so he moved operations to Denver and installed a 50bbl brewing system (a.k.a. brewhouse), collaborating on a bottling plant with John Hickenlooper (Hickenlooper, creator of Wynkoop's Railyard Ale, who would go on to become mayor of Denver, and then governor of Colorado in early 2011). Shortly after, at Thompson's behest, Stranahan commissioned famed illustrator Ralph Steadman to do some wild beer labels with the words "Good Beer, No Shit." The state of Colorado deemed the art obscene and called for a halt to production, but after five years in court Stranahan's beer survived, label intact. Today, as an investor, Stranahan's name also graces a top-shelf, Colorado-made whiskey.

As for the brewery, Flying Dog is now based in Maryland, but the Woody Creek Tavern, festooned with American flags, prized by the locals (the "Woody Creatures"), and flanked by a trailer park, isn't going anywhere. With its walls shimmering with thousands of Polaroids and margaritas as strong as mescaline, nor will you.

Ouray

OURAY BREWERY

607 Main St. • Ouray, CO 81427
(970) 325-7388 • ouraybrewery.com
Established: 2010

SCENE & STORY

In a town built at elevation 7,800 feet and ringed by peaks so high its long been dubbed the Switzerland of America (population: 900), it's fitting that the Ouray Brewery feels like a vertical affair, with a ground floor taproom leading up to a brewery and dining room mezzanine, and finally a stunning rooftop deck from which to view a cathedral of soaring 14ers (14,000-foot peaks) including Hayden and Whitehouse Peaks. The taproom has a modernized mountain house feel, with exposed beams, track lighting, and a row of heavyweight bar swings hanging from the ceiling. Once a trinket shop and home of a local newspaper, *The Ouray Plaindealer*, 607 Main is now one of the most bustling watering holes in Ouray.

But it's not just beer: Founder Erin Eddy also organizes the annual Ouray

Ice Festival, a world-famous ice-climbing weekend held every January in the Ouray Ice Park, a daredevil's playground formed each winter when the city runs gushers of water into Uncompahgre Gorge that promptly freeze in place. More than 3,000 alpinists, gear heads, and assorted outdoors mavens pile into town to watch and compete in climbing competitions. After climbing 100-foot spires of ice or tightrope walking the gorge on a nylon slack line, you can imagine one might develop a bit of thirst; so it's a good thing there's plenty of local beer.

PHILOSOPHY

Eddy's MO is straightforward. "Consistency is the philosophy I'm trying to fol-low. Same four beers on tap at all times. Never run out of beer. Never run out of food. Never give bad service. Hire the best people, and make sure they follow the vision I have."

KEY BEER

San Juan IPA, with a ruddy copper hue, ample, citrusy hop bite, and medium body is the local favorite.

DETOUR ➡ OURAYLE HOUSE BREWERY

215 7th Ave. • Ouray, CO 81427 • (970) 903-1824 • ouraylehouse.com • Established: 2005

Getting to the tiny mountain town of Ouray takes some doing. Wedged beneath a scrum of jagged San Juan Mountain passes, it's a solid two-hour drive from Aspen or Durango. But for the love of beer, you should go.

I did, en route to Durango from Aspen a few years ago, but almost made the mistake of merely passing through. In fact, I'd been hearing about this town for ages—there's the world-famous ice-climbing festival every winter, and in summer, tourists flock to ride the Durango-to-Silverton Narrow Gauge Railroad Train as it chugs up and down the 10,000-foot passes. At the time of my travels, though, I wasn't even aware there were breweries in Ouray. But its main street, lined with historic, wind-whipped facades, was too pretty to pass up. Sure enough, you can walk right into a saloon that opened in 1891, at the Old Western Hotel, and salute the portrait of "Juanita" on the floor, painted by an itinerant artist for the princely sum ent company included—it doesn't even matter what's on tap, because the place just feels like a corner of heaven.

On one evening I found the owner, James "Hutch" Hutchison, sliding side to side behind the bar on a kind of zip-line barstool with an impish grin. After studying land-use planning and the somewhat vague-sounding major of environmental economics, he began building the brewpub. It's a Reinhold Messnerian hideaway, crabbed and cabin-like, sure, but also idealistic, big-hearted, and honest about what matters. "If a kayak is missing," reads one totem, "the river is up and no one's here. *We're in a meeting*." And, on another one, "Due to factors beyond our control, major powder days may result in brewery closing at any time." I imagine Hutch chuckling as he locks up the brewhouse after a dump of snow to head out backcountry skiing. What's best about Ourayle is how merrily unconcerned Hutch is about it all. "You move down here for the lifestyle, not for the job," he explains. "I love that we have seven months of winter, three months of company. You're just nestled into the Rocky Mountains. People have said it looks so claustrophobic, like Mother Nature is giving you a big hug."

Call it a bear hug. I felt I could disappear here for a while, drinking beer with Hutch and throwing a few darts over pints of ale. "This is where the misfits kind of fit in," says Hutch. "It's real casual—you can bring your own food, you can cook here, every restaurant in town will deliver here," he says with a cheeky grin, "with the exception of the girl across the street. She has a lot of young European waitresses working for her, and apparently they never make it back."

The fact is that this is what matters in a small town: Fresh beer, and no Big Country attitude. And while Ourayle House might not have cultivated the time-consuming brewing techniques of, say, Avery, or the polish and feel-good politics of New Belgium, there was something about it that night that made me feel I might well have found the best brewpub in the world. Hutch was sliding side to side on his bar swing, clutching a giant *bierstein* from Munich's Hoffbräu Haus, a couple of regulars hooting and egging him on. "I didn't move here to see how much money I could make, or to see how much beer I could make," he said. "And I didn't come to Ourayle looking for a nice place to live—I was looking for a nice place to *die*. I get to kayak, I get to ski, snowboard, mountain climb; there's unbelievable cycling out here. You know, I brew beer when I just have to come up with money for a new toy, basically, to support what I really want to do. It's rewarding—I've done a lot of brewing, too, and I really love it."

I loved it, too, and paused for a few more minutes to hang out with Hutch and have a few sips of his Biscuit Amber, a malty, copper-hued brew that really needs to be consumed whilst seated in a rocking chair by the woodstove. This was one of the places I was looking for, long before I knew I was looking for it. But for me it was also time to make the white-knuckle drive to Durango over Red Mountain (see "The Million Dollar Highway"). On the way out, I told Hutch I'd be back and paused to contemplate one last sign. It read, "You have the free will to follow your destiny however you choose." If the good-beer life be a choice, as it was for Hutch, then I'm in. See you there.

The Million Dollar Highway

U.S. Route 550 wends between Montrose and Durango, Colorado; up, through, and over Ute Indian country, the Uncompahgre Gorge, several historic towns, and a spate of precipitous passes. The Million Dollar Highway is the route's most famous section; Russian immigrant engineer Otto Mears somehow managed to build this twenty-three-mile stretch between Ouray and Silverton, a tortuous curlicue of switchbacks following old stagecoach routes and mining roads (and lacking almost any guardrails above the plunging ravines).

It's a wonder he ever finished. Soaring skyward through a series of tight turns overlooking void-like chasms, the road tops 11,018-foot Red Mountain before easing—mercifully—down into Silverton. No one's sure if the name comes from the richness of those mines, now quiet, or the quality of the views. And while this particular road is the only direct route between Ouray's excellent breweries and Silverton and Durango beyond, it's not a drive to be taken at night, or in a gutless car, or with even the slightest buzz from one of Ouray's excellent local brews. On a good day, it's a white-knuckler; in darkness and driving sleet (as I drove it) it's a roll of the dice.

Durango

STEAMWORKS BREWING CO.

801 E. 2nd Ave. • Durango, CO 81301
(970) 259-9200 • steamworksbrewing.com
Established: 1996

SCENE & STORY

Originally built in the 1920s, the home of Steamworks Brewing Company—Durango's fourth brewery—had long been used as an auto dealership. There were cement floors, a large showroom, and a large, half-shell-like ceiling structure overhead. "There were literally GMCs and Cadillacs and Jeeps parked here," says cofounder Chris Oyler of the space, which now sports rows of taps, tables, stools, and brewing medals instead of cars. Oyler—and a cadre of some forty-seven initial investors—felt the building's industrial look was a good one for craft beer. "Having those cars parked here, I knew that the floors could hold some weight. I knew it was a solid building," he recalls. At the time, though, the exposed wooden truss beams supporting the roof were hidden above old dusty ceiling tiles. "We started pulling them down and looking up at the rafters, and we were like 'Wow, this is gorgeous.'" It is indeed.

PHILOSOPHY

Durango's soft water—low in magnesium, calcium, and other minerals—is ideal for brewing, requiring little or no adjustment during the brewing process (a luxury not all brewing towns enjoy). The company specializes in lagers, and despite the difficulty of brewing those well, there's an ease about the place. "These are beers you can sit down and have more than one or two of," he adds, mentioning the company's popular Colorado Kölsch by way of illustration. That approach has worked, at least in terms of growth and medals; today, Steamworks has a busy canning program, widening distribution, and has hauled in a spate of medals at the Great American Beer Festival and other brewing events.

KEY BEER

Colorado Kölsch—a lightly bittered golden ale (4.85% ABV) with a touch of biscuit-like sweetness in the body and a crisp, dry finish recently pulled a silver medal at the 2015 GABF.

SKA BREWING CO.

225 Girard St. • Durango, CO 81303
(970) 247-5792 • skabrewing.com
Established: 1995

SCENE & STORY

With a new, $4.8 million, ultra-eco friendly facility just south of Durango and an everybody-into-the-mosh-pit image, Ska is a fun brewery to visit. But when it comes to brewing, they're not goofing around. A visit to the sunny taproom and modernist-looking food court outside built from repurposed shipping containers may be the highlight of any beer lover's visit to Durango.

PHILOSOPHY

The well-meaning hell-raisers behind this company, a group of Colorado locals who decided to home brew because they weren't of legal age, have recently graduated to regional microbrewery status, a fact that still seems to give them a case of the giggles. They're known for pranks on other brewers (like producing a twenty-minute spoof of the Discovery Channel's *Brew Masters* show, starring their friend, Dogfish Head brewery founder Sam Calagione), and making the festival rounds with a posse in tow.

KEY BEER

Ten Pin Porter shows off Ska's more serious side: it's a fulsome, roasty black brew of 5.5% ABV with flavors of cocoa, coffee, and molasses in admirable balance.

Pagosa Springs

PAGOSA SPRINGS BREWING CO.

118 N. Pagosa Blvd. • Pagosa Springs, CO
81147 • (970) 731-2739
Established: 2006

SCENE & STORY

Heading east out of Durango toward New Mexico via Pagosa Springs, Colorado, on U.S. 160 to U.S. 84E affords one of the greatest drives in the United States—make it in daylight after leaving Ska so you can see what's around you. On arrival to Pagosa Springs Brewing Co., it's easy to see why this small seasonal resort town is such a haven for vacation-home owners and skiers. Soaring peaks ring the town; Wolf Creek, just a short drive away, is a world-class powder skiing destination that gets some of the earliest and best white stuff. And Tony Simmons's brewpub and beer garden is ideally located right off the highway coming into town. Since the day it opened, it's changed the drinking scene in this very beautiful place, and beyond.

"I don't think we realized how successful we were going to be at the time," says Simmons, who is the owner and head brewer. "We started off really as a beer bar with very limited food, and as we've evolved and kind of bootstrapped our way through this it's evolved into a full-service, made-from-scratch menu, and that's really helped tremendously as our business has grown." "Evolved" is putting it mildly: In just five years, Pagosa Brewing Company has garnered an incredible twenty-four medals at the GABF and other competitions, a testament to Simmons's in-depth training at the Siebel Institute in Chicago and Munich.

The HQ is a rustic affair. "Our building was actually a garage," he recalls. "It stored a couple of cars and it had a wood shop, but it really had no significant power, and there was no water or plumbing. That was a big investment to get it ready for a brewery." Today it maintains a down-to-earth feel, with a lazy, expansive beer garden (10,000 square feet, with some fifty tables, heat lamps, and fire pits) and a folksy kitchen-in-a-trailer setup.

PHILOSOPHY

"We're really proud of the fact that we don't filter any of our beers. It's all natural and I think it shows." Simmons is an energetic presence in the Colorado beer scene and eager experimenter; to date he's released some forty different brews. A contest sponsored by the Benjamin Franklin Tercentenary (a consortium of academic historians and museum curators) in 2006 inspired him to brew a batch of "Poor Richard's Ale," a coppery, low-hopped, colonial American brown ale utilizing corn and molasses, which was meant to approximate what Franklin would have enjoyed in the pubs of the day. A prestigious panel of brewing industry judges (including descendants of Franklin himself, "The First American") picked Simmons's recipe to be served at the gala event in Philadelphia and later brewed by more than 100 commercial brewing companies in thirty-five states and some 3,000 home brewers around the country.

KEY BEER

Every visitor should try the Poor Richard's and Kayaker Cream Ale, the brewery's top selling and most sessionable beer. It's a crisp, light-bodied Helles lager tailor-made for hot summer afternoons. When the sun drops and the air cools off, try one of Simmons's heavier-bodied brews, such as the Coconut Porter, which took the silver medal in its category at the 2010 GABF. "That was a real honor," says Simmons. "Other breweries have tried to [brew the style], but we've been really fortunate in being able to dial it in. People go crazy for it."

SCENE & STORY

Every great day of skiing is best capped off with a good beer. So why not 100? For the last fifteen years, a brother-and-sister team of beer lovers have put on this weekend of tasting, beer dinners, a home brew competition, informational brewmaster seminars, and, for those who can peel away from the action inside, skiing the world-class terrain of Vail. The fifteenth annual festival, held in 2015, featured over 100 top brewing companies (mostly from the United States, and a handful from Europe), all of which sent their founders and head brewers along. Which means for the festival attendee, it's a chance to meet some of the most well-known brewers in the land over a beer in an intimate but not too crowded environment. Chris Bauweraerts of Belgium's Brasserie La Chouffe, Avery's Adam Avery, Dogfish Head's Sam Calagione, Boulevard's Steven Pauwels, Allagash's Rob Tod, and New Belgium's Peter Bouckaert (among other luminaries) all regularly attend.

BEST *of the* REST: COLORADO

STRANGE BREWING CO.

1330 Zuni St. • Denver, CO 80204 • (720) 985-2337 • strangecraft.com

Out-of-work IT guy Tim Myers turned a home brewing hobby into a nano that just keeps getting better, culminating with a gold at the World Beer Cup in 2014 for his company's montmorency-packed Cherry Kriek (5% ABV), a highly competitive category. Head down the tasting room for one-barrel Wednesdays, when experimental beers run amok. Blackberry-bergamot golden ale, anyone?

FRESHCRAFT

1530 Blake St., Ste. A • Denver, CO 80202 • (303) 758-9608 • freshcraft.com

Iowa-born-and-bred brothers Jason and Lucas Forgy present a supereclectic menu (from tacos to barbecue to French) and a vast beer selection with twenty rotating taps and over 100 bottles; go during the "Beer Session" happy hours (3 to 7 p.m. daily) for discounts on sandwiches and 5.5% ABV-and-below draft beer pairings. This place is always packed during GABF.

HOGSHEAD BREWERY & TAPROOM

4460 W. 29th Ave. • Denver, CO 80212 • (303) 495-3105 • hogsheadbrewery.com

One of most Denver's most innovative brewpubs is also, paradoxically, one of the most traditional anywhere in the United States—at least when it comes the beer styles served. Built in a repurposed 1950s gas station and focusing mainly on the ancient art of cask-conditioned, English-style ales served at "cellar temperature" (50 degrees—cool, but not ice cold), Hogshead has been building a steady following for several years. Try the mellow Lake Lightning, a straightforward English pale ale, and work your way up.

POST BREWING

105 W. Emma St. • Lafayette, CO 80026 • (303) 593-2066 • postbrewing.com • Established: 2014

Former Dogfish Head brewer Bryan Selders signed on to help launch to this much hyped brewpub in 2014, which is a classic brewpub-restaurant, with great bar food and attention to detail throughout the interior. "With the capacity that we started out with, we have about 1,600 barrels of capacity per year," Selders told me. "We're gonna have six beers at a time, maybe eight if something lingers. I just want to make sure that we're focused on making those six beers as kick-ass as humanly possible."

WEST FLANDERS BREWING

1125 Pearl St. • Boulder, CO 80302 • (303) 447-2739 • wfbrews.com

Music-mad brewmaster Brian Lutz's resume includes the top jobs at Oskar Blues, Lefthand, Redfish Brewhouse, and research trips to Belgium with the likes of New Belgium's Peter Bouckaert. To balance all the Belgian-inflected beer you'll want to try, there's excellent, locally sourced food (order up some of the local tenderbelly pork . . . on anything). To drink? Try the Obfuscation Trippel (7.5% ABV), a style few Americans tackle well.

BRU HANDBUILT ALES

5290 Arapahoe • Boulder, CO 80303 • (720) 638-5193 • bruboulder.com

Founder and head brewer Ian Clark has an ace up his sleeve: a formal culinary education. Which means he's also the head chef. Ambitious, sure, but what might overwhelm him (and underwhelm guests) works amazingly well. The beers are very good, the food is tasty and imaginative (incorporating Clark's backyard honey, among other ultra-local ingredients), and the place is smartly put together (handbuilt, of course).

SANITAS BREWING COMPANY

3550 Frontier Ave. • Boulder, CO, 80301 • (303) 442-4130 • sanitasbrewing.com

Former Boulder Beer Co. brewer Chris Coyne and two partners opened this spotless taproom and 10,000-plus-square-foot production facility in September 2012 to make organic, canned beers year round, from easy-drinking session ales to aggressive fare like India Black Ale and just about everything else on down the line—plans include extensive barrel-aging and even a coolship. Try the Saison (5.2% ABV), which makes a compelling case that this farmhouse Belgian style, usually packed in in 750-milliliter bottles, is also a winner in "lite" form.

TWISTED PINE BREWING CO.

3201 Walnut St. • Boulder, CO 80301 • (303) 786-9270 • twistedpinebrewing.com

The diminutive Twisted Pine, established in 1995, casts a tall shadow thanks to a series of big wins at the Great American Beer Festival and a slew of well-regarded beers and experiments including Ghost Face Killah, a pepper beer made with bhut jolokia, a pepper that is also known as "Ghost Chili" and is six times hotter than a habañero. An excellent brew is the fifteenth anniversary Hoppy Knight India Black Ale (7% ABV), a fulsome, piney sipper that balances ample servings of mellow malt and spice.

THE MAYOR OF OLD TOWN

632 S. Mason St. • Fort Collins, CO 80524 • (970) 682-2410 • themayorofoldtown.com

Since you're visiting Fort Collins to hit Odell, New Belgium, Funkwerks, and others, you'd be remiss not to include this superstylish beer bar downtown opened in 2011, with an outstanding 100-tap selection of beers and a bright, clean, white subway tile interior with wide bar and cool captain's chairs, where you can post up for fresh beer, good flatbread pizzas, sandwiches, and burgers, and other fare. Look for sought-after sours from Trinity of Colorado Springs.

FUNKWERKS

1900 E, Lincoln Ave. • Fort Collins, CO 80524 • (970) 482-3865 • funkwerks.com

In 2010, award-winning Colorado home brewer Gordon Schuck and his beer-obsessed accountant friend Brad Lincoln opened this small, all-organic brewery in Fort Collins after meeting at Chicago's Siebel Institute to make saison beers, also known as farmhouse ales, starting with a tiny system and quickly ramping up production. Try the Funkwerks Saison (6.8% ABV), a tawny, grassy sipper with a clean, dry finish. In 2012 Funkwerks was named Small Brewing Company of the Year during GABF, and received two gold medals for Saison and Deceit, a Belgian-style golden strong. The latter was also awarded a silver medal in 2014 at the World Beer Cup. And in 2014, Raspberry Provincial won a gold medal at the Great American Beer Festival. My personal favorite? Tropic King, an 8% ABV "imperial" saison. Delicious stuff.

THE YAK & YETI

7803 Ralston Rd. • Arvada, CO 80002 • (303) 431-9000 • theya.k.a.ndyeti.com

Nepalese chef Dol Bhattarai specializes in "mountain food for mountain people," and the house beers are made to go with his amply spiced cuisine. Try the Chai Stout, which tastes of cardamom, cocoa, and ginger.

DRYDOCK BREWING CO.

15120 E. Hampden Ave. • Aurora, CO 80014 • (303) 400-5606 • drydockbrewing.com

Established in 2005 and connected to the Brew Hut, a home brew shop, Dry Dock anchors an otherwise flavorless suburban strip mall. The nautically themed Dry Dock has hauled up a treasure chest of top brewing awards. A boost from government stimulus money (allowing an expansion, which was later followed by another, and another), has helped to propel it to national prominence in a short time. For kicks, they've been known on occasion to serve beer from tap-enhanced hollow watermelons and once from a 208-pound pumpkin.

TOMMYKNOCKER BREWING CO.

1401 Miner St. • Idaho Springs, CO 80452 • (303) 567-4419 • tommyknocker.com

Established in 1994 in an historic mining town halfway between the ski areas of Summit County and Denver, the spacious Tommyknocker Brewery was built in the old Placer Hotel, a haven for the miners who gathered there to compare the day's work. Their Butt Head Bock is a toffeeish, raisiny 8.2% ABV lager with a creamy mouthfeel that won a silver at the 2015 GABF.

REVOLUTION BREWING CO.

325 Grand Ave. • Paonia, CO 81428 • (970) 260-4869 • revolution-brewing.com

This tiny Delta County mining town has been attracting wineries and vineyards of late; now, brewer Mike King's tiny homespun operation, with a charming little tasting room in an historic house (and beer garden out back), is consistently busy, packing the house for open mic nights and musical guests. King's TJ 60/40 Wheat Lager is a seasonal based on one of Thomas Jefferson's recipes, with 60 percent barley and 40 percent wheat (5.2% ABV).

COLORADO BOY PUB & BREWERY

602 Clinton St. • Ridgway, CO 81432 • (970) 626-5333 • coloradoboy.com

Brewing industry veteran Tom Hennessy's twenty-five-seat brewpub in a converted 1915 drugstore in tiny Ridgway—the northern entrance of the San Juan Skyway Drive—is cozy but updated with pastel orange and green walls, craftsman light fixtures, an antique bar, and art on the wall.

The inspiration for it all came from travels abroad. "My wife and I were hiking in Scotland," he recalls, "and I fell in love with the small breweries up there. This is my sixth brewery and smallest by far. Probably my most fun one also." The piney, aromatic IPA, often on cask, took bronze at the GABF in 2009 (under the ESB category). There's now a sister brewpub and pizzeria on Main Street in Montrose, Colorado, twenty-seven miles north.

GRIMM BROTHERS BREWHOUSE

547 N. Denver Ave. • Loveland, CO 80538 • (970) 624-6045 • grimmbrosbrewhouse.com

Grimm Brothers draws on Teutonic aesthetics and the wicked fun of Grimm's fairy tales. Little Red Cap is a fine version of altbier Snow Drop American Pale Wheat Ale is a brew style predating the *Reinheitsgebot*, or German Beer Purity Law of 1516, and contains wheat, oats, honey and molasses—and won a bronze in 2015 at GABF in a category with forty competitors.

WYOMING

SNAKE RIVER BREWING CO.

265 S. Millward St. • Jackson, WY 83001
(307) 739-2337 • snakeriverbrewing.com
Established: 1994

SCENE & STORY

The mere presence of great craft beer is not the first reason to go to Jackson—let's face it, the Grand Tetons are the real draw here, especially in the winter for skiers—but it does sweeten the deal. Opened in 1994, Snake River has built an excellent restaurant and award-winning brewery. The brewpub itself is a spacious, well-lit, multilevel affair with lots of windows, and frequented by locals who avoid the tourist traps in town (i.e., the Million Dollar Cowboy Bar, which, truth be told, can be a fun pit stop). It turns into a serious party around holidays like Oktoberfest, Mardi Gras, Halloween, and Saint Patrick's Day, and the food earns high marks, especially "the Roper" sandwich: braised brisket, applewood-smoked bacon, caramelized onions, white cheddar, and horseradish mayo on a housemade bun.

PHILOSOPHY

Snake River's huge popularity could have led it down the path of mediocrity in a hurry. Instead the family-owned brewery seems to be getting better every year. Since 2007, the brewery has ramped up its brewing program considerably, adding bold new styles and experiments that are gaining notice.

KEY BEER

Snake River Brewing Company has traditionally excelled in one particular style that few manage to nail or even dare to tackle: Foreign (a.k.a. Export) Stout, which is characterized by a huge roasted malt profile, a higher than usual alcohol content, and malt-given flavors of caramel, cocoa powder, and coffee. Their 6% ABV Zonker Stout has won scads of awards over the years (more than 200!), helping make Wyoming's first brewpub something of a legend in craft beer circles. But it's Le Serpent and Le Serpent Cerise that have bitten hardest into the regional, and indeed, the entire national beer landscape. A pair of limited release, Flemish-style sour ales aged in French oak barrels up to eighteen months, these two beers made surprise appearances in the top ranks of the American and international craft brewing awards circuit in 2010. The Cerise version is aged in the barrel with whole Washington cherries; both burst with funky, earthy, tart flavors of wood and fruit.

Q ROADHOUSE AND ROADHOUSE BREWING COMPANY

2550 Moose Wilson Rd. • Jackson, WY 83014 • (307) 739-0700
roadhousebrewery.com • Established: 2012

SCENE & STORY

Five miles from the famed Jackson Hole ski area between the town of Jackson and Teton Village, Q Roadhouse is part of restaurateur Gavin Fine's upscale group, with ambitious food and a range of beers that have helped Jackson locals experience styles well beyond IPA. There's a restaurant and attached Roadhouse Brewing Co., a semi-independent entity, which has been taking on a life of its own (with expansion plans brewing in 2015). While their (excellent) Cream Ale and IPA are huge sellers, brewery co-owner/head brewer Adam Chenault and assistant brewery Kyle Fleming are making great saisons, like the 2014 silver medal-winning version with apricots and peaches called Saison en Regalia (a sly reference to Frank Zappa's prog-rock epic). Meanwhile Q Roadhouse is a modernist take on the usual brewpub, in which chef Matty Melehes, who appeared on the popular cooking show "Chopped," mans the stoves with aplomb, doing exceptional high country barbecue with local lamb, pork, and beef.

PHILOSOPHY

Artful barbecue and bold beers in the Tetons, made for local skiers, beer geeks, and bon vivants. Can't go wrong there. "We focus on Belgian styles and big, West Coast style IPAs," Chenault told me. "We brew beers by different sources of inspiration; another beer, the lyrics from a song, a moment on the hill after some fresh pow turns, or a random ingredient. For instance, I was standing in line waiting for a sandwich and saw some dried apricots and peaches in packages—our GABF silver medal–winning Saison en Regalia was born. We brew beer that we want to drink. We pay attention to the history and tradition of styles but use our own techniques and sometimes unique ingredients."

KEY BEER

If Saison en Regalia isn't on, look for Sacred Creed (6.2% ABV), a Franco-Belgian style saison with ample American hops and wild yeasts imparting complex, appealing flavors.

MONTANA

THE BEST WAY TO DISCOVER MONTANA'S BURGEONING BEER CULTURE IS TO FOLLOW ALL OR PART of the Montana Beer Trail, dotted with twenty-three (and counting) breweries along some 700-hundred miles of the state's most scenic rural and wilderness areas including Yellowstone and Glacier National Parks, the Bitterroot Valley historic mining rail, and ghost towns, not to mention trout-filled rivers like the Yellowstone and Gallatin (find the map at montanabrewers.org).

When you do go, one of the first things to know about Montana, an idyllic state with pure water, some of the finest barley in the nation, and a per capita brewery density among the highest in the United States, is that for some reason, it has maddeningly confusing alcohol laws that conspire against craft brewers. Brewpubs are technically disallowed, as is production of more than 10,000 barrels (a beer barrel contains thirty-one gallons), unless they close their taprooms. At the same time, microbreweries may not sell more than forty-eight ounces of beer per consumer per day, and then only until 8 p.m. If they want to serve food and house beer from the same location, they must establish separate businesses at the same physical location that then must buy beer from said brewery. And so on, ever crazier with each new rule and exception.

The main reason for all this confusion is that the tavern lobby opposes craft brewers on the grounds that they believe craft brewery taprooms siphon off customers from their own establishments (despite the glaring differences in appeal). It all spells frustration for the small breweries, who are quite obviously offering something different. Drinking good, local, honestly made beer is an inalienable right in this country, as is the right to run or patronize a dive bar. Both can and should exist. Ultimately, craft beer is bringing better beer, jobs, and tourism to Montana and other states that are hurting financially, and it's fun to drink, explore, and manufacture. Time to wake up and smell the hops.

The good news is that even against the odds, Montana's craft beer scene is vibrant indeed. "It's growing. In Montana there's really this mentality to buy local," says Chuck Sowell, a brewer at Carter's Brewery in Billings. "So many of the small towns have their own breweries, and you don't have to be a beer connoisseur to come in and drink the local beer."

Change has come slowly, but come it has, and now you can pull into a formerly forlorn city like Billings and find craft breweries making interesting styles, barrel-aging beers, and educating consumers on life after the fizzy yellow stuff. "We're breeding a culture here where we have more home brewers, and more people that really appreciate the good craft beer, and so more breweries are now branching out beyond the basic wheat, stout, IPA, and ambers," says Sowell. "More breweries are doing barley wines and Belgian styles, and so there's an appreciation for that, too. It's really cool that there's a beer culture in Montana now."

Tony Herbert, executive of the Montana Brewer's Guild, says it's all part of the state's character. "Montanans have long had a history of liking their beer, so it's fertile ground, first of all. And a lot of the beers are coming right out of these Montana fields," he says, referring to the state's own amber waves of grain. "The water is fantastic, too. What I've seen is that people really appreciate the newness of these breweries and the beers that they make. We've been experiencing the same kind of growth that craft beer has recently. There's been a palate shift."

Time to shift into gear and get to Montana yourself.

ITINERARIES

1-DAY   Fly into Billings and hit downtown breweries within walking distance, experiencing the gamut of Montana beer culture.

3-DAY   Combine Billings with Red Lodge and the incredible drive to Bozeman near the Beartooth Highway.

7-DAY   Fly into Bozeman or Missoula and drive north to Whitefish along Flathead Lake.

Billings

MONTANA BREWING CO.

113 N. 28th St. • Billings, MT 59101
(406) 252-9200
montanabrewingcompany.com
Established: 1994

SCENE & STORY

Situated downtown in the historic head-quarters of what was once the Montana Power Company, MBC is a popular dining and sipping spot for locals and out-of-towners alike. Thanks to the refurbishment of the Babcock Theater, this part of town is becoming the arts core of the city. With a reputation for good burgers, nachos, and pizza, the portions are huge (as they are throughout Montana). The interior is traditional brewpub, and a bit dim beneath craftsman glass fixtures. But it's comfortable, with wooden booths and a large central bar area and tables in back that offer of view of a tidy brewhouse behind glass. It's quiet; the sports bar Hooligan's next door seems to siphon off the loudest cheering sections, but there's a large flat-screen in the front area for the truly devoted.

PHILOSOPHY

The whole place is festooned with banners and descriptions of the company's many GABF and World Beer Cup medals earned over the years, most recently in 2010 (the sole winner for the state, for Sandbagger's Gold—a light, smooth, biscuity ale), attesting to the effort that goes into the beer. The brewery claims it was the first in the state to do any barrel aging, a costly and time-consuming experiment for any brewery.

KEY BEER

MBC's Whitetail Wheat, a GABF winner for American wheat beers, is above par, with a clean-tasting, full-but-not-too-sweet body and a faintly spicy finish. The Sandbagger Gold and the Sharptail Pale Ale are two other beers on the lighter end of the spectrum, and a pleasingly spicy but light at 4.6% ABV amber and slightly tannic coffee stout round out the offerings nicely, too.

CARTER'S BREWING CO.

2526 Montana Ave.-B • Billings, MT 59101
(406) 252-0663 • cartersbrewing.com
Established: 2007

SCENE & STORY

Constructed in an old railroad depot storage building in the center of town opposite Billings's old hotel row, Carter's is named for owner-founder-head brewer Mike Uhrich's son; Uhrich was a brewer with Yellowstone Valley Brewing Co. before getting the itch to brew his own styles. Carter's is the young turk of the

Billings scene, with some sixteen taps from traditional kölsch to Belgian-style saisons and farmhouse ales, Imperial IPA and even an American-style sour. There are more than thirty oak barrels for wood-aging Belgian and other experimental styles strewn around the tiny 7bbl brewhouse—a marvel of space management—and it's a popular gathering place for the local beer fanatics, who come in to chat, fill growlers, and catch the occasional game.

PHILOSOPHY

"Mike experiments and brews what he wants to brew and not necessarily what people want to drink," says Chuck Sowell, one of three assistants who bartends, and a dedicated advocate for Montana's growing craft beer scene. "It's an interesting approach," he adds. "We've met a lot of brewers who brew 'to style' or they brew to win medals, or they brew to meet demand for whatever sells the most or whatever people like the most. Mike

DETOUR ➡ RED LODGE, MONTANA

A former Crow Nation redoubt and mining capital an hour out of Billings, the historic town of Red Lodge (established in 1884) is the gateway to the Beartooth Highway, a famed sixty-nine-mile ribbon of switchbacks on Highway 212 that leads south from Red Lodge into some of the most beautiful corners of Yellowstone National Park, with high glacial lakes, alpine tundra, and year-round snow. Ringed by soaring 12,000-feet peaks in the Absaroka-Beartooth Wilderness, including Montana's tallest point, Granite Peak (12,799 feet), the town itself is quintessential Old West, with 100-year-old homes and stone buildings dating from the 1880s looking over the main street (and a certain bank scoped-out—but never robbed—by Butch Cassidy, who worked the area). Despite a bit of grim history—a mining accident outside of town in 1943 remains the state's worst ever, having killed seventy-four men—it's a vibrant place today. Make sure to stop and read the roadside sign (which explains the disaster) heading into town from Billings, and stroll down Broadway, Red Lodge's main street. Red Lodge Ales hosts an Oktoberfest every September, and there are scores of other events (including annual hoe downs, a Red Lodge Festival of Nations for Native Americans, and assorted adventure races including 10K runs and a skijoring duel).

brews what he wants to brew. He's really, really passionate about his beers."

KEY BEER

De-Railed IPA, at 6.5% ABV, is a big, piney, clean brew with a bitterness-to-body ratio that approaches the heartiest of West Coast IPAs. And the Keeper, a bière de garde, pulled down a recent silver at the North American Beer Awards.

RED LODGE ALES & SAM'S TAP ROOM & KITCHEN

1445 N. Broadway • Red Lodge, MT 59068 • (406) 446-4607
redlodgeales.com • Established: 1998

SCENE & STORY

It's hard to miss the brewery along the road into Red Lodge with its jolly crimson paint job. On a busy day, depending on the season, you'll be on the heels of plenty of bikers and skiers, for starters. The taproom adjacent to the Red Lodge Ales brewery is Sam's Tap Room & Kitchen, a bright, sunny space that manages to feel both retro and modern at the same time. There are shiny metal stools and wall details of rusted and corrugated metal, a large woodstove, reclaimed barn wood, and historical photographs to warm things up. There are large viewing windows inside to the brewery, and outside space is plentiful as well, with a beer garden and separate lawn for weddings and concerts. It all feels easy-does-it and well designed, and the hops growing on all the fences outside are utilized in the brewhouse every fall. The coldest months bring some rowdy fun with a Winter Carnival (redlodge-mountain.com), complete with a local dog sled-pull contest.

Founder Sam Hoffmann, whose family comes from Germany, started out small, with a 500-square-foot facility, brewing tanks made of discarded dairy equipment, and a trio of German-style brews (alt, kölsch, and wheat), none of which are at all easy to make well. Now that the company has earned its local and regional fans and graduated to a much larger facility, the approach is much the same. There are seven year-round beers, and nine to twelve seasonals, many of them lighter to medium in body, and generally mellow in hop character, all made with Montana-grown barley.

PHILOSOPHY

German precision meets eco-minded. Head Brewer and Director of Operations Justin Moore explains that while the range of beers is somewhat traditional, there's something for everybody. "We do have the IPAs and double IPAs that we get to have fun with as well," he assures. What's more, the methods of making Red Lodge's brews are anything but traditional. "We have Montana's largest solar array," explains Moore. Among other innovations: a "free air" system which utilizes sensors and the outside air to keep beer fresh inside up to nine months a year, and an in-house biodiesel operation (to run company vehicles and delivery trucks). The brewers also crowdsource some of their own ingredients: locals are invited to bring in their own home-grown hops for use in a special fall brew called Harvest, which those same growers later enjoy at a discount.

KEY BEER

Bent Nail IPA, a juicy, piney brew at around 6.3% ABV is the biggest seller these days, but the original altbier, called Glacier Ale and pleasantly quaffable at 5% ABV, gives a look at what Red Lodge was built on. "I think it most represents us, our best year-round beer that is true to style," says Moore. Also try the 5% ABV kölsch, known as Reserve Ale, cleanly brewed and made for sessions in the grassy beer garden out back.

Bozeman

MADISON RIVER BREWING CO.

20900 Frontage Rd., Bldg. B
Belgrade, MT 59714 • (406) 388-0322
madisonriverbrewing.com
Established: 2005

SCENE & STORY

Located a stone's throw from Belgrade's Gallatin Field Airport, which serves the Bozeman area, this unassuming taproom is the ideal place to unwind with locals before a flight (or after a bumpy arrival). While the warehouse exterior isn't much to look at, the interior is inviting and busy. Drinkers chat quietly at tall tables and a small wooden bar beneath the tall ceilings. There's classic rock on the stereo, and a wall of ultracolorful hand-blown glass tankards belonging to the Mug Club members. It's for locals, but they're an amiable lot. "We get all kinds of people here," says owner Howard McMurray, the tall, gentle fellow behind the brew kettles. "We get fly fisherman, we get college students. A few days ago a little old lady came here from Butte for our Double IPA (which is a 9% ABV beer) and I actually questioned her—are you sure you want this one? And she said she'd driven an hour and a half just to drink it. It's great to see that."

PHILOSOPHY

There are six standard taps and two seasonals at any given time, and McMurray employs a workmanlike approach, researching styles and the ingredients generally used in each, to just "go with it." It's refreshing to hear a brewer speak of his own beers in this unpretentious way.

KEY BEER

Copper John Scotch Ale is a style known as Wee Heavy (akin to a strong porter), and McMurray's version is made with roasted barley and a bit of smoked malts, which gives it an appealing char kick. In 2015, this beer took a gold for Scottish-Style Ales, besting fifty-one other entries.

BOZEMAN BREWING CO.

504 N. Broadway • Bozeman, MT 59715
(406) 585-9142 • bozemanbrewing.com
Established: 2001

SCENE & STORY

Ask anyone where to drink craft beer in Bozeman and the response is, inevitably, "Dude. The BoZone." The nickname, admittedly, has a catchy ring. Nestled in a former pea canning factory in Bozeman's northeast-of-center "warehouse district"—really just a line of buildings a few blocks off the main street—it's packed every night with locals clutching pints or goblets poured off of one of the eight taps. Mondays bring bluegrass jams, and the clubhouse feel lends an added buzz. This seems like the place Bozeman's most dedicated beer drinkers and ski bums come together when it snows outside, and with charming servers and walls that were literally painted with a sort of brewer's grain-infused paint, it's easy to see why. Bottle art was derived from a variety of historic Montana breweries, and overall the place has an unpretentious, friendly feel.

PHILOSOPHY

"When I started out here, it was on a shoestring—borrowing against my house and the whole nine yards," recalls founder and head brewer Todd Scott, who brewed for the well-known (but ill-fated) Spanish Peaks brand, and scored much of its equipment after it closed. "And I was having a kid at the same time. I needed to come up with a beer that was going to start out selling well right out of the gate. I didn't have time to build a reputation for brewing awesome IPAs, or something like that. I needed a beer that was easy drinking, that people could drink three, four, five of, that was popular at the time—like Fat Tire. The idea was to brew something that looked like a Fat Tire, but didn't have that biscuity flavor. And that was our Amber."

KEY BEER

The malt-forward Bozone Amber Select is Scott's flagship today, and they've recently started canning several other beers like Plum Street Porter (six malts; no fruit added). Look for the sour Belgian tripel-style creation called Funky Virtue; at 11% ABV, it is aged with cherries in port wine barrels for three years. It's got all the sourness and power and oaky notes one expects of well-made American wild ale.

MONTANA ALEWORKS

611 E. Main St. • Bozeman, MT 59715
(406) 587-7700 • montanaaleworks.com
Established: 2000

SCENE & STORY

Spread out spaciously beneath the rafters of an 8,000-square-foot former train depot in the heart of town, Aleworks is packed nightly with locals, and its pool tables, cement bar, and outdoor patio accommodate crowds of around 300 at any given time. Still, with its cavernous wood ceilings and long layout, it doesn't feel like a mad-house even on a very busy night. The pepper-Parmesan fries have a well-deserved reputation, and the fare centers around burgers and other steakhouse specialties like bison, Wild Alaskan salmon, and a superb eight-ounce tenderloin steak.

PHILOSOPHY

Upscale but not uptight. "We're not fine dining by any means, but we do a lot

of really nice food, and one of the big things for me is keeping it affordable for locals—for everybody," says managing partner Roth Jordan. "We're really preaching that we take as much pride in a nine-dollar hamburger as we do in a thirty-six-dollar Kobe rib-eye steak."

KEY BEER

There are thirty-two mostly local taps and eight rotating guest taps weighted toward regional brews from Belgrade, Missoula, and Big Sky. There's always a cask-conditioned beer (recently, Madison River Oatmeal Stout) and several seasonals like Bozeman Brewing Company's piney Harvestfest märzen.

Butte

QUARRY BREWING CO.

124 W. Broadway St. • Butte, MT 59701
(406) 723-0245 • wedigbeer.com
Established: 2007

SCENE & STORY

Chuck Schnabel and his wife, Lyza, opened a little (seven-barrel system) brewery in Butte against what some would call considerable odds. Butte was once home to five breweries at the turn of the last century (when "the Richest Hill on Earth" had made it a fantastically rich mining metropolis), but none survived past the mid-1960s, and the rough-around-the-edges town wasn't the place to try anything newfangled.

But today the Schnabels' taproom is a kind of testament to the steady community-building power of craft beer. It's in the old Grand Hotel, which was built in 1915 but gutted by fire in 1992 and vacant ever since. Plans for a ten-room bed and breakfast would make it Butte's first brewery B&B in the modern era. Chuck or Lyza can usually be found tending bar, and it's a good stopping point between Bozeman and Helena. Quarry's beers are named for types of local rock (basalt, granite, mica, calcite, etc.); Chuck experiments with new recipes to meet the rising expectations and changing palates of beer lovers.

PHILOSOPHY

Chuck Schnabel is a pragmatist, even a bit curmudgeonly, and his beers reflect a utilitarian approach. "I try to keep it simple," he says. "There's no sense in overcomplicating recipes, overcomplicating brews. I don't even send beers to competitions. I don't believe in them. My biggest thing is this: If the beer sells, it's good. We gotta be doing something right." True enough. He risked a lot to get a craft brewery going in a macrobrew tavern town, and seven years in, business is booming.

KEY BEER

Schnabel is particularly proud of his Gneiss IPA (6.8% ABV), made with Chinook and Cascade hops.

A Wild Rider's Party Town

Robert Craig Knievel, a.k.a. Evel Knievel, was born and raised in Butte (Oct. 17, 1938 to Nov. 30, 2007). Evel Knievel Days, a festival in his honor, occurs the last weekend in July, drawing some 50,000 every year. As the story goes, eight-year-old Knievel attended a daredevil show in town, and the rest is history—thirty-five broken bones later. On St. Patrick's Day, Butte, which has no open container law, becomes a massive open-air street party, and Quarry sells a great deal of beer every single second of it.

Missoula and the Bitterroot Valley

Southwestern Montana's Bitterroot Valley, a 100-mile stretch from Missoula in the north down to Lost Trail Pass (7,014 feet), straddling the Bitterroot River and flanked by the Bitterroot and Sapphire ranges, is not to be missed. With its world-class fishing holes and kayaking streams, jagged mountain vistas, easily accessible hot springs, swaths of cotton-wood forest, historical attractions (Lewis and Clark paused in the area, and the Daly Mansion—a 24,000-square-foot, fifty-room palace—draws many visitors), it's one of Montana's prettiest corners. Missoula is home to a vibrant literary tradition (Norman Maclean, author of *A River Runs Through It*, was from here, and the yearly Festival of the Book is a major draw) and has a growing beer scene, nourished by the University of Montana, and features the Garden City Brewfest held every year on the first Saturday in May.

BITTER ROOT BREWING CO.

101 Marcus St. • Hamilton, MT 59840
(406) 363-7468 • bitterrootbrewing.com
Established: 1998

SCENE & STORY

In what used to be an old apple warehouse, this brewery in the sleepy former copper mining capital of Hamilton is bright and cheerful, with high wooden tables and metal stools—something of a Montana brewpub standard—and interesting old historical artifacts and photos, chalkboards, even a few big peacock feathers for good measure. Owner Tim Bozik, a commercial furniture manu-

facturer who moved to the area fifteen years ago, saw a wide-open opportunity to serve a thirsty local clientele who had few local options for craft beer. He utilized old dairy tanks and other hand-built equipment and began winning over the locals, crank by crank. "Old timers would come by and ask me, 'Are you gonna be brewing that dark sh—t?' Yep, I said. And most of those guys are still regulars." Bozik and his daughter, Nicol, are big music fans as well. There's a stage in the corner for live music twice a week; Huey Lewis (of '80s rock band fame) lives nearby, so if you're lucky you'll catch one of his impromptu appearances.

"There's such an eclectic crowd that comes in," says Bozik. "Walk in at any given time and you're bound to see the local pig farmer sitting next to the town judge and maybe a highway patrol guy."

PHILOSOPHY

"We're strictly about quality. I don't want someone coming in here and ordering a porter or IPA and hearing them say, 'You missed it,'" says Bozik. In other words, the brewing ethos is more or less directly to style, with an emphasis on clean, balanced beers. With the "whims," or seasonals, and experiments though, expect to see some more innovative styles like India Black Ale, smoked beers, and other departures. "The whims allow our brewers to try new things, try something that excites them. Sometimes we have guest brewers. And we do the same thing with our kitchen," says Nicol Bozik.

KEY BEER

The juicy 6.2% ABV IPA is the flagship, but look for what's on the seasonal and whim list for a taste of what the brewery can really do. Additionally, the 5.1% ABV porter is especially interesting for its use of smoked malt, which gives it an almost leathery, earthy bite.

BIG SKY BREWING CO.

5417 Trumpeter Way • Missoula, MT 59808 • (406) 549-2777 • bigskybrew.com
Established: 1995

SCENE & STORY

Two good friends who spent all their spare time home brewing and visiting breweries moved to Missoula in 1990 and met a third friend who was working in a ski shop. The trio got serious about beer (when not backcountry skiing) and their by-the-bootstraps creation, Big Sky, has grown so rapidly that today it likely brews more beer in one facility than the rest of Montana's combined. Not bad for "a bunch of yahoos up here having a good time," says cofounder Bjorn Nabozney. To certain Montanans who rue progress, the sudden success and size, can seem off-putting, but it's hard to begrudge their good-natured success. "We've sort of become the Schmidt Brewery of the craft scene with all of our animals," says Nabozney, whose mother designs the cartoonlike label art for the brewery. A visit to the bright, modern taproom is a fun affair, because every visitor is allowed four samples, which are no mere sips. Despite the location in an industrial park, there's often a sizeable crowd on hand. And check out the summer concert series, which brings major acts to Missoula (like Wilco, a couple of years ago) for outdoor performances that are surprisingly intimate.

PHILOSOPHY

Ultimately, Big Sky is in it for the beer. "We don't brew to get medals," says Nobozney. "We brew for ourselves. We brew what we like. Which is very similar to a lot of craft brewers. We don't brew a West Coast–style beer; we don't brew an East Coast–style beer. We're kind of monkeys-in-the-middle with regard to our hops and our malt characters. Our alcohols are pretty manageable; we don't brew a bunch of extreme beers. When I'm having a beer, I want to enjoy my third beer and not feel like I'm overly full or like I can't have another one. After I'm done skiing or getting off the river, I want to be able to have a couple."

That approach has paid off. "We know that because of our size, we're not the local beer anymore, we're more like Montana's beer. We're an apple in a basket of oranges—distinctly different," he says.

KEY BEER

The success of Big Sky has been built largely on the huge sales of Moose Drool, a slightly sweet-tasting 5.3% ABV American Brown Ale made with a tangy touch of Willamette hops from the Pacific Northwest, but the brewery's more ambitious barrel-aged barley wines, Belgian-style saisons, and other limited releases are worth trying, too.

Local Hero

Brennan's Wave: Missoula and the Bitterroot area are famous for whitewater rafting, kayaking, and river boarding. In the taprooms and bars of Missoula, you'll inevitably hear of this man-made whitewater kayaking destination downtown on the Clark Fork River at Caras Park. Local Brennan Guth was a star high school athlete who later discovered whitewater and created a Montana-based kayaking school. He died in a boating accident in Chile in 2001, and a major community effort, including donations from Big Sky Brewing Co., resulted in the construction of this $300,000 play spot in the river (for experienced paddlers only), which has been the site of the U.S. Freestyle Kayaking Championships. It's a meaningful local landmark.

BAYERN BREWING

1507 Montana St. • Missoula, MT
59801-1409 • (406) 721-1482
bayernbrewery.com • Established: 1987

SCENE & STORY

Think: Little Bavaria. Owner and head brewer Jürgen Knöller, who bought the operation from its original owners in 1991, is a born-and-raised Bavarian brewmaster, and he has taken great pains to create the atmosphere of a traditional German bierstube here, with wooden tables, German breweriana, hop garlands, and a barrel on the bar. The space is clean, with a wide bar and plenty of tables and stools inside. There are some traditional snacks available, like German Landjaegers (Bavarian beef jerky), and on Fridays, during the warm months, brats and sauerkraut are served outside. It's popular with firefighters in very dry years, reports Knöller, and there's a strong local contingent of fans as well. And like many German breweries back in the fatherland, Bayern is now working with a recycle/reuse program for their bottles.

PHILOSOPHY

"We're a lot different than the other breweries. For one, it's the good old way of brewing German beer, following the *Reinheitsgebot* [the German Beer Purity Law of 1516]," says Jürgen. Reinheitsgebot, still followed in spirit if not to the letter of the law in southern Germany, means the only ingredients used are malt, hops, yeast, and water, with nothing else in the brew. What's more, he's super dedicated to traditional styles like pilsner and Dopplebock while adhering to extremely tight protocols for making and serving beer, but he's equally as vigorous in the fun department, sponsoring a raucous Oktoberfest and other events.

KEY BEER

Bayern Pilsner, at 5% ABV, is exactly true to style, and has a bready taste with good, ample, noble hop flavor, which is on the spicy side.

KETTLEHOUSE MYRTLE ST.

602 Myrtle St. • Missoula, MT 59801 •
(406) 728-1660, ext. 201 • Established: 2009

KETTLEHOUSE NORTH SIDE

313 N. 1ˢᵗ St. W. • Missoula, MT 59802 •
(406) 728-1660, ext. 222 • Established: 1995

SCENE & STORY

The original location of Kettlehouse, a brew-on-premises facility where cus-

tomers could make their own beer in small batches, has a gritty, backcountry ski hut feel, and newcomers are likely to find the crowd at least two-deep around the bar. It's there you'll find the magnificently named Al Pils—bartender, in-house philosopher, and the bearded inspiration behind a house beer bearing his own name. Pils and his cohorts serve an ultradedicated fan base that sometimes refer to their favorite establishment as the "K-Hole," mingling as they sip on taproom-only offerings like the kookily named (but seriously brewed) Fresh Bongwater Pale Ale, Hemptober Spliff, and Discombobulator Maibock.

The newer north side location, necessitated by the company's steady growth, is a sleeker affair straddling the Orange Street underpass and built in an old train building, with high ceilings, exposed brick walls, and a wooden bar that must be one of the longest in Montana. It's a slightly more serene atmosphere, but not stuffy by any stretch of the imagination.

PHILOSOPHY

Tim O'Leary, Kettlehouse's founder, set out to match the quality of his beer to that of Montana's outdoor bounty. "I guess I don't call myself a brewmaster because I have a degree in physics," says the Helena native. "And I didn't go to formal brewing school, but we've taken recipes that I've created, and those that our staff has created, and refined them. A core principle of ours is to buy local ingredients whenever possible. The barley that we use is grown in Montana, across the divide. The hops come from the Willamette and Yakima valleys, and then we use pure Montana water. I spend most of my thinking, working, and worrying time on the quality of the beer. Montana's like a small town. If I put my name on a beer, I want to be proud of it, because I might see someone on the street, and they have no qualms about coming up to me to say, 'Hey, your beer's great!' or 'Your beer sucks.' If we're not making award-winning beer, I'm not doing my job. You've got to listen to people."

KEY BEER

"Cold smoke" is a skier's term for the sort of snow that forms with low humidity and low-temperature conditions, creating the best powder. It's light, buoyant, and rare outside the Rockies. Kettlehouse's

award-winning beer of the same name isn't overly heavy, nor is it airy and light. It's a Scotch Ale that has fulsome, malty body with a slight smoky character. Spicy accents from East Kent Goldings hops (a British version also grown in the American West) balance it beautifully.

MISSOULA BREWING CO.

200 International Dr. • Missoula, MT, 59808 • (406) 549-8193 • missoulabrewing company.com • Established: 2009

SCENE & STORY

The popular regional brand of Montana was Highlander, brewed from 1910 to 1964, nudged into obscurity by big national brands. In 2009, Bob and Shannon Lukes teamed up to build Missoula Brewing Co. and resurrected it, starting

DETOUR ➡ BIG DIPPER ICE CREAM

631 S. Higgins • Missoula, MT 59801 • (406) 543-5722 • bigdippericecream.com

Big Dipper, a classic old-fashioned ice-cream stand which opened in the back of the original Kettlehouse brewery location in 1995, has become a staple in Missoula and achieved fame far beyond thanks to its retro feel and occasional ice creams made with (nonalcoholic) beer ingredients from Montana breweries like Kettlehouse, Angry Hank's, and Big Sky. Today, the company has a new location in Billings as well as Helena's Last Chance Gulch downtown, and a truck ("Coneboy") that's parked in Missoula.

with a contract brew and later building out a 17,000-square-foot showpiece brewery. This is a huge facility with a lot of polished cement floors, salvaged barnwood, a glassed-in modern brewhouse, and a 1947 Chevy overlooking the taproom. Breweriana from Highlander is all over the taproom. Fill up on artisan pizzas, grab a beer, and head out to the huge beer garden overlooking Grant Creek.

PHILOSOPHY

They make 'em like they used to, only better.

KEY BEER

Highlander is the "brand," i.e., logo, of Missoula Brewing Co., and the individual beers are named for local peaks like Mount Jumbo, Devil's Hump, and Lost Peak. For now, the list looks Montana-malt forward.

GLACIER BREWING CO.

6 10th Ave. E. • Polson, MT 59860-3219
(406) 883-2595 • glacierbrewing.com
Established: 2003

SCENE & STORY

Located on the southern end of Flathead Lake (at 192 square miles the largest freshwater lake in the United States), Polson (population: 4,000) is part of the Flathead Indian Reservation. It's also home to the nation's largest fiddle compe-tition, and in the summertime the town becomes a major tourist thoroughfare. From the ground up, Glacier Brewing Company has a wonderful Old West feel, with swinging saloon doors and a historic brewery sign over the entrance (which came out of Montana's first brewery, the H.S. Gilbert Brewery in Virginia City), antique brewing posters, and wooden truss rafters. The owners expanded the taproom a few years ago, and today there's a small wooden stage in the beer garden outside for all those fiddlers.

PHILOSOPHY

Unfussy and stylistically simple, hitting several major beer styles from kölsch and pilsner to altbier and stout, with friendly, smiling service.

KEY BEER

Cherries grow in the area, but the very popular, very sweet Flathead Cherry Ale is made with a grenadine-like cherry additive, which seasoned craft beer aficionados might have difficulty enjoying, hoping for a balancing tartness. Also try the Slurry Bomber Stout, at 5.5% ABV, a dry roasty sipper, and the Glacier Select Oktoberfest (6.7% ABV), a dark amber with some spicy hop character that is, despite the seasonal-sounding name, one of the company's most popular year-round beers.

TAMARACK ALEHOUSE & GRILL

105 Blacktail Rd., Ste. 1 • Lakeside, MT 59922 • (406) 844-0244
tamarackbrewing.com • Established: 2006

SCENE & STORY

Heading along the west side of Flathead Lake, it's a short drive onto Lakeside, with the turn for "the Rack," as locals call it, at the beginning of town. In the winter, this is a popular spot for skiers at nearby Blacktail Mountain Resort. The attractively modern two-level facility is situated on the side of Stoner Creek, and out back there's a shady patio that beckons in the summer months.

There's an open viewing area from the second floor looking into the brewhouse and the lack of a barrier between the brewery tanks and the bar area itself (a feature borrowed from Four Peaks Brewery in Tempe, Arizona, where Northern California-raised co-owner/operator Craig Koontz met his founding business partner). With the beautiful copper-clad kettles and seven shiny fermenters, there's a cheery confidence about the place and a hum of activity even on weekday afternoons. One of the best features is a wood-burning indoor-outdoor fireplace with seating on each side—on the patio and inside the restaurant.

And while the Alehouse & Grill area is technically a separate business from the brewery, it's really only on paper that the two are distinct from each other. "You can hear it, and you can smell it," says Koontz proudly of the open-plan design. The food menu is extensive, from burgers to pizzas made with handmade beer dough and even a few Southwest items. Several beer dinners per year stretch the kitchen's repertoire with local Willow Spring Ranch lamb shanks, seasonal vegetable tortes, and cured meats. In 2011 Tamarack opened a second taproom location in Missoula.

PHILOSOPHY

Koontz is an eager experimenter with his ten-barrel facility, with recent forays into making pilsner with Sorachi Ace hops (developed in Japan), which have a distinctive lemongrass quality. But most of the beers are true to style. "There's stuff that sells for a reason," he says. With that in mind, the ten standards hew to familiar styles such as amber, wit, hefeweizen, and stout.

KEY BEER

Yard Sale Ale. "We describe it as a robust amber ale," says Koontz of his 5.6% ABV top seller. "It's bordering on a brown if you look at it in the glass, which separates it from the Fat Tires and Alaskan Ambers out there on the shelf," he says. "It's got heavy amounts of chocolate malt and a little roastiness to it, as well." Ask if Old Stache is available; it's a super limited-quantity porter aged in bourbon barrels.

THE GREAT NORTHERN BREWING CO. & BLACK STAR DRAUGHT HOUSE

2 Central Ave. E. • Whitefish, MT 59937
(406) 863-1000 • greatnorthernbrewing.com
Established: 1994

SCENE & STORY

The mostly automated, 8,000-barrel-capacity brewery itself is unmista.k.a.ble; for one, it's the tallest building in town (three levels), and for another, it's more or less completely made of glass, which shows off a gravity-flow brewing setup (using few pumps) unlike any other in the state. It's a striking contrast to the less lofty wood clapboard buildings around it, and it means the brewers have the best view. A tour up and down the winding circular stairs is recommended, building a thirst for refreshment.

PHILOSOPHY

Solid, malt-forward, cleanly made brews. Founder Minott Wessinger, the great-great-grandson of Henry Weinhard—whose own Blitz-Weinhard Brewery was a Portland institution from 1856 until it closed for good in 1999—built Great Northern Brewing in 1994 as a vehicle for Black Star Golden Lager, with a hoppy lager recipe akin to the great

Weinhard's Private Reserve, which had made his family's fortune. It's a hop-accented golden lager designed to appeal to discerning drinkers in both the macro and craft segments.

KEY BEER

"Black Star Golden Lager built this brewery," says General Manager Marcus Duffey, by way of explaining why they brought the 4.6% ABV brew back after a seven-year hiatus (see the "Detour" below for more on founder Minott Wessinger and his inventions). It's a slightly sweet, malty golden lager with some discernible, grassy hop character, good for a session down at the bar, but nothing particularly astounding.

THE GREAT NORTHERN BAR & GRILL

27 Central Ave. • Whitefish, MT 59937
(406) 862-2816 • greatnorthernbar.com
Established: 1919

SCENE & STORY

Right across the street from the Great Northern brewery, this is the kind of place that every town needs but too often lacks: a classic establishment with a beat-up old bar, cool signage from days and businesses gone by, a patio, a full menu, and a stage. It's got a roadhouse feel, with pool tables, shuffleboard, and ping-pong, and the atmosphere of a glorious dive without too much of the grime. And because it's the social center of town in Whitefish, it's typically filled to the brim with Whitefish citizens and tourists young and old. The locals are appropriately proud of the day The Boss—Bruce Springsteen—jumped on stage with the band to play "Mustang Sally" . . . way back in August, 1996 (some legends never die).

PHILOSOPHY

Officially? "If we ain't got it, you don't need it."

KEY BEER

Of the tap brews, most are local to Montana, or at least the Pacific Northwest, so ask what's freshest and take your pick. Kettlehouse's Double Haul IPA is a mainstay, as is Big Sky's Moose Drool.

A BEER WITH
MINOTT WESSINGER & FAMILY

Whitefish, Montana—like Aspen, Taos, and Sisters, Oregon—is an ultrapictur-esque western town that lures hordes of affluent, influential types to soak up the vibes and spread their empires. Minott Wessinger is one of those sorts himself. There are several very well-made beers in his lineup, and, taking cues from the Empire Builder train line that serves Whitefish, there is some dynasty-building going on that might come as a surprise to lovers of craft beer.

Wessinger had struck gold developing St. Ides (a "malt liquor") under a contract arrangement with another brewery in the late 1980s, and rap artists such as Snoop Dogg, Tupac Shakur, and Biggie Smalls expounded on its qualities in their music. In 2001, Wessinger decided to capitalize on this success, sell Great Northern Brewing Company, and cease brewing Black Star Lager in order to pursue other projects, notably a youthfully marketed alcoholic soda pop called Sparks (which caused much consternation among watchdog and parent groups). After launching it in 2002, Wessinger later sold Sparks to Miller in 1996 for a reported $220 million. Perhaps sensing his legacy and lineage—and sensing new opportunity in craft beer—Wessinger returned as a partner to Great Northern and helped relaunch Black Star Golden Lager in February 2010. Who knew craft beer and gangsta rap were bedfellows in Whitefish, Montana?

BEST *of the* REST: MONTANA

WORDEN'S MARKET

451 N. Higgins Ave. • Missoula, MT 59802-4522 • (406) 549-1293 • wordens.com

Missoula's very first grocery store, now in its fifth location, originally opened in 1883 and has played a key role in the development of Montana's beer scene. For starters, it has long stocked a good selection of kegs, stoking many a local party, but more important, its owners have introduced locals to hundreds—perhaps thousands—of imports and American craft beers, lovingly curated by the talkative and knowledgeable Mark Thomsen. Popular with locals of every stripe, it's a friendly, bustling place. In October 2009 another of Montana's backward beer laws was amended, finally allowing the sale of beer up to 14% ABV, a threshold that is common with many of the most sought-after styles of Belgian and English beers.

LOLO PEAK BREWING CO.

6201 Brewery Way • Lolo, MT 59847 • (406) 493-6231 • lolopeakbrewery.com

There's a wildlife spotting scope on the deck railing of the original location of this popular brewery opened in 2014, which tells you something about everyone involved, from the owners to the locals and the animals of the area. Live music is a staple here, and the brewery has been so successful that in 2015 it announced plans to expand into a second location in Missoula's Old Sawmill District. Try the toffee-ish, roasty Old Toby Porter (5.6% ABV).

FLATHEAD LAKE BREWING CO.

116 Holt Dr. • Bigfork, MT 59911 • (406) 837-2004 • flatheadlakebrewing.com

One of Montana's most beloved breweries is Flathead Lake because of—you guessed it—its awesome location overlooking the largest freshwater lake West of the Mississippi—even bigger than Lake Tahoe. The brewery has done so well that they've added a production brewery in Bigfork and a new taproom in Missoula. But it's the original lakeside taproom you want to hit, for sixteen taps, good food . . . and that view.

KALISPELL BREWING CO.

412 Main St. • Kalispell, MT 59901 • (406) 756-2739 • kalispellbrewing.com

Opened in 2014 in the Flathead Valley—home to Glacier National Park, Flathead Lake, and the Bob Marshall Wilderness Complex, for starters—Kalispell Brewing Co. was founded in a cool old brick building on Kalispell's main drag by husband and wife Cole Schneider and Maggie Doherty ("English majors, telemark ski racers, and home brewers") with a 10bbl system. Try the Two Ski Brewski Pils, and venture out from there.

the SOUTHWEST and TEXAS

WITH ITS PIÑON-DOTTED HIGHLANDS, SUN-BAKED MESAS, AND LABYRINTHINE CANYON lands, the American Southwest is mesmerizing from 30,000 feet, the distance from which most travelers view it as they whiz by from L.A. or S.F. to the East Coast or back again. But the best way for a beer lover to experience its incredible bounty is to spend some time on the ground in the cities and small towns. The soulless casinos, strip malls, and tacky strip joints are just side effects, like jet lag, because a vanguard of hard-working beer lovers has propelled the Southwest's craft beer scene from tumbleweed to tornado, from Austin to Albuquerque, Reno, and even Sin City—Las Vegas. It used to be the kind of place where beer meant only a frosty can of Tecate with lime, the follow-up to a good tequila (which, to be honest, is still not a bad way to go). But beyond the old standbys there's now a new wealth of great American craft beer breweries and internationally savvy beer bars springing up like Christmas cactus flowers in a dried-up arroyo, even along the iconic Route 66 amid the old adobe of New Mexico. In the end, there's nothing better than a brewery-fresh beer and a high desert sunset, but roadside tacos and Texas barbecue aren't far behind. Time to hit the road. Just don't forget the sunscreen.

ARIZONA

ARIZONA WILDERNESS BREWING COMPANY

721 N. Arizona Ave., No. 103 • Gilbert, AZ
85233 • (480) 284-9863
azwbeer.com • Established: 2012

SCENE & STORY

Located in a banal strip mall twenty-one miles southeast of the center of sun-baked Phoenix, Arizona Wilderness is the unlikely creation of bearded founder (and former window washer) Jonathan Buford, which sprang forth out of his home's little garage brewery with a sense of dreamy yet indomitable mission. On the brink of personal bankruptcy, he became inspired while watching the short-lived *Brew Masters* show on the Discovery Channel about Dogfish Head founder Sam Calagione's wild travels, beery inventions, and financial success. What he and his team would succeed in doing in a short time is nothing short of amazing. Home brewing became an obsession; the beers kept getting better and better. Friends and family encouraged him to go pro, and working with a couple of partners, he went for it.

The reception by locals (and beer geeks who got to taste the early beers at prestigious off-site tastings) was, fair to say, rapturous. Working in tight quarters, Buford and Co. took to embarking on mountain hikes to dream up recipes, over 100 in a year. Word-of-mouth was growing like thunderheads behind a mountain range. When RateBeer, one of the two largest websites in the world on craft beer, named AWBC the World's Best New Brewery in 2014, the beautiful deluge began. Lines at beerfests, chatter online, a profile in *Esquire*, and high-profile collaborations with the likes of Danish gypsy brewer Mikkeller followed. Now there's talk of another location in the summer of 2016. The brewpub menu is impressive, with an emphasis on cheff-ed up (but not pretentious) southwestern fare (pork, especially) laced with piquant chile and spices.

PHILOSOPHY

This is new school brewing at its finest, informed by Buford's deep-seated love of the woods and wild places. Think: extensive use of wild yeast, foraged ingredients, heritage grain projects, and other interesting forays into the hinterlands of beer making.

KEY BEER

Refuge IPA has been a huge hit for AWBC, but it's the unusual foraged-ingredient beers that are truly setting Buford and his team apart, like a recent project even Michael Pollan—best-selling author of *The Omnivore's Dilemma*—noticed, using white Sonoran wheat berries (a tangy, heirloom grain said to be the oldest in North America) and wild juniper berries.

Tempe

FOUR PEAKS BREWING CO.

1340 E. 8th St., No. 104 • Tempe, AZ 85281
(480) 303-9967 • fourpeaks.com
Established: 1997

SCENE & STORY

Just east of ASU's campus, Four Peaks Brewing Company (and a good percentage of ASU students on weekend nights) calls a huge 1892 Mission Revival–style barn home. Formerly housing a series of creamery businesses, it's got weathered brick walls and high wood ceilings with a thirty-five-foot-high glass clerestory, the rafters festooned with banners for the Minnesota Vikings and ASU Sun Dev-

ils. There's three other locations now: the Grill & Tap in Scottsdale, a brewery and tasting room in Tempe, and an airport bar in the Sky Harbor International Airport in Phoenix.

PHILOSOPHY

The All-American brewpub. Nothing wrong with that: expect eight tasty beers of a fairly standard lineup (kölsch to stout), plus occasional seasonals and cask-conditioned beers, and the full complement of brewpub fare.

KEY BEER

If it's 110 degrees Fahrenheit in the shade, go for the hazy, clovey 5.5% ABV hefeweizen; any cooler, go for the Kilt Lifter, a 6% ABV Scotch ale with rich malt and smoky notes. Extra points for locating the Elvis shrine.

BEST *of the* REST: ARIZONA

FATE BREWING CO.

7337 E. Shea Blvd., Ste. 105 • Scottsdale, AZ 85260 • (480) 994-1275 • fatebrewing.com

Opened in 2012 by Steve McFate (and not to be confused with Boulder, CO's, brew-pub of the same name, also opened in 2012), Fate of Arizona has become the focal point of Scottsdale beer culture in short order, adding an 11,000-square-foot second location, brewery, and barrel cellar in 2015. The mission of both: great small-batch beer and wood-fired pizza. Try the Single Hop Sour (4.6% ABV) if they have it on; otherwise, the Candy Bar milk stout brewed with honey roasted peanuts, cacao nibs, vanilla bean, and sea salt.

PAPAGO BREWING (BEER BAR & BOTTLE SHOP)

7107 E. McDowell Rd. • Scottsdale, AZ 85257 • (480) 425-7439 • papagobrewing.com

Hidden among the car dealerships and dusty palm trees of Scottsdale Avenue, inside a faux-adobe mini mall, is a beer lover's dream, a solid brewpub that also stocks a massive tap row and more than 500 varieties of beer in bottles carefully arranged in coolers. The servers are trained to know their stuff on beer, which helps when the selection is this vast. You're going here to drink Orange Blossom Mandarin Wheat Ale. But also give the 2005 bronze medal winner at the GABF in the nebulous "other strong ale or lager" category, the 8% ABV Papago El Robusto Porter a try.

TOPS LIQUORS & TASTE OF TOPS

403 W. University Dr. • Tempe, AZ 85281 • (480) 967-2520 • topsliquors.com

What's better than a bottle shop with 1,000 selections comprising every foreign and domestic style and region imaginable? A bottle shop with a beer bar attached, drawing from its riches, that's what. The wood-paneled Taste of Tops bar has twelve rotating taps, over 100 different bottled beers chilled in 750-milliliter, twenty-two-ounce, and twelve-ounce sizes, and a few small booths and two couches. There's a limited food menu, but the owners don't mind if you get takeout from next door.

NEVADA

NEVADA, LAND OF LADY LUCK AND THE LONG DOUBLE-YELLOW LINE, DEADLY DRY DESERTS AND the lights of Las Vegas, has a beer industry going back to 1860, but a bit less going on compared to other western U.S. states. It's no surprise that the active Tahoe region, and Reno, with its abundance of affordable industrial buildings, would, like Albuquerque or, say, Billings, Montana, become a hub for craft breweries. There are about three dozen in the state now, mostly brewpubs concentrated in Reno and Las Vegas. There's been a fair amount of change as the industry rolls into motion, and, with a few home brewing shops open, a genuine beer culture is taking root.

BRASSERIE ST. JAMES

901 Center St. • Reno, NV 89501
(775) 348-8888 • brasseriesaintjames.com
Established: 2012

SCENE & STORY

After just two years in business, Brasserie St. James has gained major national notice for its line of Belgium-inspired saisons, sour beers, and other whimsies. Built in the historic Crystal Springs ice and water building in Reno's slightly down-at-the-heels midtown, the building has all the classic-looking lines of a brewery in Europe. No matter: named best midsize brewpub in the country at the 2014 GABF, things are going fabulously well there, and among the new ventures planned are a music venue and bar nearby, a distillery, and a second location in the Mission area of San Francisco, serving housemade sausage, burgers, traditional cassoulet, and moules frites. Not a bad first few years.

PHILOSOPHY

In the tradition of a classic French estaminet, or café that sells good things to drink, Brasserie St. James is harnessing an Old World feel, but with modern sensibilities (and brewing methods). All the beers I tasted in 2014 and 2015 during GABF were excellent, some world-class.

KEY BEER

Daily Wages, a classic saison with three yeasts including *Brettanomyces* (wild yeast), or "brett," is what you hope for when you think "saison": at once barnyardy, grassy, wheaty, herbal, and refreshing.

NEW MEXICO

Albuquerque

MARBLE BREWERY

111 Marble Ave. NW • Albuquerque, NM
87102 • (505) 243-2739
marblebrewery.com • Established: 2008

SCENE & STORY

A hoppy oasis in a dusty warehouse area of Albuquerque not far from the main drag of Lomas Boulevard, Marble has become one of the most watched breweries in the West. The original brewpub has hardwood floors, deep red walls, a forty-inch-wide bar, and a spacious, umbrella-equipped seating area outside, with terrific food carts. "It's a great scene," says founder Ted Rice. "We get blue-collar guys coming in from the machine shops that are right around the corner. But then we're also right next to the courthouse facility, so we'll get lawyers coming in, too. And we get the local beer nerds—all walks of life, all comingling and just gathering around a great local flavor." This is a short drive from the airport, so it would make a great first or last stop in the Land of Enchantment.

In the summer of 2015, Rice and Co. broke ground on a $1.5 million expansion that will more than double its beer-making capacity and add a rooftop deck, plus another taproom across town, moves which follow a 2014 Small Brewery of the Year award at the GABF and the addition of a second taproom on the west side of town in 2012. Between 2011 and 2014, Marble won no less than nine medals at GABF, which is testament to all the hard work Rice and head brewer Josh Trujillo have been doing.

PHILOSPHY

Rice and Co. have helped New Mexico embrace the tang and bite of beers. "We want the malt character and the residual sweetness to be low, to allow layers of hop flavors to shine through," Rice says. "So, when you have those layers of hop flavors and that low residual sweetness, the malt base is dry, and you have drinkability." The water in Albuquerque is fairly alkaline and fluctuates depending on whether the city is drawing from surface or well sources; turning a potential liability into a strength, Marble runs brewing water through a reverse osmosis filter and then adds back in necessary minerals, allowing them to mimic classic brewing styles.

KEY BEER

Marble Red is a chewy, 6.2% ABV sipper with ample caramel malt body enfolded by juicy Cascade, Crystal, and Simcoe hops, and the pilsner is simply outstanding.

Santa Fe

SANTA FE BREWING CO.

35 Fire Pl. • Santa Fe, NM 87508
(505) 424-3333 • santafebrewing.com
Established: 1988

SCENE & STORY

The road leading to New Mexico's oldest brewing company was known as a section of Route 66 as it passed through town during the 1920s and '30s. Today it's known as Route 14, a.k.a. Cerrillos Boulevard, and the Turquoise Trail National Scenic Byway. Time your visit (it's about a fifteen-minute drive from the city center) for sunset, because the taproom and its outdoor tables have ideal west-facing views overlooking the vast, high-desert plateau Bandelier National Monument. The original brewery taproom is cozy, quiet, and congenial, with stools and high ceilings. Free guided brewery tours are offered on Saturdays at 12 p.m., and there are ten house beers on tap plus one guest tap and growler sales. Once an almost unknown brand outside of Santa Fe, the addition

of new tanks and a bottling line and canning capability for the IPA and Oktoberfest brands have revved up this company (and it didn't hurt when the owners put the 6.6% ABV IPA in a can prominently featuring the New Mexico state flag's red, stylized sunbeam "Zia" against a bright yellow field). Recently, the beers have gone from banal to barnstorming, incorporating barrel aging, wild yeasts, and other tricky techniques, and they've opened a second Santa Fe taproom as well as an innovative tasting bar in Albuquerque, right off of I-40 and Carlisle, created entirely from recycled shipping containers, with twenty-seven taps in addition to hard cider, and wines.

KEY BEER

The Imperial Java Stout (8% ABV) is a very good, massive brew of American and British hops, heavily roasted malts, and locally roasted, organic East Timor and New Guinea coffee beans. Last time I visited, brewer Ty Levis's Zotte Berten series was also showcasing the brewery's sour and experimental side, such as #5, a tart brew resembling the Belgian style of geuze, made from blends of aged and young lambic, or spontaneously fermented beer.

SECOND STREET BREWERY

1814 Second St. • Santa Fe, NM 87505
(505) 982-3030 • secondstreetbrewery.com
Established: 1996

SECOND STREET BREWERY AT THE RAILYARD

1607 Paseo De Peralta, No. 10 • Santa Fe, NM
87501 • (505) 989-3278
Established: 2010

SCENE & STORY

Caught unawares amid the hordes of tourists, it can be easy to want to run for the hills. While 9,000-foot Atalaya Mountain just behind town makes a very good day hike, there is no brewery on the summit at present, so instead, hang with the laid-back locals who make Second Street a kind of second home. The original is housed in a warehouse structure next to some old train tracks with outdoor seating, and the décor might be described as 1980s meets 1880s: sponged sienna paint, wagon wheels for chandeliers, and arty photos on the wall. There's a more updated location, too, at the Railyard near downtown, home of Santa Fe's farmers' market (which supplies the restaurant in season) and the REI store, should you still need gear for that hiking escape. The patio is a nice spot for al fresco beers when the temperature's right. Both locations have full menus; try something with green chile, like the juicy burger.

PHILOSOPHY

Strength in numbers. Brewer Rod Tweet has a huge repertoire, with about fifty different beers so far, though results are still a bit uneven.

KEY BEER

Start with a crisp kölsch (4.6% ABV), which will put out the fire if the green chile takes you for a ride.

THE COWGIRL HALL OF FAME

319 S. Guadalupe St. • Santa Fe, NM
87501-2613 • (505) 982-2565
cowgirlsantafe.com • Established: 1993

SCENE & STORY

Known simply as "the Cowgirl," this great bar is filled with creaky old wood floors, an incredible array of western bric-a-brac, cowgirl photos, and the aromas of mesquite barbecue. Santa Fe's most popular watering hole, with nightly live music and entertainment, a huge billiard parlor, private party rooms, and breezy brick patio, it's also one of the West's perfect places to drink a good beer on a hot afternoon. Based on a southwestern barbecue restaurant opened in New York City under the watchful eye of the late Margaret Formby, the founder of the National Cowgirl Hall of Fame and Western Heritage Museum in Hereford, Texas, the Cowgirl Hall of Fame of Santa Fe is located in a 100-year-old building in Santa Fe's historic Guadalupe district. Try for the Bob Dylan Brunch starting Sundays at noon.

PHILOSOPHY

Beer, bluegrass, and barbecue, Annie Oakley-style.

KEY BEER

This isn't exactly a craft beer bar, but you won't go thirsty. Santa Fe Brewing Company's 6.4% ABV State Pen Porter is so good, so nutty, and so chocolate-like, you'll have to be careful not to drink too much of it, or end up in the clink yourself.

Embudo

BLUE HERON BREWING COMPANY

2214 Hwy. 68 • Embudo, NM 87531
(505) 579-9188 • blueheronbrews.com
Established: 2010

SCENE & STORY

Housed in a tiny adobe overlooking the Rio Grande along the road up to Taos (the main road, not the "High Road to Taos"), this adorable little brewery was founded by dedicated home brewers in a building formerly used as a gas station, vet clinic, and art gallery. It's a teeny affair, with colorful framed art, track lighting, a lit

DETOUR → HEAVEN'S DRIVE-THRU EL PARASÓL

1833 Cerillos Rd. • Santa Fe, NM 87505 • (505) 995-8015 • elparasol.com

Founded in 1958 in nearby Española by the Atencio family, there are now seven locations in this miraculously talented family's mini chain. Santa Fe's oldest (of two) is an unassuming little cinder block drive-through on Cerrillos Boulevard; you may also walk in to order, which can be quicker when the cars are backed up or you've called ahead. The tender pork and beef tacos are sublime, but there's simply no way to adequately describe how good the burrito with roasted white meat chicken and guacamole with green chile tastes. Don't miss a taste of this New Mexico road food paradise.

tle three-tap bar for the three beers on at any given time (brewed in a back room on a 100-gallon system), and at least three little kids with brewing in their futures. Parent-owners Kristin Hennelly and her husband, Scott, a biochemist, use locally grown hops. They also recently added a taproom and eatery in nearby Española.

PHILOSOPHY

This is community brewing with a sense of history—and humor. Scott Hennelly characterizes the clientele and the mission with a wink. "It's an art community, it's an old Hispanic community, it's a kind of a hippie community, and it's kind of a hipsters-escaping-the-world community. There's writers and artists from a couple of generations here. Kristin's parents have a winery—one of the earliest in New Mexico. It's probably one of the main reasons we're doing this, because they want to corner the local market in sin."

KEY BEER

Embudo Gold, using Perle and locally grown Cascade hops.

Taos

ESKE'S BREW PUB & EATERY

106 Des Georges Ln. • Taos, NM 87571
(575) 758-1517 • eskesbrewpub.com
Established: 1992

SCENE & STORY

New Mexico's oldest brewpub is still one of the oddest and most fun to visit. Founded in funky Taos by ski patroller Steve "Eske" Eskeback in a little old adobe house a short walk from the plaza, it's just a few booths and tables and a small outdoor patio served by a nano-size brewhouse down some stairs next door. But there's something very comforting about the whole lack of pretense here. The food is good, homey, and cheap (try the green chile stew), and the best way to see what's been brewing is to order up a sampler and chat with the servers.

PHILOSOPHY

Eske is a local character who has seen the entire history of New Mexico's craft brewing industry unfold through recessions, booms, and waves upon waves of tourists. "I set out to capture what I thought would be a European-style brewpub or English brewpub, because I hated American bars," Eske says. "Dark and dingy and sometimes weird. We wanted a place where we could have friends and family over and have a good time. We still don't filter, we don't pasteurize, and with good healthy food, not too much frying going on, all ingredients are fresh, especially during summer from local markets. We have hula-hoops for kids outside, a sandbox, ping-pong tables, and board games. Anybody can come in and you don't have to drink."

KEY BEER

A long-lost narrow-gauge railroad in the area was called the "Chili Line," running from Antonito, Colorado to Santa Fe, with a branch near Taos. Eske's homage to the local favorite tradition is Eske's Taos Green Chili Beer (4% ABV, a bronze medal winner at the 1993 GABF), made with whole roasted Sandia Hatch green chile added just after the yeast is pitched.

DETOUR → RIDE ON THE WILD SIDE: THE SOUTH BOUNDARY TRAIL

Gearing Up Bicycle Shop • 129 Paseo del Pueblo Sur • Taos, NM 87571
(575) 751-0365 • gearingupbikes.com

Taos is world famous for mountain biking trails, none more vaunted than the South Boundary Trail, twenty-two miles of serpentine roller coaster bounding through steep glades of aspen, lush evergreen forest, and leafy meadows with widescreen views of soaring peaks and plunging valleys. Late September is prime season, just as the aspens reach their Technicolor best. To rent quality gear, hire a guide, or join a group, visit Gearing Up, right down the alley from Eske's. For $105, you can secure a seven-passenger van shuttle to and from the trailhead departing at 7 a.m. If you don't have a big group, call ahead to be added to a waiting list for your desired day, which ought be capped off with beers—where else?—on the patio at Eske's.

BEST *of the* REST: NEW MEXICO

CHAMA RIVER BREWING CO.

106 2nd St. SW • Albuquerque, NM 87103 • (505) 842-8329 • chamariverbrewery.com

These guys earned a gold in 2014's GABF in a supercompetive category, Bohemi-an-style pilsner, for Class VI Golden Lager, a 5.5% ABV sipper spiced liberally with noble Saaz hops. Taste it in the upscale brewpub with an ambitious steak house menu (petite sirloin; pan roasted striped bass) and even more ambitious young brewers.

LA CUMBRE BREWING COMPANY

3313 Girard Blvd. NE • Albuquerque, NM 87107 • (505) 872-0225 • lacumbrebrewing.com

Based in an industrial park, this is a local institution, with a cozy taproom and a patio with food trucks outside. In 2015, a new, custom 30bbl system was coming online. For fans (and the makers of) the much-loved "Project Dank," a 7.5% ABV IPA bursting with Chinook, Simcoe, Mosaic, Citra, Sorachi Ace, Meridian, and other exotic vari-eties of hops, it's good news indeed.

BOSQUE BREWING COMPANY

8900 San Mateo Blvd. NE • Albuquerque, NM 87113 • (505) 433-3889 • bosquebrewing.com

This young crew of former home brewers launched this brewery in 2010. By 2014, they were toasting a GABF gold in 2015 for the Acequia Wet Hop IPA. Their beers are on tap all over town, and there are already three locations—two in Albuquerque and one in Lac Cruces—to drink from the source amid salvaged-wood and hop-col-ored walls.

TEXAS

THANKS IN LARGE PART TO WAVES OF GERMAN IMMIGRANTS WHO MADE TEXAS HOME, THE Lone Star State has long been synonymous with beer, especially a couple of inexpensive, mass-produced lagers, Shiner Bock (from San Antonio's Gambrinus Corporation) and Pabst's Lone Star. No disrespect to those ubiquitous brews, but there's much, much more to discover in the new world of Texas craft breweries and beer bars today, especially in Austin, which has embraced pathbreaking brewing styles with the force of a Texas twister. These bold, natural beers go especially well with Texas Hill Country cuisine and languid afternoons with friends and great music.

Austin & Hill Country

JESTER KING CRAFT BREWERY

13005 Fitzhugh Rd., Bld. B • Austin, TX 78736 • (512) 537-5100
jesterkingbrewery.com • Established: 2010

SCENE & STORY

Few breweries have to remind visitors to leave pets at home so as not to spook the livestock. Located fifteen miles outside of town on a ranch in the beautiful Texas Hill Country, Jester King is a first for the American South: an ambitious farm house brewery working primarily in the rarified world of oak-barrel aging and second fermentations in the bottle. With a massive 8,000-square-foot barn next to the new stone-walled brewery, the owners opened for business with a rapid-fire release of highly rated beers including a collaboration with Dane Mikkel Borg Bjergsø of Mikkeller, the acclaimed globe-trotting brewer.

What happened in this brewery's first few years is remarkable. Much of the brewhouse was hand-built or modified—even the boiler—thanks to one of the founders learning how to weld. The brewing shed was uninsulated, causing havoc in the brewing process. The first beer released was a conservative-sounding English mild ale. But by calling it, punkishly, "Commercial Suicide," Jester King seemed to capture the hearts of all of Austin's beer drinking public in one fell swoop. Soon came the pizza place next door (Stanley's Farmhouse Pizza), the cornhole games, and a growing sense that something truly special was coming to life.

While some early beers like Commercial Suicide relied on dried, lab grown English ale yeast at first, the Jester King crew has now moved almost exclusively into wild-yeast territory, harnessing the unique microflora of the area in a line of superdistinctive beers. Under the watchful eyes of brothers Jeffrey and Michael Stuffings, and longtime beer industry maven Ron Extract (plus a talented team of brewers, blenders, and staff, and various do-gooders helping out), Jester King has, in just a few short years, vaulted into the upmost ranks of breweries worldwide, among those that focus on wild and sour ales. On weekends, crowds of hundreds, even thousands show up at the brewery (so plan ahead). What's more, the owners have been tireless in working for legal reforms to Texas's antiquated beer laws, and seem to be perpetually "on tour" at beer tasting events around the globe.

Lately collaborations have been a major focus, with the brewery team heading to Europe, as well as crisscrossing the United States to work with breweries like Sante Adairius, and Florida's Green Bench and St. Somewhere breweries. The beer is great, the labels are superb, the setting is incredibly unique, and the staff is a garrulous, dedicated bunch. Do I seem biased? I am. The current brewing team visited me in the early months of 2016 to brew a collaboration of our own.

In early 2016, Jester King announced it had acquired a major parcel of land adjacent to the brewery, which will be farmed for fruits and herbs used in the brewing process and save the land from development.

PHILOSOPHY

Belgium comes to Hill Country. By Texas standards these are wild, experimental beers, but the Belgian and French traditions at work here are time-tested. The founders also espouse deep philosophical underpinnings of conservation, pledging to use organic and local raw materials at every turn, even rainwater in the brewing kettles.

KEY BEER

Boxer's Revenge Farmhouse Provision Ale (9% ABV) is a dry, Champagne-like farmhouse ale dry-hopped with spicy Hallertau and floral Cascade and Centennial hops. The beer is refermented in French oak wine barrels with wild yeast for up to a year. And if you can find a bottle of Atrial Rubicite, a raspberry-infused wild ale aged in oak, grab it before one of the rabid beer collectors can.

THE GINGER MAN

301 Lavaca St. • Austin, TX 78701
(512) 473-8801 • aus.gingermanpub.com
Established: 1994

SCENE & STORY

This large, dimly lit bar consists of a long stone bar, couches, dark wood paneling and tables, a tasteful collection of beer trays on the walls, and a busy outdoor seating and stage area, well retaining the charm that made the original (close by and now called the Ghost Bar) one of Austin's most beloved spots. There are eighty taps and more than 100 bottles to choose from, with a strong selection of American craft beers and choice international marks.

PHILOSOPHY

Founder Bob Precious took his inspiration for the Ginger Man family of bars from J. P. Donleavy's novel of the same name, in which the character of Sebastian Dangerfield is a young American abroad at Trinity College. But thankfully, the maudlin shtick doesn't get the better of this loose-knit family of bars. Of the original Ginger Man, in Houston, Michael Jackson memorably wrote, "it is a true pub, where it is possible to indulge in conversation without having dubious entertainments or food pressed upon one. Despite its name, it has no oppressive theme, either as a literary bar or as an Irish tavern."

KEY BEER

Look for local taps from surging Texas breweries like Dallas's Community, Lakewood, St. Arnold, Karbach, and Real Ale.

DRAUGHT HOUSE PUB & BREWERY

4112 Medical Pkwy., No. 100
Austin, TX 78756 • (512) 452-6258
draughthouse.com • Established: 1968

SCENE & STORY

Austin's most famous beer destination, the Draught House is an old Anglo-German-style bar with a Tudor half-timber exterior. Inside is a softly-lit, exposed-beamed space furnished with rough-hewn wood tables and straight-backed wood chairs, and a bar with seventy taps, eighteen bottles, and a few casks on at a time, along with pub grub like made-to-order pizza, nachos, and calzones. Outside, there's a massive beer garden that often fills with a chilled-out crowd.

PHILOSOPHY

Funky Old World meets Craft Beer Nation, U.S.A. Instead of lining up along the bar, locals know to form a single-file line, as if purchasing train tickets, but they're quite happy in the process. You will be, too.

KEY BEER

There are always several inventive house beers on like a recent stout, Funkhouser, aged with the famed Drie Fonteinen brett strain for eight months.

BEST *of the* REST: TEXAS

REAL ALE BREWING COMPANY

231 San Saba Ct. • Blanco, TX 78606 • (830) 833-2534 • realalebrewing.com

Founded in 1996 out in quiet, quaint Blanco in the Texas Hill Country an hour or so from Austin, Real Ale is one of the state's biggest craft beer success stories despite humble beginnings. Working on a ramshackle setup in the basement of an antique store (with offices in an airstream and storage in shipping containers), Real Ale came up with great brews like Brewhouse Brown, and shunned filtration and pasteurization all the way to a vast (and still growing) market.

KAMALA BREWING AND THE WHIP IN

1950 S. Interstate 35 • Austin, TX 78704 • (512) 442-5337 • whipin.com

"Hindu Hillbilly" themed honky-tonk and gourmet beer garden, anyone? The Whip In exemplifies Austin's freewheeling spirit by combining an authentic, family-owned Indian *dhaba* (roadside café)–style restaurant (founded in 1986) with a cigar counter, bottle shop, seventy-two-tap beer garden, and two-stage music venue. There's also a small, ambitious brewery on site, Kamala, which, operating formerly as Namaste Brewing, nabbed a gold in Herb & Spiced beers at the 2013 GABF.

AUSTIN BEERWORKS

3009 Industrial Terrace • Austin, TX 78758 • 512-821-2494 • austinbeerworks.com

Opened in 2011, Austin Beerworks has the quintessential modern brewery tap-room feel, with warm lighting, retro art like a big carnival-style lights sign reading "WARES," stainless-steel tanks everywhere inside and great food trucks outside (and a black velvet painting of Sloth from *The Goonies*). The brewery *only* packages beer in cans. Try the killer Fire Eagle IPA, a 6.8% ABV American style IPA with German Magnum, Columbus, Centennial, and Citra hops, a GABF silver medalist in 2014. Their most eye-catching stunt? An actual ninety-nine-pack of beer released locally, for ninety-nine dollars, naturally.

HOPS & GRAIN BREWING

507 Calles St., Ste. 101 • Austin, TX 78702 • (512) 914-2476 • hopsandgrain.com

For a recent experimental series of brews, the fun-loving Hops & Grain crew (founded in 2011) featured a different dry hop every month, released only in 300-case batches locally (yup: time to book a trip, pardner). But which hops? After the resinous, Mosaic-rich release #1, the cans remained mysterious, encouraging drinkers to guess (or scan the can's QR-code to learn more). This brewery, built in a big warehouse and doubling as a coffeehouse, is packed with big time Texas and U.S. pride.

LIVE OAK BREWING CO.

3301-B E. 5th St. • Austin, TX 78702 • (512) 385-2299 • liveoakbrewing.com

Founded in a bare-bones two-room warehouse of a brewery in southeast Austin in 1997, Live Oak has gained a reputation for making some of Austin's—and the entire Southwest's—best beer, thanks to their luscious Live Oak HefeWeizen (4.1% ABV). The secret to their success? Ultratraditional old-world methods including open fermenters made from repurposed dairy tanks, secondary lagering (cold aging), and decoction mashing, a technique described in detail on a super popular, reservations-required ninety-minute tour. In late 2015 they were preparing a massive new facility on twenty acres near the airport.

(512) BREWING CO.

407 Radam Ln. • Austin, TX 78745 • (512) 922-8093 • 512brewing.com

This seven-year-old (as of 2015) upstart named for the local area code is making some of Austin's best beer. Reserve a spot on a weekend tour and drink some of their 6.8% ABV Pecan Porter at the source. Otherwise, look for it and the other (512) beers in Austin bars.

COMMUNITY BEER COMPANY

1530 Inspiration Dr., No. 200 • Dallas, TX 75207 • (214) 751-7921 • communitybeer.com

Located near downtown Dallas on Stemmons Freeway, across from the American Airlines Center and on the edge of the Design District, Community sprang to life in 2013, with the tasting room opening in 2014. It's a 21,000-square-foot facility with cornhole and pool table, giant Jenga game, art exhibits, live music, food trucks, and other diversions. Try the Mosaic IPA.

LAKEWOOD BREWING COMPANY

2302 Executive Dr. • Garland, TX 75041 • (972) 864-2337 • lakewoodbrewing.com

Belgium-born founder Wim Bens was raised in Texas and his brewery and 4,000-square-foot beer garden opened in 2011, with a music stage and vast amounts of seating. If you want to take a tour, go early on a Saturday or Sunday. Styles aren't strictly "Belgian" per se. Start with the sessionable Hopochondria IPA (3.5% ABV) and work your way up to the flagship, a rich, 9.1% ABV milk stout called the Temptress.

FREETAIL BREWING COMPANY

4035 North Loop 1604, No. 105 • San Antonio, TX 78257 • (210) 395-4974 • freetailbrewing.com

Named for a species of large bat and launched as a brewpub on the outskirts of town in 2008 by economics professor turned brewer Scott Metzger, Freetail filled a gaping void in San Antonio. The spacious hillside taproom and tailgater-like patio was so popular, Freetail opened a 30,000-square-foot production facility and thirteen tap tasting room twenty-four miles away in 2014, with attached barrel-aging and sour-beer program. Try the latest American wild ales and hoppy pale ales and IPAs.

RAHR & SONS BREWING CO.

701 Galveston Ave. • Fort Worth, TX 76104 • (817) 810 9266 • rahrbrewing.com

Located on the south side of downtown Fort Worth since 2004, this brewery has an eventful history, to say the least. Current owner Frederick William "Fritz" Rahr Jr.'s great-great-grandfather William opened the first lager brewery in Wisconsin in 1847, but was killed due to burns suffered in a tragic brewing kettle fall. Fritz resurrected the family beer company name in 2004 to make German-influenced beers with Texas twang and a sense of off-beat humor, as evidence by beers named Ugly Pugg and Buffalo Butt. Look for the Iron Thistle, an 8.5% ABV Scotch Ale with hints of fig, raisin, chocolate, and smoke.

UTAH

LITTLE-KNOWN FACT: AS OF JULY 1, 2009, THE NOTORIOUSLY CONSERVATIVE STATE OF UTAH'S beer laws took a great leap forward. For the state's twenty-plus breweries and brewpubs, beers over the notorious limit of 3.2 percent alcohol by weight (4.0% ABV) were made *legal*, though they must be bottled and sold in a place with the right license (which could be a brewpub, bar, or restaurant). The irksome "private club" law was dropped (it required drinkers to pay a membership fee for bars and sign a registry), but a few bars and other establishments still hew to the practice. "Taverns" must still sell only 4.0% ABV or weaker beer, and no wine or hard liquor. Keg sales are verboten, as is sampling at a brewery-only location, but home brewing up to 200 gallons per year per household is A-OK. It all makes perfect sense, doesn't it? So it goes. Time for a beer—might as well make it a strong one.

Salt Lake City

SQUATTERS PUB BREWERY

147 W. Broadway (300 South)
Salt Lake City, UT 84101 • (801) 363-2739
squatters.com• Established: 1989

SCENE & STORY

Utah's most famous beer spot owes part of its fame to its central location in downtown Salt Lake City. There are nine taps and six bottled beers available, with occasional casks, and a huge menu of good pub grub. It's big inside with exposed timber, corrugated metal details, tastefully modern lighting, and wide, polished blonde wood bars. Growler refills are a mere $7.99 (bring your own empty), which makes them a good idea for après ski libations up in the whisper-quiet Little Cottonwood Canyon. Squatters added a Park City location, as well as a pub at the airport in Salt Lake City.

PHILOSOPHY

Under the draconian limitations of the "3.2 laws," Squatters had to do a lot with a little for a very long time. Former brew master Jenny Talley, in the role from 1994 to 2011, rose to the occasion, racking up a war chest full of medals for lower strength beers like her crisp 4% ABV Provo Girl Pilsner. She also ventured into wilder terrain, with meatier Old World styles and New World variations thereof, like her 529, a Flanders oud bruin-style beer (or "old brown") aged for 529 days in oak barrels with wild yeasts (7.15% ABV).

The first brewer in Utah to venture into such tricky stylistic terrain, Talley was recognized in 2011 as the first female recipient of the Russell Schehrer Award for Innovation in Brewing, a prestigious honor from the Boulder, Colorado-based Brewers Association, which oversees the craft brewing industry nationwide. She left Squatters for Red Hook in 2011.

KEY BEER

Start with a Provo Girl, then look for reserves and one-offs like Hell's Keep, a Belgian Strong Specialty Ale, which took a gold in the 2014 GABF.

UINTA BREWING COMPANY

1722 Fremont Dr. • Salt Lake City, UT
84104 • (801) 467-0909
uintabrewing.com • Established: 1993

SCENE & STORY

From its catchphrase alone ("save water—drink beer"), it's clear this Salt Lake City microbrewery and brewpub a short drive southwest of downtown makes good beer without wrecking the neighborhood. Named for the soaring, east-west situated Uinta peaks in the north of the state, UBC is 100 percent wind powered and repays customers that reuse six-pack carriers with swag from the gift shop, the Little Big Beer Store, which has seven varieties of beer to go. All the spent grain goes to ranchers rather than landfills.

PHILOSOPHY

Recently the brewery has also moved the beers in a more progressive direction. The minimalist labels of the Four+ series belie more complex beers within, such as the Wyld, a dry, citrusy, and faintly honeyish 4% ABV American pale ale. With somewhat mixed results, the 750-milliliter Crooked Series line wanders farther away from the old standards of pale, wheat, and stout, with an imperial pilsner, double IPA, and 13.2% ABV black ale called Labyrinth, all labeled by hip local artists.

KEY BEER

Sum'r, from the Four+ series, is a 4% ABV blonde ale with a distinct lemony zing, excellent for a hot day.

BEST *of the* REST: UTAH

←——————→

EPIC BREWING COMPANY

825 S. State St. • Salt Lake City, UT 84111-4207 • (801) 906-0123 • epicbrewing.com

The first high-strength brewery in Utah since Prohibition, Epic was established in 2010 to brew exclusively bigger beers like the Brainless Belgian series (around 9% ABV) which are strong golden ales, sometimes later aged with cherries, peaches, and other fruit in wine barrels for added complexity. The beers come in three categories, Classic, Elevated, and Exponential, and are sold directly from the brewery in twenty-two-ounce bombers, but no sampling is allowed on the premises. No matter. Demand soared from Day One and Epic's distribution quickly spread throughout Utah, and into Idaho and Colorado as well. Now Denver's taproom in the RiNo district is open, as well. Look for Brainless on Peaches, which is a big beer aged in white wine oak barrels with peaches and Champagne yeasts (7.3% ABV).

THE BAYOU

645 S. State St. • Salt Lake City, UT 84111 • (801) 961-8400 • utahbayou.com

A busy taproom near downtown in a funky, old brick building with thirty drafts and some 300 bottles to choose from (including some two dozen brews from Epic and another fifty-odd Utah-brewed beers), the massive selection is the real draw here, but a huge, Cajun-themed food menu, live jazz and blues performances, and free week-night pool also draw hordes of locals.

The Midwest

The MIDWEST

THE AMERICAN HEARTLAND HAS LONG BEEN THE NATION'S BEER CELLAR AS WELL AS ITS BREAD-basket. (And of course, the cheese counter, too.) But until very recently, nearly all the beer coming out of the lake-dotted countryside and prairies of Middle America was bland, industrial lager made with cheap adjuncts like corn, rice, and other profit-driven shortcuts, spending millions on ads instead of quality beer, even employing chemical foam enhancers. The craft beer revolution came on slowly here, but now more than ever, the area we sometimes call the Corn Belt, and especially the Great Lakes region, has discovered the true joy of drinking all-natural craft beer. And if you haven't had the pleasure of drinking beer with native Midwesterners, you're in for a treat.

The German and Central European immigrants who settled here certainly engrained a cultural thirst for the good stuff, and now breweries and beer bars are delving into life beyond—light years beyond—pale, watery lagers. It's a wild time: in 2011, Anheuser-InBev, the once proudly midwestern but now foreign-owned makers of Budweiser, took control of the most famous craft brewery in the region, Goose Island, for a cool $38.8 million. Craft beer's march keeps gathering steam, and ambitious new breweries emerge almost monthly. From Chicago and its world-famous Map Room bar to Nebraska and Missouri, where a bunch of rebel upstarts are helping remake the beer landscape from the geographical center of the nation, it's nothing short of a sea change. Or perhaps wardrobe change is the better phrase: Beer Belt has a nice ring, doesn't it?

ITINERARIES

1-DAY   The Local Option, Map Room, Pipeworks, and The Publican (Chicago)

3-DAY   One-day itinerary plus Hopleaf (Chicago), and New Glarus (WI)

7-DAY   Three-day itinerary plus Boulevard (MO), the Rathskeller (IN), Heorot (IN), and Jolly Pumpkin (MI)

MISSOURI

Kansas City

BOULEVARD BREWING CO.

2501 Southwest Blvd. • Kansas City, MO
64108 • (816) 474-7095 • boulevard.com •
Established: 1989

SCENE & STORY

John McDonald, a mild-mannered furniture maker, started with some used Bavarian equipment in a 100-year-old converted warehouse. His modest goal was to turn out enough beer for the diehard beer lovers in Kansas City, perhaps topping out at 6,000 barrels a year, but the local thirst for Boulevard Pale Ale and Unfiltered Wheat was seemingly unquenchable. Fifteen years later, in 2005, he broke ground on a three-story, 70,000-square-foot expansion adjoining the original, where Belgian-born brewmaster Steven Pauwels can really spread his wings. There was another major expansion in 2011, too. Boulevard is now among the largest locally owned craft breweries in the American Midwest (making over 600,000 barrels annually), with Unfiltered Wheat as the flagship. The Smokestack series, a line of experimental styles, many aged in wood, set tongues wagging in the beer-geek community. To tour the operation is to see what happens when a fully modern brewery puts ancient techniques into action. The tour even includes a taste of beers in development along the fifty-minute stroll (free, including at least four samples; reservations required). On occasion Boulevard also works with local restaurant partners to create beer and food pairings for a tour and luncheon with brewmaster Pauwels for thirty-eight dollars, which includes a tour, three-course lunch, and a souvenir pint glass. In 2013, Belgian powerhouse Duvel Moortgat bought Boulevard for an estimated $100 million, all but guaranteeing its success for decades to come.

PHILOSOPHY

Balance is everything. Pauwels brews so that countervailing sensory aspects in his beers—such as bitterness and residual sugars—play off and against one other, no matter how rudimentary the style.

KEY BEER

Tank 7 is an 8% ABV saison beer named for a fermenter that seemed to be giving Pauwels some problems for a new batch, but instead yielded one of the brewery's best beers yet. It's the color of hay with an aromatic fruit orchard of flavors and a peppery, dry finish. Saison-Brett (8.5 % ABV) takes this superb beer one better: it's dry-hopped and bottle-conditioned with earthy *Brettanomyces* (wild yeast), or "brett," then aged three months before leaving the brewery.

St. Louis

SCHLAFLY BOTTLEWORKS

7260 Southwest Ave. • St. Louis, MO 63143
(314) 241-BEER • schlafly.com
Established: 2003

SCENE & STORY

There are dozens of breweries in Saint Louis, home of the Big One (Anheuser-Busch), but Schlafly (pronounced schlaff-lee) is one of the best. Built in an atmospheric old wood and brick building on the National Historic Register, it has gloriously worn-in floors befitting the original microbrewer in the state, the first to set up shop after Prohibition. It's a short walk away from both the Gateway Arch and City Museum, home of a massive, interactive monkey bars installation and the world's largest No. 2 pencil (citymuseum.org), and makes a great stop for unwinding after both.

In 2003 Schlafly took over the former home of an old grocery store to create Bottleworks, which boasts a cool, little brewing history museum with historic cans and breweriana, a selection of beers to go in coolers, movie nights in a meeting room, and a farmers' market on occasion in the lot. There are twelve taps and a good little pub for eats, as well. Tours (of Bottleworks) are free every Friday through Sunday from 12 to 5 p.m., and there's also a third Schlafly pub in Lambert International Airport if you'd just like a chance to try the beers en route to or from St. Louis.

PHILOSOPHY

Good local beer for good folks. To give you an idea of their scale, consider that Anheuser-Busch produces well over 100 million barrels of beer a year. The Bottleworks location produces just 40,000 (1.2 million gallons), making it 1/100th the size, and the Tap Room brewery is even smaller.

KEY BEER

Try the 4.8% ABV Pilsner for a taste of the style of beer Anheuser-Busch might have been making 100 years ago. Also excellent: the 5.9% ABV Dry Hopped APA, or American Pale Ale, grainy and reminiscent of citrus and honey.

BEST *of the* REST: MISSOURI

PERENNIAL ARTISAN ALES

8125 Michigan Ave. • St. Louis, MO 63111 • (314) 631-7300 • perennialbeer.com

Phil Wymore, formerly Goose Island's cellar master as well as the head brewer at Half Acre, tapped Cory King, a home brewer with no professional experience, to become the head brewer at his new brewery Perennial, in 2011. It was a move that would prove to be brilliant for both. With artful saisons and Belgian ales with Brett (as well as oddball projects like a squash-infused brown ale and Abraxas, a stellar stout with cacao nibs, ancho chiles, cinnamon sticks, and coffee beans), Perennial vaulted into the national beer conversation in short order. Abraxas, one of Cory King's home brewing recipes, took a silver in the experimental category at Chicago's Festival of Barrel-Aged Beers in 2012, and Savant Blanc pulled a gold in the American-style sour ales category in 2015.

THE SIDE PROJECT CELLAR

7373 Marietta Ave. • Maplewood, MO 63143 • (314) 224-5211 • sideprojectbrewing.com

Side Project is Cory King's gypsy beer brand, which started (at Wymore's invitation) within Perennial, and he now has his own attractive tasting room, opened in 2014. On offer, superbly blended, 100 percent barrel-aged (and mostly barrel-fermented) saisons, wild ales, and stouts aged in spirits barrels.

INTERNATIONAL TAP HOUSE

1711 S. 9th St. • St. Louis, MO 63104 • (314) 621-4333 • internationaltaphouse.com

A mile and a half south of Busch Stadium (home of the Saint Louis Cardinals) "iTap" (as this sleek beer bar is known) has a spacious patio with Christmas lights hanging in draped rows outside and a long row of black captain's chairs inside facing the main event: coolers and forty-four taps totaling 500 selections inside, with a world-class selection of craft brews, not a macro in sight. It's a long, narrow space with exposed brick, low lighting, and frequent live acoustic music (no food is served). Tuesdays feature Missouri brews, with extra rarities from Boulevard, Schlafly, and other locals. There are two more locations in St. Louis, and one in Columbia, Missouri now, too.

BRIDGE TAP HOUSE & WINE BAR

1004 Locust St. • St. Louis, MO 63101 • (314) 241-8141 • thebridgestl.com

With arty chandeliers, heavily framed black-and-white photos, polished wood, and a leaning library ladder behind the bar, this downtown St. Louis bar draws a young, casual crowd. Open every night until 1 a.m. (midnight on Sundays), it's the best place in the city to grab dinner from the chef-driven menu or just a bite of local and house-cured charcuterie, duck, pickles, and whole raw cheeses. In addition to a comprehensive wine and farm-to-table menu, there are fifty-five taps and more than 200 bottled beers, with a full complement of Boulevard and a half-dozen Founders taps, including Goose Island's food-friendly Sofie, an oak-aged Belgian-style farmhouse ale aged with orange peel (6.5% ABV).

ILLINOIS

Chicago

PIPEWORKS BREWING CO.

1675 N. Western Ave. • Chicago, IL 60647
(773) 698-6154 • pdubs.net
Established: 2012

SCENE & STORY

It's the ship that launched a thousand tippy Kickstarter canoes. Founded in 2012 by Gerrit Lewis and Beejay Oslon, home brewers who met while working at Chicago's West Lakeview Liquors, Pipeworks was the first ever crowd-funded brewery, raising an eyebrow-raising $40,075 (on their wished-for $30,000) in January of 2012, plus a reported $40,000 through PayPal from friends, family, and supporters who missed the initial thirty-day window. Neither brewer had real-world experience beyond a brief apprenticeship with acclaimed De Struise, in Belgium, but the duo hit full speed with beers like Ninja vs. Unicorn, a resinous double IPA, and, a few months later, a whiskey barrel-aged smoked porter. Pipeworks' beers have sold out again and again.

PHILOSOPHY

Sometimes having no experience means going no-holds-barred. Since their formation, Pipeworks has hewed to a rarely used commercial model: almost every single batch is totally unique. (The surging Gigantic, in Portland, Oregon, is also an adherent to this model.) What it means for fans of the Bucktown brewery is that every week or two a new beer lands. And that's just how locals like it. "It's very much a home-brew mentality," says Cicerone (the beer equivalent of master sommelier) Chris Quinn of Avondale-area, 800-label bottle shop, the Beer Temple. "They experiment constantly. Last Kiss, for example, was a wonderfully clean and malty wee heavy brewed with molasses. Sonorous was an 'Imperial English Summer Ale.' I have no idea what that is—but it tasted darn good, and showed you can balance hop and yeast character in an over-the-top, imperial beer."

KEY BEER

The guys are fond of goofy, pop-culture references (i.e., naming a "White Russian" imperial milk stout "Hey Careful Man, There's a Beverage Here" after the classic *Big Lebowski* line). But Pipeworks' brewing experiments are more bold than simply weird, skewing into the culinary (i.e., Zommelier, a smoked wheat wine with black cardamon, lemon, and black peppercorns). And with Brown & Stirred, a recent rye strong ale aged in Heaven Hill rye whiskey barrels with cherries and bitter roots—a Manhattan cocktail in beer form brewed in collaboration with Longman & Eagle, a stylish Chicago inn and whiskey bar—Pipeworks is veering into mixology terrain.

LOCAL OPTION

1102 W. Webster • Chicago, IL 60614
(773) 348-2008 • localoptionchicago.com
Established: 1988

SCENE & STORY

With black walls, a tattoo-like skull illustration on the wall, and a good-size chalkboard of hard-to-find beers that unfailingly makes the savviest beer lovers weak in the knees, this Lincoln Park beer bar has another quality many of the top beer bars in this country haven't quite nailed: humility. Service is knowledgeable and friendly without being overly solicitous nor irritatingly aloof. There are thirty taps and over 100 bottled brews drawn from the most eagerly savored American, Dutch, and Belgian makers, such as Denmark-based Mikkeller, always an educational choice, as many of the beers are often formulated to highlight a single defining element, such as a hop variety or yeast strain. And their own line of beers, especially pathbreaking sours, is excellent. It's even vegan-friendly.

PHILOSOPHY

As the motto in the skull says more colorfully (if inaccurately) in German, bad beer can be fatal. (Note: If jokey references to the Prince of Darkness/Satan offend you, you might want to pick another spot. These low-key guys, Jack Black–like, are all about referencing the heavy rock symbolism of 666.) Brand Ambassador Alexi Front is, in addition to being a really nice guy, a Swedish death metal aficionado. To hear the place as described by the hallowed *New York Times*: "Stepping in the door was like passing through a portal from a Catholic college into a disaffected teenager's basement hideout. The walls of the dim, crowded hallway of the bar were decorated with painted flaming skulls. Death metal music roared. I waded into the mosh pit to shout an order to a tattooed bartender. . . ." What a country.

KEY BEER

Jolly Pumpkin's Oro de Calabaza. Technically speaking, this is a bière de garde, or French for "beer to keep." It's earthy, oaky, spicy, floral, slightly tart, and incredibly delicious. Feeling local and devilish? Try the tasty Exorcist! foreign extra stout, which, at 8.5% ABV, "pours black as Satan's heart." You've been warned.

THE MAP ROOM

1949 N. Hoyne • Chicago, IL 60647
(773) 252-7636 • maproom.com
Established: 1992

SCENE & STORY

True to its name, the Map Room is equipped with old issues of *National Geographic* and huge colorful topographic charts, and the twenty-six taps and 230 bottled selections (and one cask at all times) reflect the worldly outlook. A Bucktown neighborhood standby, the cash-only bar has high ceilings with black tin tiles hung with various flags, red walls, and a half-dozen round tables along a polished wood bar, and chalkboard tap lists that require a lot of attention, because beers turn over so often. The Map Room's owners freely admit they had no idea what they were doing when they started, but quickly fostered a community of committed beer lovers who held beer club meetings, brought back travelers' tales, and even taught "beer

school" classes, a tradition that continues in the bar to this day, led by brewer Greg Browne of Mickey Finn's Brewery in Libertyville, north of the city.

PHILOSOPHY

The best kind of journey is one for the love of interesting beer. The Map Room's owners and staff go to great lengths to bring back treasures they can share. As founder Laura Blasingame writes on the pub's home page, the Map Room started out as a place "where ideas could be exchanged, where people could come to get some good social nourishment. What a better beverage to feature than beer?"

KEY BEER

Muncie, IN's, Three Floyd's Dreadnaught, a 9.5% ABV Imperial IPA, a lush panoply of tropical and fruit flavors like mango and peach balanced with a hefty dose of resinous hops.

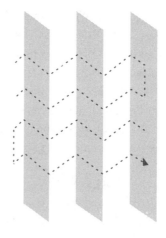

SHEFFIELD'S BEER AND WINE GARDEN

3258 N. Sheffield Ave. • Chicago, IL 60657
(773) 281-4989 • sheffieldschicago.com
Established: 1980

SCENE & STORY

With three distinct bar areas and a beer garden for fair-weather days, this well-established Windy City watering hole in the Lake View area of town is known for both its great beer lists and its "Backroom Barbecue." The whole place has red tile floors, warm, mustard-yellow walls, antique trim, old craftsman-era light fixtures, and an incredible selection of beers (thirty-eight taps; 150 bottles) from close-by favorites like Bell's and Goose Island to West Coast cult beers and abroad to Belgian, German, and Japanese imports such as Hitachino.

PHILOSOPHY

Options make the meal. Late founder Rick Hess worked hard to give diners the choice of the best Memphis-, Texas-, and Carolina-style sauces to dress the house-smoked ribs, brisket, and other barbecue fare, and the mostly American draft beer list reflects a similar attention to detail and quality, with cask-conditioned beers, growler sales to go, and a "new and notable" list for customers.

KEY BEER

Furious, from Surly Brewing in Minnesota is, a 6.2% ABV American IPA. It's perfect for cutting the tangy spice of the ribs.

THE PUBLICAN

837 W. Fulton Market • Chicago, IL 60607
(312) 733-9555 • thepublicanrestaurant.com
Established: 2008

SCENE & STORY

All together now! Among the most impressive aspects of the Publican is the huge square of walnut-hewn, communal table space in the center of the dining room, which seats 100 and is ringed by tiered booths and walls glowing with an earthy, ochre color and lit by striking, globelike light fixtures. The space was designed by James Beard Award winner Thomas Schlesser, and the bar area is a marvel of polished steel and brass fixtures, chic wooden tap handles, and gleaming delicate glassware for the carefully curated list of twelve taps and eighty-five bottles. Impressively, all servers, managers, and bartenders have achieved at least level-one certification on the dauntingly long path to becoming Cicerones.

PHILOSOPHY

Beer and food deserve equal thought and care. Executive Chef Paul Kahan's beer-centric menus center upon sustainably sourced seafood, certified-organic pork from Dyersville, Iowa (made into, among other things, terrine and charcuterie), seasonal vegetables, and daily aioli. Other beer-friendly specialties include housemade black and white sausages, steak tartare, pork shoulder, pot-au-feu, and wood-roasted chicken with frites. Special beer dinners are common, with recent appearances by Los Angeles's the Bruery and American barrel-aging pioneer Allagash.

KEY BEER

Order up Thiriez XXtra (Brasserie Thiriez, of Esquelbecq, France), a wonderfully aromatic and spicy food–friendly beer in 750-milliliter bottles (4.50% ABV).

GOOSE ISLAND BEER CO.

1800 N. Clybourn • Chicago, IL 60614
(312) 915-0071 • gooseisland.com
Established: 1988

SCENE & STORY

At this point, it's almost a household name. And the elephant in the room? In 2011, owner John Hall sold out to Anheuser-Busch for a cool $38.8 million, prompting howls of protest, but the beers—especially sours and other barrel-aged specialties—have continued to be good, with a few greats since the merger. So. One must simply decide: is it now perfectly okay to drink beer from a global corporation that has relentlessly mocked and conspired against small craft breweries by controlling distribution and shelf sets in stores for *decades*? Now that Anheuser-Busch is snatching up respected craft

breweries (i.e., Elysian, Golden Road, and many, many more), the wolf of monopoly-like distribution now comes wearing once-trusted craft beer clothing.

No matter who bought them out, Goose Island deserves credit for growing and shaping the national craft beer conversation. The original Goose Island opened in Lincoln Park and has racked up well over 100 prestigious brewing medals. In the handsome wood-paneled pub with its huge, central oval-shaped bar, there are at least twenty taps, many only available there (including occasional cask-conditioned ales), in addition to bottle, growler, and keg sales to go. The pub grub consists of higher end pub fare including duck and rabbit, mussels, andouille, and cassoulet. There are often beers on tap that have been created as collaborations with local chefs including Rick Bayless and Paul Kahan of the Publican. A second brewpub, in Wrigleyville, opened in 1999. Tours of both locations (seven dollars; about an hour) can be reserved on weekends at various times.

PHILOSOPHY

Innovative and quality-minded. In recent years the company has made strides with Belgian-style ales such as Matilda, a 7% ABV Belgian pale ale with earthy Brettanomyces yeast.

KEY BEER

Goose Island has been steadily expanding its ambitious sour program, launched in 2007. Halia, (Hawaiian for "remembrance of a loved one") was brewed in memory of a close friend of the brewery who loved peaches. This straw-hued, slightly funky Belgian-style wild ale is aged in white wine barrels with 12,000 pounds of fresh Michigan peaches. Flaxen-yellow, it smells like a wicker basket of those ripe peaches, with a bright, citrusy, mouth-watering smack on the finish (7.5% ABV).

BEST *of the* REST: ILLINOIS

←——→

PIECE BREWERY & PIZZERIA

1927 W. North Ave. • Chicago, IL 60622 • (773) 772-4422 • piecechicago.com

One of the best all-time pairings for pizza is dry, hoppy American-style pale ale and IPA, and this artisan pizzeria and small batch craft brewery excels at both, even winning top honors during the World Beer Cup in American pale ale in 2014. Brewer Jonathan Cutler, who trained at the Siebel Institute and Master Brewers Association of America, opened Piece in 2011 with over a decade of brewing experience. The pizzeria is a large, renovated loft-like room (formerly a roofing supply house) with skylight, flat-screen TVs in every direction, and a sunken bar area. Hit it on Sunday for a large pie and a sixty-four-ounce growler, twenty-five dollars.

DELILAH'S

2771 N. Lincoln Ave. • Chicago, IL 60614 • (773) 472-2771 • delilahschicago.com

The black, Old West exterior resembles a saloon a gunslinger might have preferred, but inside it's pure rock and roll. With punk, rock, ska, and alt-country blasting from an excellent jukebox (plus pool tables upstairs), this bar (established in 1994) offers a refreshing break from the sometimes too-precious vibe of new-school beer bars (but still organizes cool, special events and tastings five times a year). Owner Mike Miller rotates a selection of 20 taps and 150 bottled crafts and imports, like Daisy Cutter Pale Ale (5.2% ABV) from Chicago's own Half Acre Brewing Company.

HALF ACRE BREWING CO.

4257 N. Lincoln Ave. • Chicago, IL 60618 • (773) 248-4038 • halfacrebeer.com

A group of beer-loving friends living in Bucktown (home of the Map Room) started Half Acre as a contract brewing arrangement in 2006. Within two years the crew was ready to move into a big converted brick warehouse, and were soon brewing an impressive arsenal of beers including the peachy, pungent, and eminently drinkable Daisy Cutter Pale Ale (5.2% ABV). Along the way the brewery has propelled the Half Acre's competitive cycling team to new heights. The beers are finding wider distribution in the area every day. Brewery tours are offered on Saturdays at 1 p.m. by reservation only, with a maximum of sixty adults per day.

HOPLEAF

5148 N. Clark St. • Chicago, IL 60640 • (773) 334-9851 • hopleaf.com

With warm, weathered wood throughout, Hopleaf (opened in 1992) is broken up into three areas—a front bar, dining area, and loft-like seating area upstairs—offering 41 taps and 260 bottled selections. The beer selection is heavily influenced by Belgian styles, as is the menu: standout dishes include the mussels, frites, rabbit with dumplings, duck meatballs, and cod croquettes. Look for Lost Abbey beers (from California), such as the cloudy gold Carnevale on draft, a 6.5% ABV saison beer with hints of orange peel and a delicate floral aroma from ample Amarillo and Simcoe hops.

REVOLUTION BREWING CO.

2323 N. Milwaukee Ave. • Chicago, IL 60647-2924 • (773) 227-2739 • revbrew.com

Opened in 2010 with a faux Bolshevik attitude, this Logan Square brewpub roared into high gear under the leadership of former Goose Islander Josh Deth. With its tin ceilings, contemporary-classic dark wood bar island, defiant fist tap handles, and locally sourced pub grub, it's cool enough for the young folk yet classy enough to take the parents (on a quiet afternoon that is; it gets mobbed at night). So quick and sure has the Revolution swept over Logan Square that they planned a 35,000-square-foot production brewery for 2011 with a row of 800 barrel outdoor fermenters (800 barrels each!), room for barrel aging, and a slew of styles leaving chinks in the armor of macrobrew hegemony. The 6.5% ABV Anti-Hero IPA is madly popular, with massive amounts of tangy and floral hops.

TWO BROTHERS

30 W. 315 Calumet Ave. • Warrenville, IL 60555 • (630) 657-5201 • twobrosbrew.com

Brothers Jim and Jason Ebel were obsessed with craft beer after living in Europe; when they returned home, they opened a home-brew shop, which led to plans to brew commercially. One brother completed a law degree while the other mastered brewing science; using borrowed money, gear, and some dairy tanks their grandfather handed down, Two Brothers was born in 1997 in the western suburbs of Chicago, and has grown like a beanstalk ever since. Starting in 2009, the duo acquired a beautiful collection of wooden tanks called *foudres* for making far more complex beers than the hefeweizens (cloudy wheat beers) that put them on the map. Look for their flagship, Cane & Ebel Red Rye Ale, made with a bit of Thai palm sugar, rye malt, and unusually aromatic hops (7% ABV).

SOLEMN OATH BREWERY

1661 Quincy Ave. No. 179 • Naperville, IL 60540 • solumnoathbrewery.com

Launched in 2012 by a man called John Barley (really) to brew Belgian-style ales and various experimental excursions into the brewer's art, Solemn Oath has done a lot of cool things, including "Oath Day" tours where guests help create spice blends for Whisper Kisses, a saison that will be poured later on in the taproom. Wend your way through the ever-changing list.

SCRATCH BREWING CO.

264 Thompson Rd. • Ava, IL 62907 • (618) 426-1415 • scratchbeer.com

A farmhouse brewery and restaurant located five miles from Shawnee National Forest, Scratch works with a purist focus on farmhouse styles brewed with homegrown, locally farmed, and foraged ingredients such as nettle, elderberry, ginger, lotus, dandelion, hickory, and honey. Enjoy equally adventurous wood-fired pizzas and breads from the brick oven, plus locally produced charcuterie and cheese.

NEBRASKA

Lincoln

ZIPLINE BREWING CO.

2100 Magnum Cir., No. 1 • Lincoln, NE 68522 • (402) 475-1001
ziplinebrewing.com • Established: 2011

SCENE & STORY

Marcus Powers was a water and natural resources attorney working with water engineers and hydrologists of groundwater and surface water interaction. Good background for a brewery, you might say. Home brewing gibed with his science background and soon his recipes were taking shape. Around 2011, with a pair of partners, Powers began the build-out of Zipline Brewing Co. The taproom is adorned in a combination of concrete, wood, and steel; two walls are covered in pallet wood that stretches up and gets lost in a high, dark warehouse ceiling. Exposed concrete floors are set off against steampunk tables made with sawmill timbers and galvanized pipe. The warm, low light of Edison bulbs hanging from cloth cords glows in the space, which has eight taps and a beer engine.

PHILOSOPHY

"Our slogan is Brave New Brew," says Powers. "[It] enshrines our focus on making high quality, progressive beer. If we wouldn't buy it, we wouldn't ask you to either."

KEY BEER

Fans of their Double IPA might race you to the door. Copper Alt won a gold medal at the GABF in 2015; also try the 4.5% ABV Gin Barrel-Aged Hibiscus Saison, a bright pink, effervescent brew of tart hibiscus flowers, gin spiciness, and wooden barrels.

Papillion

NEBRASKA BREWING CO.

Shadow Lake Towne Center • 7474 Towne Center Pkwy., Ste. 101 • Papillion, NE 68046
(402) 934-7100 • nebraskabrewingco.com
Established: 2007

SCENE & STORY

Should you find yourself driving from the Midwest to Colorado across the vast expanse that is the Cornhusker state, it's just a short detour off of I-80 to the French-influenced prairie town outpost of Papillion (population: 24,000) outside of Omaha. Thanks to low unemployment, crime, and traffic, it has been considered one of the best places to live in the United States by *Money* magazine. In 2007, life improved with the arrival of an adventurous brewery in a nondescript shopping center just down the sidewalk from T.J. Maxx and Bed, Bath & Beyond.

Inside, there's a beauty of a 10bbl brewhouse made in Japan behind glass and a spacious eight-tap pub with locals at the bar who look a lot like reformed lager-swilling college football junkies. But founder Paul Kavulak and his team of brewers have done more than just get the attention of the local drinking populace. They've found distributors willing to take a chance on their beer in markets as demanding as Oregon, and started winning awards in competitions. Whoever said there's no good beer in the heartland hasn't been to Nebraska lately.

PHILOSOPHY

No risk, no reward. Nebraska Brewing undoubtedly raised some eyebrows in town when they started serving up beers aged in wood, like wines. But their timing was impeccable. Across the country the taste for barrel-aged beers was spreading like wildfire. The experiments continue, the fans and medals multiply, and the beers keep improving. Now they're can-

ning, too—fuel on the beer sales fire, as any brewer will tell you.

KEY BEER

Mélange à Trois Reserve Series, a 10% ABV strong Belgian pale ale aged in chardonnay barrels for six months, is full-bodied in the mouth, mingling pear and tropical fruit with vanilla, spice, and a faint, oaky woodiness.

INDIANA

Munster

THREE FLOYDS BREWING CO.

9750 Indiana Pkwy. • Munster, IN 46321
(219) 922-3565 • 3floyds.com
Established: 1996

SCENE & STORY

Home-brewing brothers Nick and Simon and their father, Mike Floyd, started their brewery the old-fashioned way: with a kettle fired by a wok burner and some old, open swiss-cheese tanks for fermenting the beers five barrels at a time (155 gallons). That was back in Hammond, Indiana. Four years later they were ready to move up to a larger facility, which is located behind an office park near a hospital. As far as their cultishly devoted fans are concerned, the Floyd brothers could have built that brewery three levels below the hospital in a moldy mop closet: in 2010, for the annual release party of Dark Lord, a buck-strong stout of 15% ABV topped in colored wax, 8,000 people showed up.

Call it beer-geek Brigadoon.

Inside, the brewpub and taproom is equal parts stoner man cave and chef's pantry. Just when you expect to see corn dogs and tater tots come out of the kitchen, plates of cassoulet, duck-fat frites and whole roasted Wisconsin lake trout appear. Amid the psychedelic murals and flags, metal on the hi-fi, and projectors showing '80s movies like *The Karate Kid*, there are eleven excellent taps and twenty-one bottles to sample across the entire brewable spectrum. In 2015, Three Floyds teamed up with Danish brewing phenom Mikkeller to open Warpigs, a barbecue and craft beer emporium built in the old meatpacking district of Copenhagen.

PHILOSOPHY

Officially, the *modus operandi* is, "It's Not Normal." Three Floyds has unleashed dozens of intense beers pushing the envelope of hops, malt, and other flavor components. If they were to brew too many beers on the lighter side, their fans would be confused, even irritated.

KEY BEER

Gumballhead is an American pale wheat

ale, and on the low end for FFF (5.5% ABV). But its lemony gold flavors and hemp-like aroma is no less desirable for the restraint.

Indianapolis

THE RATHSKELLER

401 E. Michigan St. • Indianapolis, IN 46204
(317) 636-0396 • rathskeller.com
Established: 1894

SCENE & STORY

Of the many things the Rathskeller is, subtle isn't one of them. With history as rich as its oversize, dark wood décor, the Rathskeller is a like a true Bavarian castle encased in a massive nineteenth-century brick building (designed by, among others, Kurt Vonnegut's grandfather) in downtown Indianapolis. Once you head inside and take in the gorgeous interior of polished wood archways and creamy walls, it's time for a beer. There's something mightily satisfying about drinking from a thirty-two-ounce German stein while sitting underneath a mounted moose head. There are twelve rotating imported drafts and fifty-some bottles of German, European, and American craft beer to choose from, along with a celebrated menu of authentic German fare, so the *gemütlichkeit* ("cheerful belonging") is not far behind. In summer, don't miss the rooftop biergarten, featuring a wide-screen view of the city, live music, and plenty of locals raising a stein or three. If you go on a weekend, chances are you'll get to ride the endorphins of somebody celebrating a wedding or class reunion in one of the banquet rooms. And if you're hungry, for the love of Klaus, do not leave without trying an oversize, pillowy pretzel coated in salt and served with a side of sinus-clearing hot mustard.

PHILOSOPHY

Auf freundes wohl! To the good health of friends! The Rathskeller is authentically German, with a side of Hoosier pride—check out the bust of the late author Vonnegut.

KEY BEER

Something German in a stein, naturally, like the Mönchshof Kellerbier; its creamy, caramel taste shines through the cloudy texture of this unfiltered, traditionally brewed lager (5.4% ABV).

BEST *of the* REST: INDIANA

←————————→

UPLAND BREWING CO.

350 W. 11th St. • Bloomington, IN • (812) 336-2337 • uplandbeer.com

Bloomington is a college town for Indiana University, and this sunny, brick-sided brewpub draws youthful imbibers in with great burgers and an outdoor patio, where locals sip on cloudy gold glasses of Upland Wheat Ale, a 4.5% ABV Belgian *wit* (white beer), made with organic coriander, chamomile, and orange peel. Lately, the brewery has delved into more exotic Belgian and other brewing styles with strong results and opened two more locations. Indiana still doesn't allow beer or alcohol sales on Sunday except from breweries or wineries, so during the summer, it's common practice for locals to buy a growler of the slightly tart and quenching Wheat and head to a local lake, sit in the sun, and sip beer straight out of the bottle—Indiana summer at its best.

SUN KING BREWING

135 N. College Ave. • Indianapolis, IN 46202 • (317) 602-3702 • sunkingbrewing.com

Sun King's original Indianapolis location opened up with a twelve-tap tasting room with a fifteen barrel brewhouse in half of an unused warehouse space. Today they've expanded, they're canning, they're making a beer with the Indiana Pacers, they're filling growlers like mad and selling a great deal of beer across the state, and they're pulling down gold medals at almost every GABF and World Beer Cup. Pay a visit and taste some Sunlight Cream Ale at the source.

HEOROT

219 S. Walnut • Muncie, IN 47305 • (765) 287-0173 • theheorotpub.com

What is the airspeed velocity of an unladen swallow? If you comprehend this *Monty Python & the Holy Grail* reference, you'd probably like this place, named for the mead hall of heroes in the epic poem, *Beowulf*. This beer bar in the home of David Letterman's alma mater Ball State University comes complete with a dragon sculpture curling in and out of the wall, stuffed animal heads, shields, skulls, various faux-medieval bric-a-brac, and Basil Pouledouris's soundtrack to Conan the Barbarian on the stereo. The service is spotty and the whole thing is a bit hokey, sure. But when you have fifty-four-plus incredible taps and over 600 bottles to choose from, including vintage ales in casks the likes of which are found almost nowhere else in the world, a sword on the wall lancing through cans of macro-brew for inspiration, and a house brewery coming online, who really cares? Order up a Dogfish Head Midas Touch (based on a 2,700-year-old Turkish recipe found in the tomb of King Midas; 9% ABV) and call your Round Table to order.

SHALLO'S

Country Line Shoppes • 8811 Hardegan St. • Indianapolis, IN 46227
(317) 882-7997 • shallos.com

A cluttered, dimly lit and very old place on the south side of Indianapolis that's connected to the Old Time Pottery store in a desolated strip mall, Shallo's is the craft beer bar as imagined by David Lynch, with smoke-darkened, wood-paneled walls, pressed tin ceilings, deep padded booths, and a beer cooler with a neon sign reading "INSURANCE." With 300 bottled beers and forty drafts (presented on a perpetually outdated list) including the likes of Indiana's own Three Floyds, Mikkeller of Denmark, and San Francisco's He'brew ("the Chosen Beer"), it's a holy land for beer lovers if there ever was one.

IOWA

Des Moines

EL BAIT SHOP

200 SW 2nd St. • Des Moines, IA 50309
(515) 284-1970 • elbaitshop.com
Established: 2006

SCENE & STORY

For a bar with such a kooky mix of blue Formica, faux-wood paneling, retro video games, Maurice Sendak murals, and other late-period Greg Brady–era stylings (lacquered marlin; plastic grapes, assorted tchotchkes), El Bait Shop has an incredibly up-to-date beer list, with 180 taps and hundreds of bottles from over thirty countries. Especially strong is the draft list from the Midwest—Boulevard, Bells, and Goose Island.

PHILOSOPHY

The vinyl booths may be cheap, but there's no skimping on the beer, and the two-tiered tap row is a thing of organizational beauty. Neither college clown show nor meat market, this is a bar to love for one reason above all: almost everyone's here for the beer.

KEY BEER

This would be the perfect place to drink Boulevard's Long Strange Trip, a 9% ABV tripel that has a heady sweetness and a puff of delicate noble hop character.

BEST of the REST: IOWA

TOPPLING GOLIATH BREWING COMPANY

310 College Dr. • Decorah, IA 52101 • (563) 387-6700 • tgbrews.com

Home brewers Clark and Barb Lewey founded their "David"-size brewery in a quiet northeastern part of the state in 2009 "after months of dangerous experimental home brewing projects" that overtook their garage. Brewing three times a day on a half-barrel nano-system, the Leweys built up a local following, then graduated to a ten-barrel system, and quickly outgrew that as well. Today they've got a four-vessel, thirty-barrel system and state-of-the-art packaging gear, and a taproom open seven days a week. Look for clean, hop-forward ales, pungent double IPAs, and acclaimed barrel- and wood-aged beers like their giant-killer, Kentucky Brunch Brand Stout, a 12% ABV aged in bourbon barrels with coffee.

THE ROYAL MILE

210 4th St. • Des Moines, IA 50309 • (515) 280-3771 • royalmilebar.com

A glorious array of weathered, old wood tables, English breweriana, stained glass, a Union Jack, and London Underground signs help make this the unofficial "living room" of Des Moines, an ideal place for storytelling among old friends. Along with a stream of special firkin nights from top craft brewers like Colorado's Left Hand and New Belgium, regulars gather inside (and out on a quaint brick patio) for hearty bites like English pork pie and bangers and mash, washed down with rare beers, including the delicately hoppy and refreshing Coniston Bluebird Bitter (4.2% ABV) from Cumbria, England.

MICHIGAN

Ann Arbor

JOLLY PUMPKIN CAFÉ & BREWERY

311 S. Main St. • Ann Arbor, 48104
(734) 913-2730 • jollypumpkin.com
Established: 2004

SCENE & STORY

Across the country, American craft brewers have followed Ron Jeffries' quiet but confident lead, embracing tricky, Belgian-influenced techniques like the use of oak barrels and wild yeast strains that are lethal to beer in the wrong hands. He started his odyssey toward becoming one of the nation's best brewers of Belgian-style ales around 1991 with the goal of opening his own brewery. By 1995, he had made a name for himself in Michigan's emerging scene, and by 2004 he was ready to unleash his vision: a brewery dedicated to wood-aged artisanal beers. Trouble was, he hadn't settled on a name.

On a warm, early spring afternoon with snow on the ground and ample heat in the air, Jeffries, who is tall and thin with the quiet, placid demeanor of an English Lit professor, thought of a name that encompassed everything he intended to do: Jolly Pumpkin Artisan Ales, a mishmash of concepts encompassing Halloween, pirates, his low-key, slow-paced Hawaii, and the kind of beer he wanted to make. He and his wife laughed. It grew on her. Jolly Pumpkin it was.

Today, Jeffries oversees operations of the original Dexter, Michigan, location (where a new pub was under way in 2011), a brewpub in Traverse City, and a brewpub in Ann Arbor, which has a lovely bar, roof deck, and full menu of beer-friendly cuisine, and a new pizzeria and brewery, which opened in Detroit in April 2015 with thirty-two beers on tap. It's the only brewery in Detroit making a sour. Both the Ann Arbor and Traverse City locations have Jeffries's beers on tap or in bottles, and both allow growler and bottle sales to go.

The beer that Jeffries has been brewing from the start is some of the most interesting and innovative in the country. These days it's relatively common to hear about wood-aging experiments, sour beers, bourbon barrels, and the like, but Jeffries was the first modern American brewer to be fermenting all of his beer in huge wood fermenters from the start, which is incredibly risky—one runaway infection in a barrel and tens of thousands of dollars' worth of beer can turn into vinegar. It's not easy to grapple with wild yeasts, which can bore into wood and wreak havoc in a brewhouse, nor to bottle-condition the beer as if it were Champagne, but Jeffries doesn't go around crowing about it. He doesn't have to. The beers—complex, flavorful, original, by turns elegant and edgy—speak for themselves.

PHILOSOPHY

Traditional, small-scale production with deep, pleasing complexity as the ultimate goal. Not every experiment is perfect, but that's part of the beauty of Jolly Pumpkin.

KEY BEER

Luciernaga (6.5% ABV) and Luciernaga Grand Reserve (7% ABV). With a hearty helping of exotic spices like grains of paradise and coriander, Luciernaga is an annual, spicy-tart Belgian pale ale arriving in summer, like the wondrous insect for which it's named. It pours radiant, ruddy amber with a huge pillow of head. The Grand Reserve version is aged in bourbon barrels for fourteen months, deepening the flavors with curling, vinous notes of vanilla and smoke. And if those aren't available, look for the superb Bam Biere, a farmhouse-style golden ale, naturally cloudy, bottle-conditioned, and dry-hopped (4.5% ABV).

Grand Rapids

FOUNDERS BREWING CO.

235 Grandville Ave. SW • Grand Rapids, MI 49503 • (616) 776-1195
foundersbrewing.com • Established: 1997

SCENE & STORY

Like a lot of great American craft brewers, Mike Stevens and Dave Engbers started their dream company while working day jobs they couldn't wait to quit, and with a giant loan from the bank. With beers that were balanced but frankly timid, they teetered on bankruptcy soon after opening the doors, so Stevens and Engbers decided to go all-in, releasing the sort of uncompromisingly bold beers that got them interested in brewing in the first place. After a remarkable turnaround, their brewery and airy taproom (a glorious space of weathered hardwood floors, tall glass windows looking into the brewery, and a polished, serpentine mahogany bar), is one of America's top beer destinations. For several years, Founders has been burning up the awards circuit and, around 2009, became the fastest growing American craft brewery. Today it occupies an entire city block and just embarked on a $40 million expansion driven largely by a session beer called All-Day IPA, which is delicious stuff.

PHILOSOPHY

The stated credo: "We don't brew beer for the masses. Instead, our beers are crafted for a chosen few, a small cadre of renegades and rebels who enjoy a beer that pushes the limits of what is commonly accepted as taste. In short, we make beer for people like us." Good call.

KEY BEER

Founders' KBS (Kentucky Breakfast Stout) is an 11.2% ABV brew released annually on the Saturday closest to the Ides of March (the 15th), an event at the brewery that draws hordes of beer fans. It's got a massive quantity of chocolate and coffee and is cave-aged in bourbon barrels before bottling. And unfortunately, you'll have trouble finding it outside the brewery. All-Day IPA is aptly named, and easier to come by. This grainy, citrusy, supersociable India pale ale of 4.7% ABV deftly balances three types of juicy, aromatic hops.

HOPCAT

25 Ionia Ave. SW • Grand Rapids, MI 49503
(616) 451-4677 • hopcatgr.com
Established: 2008

SCENE & STORY

With its seasonal outdoor patio, exposed brick walls, bare wood and pressed-tin ceilings, wooden floors and tables, and narrow, wrought-iron support columns, HopCat is inviting before you even get to the bar. Then there's a series of inviting padded booths and tables and a loft-like seating area with couches upstairs. When you get to the bar, with its clover-honey-hued Italianate woodwork and mirrors and epic forty-eight-tap row (featuring a slew of Michigan locals, ten or more house brews, and 150 more bottles, not a macrobrew in sight), the hard part begins: What to drink? There's at least one thing you must order from the food menu: their house beer-battered Crack Fries (entirely as advertised though quite legal and only $4.95).

In recent years, HopCats appeared like rabbits, with six additional locations (Ann Arbor, Broad Ripple, Detroit, East Lansing, Grand Rapids, East Lexington, and Madison) opening in quick succession. But the real kicker was HopCat announcing, late in 2015, *a thirty-location, $25 million expansion* across the entire Midwest (whoa!). Now that is a clowder of cats.

PHILOSOPHY

Experiment and learn. With beer education classes and an ever-changing list, HopCat is a benevolent master. The Crack Fries, however, own you completely. You are powerless to resist.

KEY BEER

Every great midwestern brewery from the nano-of-the-minute to massive regional heavyweights is represented, so take your pick.

Kalamazoo

BELL'S BREWERY ECCENTRIC CAFÉ

355 E. Kalamazoo Ave. • Kalamazoo, MI 49007 • (269) 382-2332 • bellsbeer.com
Established: 1985

SCENE & STORY

Larry Bell's operation is a household name in these parts, but it started as a mere Kalamazoo home-brew shop in 1983 and sold its first beer—quite literally made in a fifteen-gallon soup kettle—in 1985. Bell, a self-described failed jazz musician and occasional radio broadcaster, had started the first craft brewery east of the Rockies and by 1993 became the first brewer in the state of Michigan

to serve beer on-site at a brewery.

Now the commercial production is housed in nearby Comstock, Michigan, cranking out a wide array of beers 24/7 on a system that brews 1,500 gallons per batch, around 170,000 barrels per year—or five million gallons, double the output of 2005. The original brewery location in Kalamazoo is home to the Eccentric Café, with 130 seats, beer garden, and newly expanded, warehouse-size music venue. One really cool thing the brewery does? Host a home-brew competition and send the winner to GABF on the brewery's dime. It's a super communal idea that builds the tight community Bell's has developed.

PHILOSOPHY

The official motto is "Inspired Brewing," but Larry himself is a no-nonsense kind of guy, more focused on the business of brewing beer than flights of commercial fancy. Inspired by the successes of Sierra Nevada and Anchor, his goal was to open a brewery that made at least 30,000 barrels a year. Mission accomplished, and a whole lot more.

KEY BEER

Bell's Expedition Stout is one of the early American versions of a Russian imperial stout, chewy and laced with flavors of black patent brewers' malt, chocolate, licorice, and stone fruit (10.5% ABV).

BEST *of the* REST: MICHIGAN

ASHLEY'S RESTAURANT & PUB

338 S. State St. • Ann Arbor, MI 48104 • (734) 996-9191 • ashleys.com

With seventy-two taps and fifty bottled selections, this cozy and often crowded college bar with an unremarkable interior has one of the best tap rows in the state. The sponsors of a Michigan cask ale festival (held at the newer Ashley's location, twenty-five miles away in Westland), Ashley's is credited with bringing the level of Michigan craft beer appreciation up overall since 1983, when it first opened. There's a rotating selection from the excellent Short's Brewing Company in Bellaire, Michigan, which ought to be your first choice. In 2015, the founders were awarded the Ridderschap van de Roerstok der Brouwers in Belgium, or the Knighthood of the Brewers' Mash Staff. The knighthood, bestowed in a ceremony during a massive three day beer festival in Brussels, recognizes "individuals who have rendered loyal services" to the Belgian brewing profession. In other words, you're in good hands.

ARCADIA BREWING

103 W. Michigan Ave. • Battle Creek, MI 49017 • (269) 963 9520 • arcadiaales.com

The centerpiece of Arcadia brewing company (established in 1996) is the impressive wood- and brick-sided brewing system visible from behind glass in the British-style restaurant and T.C.'s Pub in the back, where you can snack on wood-oven pizzas and pita bread with hummus. Take a free tour of the brewery itself most Saturdays at 1 p.m. (and please call ahead). Built by influential British brewer Peter Austin, it's the birthplace of a wide array of ales, like the 7.2% ABV Arcadia London Porter, which is sweet and full-bodied with notes of cocoa and smoke. Arcadia built a second location in Kalamazoo in 2014.

BLACKROCKS BREWERY

424 N. 3rd St. • Marquette, MI, 49855 • (906) 273-1333 • blackrocksbrewery.com

David Manson and Andy Langlois launched Blackrocks as a nano in 2010 in a little yellow house on a quiet corner of Marquette. Wired into the local music and mountain biking scene, these fun-loving guys were so slammed so fast that a 3bbl pub system and 20bbl production system (housed a mile away in an old Coca Cola plant) weren't far behind. Now they help host live music five nights a week, sponsor big bike races, and seem to have a grand old time. Try the 51K IPA, a dry, dank, 7% ABV citrus and pine bomb.

BREWERY VIVANT

925 Cherry St. SE • Grand Rapids, MI 49506 • (616) 719-1604 • breweryvivant.com

Built in 2010 around the striking chapel of a former funeral home—read: exposed beams, stained-glass, and Gothic-looking arches—Brewery Vivant was inspired by farmhouse breweries from Wallonia, the farm-dotted hinterlands between Belgium and France, where founder Jason Spaulding fell in love with the saison beers after selling his stake in New Holland Brewing Co., of which he was a founder. The Grand Rapids farmers' market is close by, supplying the restaurant/pub and beer garden, too. Try the various saisons on draft or a can of Triomphe Belgian-style IPA (6.5% ABV).

OHIO

Cleveland

GREAT LAKES BREWING CO.

2516 Market Ave. • Cleveland, OH 44113
(216) 771-4404 • greatlakesbrewing.com
Established: 1998

SCENE & STORY

The first microbrewery in the state of Ohio since the last of the old-line companies closed in the early 1980s, Great Lakes opened in 1998 in a massive Victorian complex. With its antique 1860s tiger mahogany bar, beer garden with retractable canvas roof, and atmospheric *rathskeller* (or cellar bar), it's a superb spot for an afternoon pint and a bite.

PHILOSOPHY

Proud and feisty. Raise a glass of Eliot Ness Amber Lager to the Untouchable himself, who drank here and might—just might—be responsible for some bullet holes in the bar.

KEY BEER

Burning River Pale Ale is a great name; unfortunately it's also a reference to the worst days of the Cuyahoga River, once so befouled by coal plants on its banks that it periodically caught fire. But not to worry: there's nothing remotely toxic in this beer. It's a perfectly carbonated pale ale of 6% ABV with the mellow sweetness of British-style pale ale but the flash and brightness of an American IPA.

McNULTY'S BIER MARKET

1948 W. 25th St. • Cleveland, OH 44113
(216) 274-1010 • bier-markt.com
Established: 2005

SCENE & STORY

Ohio's first Belgian beer bar set up shop in the center of the entertainment district, and stays open every day of the year until 2 a.m. The dark, alluring interior design is a feast for the eyes, simultaneously classic and futuristic, with red-trimmed windows against warm, earthy walls and jet black tin ceilings, elaborate paneling in other sections, and elongated Edison bulbs hanging over the curved main bar.

PHILOSOPHY

Meet the new boss: With brewery nights from the likes of Ommegang and Victory, a deep and mouthwatering list of gastropub fare, and a ninety-nine-label Belgian list, it's safe to say the Cleveland beer scene will never be the same again.

KEY BEER

Look for the Caracole Nostradamus, a deliciously complex 9.5% ABV Belgian brown ale.

Columbus

SEVENTH SON

1101 N. 4th St. • Columbus, OH 43201
(614) 421-2337 • seventhsonbrewing.com
Established: 2013

SCENE & STORY

Seventh Son is located in the historically Italian neighborhood of 4th and 4th, constructed in a big, boomerang-shaped former auto garage with huge, roll-up doors, making it an awesome place to hang out on a sunny day. With a spacious tasting room and patio areas, head brewer Colin Vent and Co. create distinctive, experimental beers in a cool, clean setting with food trucks deployed at critical weekend junctures, like brunch.

PHILOSOPHY

"We wanted to start a brewery but we also wanted to create an environment," reads the founders' mission statement. "We believe that beautiful and vibrant surroundings will reflect and create beautiful and vibrant beer."

KEY BEER

Vent describes his flagship, Seventh Son American Strong Ale, as a "a ruddy amber American Strong clocking in at 7.7% ABV. Grapefruit and stone fruit hop aroma and character are balanced by a rich, red malt backbone. A precise blend of seven hops go into the brewing and dry-hopping process including Nelson Sauvin, Mosaic, Horizon, Palisade, Citra, Willamette, and Columbus."

BEST *of the* REST: OHIO

JACKIE O'S

25 Campbell St. • Athens, Ohio 45701 • (740) 592-8696 • jackieOs.com

This avidly experimental brewery founded in 2006 in the heartland has used ingredients such as black walnuts, maple syrup, lemon verbena, coffee, and pumpkins in their various one-off beers, and has collaborated with Hill Farmstead, one of the most talked-about breweries in the world. They've gotten seriously into barrel aging, and operate a farm outside of town. Look for Firefly (a 4.5% ABV amber), Chomolungma (a 6.5% honey brown ale), and rotating reserves. A canning line and big production brewery added in 2015 means Jackie O's is going big.

RHINEGEIST

1910 Elm St. • Cincinnati, OH 45202 • (513) 381-1367 • rhinegeist.com

Rhinegeist translates to "Ghost of the Rhine" and refers to the historic, once brewery-filled, Over-the-Rhine Brewery District in Cincinnati, where in 2013 this juggernaut was constructed in the massive old Moerlein bottling plant, which dates to 1895. The timing could not have been better, as Cincinnati had largely been bypassed by the craft beer craze. Starting with 20bbl batches, Rhinegeist experienced pegged demand since day one, leading to some eye-popping changes. They've already launched a $10 million expansion, *bought* the 100,000-square-foot-plus building they were leasing, leaped to a 60bbl BrauKon system (the Mercedes-Benz SLK class of breweries), and built a 7,000-square-foot roof deck, just to name a few. Special bottle releases have drawn crowds of 4,000. Try the 5.2% Puma Pilsner and move up from there. Who knows just how high this ghost will get?

MINNESOTA

THE HAPPY GNOME

498 Selby Ave. • St. Paul, MN 55102 • (651) 287-2018 • thehappygnome.com
Established: 2005

SCENE & STORY

With its facade covered in climbing creeper vine, a spacious patio, vintage-inspired interior of plush brown leather booths, acres of dark and unvarnished wood surfaces, and framed poster art, the Happy Gnome is getting it right on multiple levels before you even sit down.

PHILOSOPHY

Beer is happiness. The beer and food here will make you even happier, with seventy adventurous, fresh taps, 400 bottle selections, and occasional firkins (the nine-gallon British vessels used to dispense cask-conditioned beers through a hand pump). There are monthly brewery dinners and a chef-driven menu daily, featuring expertly prepared fare like chestnut-stuffed quail with roasted squash puree, braised kale, and cherry-rye whiskey reduction.

KEY BEER

Look for the Furthermore Fatty Boombalatty Belgian pale ale (Wisconsin), which, besides being a lot of fun to order, is a 7.2% ABV brew of amber with wheaty, zesty notes and peppery bite.

SURLY BREWING

520 Malcolm Ave. SE • Minneapolis, MN
55414 • (763) 999-4040
surlybrewing.com Established: 2006

SCENE & STORY

After a trip to Oregon to tour breweries, founder Omar Ansari (a home brewer with big dreams) returned to build Minnesota's first new brewery since 1987. That was in 2006, and his beers and tours were so incredibly popular—*Beer-Advocate* magazine named Surly Brewing the Best Brewery in America, and RateBeer named Surly Darkness the best American beer only sixteen months after they sold the first keg—that by 2011 he was leading a pitched battle to get the state and local government to approve a major new destination brewery, bar, restaurant, and event center, which is now open as of 2014. Detailed, hour-long tours are five dollars and include a taster glass and four samples, plus a donation to a local charity; register on the website. There's a beer hall with food served (brisket, burgers, and sausages, etc.) and a finer restaurant, Brewer's Table, with dishes like seared *foie gras* with pan perdu, walnut gravy, candied cranberry or duck with Szechuan pears, toasted barley, carrot jus, and a grilled short rib with beluga lentils, salsify, and frisee (all paired with beers, of course).

PHILOSOPHY

Big beers, big picture. Ansari led a pitched battle to get the right for breweries to sell beer on site. In 2011, Governor Mark Dayton signed the "Surly Bill" into law, making it possible for breweries that produce less than 250,000 barrels each year to sell pints of their beer at their brewery.

KEY BEER

Head brewer Todd Haug, is a brewer of heavy metal flavors with a deft touch. Furious is a 6.2% ABV American IPA brewed with five different malts and four tangy, grapefruity hop varieties working in surprisingly peaceful tandem.

BEST *of the* REST: MINNESOTA

THE MUDDY PIG

162 Dale St. N. • Saint Paul, MN 55102-2028 • (651) 254-1030 • muddypig.com

An easy-to-find corner bar with a casual, neighborhood feel and weathered old booths, books, a cozy outdoor patio, and lots of dark wood, the Muddy Pig has the best beer selection in the Twin Cities—around fifty taps and a similar number of Belgians. Stick to the beers like Flying Dog's 8.3% ABV Raging Bitch Belgian-style IPA, which has the peppery bite of a great Belgian and an aromatic whiff of Amarillo hops.

INDEED BREWING COMPANY AND TAPROOM

711 NE 15th Ave. • Minneapolis, MN, 55413 • (612) 843-5090 • indeedbrewing.com

In the summer of 2012, three friends opened an attractive 12,000-square-foot brewery and taproom in a century-old building at the heart of the Northeast Minneapolis Arts District. It was the culmination of a dream for the three founders—Tom Whisenand, Nathan Berndt, and Rachel Anderson—who met at the University of Minnesota, and who make everything from light, crisp APA to beers like Hot Box Imperial Smoked Pepper Porter, a 9% ABV collaboration beer brewed with hickory-smoked peppers and malt smoked over alder, maple, and apple woods. They've added an extra taproom area on site and pulled down a silver at GABF in 2014 for a honey beer.

WISCONSIN

New Glarus

NEW GLARUS BREWING CO.

2400 State Hwy. 69 • New Glarus, WI 53574
(608) 527-5850 • newglarusbrewing.com
Established: 1993

SCENE & STORY

After the tiny New Glarus brewery was founded by the straight-talking Deb Carey and her brewer husband, Dan, something wonderful happened. Their little brewery in the countryside grew so quickly throughout the state and into several others that by 1998 the couple was rethinking a strategy of unchecked growth, and pulled distribution back to Wisconsin only, creating an uproar. The Careys were unfazed; they wanted their brewery to stay strong and local. And so the only way to drink some of the best beer in America is to go to Wisconsin, and ideally, New Glarus, to see where it comes into the world.

It's a testament to ingenuity and the power of a brewery to pull together a community. Rather than stifling sales, limiting their sales market propelled sales higher, and by 2007, the Careys constructed one of the country's most appealing breweries, a 75,000-square-foot Bavarian-style brewery on a hill about a mile from the original location, which cost the couple $21 million. It's a fairy tale of steep-pitched roofs, creamy exterior walls with exposed beams, stone-stair approaches, and gleaming copper kettles inside. Free, self-guided tours are offered Monday through Sunday from 10 a.m. to 4 p.m.; "Hard Hat" tours depart every Friday at 1 p.m. from the original Riverside brewery location, where pilot batches are still developed and wood aged in some cases (twenty dollars per person and reservations required). Recently the family added the "wild fruit cave," a wood barrel-aging cellar for sour and fruited sour beers.

PHILOSOPHY

Down to earth, experimental, fun, and delicious. As Dan puts it, "Some people paint, some sing, others write . . . I brew."

KEY BEER

Spotted Cow, a pale, mellow, and wheaty lager is the flagship, but it's the waxed-top, 750-milliliter bottles of Wisconsin Belgian Red that ends up in the trunk of the most choosey visitors. It's a racy, scarlet ale of 4.0% ABV brewed with a pound of whole sour Montmorency cherries per bottle, local wheat, and Belgian malt, then aged in oak tanks and balanced by German Hallertau hops which have been aged for a year in the brewhouse. It's as bright and jammy as a Wisconsin cherry pie.

Madison

THE OLD FASHIONED

23 N. Pickney St. • Madison, WI 53703
(608) 310-4110 • theoldfashioned.com
Established: 2005

SCENE & STORY

Befitting its name, the Old Fashioned channels the feel of an old-timey supper club rich with Wisconsin history. It's located in the heart of Madison, with a view of the capitol building. Authentic Miller and Schlitz banners—along with maps of Wisconsin and a mounted walleye fish or two—adorn the walls, and dark, natural wood gives the spacious 100-seat dining room a convincingly homey, old-school vibe.

PHILOSOPHY

The Old Fashioned is Wisconsin, through and through. Their beer list—fifty taps, 150 bottles—is stocked entirely by Wisconsin breweries, save one bottle of the oft-requested Grain Belt Premium from Minnesota—the sole "import." Their food menu follows suit: Everything is made from local ingredients or picked up directly from local purveyors. They don't even have tomatoes when they're off-season in the Badger State. When it comes time to order, go for the fried walleye sandwich, or perhaps something involving the official state food, cheese. "The batter-fried cheese curds are out of this world," said waitress Jessica Carrier on a recent visit, "and I'm not just saying that. I have literally had a dream about the cheese curds."

KEY BEER

Sprecher Black Bavarian Lager, an authentic, German-style black beer that practically dances on the tongue, a far more delicate brew than the hue would suggest (6% ABV).

BEST *of the* REST: WISCONSIN

ALE ASYLUM

2002 Pankratz St. • Madison, WI 53704 • (608) 663-3926 • aleasylum.com

Home brewer Dean Coffey built this popular brewpub in 2006. Ale Asylum's Bedlam, a 7.5% ABV Citra-hopped Belgian IPA, is just one of many good beers propelling this little but pioneering Madison micro into the spotlight, along with Hopalicious, an American pale ale hopped eleven times with piny, grapefruity Cascades.

TYRANENA BREWING CO.

1025 Owen St. • Lake Mills, WI 53551 • (920) 648-8699 • tyranena.com

A short drive from Madison leads to sleepy Lake Mills and the sleek Tyranena (pronounced tie-rah-nee-nah) brewery and taproom, opened in 1998. (The company is named for some mysterious rock formations at the edge of a nearby lake.) No one's quite sure who or what's behind their design, but no matter, the beer's good and the owners have a nice beer garden, steady live music, and a sense of humor, sponsoring can't-miss events such as Sweater Vest Appreciation Night (really). There are free tours Saturdays at 3:30 p.m. and ten taps to sample (in addition to six packaged beers, growlers, and specials). Chief Blackhawk Porter, named for the Sauk Indian chief who led the last armed conflict between Native Americans and Europeans east of the Mississippi, is a fulsome 5.5% ABV brew with notes of coffee, toffee, and chocolate.

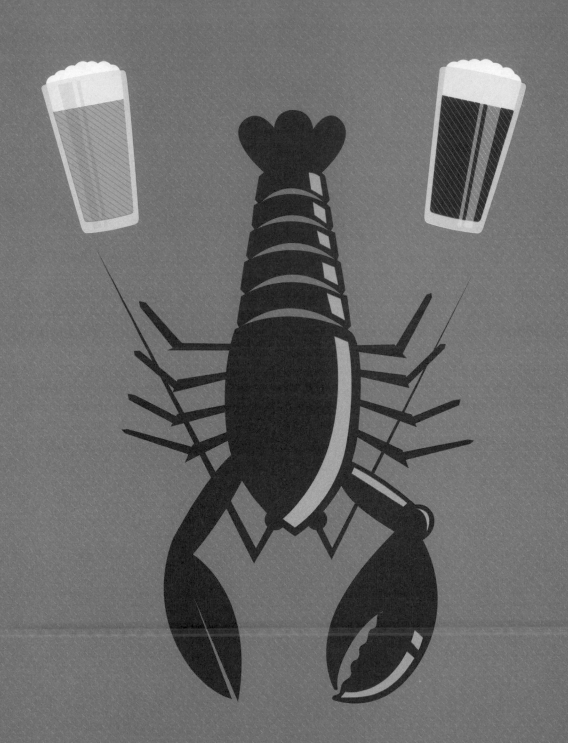

The NORTHEAST

WHILE IT'S TRUE THAT THE WEST HAS A LOCK ON MODERN CRAFT BREWING HISTORY AND has long been at its leading edge, the Northeast offers tastes of America's oldest historical beer traditions and its most delicious, innovative present tense all at once. From rural Vermont to the rocky shores of Maine, there's a new craft beer tapestry to explore that is every bit as diverse as the population itself.

What else to expect from the hardy types that call New England home? Head to the coast for raw oysters and innovative stouts or deep into the Northeast kingdom for hoppy ales like Heady Topper, a canned sensation of rare intensity. The leafy byways and small towns of Maine and Vermont, especially, offer beer travelers a lot of great options. Spring and fall are the times to go (winter extremes make travel and brewery hours variable, and summer can be stiflingly hot); be sure to plan ahead for the sometimes long drives between breweries and beer bars, and look into lodging options well in advance, especially in peak tourist season (when all leaves turn kaleidoscopic). Trust me: You haven't witnessed fall until you've walked in a forest in upstate Vermont or New Hampshire in, say, October. The colors are indescribably vivid, varied, and inspiring.

So, whatever you do, make the trip. What was once a quiet corner of the United States when it comes to beer has become a world-class beer region, with true farmhouse breweries like the celebrated indies Hill Farmstead and Oxbow joining urban innovators in the Boston area like Trillium, Mystic, and Jack's Abby. Early pathbreakers—including the Belgian-styled Allagash in Portland, Maine—keep pushing into new territory with their all-spontaneously fermented ales that are as rare, delicious, and sought after as any beers in the world today. The local seafood alone—fresh lobster roll, anyone?—is worth the trip. World-class beers now make this region not just interesting but truly bucket-list worthy.

MAINE

ALLAGASH

50 Industrial Wy. • Portland, ME 04103
(800) 330-5385 • allagash.com
Established: 1994

SCENE & STORY

Rob Tod's Allagash Brewery helped usher in the American craze for Belgian brewing styles with its first of many insanely drinkable beers, Allagash White, a traditional 5% ABV wit containing wheat (in place of barley), coriander and other spices, and curaçao orange peel. Since then, Tod, along with brewmaster Jason Perkins, have created an array of new standards and superb bottle-conditioned beers. The brewery features free thirty-minute tours (call ahead just to make sure they're on) and a tasteful merchandise and bottle shop. It's not much to look at on the outside, but the beer is extraordinary in every way, and has influenced and inspired countless young American brewers.

PHILOSOPHY

Of all the American craft breweries inspired by Belgium's funky brewing practices, Allagash has made some of the boldest leaps, utilizing herbs, spices, and starchy vegetables usually only eaten on Thanksgiving. Some are wood-aged and then bottle-conditioned, meaning the beers have rested quietly in oak barrels before bottling with some yeast and a small measure of special brewing sugar to carbonate in the bottle. Inspired by Belgian classics but going in new directions, too, these beers boast wine-like complexity and higher alcohol levels, pushing the limits of what's considered sane and desirable in American microbrewing. They're also often very good with food, exhibiting tannins, vinous notes of vanilla and various acidic dimensions (and accents of whatever liquid was in the barrel before beer, usually red wine or bourbon). Incredibly time-consuming and expensive to produce, barrel-aged beers expand the sensory horizon of beer almost exponentially, and Allagash has been at the forefront of this practice, inspiring countless imitators.

KEY BEER

Part of the (not barrel-aged) Serie de Origine experimental series, Confluence (7.5% ABV) combines the house Belgian yeast strain with *Brettanomyces* (wild yeast), or "brett," two kinds of traditional English hops, and a transatlantic medley of grains (including German-style pilsner malts) for a totally deracinated, fully delicious evening sipper. This is a beer that shouldn't work—it sounds like the recipe came from a few rolls of some cloak-wearing home brewer's twelve-sided dice—but does. It's tart and wine-like on the front end, warm and creamy on the back end, and delicious throughout.

OXBOW BLENDING & BOTTLING

49 Washington Ave. • Portland, ME 04101 • (207) 350-0025 • oxbowbeer.com
Established: 2015

OXBOW BEER

274 Jones Woods Rd. • Newcastle, ME 04553
(207) 315-5962 • Established: 2011

SCENE & STORY

Picture, if you can, a rocking street party with a massive stage, DJs pumping dubstep, face-masked graffiti artists wielding poppling paint cans, glass (pipe) blowers, hordes of raucous locals and, to top it all off, a skater launching a perfect kick-flip over a flaming whiskey barrel. Now imagine that this party, attended by more than 2,000 beer lovers recently in Portland, Maine, has been organized by a tiny farmhouse brewery fifty miles from town on eighteen acres whose connoisseur-ready beer styles hail from the sleepy Belgian countryside—saison, grisette, and other mellow stripes normally served alongside a good cow's milk cheese. That's exactly the beautiful paradox Newcastle, ME, Oxbow embodies every day, which is why, like that flaming whiskey barrel stunt (true story, by the way), it's on fire.

While the beers are still sold only in Maine, Adams and partners Geoff and Dash Masland have begun collaborating with Italy's Birrificio del Ducato and Naparbier in Spain's Basque region, as well as opening a new 10,000-square-foot Portland warehouse to use for barrel aging, blending and bottling, on Washington Avenue. Meanwhile, "the Newcastle brewery and tasting room are very small, but sit on an eighteen-acre plot in the middle of the woods," says Adams. "We have a pond (swimming in the summer, hockey in the winter!); we have bees for honey, grow fruits for our beers and raise pigs on our spent grains. It is quiet and peaceful."

Best of all: you can rent out the crisply appointed three-bedroom farmhouse at Oxbow Beer (sleeps nine) for $255 a night, which has a full modern kitchen, full bathroom, laundry facilities, and wireless Internet. It even comes with a twenty-five-dollar credit for the taproom.

THE COOLSHIP REVOLUTION & THE SLOW BURN of AMERICAN WILD ALES

For some craft brewers innovation means slowing down—way down. Instead of finding ways to get more people to buy their beer faster, they're aging ales for months or even years with monkish consideration. You've heard of slow food? This is slow *brewed*.

For Allagash, mere months of barrel aging wasn't enough; in 2008, following Tod's trip to Belgium and tours of funky artisanal operations, Allagash installed what is thought to be the first modern *koelschip*, or "coolship" in the United States. A shallow-bottomed steel vessel used to cool a rich wheat-, barley-, and aged-hops-infused wort (unfermented beer), expose it to the outside air, and kick off a spontaneous wild yeast fermentation, coolships are still used in a handful of breweries in Belgium (including Cantillon, the granddaddy of them all) in the making of *lambic*, the traditional sour beers of the Zenne Valley outside of Brussels.

It's a remarkable process to observe. Freshly brewed beer is moved into the *koelschip* following a long boil—up to four hours— of a mash using unmalted wheat (to facilitate a super-long fermentation). The brewer then opens louvered vents or windows to allow ambient air to cool and to let naturally occurring yeasts aloft to settle in the beer. The next day the now-inoculated beer is racked into preused wood barrels (often formerly containing red wine), whereupon the wild yeasts and bacteria begin—very slowly begin—to chew on the starches inside. Anywhere from hours or days to several months later the fermentation erupts and the beer begins a voyage of drying, souring, and evaporation through the oak walls of the barrels, leaving behind an ever tarter and more complex beer as time goes on. It's a mysterious, near-mystical process, one far more gnostic than most traditional brewmasters can stomach. Later those beers are sometimes blended with younger beers to make what Belgians call *Geuze*, or aged again with fresh fruits to make *kriek* (cherry), *framboise* (raspberry), *cassis* (currant), and other tart-sweet creations.

Allagash's bold experiment succeeded, and in so doing challenged long-held beliefs. There are many who still object that the Allagash beers (and subsequent, similar projects popping up all over the country) shouldn't be called Lambic, an appellation akin to Champagne or Parma ham. Tod and Russian River's Vinnie Cilurzo (among others) who are leading the American revival of the style (and variations thereof) prefer to call them wild ales or spontaneous fermentation beers, a solution which seems respectful and useful, especially as the beers—owing to the difference in local microflora—are unique, even if the methods are similar. And today the approach is one of the most talked-about directions in craft beer. Now the excellent Allagash beers are trickling out (the aging and blending period can take up to three years). Tod and Perkins have proven that Americans can make wild ales without physically adding yeast, a development the most enlightened Belgian producers—such as Cantillon's Van Roy—applaud and support. And thanks to the success of Tod's *koelschip*, other breweries are trying them out, too. Among them: Jester King, Crooked Stave, Prairie Artisan Ales, and Wolves & People.

PHILOSOPHY

Officially: "Loud beer from a quiet place," which is just the kind of clever catchphrase fans have come to expect. But it's a subtle approach, too. "We have a very specific focus: farmhouse ales," Adams told me. "Our inspiration comes mainly from classic styles of beer, and not just those from Belgium. I drink a lot of German lagers and love them for their balance and their ability to showcase quality ingredients in the most beautiful way. We try to apply that to our take on farmhouse ales. We strive for balance and refreshing drinkability, but unlike the lagers of Germany our beers display an incredible amount of complexity from their fermentation character."

In 2015, Oxbow launched a coolship-led sour program using the farm's and other local fruit including raspberries, cherries, elderberries, and strawberries, for starters. "I think it's very much in line with what we do: not being scared to take chances and to take the time to make the best possible beer we can," Adams says. "It's the ultimate extreme of taking chances and taking time. It's not the road most traveled, but I think spontaneous beers are the finest out there."

KEY BEER

Adams's favorite, and the company flagship, is Farmhouse Pale Ale, a 6% ABV saison with American hops.

NOVARE RES BIER CAFÉ

4 Canal Plaza • Portland, ME 04101 • (207) 761-BIER (2437) • novareresbiercafe.com • Established: 2008

SCENE & STORY

With twenty-five rotating taps, two hand pumps, and some 300 bottles on its list, Novare Res is a craft beer lover's refuge down an alley in the Old Port area of town off of Exchange Street. Inside the bar is an array of beer signage, warm, wood tones, exposed brick, oak barrels, and tin ceilings. Outside there's an elevated wood patio area, which fills up on sunny days. Every May, an annual Belgian Beer fest brings nothing but Belgian brews to the taps for three weeks, and the owners—who were inspired to open the bar after extensive travels in Europe—organize frequent events year-round with noted brewmasters and extremely hard-to-find beers. The combination has resulted in a beer bar with something of a special reputation: seemingly no matter where you travel in craft beer America, people are either talking about a recent visit to Novare Res, or planning to go. According to Dan Shelton, the outspoken writer and importer of Cantillon and over 100 other very special European beers, owner Eric Michaud is running "the best beer bar in Maine," which, coming from the famous Europhile, is no faint praise. There's a menu of relatively simple but hearty fare (stew, sausages, artisan meats and cheeses, hot sandwiches), and ambitious desserts cooked with sought-after Belgian ales like Cantillon.

PHILOSOPHY

Novare Res means "to start a revolution" in Latin, and the owners cheekily define the bar by what it is *not*. It's neither British pub (though there are dartboards and cask ales), nor German biergarten (though there are the appropriate picnic tables outside), nor Belgian bière café (though Belgophiles will love its selection). It is instead a hybrid of approaches dedicated to great beer, no matter where or how it may have been brewed. Founder Eric Michaud previously managed the Moan & Dove, and there's a fond fellowship between the two bars.

KEY BEER

The Belgian list is deep; the creamy-bodied Moinette Blond from the makers of Saison Dupont is an enormously complex but sociable pale ale (even at 8.5% ABV) with yeasty, funky, fruity notes up front and a snappy hop finish.

MARSHALL WHARF BREWING CO. / THREE TIDES

2 Pinchy Ln. • Belfast, ME 04915
(207) 338-1707 • marshallwharf.com
Established: 2003 (bar) and 2007 (brewery)

SCENE & STORY

Located smack on the pier next to the tugs of Belfast—a fishing village first settled in 1770—the Marshall Wharf brewery was built in the town's original granary in 2007. A combination patio- and bocce-court-equipped beer bar, seven-barrel brewhouse with eight-spigot taproom and lobster pound (so you can buy some fresh-caught on summer mornings to take home), and a twelve-tap seasonal beer garden with repurposed bus station benches and upended logs for seats, Marshall Wharf is truly a one-stop affair. There's even a heap of oyster shells, a midden, an ancient coastal tradition. Brewing around thirty unusual styles and aging certain brews in Heaven Hill distillery barrels with increasingly assured results—especially in the IIPA, brown, stout, and Baltic Porter genres—founder David Carlson and brewer Danny McGovern have been helping remake coastal Maine's beer scene for some time. McGovern, the former owner of Lake St. George Brewing Company and brewer for Belfast Bay Brewing Company (and a trained butcher), brought Carlson's operation a number of interesting recipes. And Carlson's waterfront Three Tides bar next door (which now serves seventeen Marshall Wharf beers and is sometimes known by locals as the "Lampshade Bar") had been the first bar in Maine to serve beers from Anchor, Unibroue, and Ayinger on draft.

PHILOSOPHY

Good beer, fresh seafood, and a bocce ball court are the only necessities of life.

KEY BEER

Cant Dog, an Imperial IPA released in 2004, was one of Marshall Wharf's early beers, and came about when Carlson and McGovern scored a haul of Simcoe hops from an Idaho brewer in distress. It's a golden amber, 10% ABV hop bomb with such dangerous drinkability that patrons are limited to two per day.

EBENEZER'S PUB

44 Allen Rd. • Lovell, ME 04051
(207) 925-3200 • ebenezerspub.net
Established: 2004

SCENE & STORY

One of the country's most celebrated beer bars, Ebenezer's—named for a late-eighteenth-century trapper said to have survived a duel with a bear but lost an arm—is located in the attached barn of an old farmhouse on a rural golf course, meaning it will take some planning (and driver's GPS) to reach. With its screened porch, copper-topped bar, thirty-five taps (about two-thirds Belgian) and more than 700 labels in the cellar, it's a bucket list beer bar with well-regarded food and a reputation for impromptu, eye-popping cellar tours. It's not just that the list is long, it's ridiculously deep, varied, and unusual. The location makes it a pilgrimage (and it's easy to part with a great deal of money here), but those who make the effort are rewarded.

PHILOSOPHY

"We may be located in a small Maine town, but we've always dreamed big. From day one, it was our goal to build the best beer pub in the world," says owner Chris Lively, who, with his wife, Jen, is a constant presence in the bar. This translates to cheerful service and a massive selection, care for the beer on hand, and a tradition of over-the-top events and beer dinners.

KEY BEER

The house beer is Black Albert, a resinous, roasty, coal black 13% ABV Russian Imperial Stout brewed by De Struise of Belgium. Lively's selection of large-format bottles will no doubt be tempting, too, especially for groups who make this pilgrimage, and the draft choices are beyond unusual, like a recent tapping of 2006 Cantillon Kriek, a sour Belgian ale aged with whole cherries in oak casks for up to three years before it is released.

BEST *of the* REST: MAINE

BISSELL BROTHERS BREWING

1 Industrial Way, Ste. 1 • Portland, ME 04103-1072 • (207) 279-0346 • bissellbrothers.com

Working in an old industrial warehouse space within walking distance of five other breweries, Bissell Brothers Brewery is one of Portland's hottest new upstarts, thanks to sought-after cans of the Substance, a dank, 6.5% American-style IPA that caught on like wildfire in 2014, and Swish, its bigger DIPA brother. The taproom is all about uplighting, graffiti, and the ping-pong table in a back room. Anticipate and plan for long lines for beer on release days.

MAINE BEER CO.

525 U.S. 1 • Freeport, ME 04032 • (207) 221-5711 • mainebeercompany.com

Opened in 2009 just south of Exit 20 off I295, Maine Beer Co.'s tasting room affords the chance to try one of the best breweries in the Northeast. There are eight beers on tap and some brewery-only releases. Snacks from local vendors, bottles to go, and stylish swag are all available. Gaze through glass at the brewery and start with Peeper, a floral and citrusy but dry American Pale Ale (APA) which ups the ante on the old English style. Read: more hops, cleaner finish.

THE GREAT LOST BEAR

540 Forest Ave. • Portland, ME 04101 • (207) 772-0300 • greatlostbear.com

A dimly lit British-style pub packed with ephemera and breweriana, the Great Lost Bear opened in 1979 and arguably helped Maine's nascent brewing industry take shape throughout the 1980s. With some seventy taps, fifty of which are from the Northeast (including fifteen from Maine), it's still a favorite destination for beer lovers in the area and tourists, and its "Allagash Alley"—a tap row proudly dedicated to the local brewer's beers—is a nice touch.

MASSACHUSETTS

GOING BACK TO THE DAYS OF THE MAYFLOWER AND THE FOUNDING FATHERS, BEER HAS LONG played a central role here. Today the earliest breweries are long gone but thanks in part to Jim Koch, the energetic founder of Boston Beer Company, the homegrown tradition is alive and well. "Boston was one of the original brewing centers in the United States," explains Koch on a recent afternoon visit to his south Boston headquarters, a renovated, 25,000-square-foot brewery that gets about 50,000 thirsty visitors per year. "The first brewery in the English colonies was built here in Boston, in 1635, the year before Harvard was founded," he says. "I guess you can't have college if you don't have beer."

Koch, a sixth-generation brewmaster who holds BA, MBA, and JD degrees from Harvard, describes why beer has always been so important to Boston life. "From the day the Pilgrims landed, beer was a part of the social fabric here," he says. "For one, it was a nutritional necessity; water was polluted. By the 1600s, one of the duties of the president of Harvard was for his wife to brew beer—for the students. Today there's a street in Cambridge called Alewife. There was even one president who got kicked out—because his wife made bad beer," Koch says.

Flash-forward 100 years, at which point Boston was welcoming waves of European immigrants, including scores of brewers. "At the turn of the twentieth century, there were thirty-one breweries inside the city limits, mostly in this area," says Koch. Inspired by Samuel Adams's story, Koch decided on the Boston area to carry on the family tradition. "The whole idea was insane. No one had heard of microbrews," Koch remembers. "Back then, the whole beer world was mass-produced domestic beers: Bud, Miller, Coors, and imports. There was nothing else."

BOSTON BEER COMPANY

30 Germania St. • Jamaica Plain, MA
02130 • (617) 983-9036
bostonbeer.com • Established: 1984

SCENE & STORY

A tour of Boston Beer Company paints the picture of a remarkable craft brewing story. Starting in 1984, Jim Koch (and two business partners he met at Harvard) has built what is now the nation's largest craft brewing company, if you accept the metrics put forth by the Brewers Association (six million barrels). The Boston facility operates as a test brewery and barrel aging facility; the firm's commercial beers are brewed elsewhere. Through a remarkable combination of a great story and a standout recipe (the recipe for Boston Lager was based on a recipe created by his great-grandfather, Louis Koch), quality control, timing (the microbrewing wave was simmering nationwide), ready investment capital, hard work (he pounded the pavement and learned to drive a forklift himself), Koch and company created a barnburner of a brand and haven't looked back.

Today, more than 800 local bars serve the company's beers (and tens of thousands nationally). The company's lineup has expanded to dozens of styles, including one bi-annual release that ranks among the world's strongest: Utopias, a costly elixir aged for years in oak barrels and costing hundreds of dollars per bottle. Visitors wend through display cases brimming with medals, accounting sheets from the early days, and prototype bottles before settling in with some tasters at a small bar area. It's hard to believe how much has changed in America's brewing scene in just twenty-seven years. A Cincinnati native, Koch is proud of the role he's played in the advent of craft-brewed beer in Boston and around the country. In 1989, Boston Beer Company was cranking out some 60,000 barrels of beer. In 2015, that number stands at more like $4 million annually; Koch became a certified billionaire in 2013. That's *billion*.

"In a lot of ways, American craft brewers have become sort of the Noah's Ark of the world's brewing traditions," Koch says. "We are preserving and developing them here at the same time as they are dying out in their home countries," he says. "I'd like to think that we're one of the few pioneers of the industry left that still has that passion for innovating, experimenting, and pushing the envelope."

PHILOSOPHY

No stone unturned. There are plenty of Sam Adams beers that aren't all that good, but for all the experiments and misfires, there's an overall ratio of excellence. A couple of years ago, Koch had a 500-pound bale of fresh hops delivered, literally picked off the vine earlier in the day, which is a remarkable feat (the flowerlike cones, which are best when fresh, give beer its bitterness, aroma, and aftertaste, and must be carefully kiln-dried and packed into bales for shipment).

Even more remarkable? Koch only uses delicate European noble hops. As the vividly fresh, spicy tangy smell of Hallertau Mittelfrüh hops infused the room, Koch described how the Stanglmair clan, a hop-growing family in Bavaria supplying the hops used in Boston Lager, had helped him arrange an unprecedented air drop so he could be the first American brewer to brew with European hops picked *the same day*. It was a stunt, sure, but one that underscored his daring side, and one that guaranteed an extraordinarily aromatic finish to a batch of pilsner already steaming out of the copper-clad kettles. Chalk it up to old-fashioned Yankee optimism, and Koch's flair for marketing the craft of brewing.

"It's a lot of work for 700 cases of beer," he added, making an obvious point, but one that truly illustrates what separates craft brewers—the revolutionaries of beer making—from the old guard. "To me, it's like a responsibility. We're big enough so we have the resources to try something like this, yet we're still small enough to be crazy. That's what makes it fun."

KEY BEER

Koch has overseen the development of some 100 different beers of almost every conceivable style and some that didn't really exist before, for better or worse. But it's still the Samuel Adams Boston Lager, a smooth, 4.9% ABV lager now ubiquitous in the United States that has held up the best since it was introduced in 1985, when it won a GABF gold medal mere weeks after Boston Brewing Company opened for business. It's a spicy, malty, and faintly nutty-fruity elixir with a gorgeous, new-penny color, fluffy white head, and smacking dry finish.

MYSTIC BREWERY

174 Williams Ct. • Chelsea, MA 02150
(617) 466-2079 • mystic-brewery.com
Established: 2011

SCENE & STORY

Fascinated by preindustrial techniques yet trained in biotechnology, fermentation scientist Bryan Greenhagen founded Mystic Brewery in 2011 after a honeymoon in beer-blessed Belgium. Living in greater Boston's Mystic River Valley, he also knew he wanted his beers to reflect the time and land and place they came from. Inside the brewery's "Fermentorium," Greenhagen and Co. ferment wort (brewed offsite and transported to their facility) with wild yeast propagated from wild Maine blueberries and Vermont grapes, among other sources. In 2013 Mystic opened a beer café, bringing their rustic saisons (and charcuterie) to the suburbs of Boston.

PHILOSOPHY

Says Greenhagen, "In a world of ingredient homogenization, we aim to brew beer using the methods used for thousands of years, before modern industry. In that effort we'll develop exciting and distinctly local new styles."

KEY BEER

Vinland Two, fermented using native yeast from a Maine lowbush blueberry was delicious, and took gold in the Indigenous category at the 2013 GABF.

A BEER WITH
THE BOSTON BOY: JIM KOCH

"**Boston's a great beer town because it's a community that combines so many** different elements. It's a basic, blue-collar town, with the neighborhoods like Southie and Charlestown that you see in the movies—those are real places. You've got *Good Will Hunting* going on there. And Boston's also the world's center of higher education. Boston is able to put them together in this extraordinary way.

That's the essence of beer. Beer is democratic; beer is the alcoholic beverage equivalent of Andy Warhol's Coke bottle. People asked him, 'Why a Coke bottle?' And he said, 'This is an icon that is uniquely American.' Because in America no matter who you are—you can be Bill Gates, you can be Barack Obama, or you can be the janitor at the elementary school—everybody in the country gets the same Coke. Beer is that way, too. No matter who you are, you cannot get a better Sam Adams Boston Lager than anybody else.

If you have to leave the brewery and find another place to drink, you don't have to go very far. Just down the street is a bar called Doyle's. Doyle's has been a bar since the 1880s. It's owned by a family of Irish guys—wonderful people—the Burkes. They grew up running bars, and their dad had the beer concession at the zoo. All they ever wanted to do was run a great bar, and they've done that. It's this complete, wonderful melting pot, what a bar should be. That's where Ted Kennedy used to spend St. Patrick's Day. Mayor Flynn [Boston mayor from 1984 to 1993] went to Doyle's. I was there once when Mayor Flynn was tending bar on Saturday night. If there were a real *Cheers* bar, it would be Doyle's."

DOYLE'S CAFÉ

3484 Washington St. • Jamaica Plain, MA
02130 • (617) 524-2345
doylescafeboston.com

Low tin ceilings, acres of dark wood, Kennedy campaign posters, and fresh Sam Adams brews—this was Jim Koch's first account in 1984—make this stop essential for anyone touring the nearby Boston Beer Company. There's a small draft list with Sam Adams and Wachusett seasonals, the obligatory Guinness, and bottles of Samuel Smiths and Chimay, among others.

BEST *of the* REST: MASSACHUSETTS

NIGHT SHIFT BREWING

87 Santilli Hwy. • Everett, MA 02149 • (617) 294-4233 • nightshiftbrewing.com

Founders Michael Oxton, Mike O'Mara and Rob Burns are regularly brewing everything from pink hibiscus IPA to habañero-agave rye ale. The Sour Weisse Collection, consisting of Berliner weisses amped up with kiwi-strawberry and lemongrass-cinnamon flavors, was released in 2012. The new brewery and taproom, opened in 2012, is one of Boston's finest beer spots, with a huge bar, picnic tables, cornhole, and a steady rotation of food trucks.

TREE HOUSE BREWING COMPANY

160 E. Hill Rd. • Monson, MA 01057 • (413) 523-2367 • treehousebrew.com

Treehouse Brewing is a destination brewery on a cute little farm out in western Massachusetts that sees a great deal of traffic thanks to crowds in search of one beer: Julius, a bright, citrusy IPA ranked at 100-points on BeerAdvocate.com. With a koi pond, growler-filling station, warm, woody pub, and new brewing facility and canning line coming online, things are looking up in Monson.

DEEP ELLUM

477 Cambridge St. • Allston, MA 02134 • (617) 787-BEER (2337) • deepellum-boston.com

With its light-beige walls, beautiful polished bar, and dark wood accents, white tile floors, airy garden patio, and reasonably priced upscale comfort fare (meat loaf, mac 'n' cheese), Deep Ellum would be a go-to spot even without its excellent, even world-class, tap and bottle list. But what a list. There are twenty-eight taps and about 100 bottled varieties at any one given time (with matching logo glassware); look for beers from such insiders-only producers as High and Mighty and Pretty Things, both of Massachusetts, and Belgium's De Ranke.

LORD HOBO

92 Hampshire St. • Cambridge, MA 02141 • (617) 250-8454 • lordhobo.com

One of the most hyped craft beer bars to come along in the Northeast in some time (from Daniel Lanigan, former owner of the Moan & Dove in Amherst and the Dirty Truth in Northampton), Lord Hobo took over the space of B-Side, a fabled cocktail bar in Inman Square, in late 2009. With forty taps balanced between obscurities and crowd-pleasers, three hand-pump lines, regular appearances by well-known craft brewers, a small but connoisseur-ready bottle list, and a few bar-top casks, the beer bona fides are absolutely solid. The beer selection is complemented by an ambitious (and accordingly priced) menu of haute-comfort food (boquerones, pork belly, pan-seared scallops, grilled rib-eye) served in a dark, arty environment. Now Lanigan's running a 47,000-square-foot production brewery, Lord Hobo Brewing Co. in Woburn (5 Draper St.; 781-281-0809), to brew, among others, Boom Sauce, a brashly hopped 7.4% ABV American-style IPA in cans.

THE PUBLICK HOUSE

1648 Beacon St. • Brookline, MA 02445 • (617) 277-2880 • eatgoodfooddrinkbetterbeer.com

With thirty-six taps and about 150 bottle selections, the Publick House has garnered rapturous reviews since 2002 from beer geeks and casual fans alike, drawn in by its vast menu, candlelit interior, and broadly Belgian-influenced pub-grub menu. The beer list is divided into Belgian, Belgian-style, Here (domestic craft) and There (imported craft), and yields some very unusual treats, such as a recent sour, dark Flemish red beer called Cuvée Des Jacobins Rouge (5.5% ABV) from Brouwerij Bockor.

REDBONES

55 Chester St. • Somerville, MA 02144 • (617) 628-2200 • redbones.com

A dependable, down-to-earth barbecue place open since 1987 and serving up big heaping piles of Memphis-, Texas-, Arkansas-, and St. Louis–style ribs, Redbones has always had a strong beer list. And with beer bars all over the country raising the bar to unheard-of heights in terms of hard-to-find beers, this affably rough-hewn two-story place has kept pace, adding a total of twenty-eight taps, a smart little bottle list, and cask-conditioned ales. Recent drafts have included such California cult beers as Lost Abbey and Ballast Point, two makers of big-hearted beers that go well with the spicy, juicy barbecue feast coming off the grill.

ARMSBY ABBEY

144 Main St. • Worcester, MA 01608 • (508) 795-1012 • armsbyabbey.com

Chef-owner Alec Lopez opened this elegant gastropub in 2008, developing a rock-solid local following for his epicurean bites and esoteric, sought-after brews. Then the place went "global" in 2012, when the Shelton Bros. importers' first annual "Festival" was staged in town. For several days straight, Lopez's bar was jammed with international brewing stars (and their beers), cementing the bar's reputation. If you make it here, don't miss The Dive Bar, another low-key Lopez masterpiece in Worcester.

CAMBRIDGE BREWING CO.

1 Kendall Sq., Bldg. 100 • Cambridge, MA 02139 • (617) 494-1994 • cambridgebrewingcompany.com

The oldest brewpub in the Boston area (est. 1989) has been spreading its wings in recent years, broadening from the ambers, porters, and stouts that won it early praise into tasty farmhouse styles and herb-and-spiced brews that are harder to brew than to love. Look for longtime brewmaster Will Myers's hits like Sgt. Pepper, brewed with four kinds of pepper, and Le Saisonierre, a traditional saison.

TRILLIUM BREWING CO.

369 Congress St. • Boston, MA 02210 • (617) 453-8745 • trilliumbrewing.com

Opened in March 2013 with the support of "family, volunteers, two babies, and three employees," Trillium has found a massively appreciative audience in Boston, allowing the upstart to expand into a 16,000-square-foot production brewery and tasting room in nearby Canton in 2015 (about 20 miles south). The beers in both locations range from pale ales, "dank, juicy" IPAs, and stouts, to a handful of wild ales, farmhouse-inspired saisons, and other barrel-aged adventures.

JACK'S ABBY

100 Clinton St. • Framingham, MA 01702 • (774) 777-5085 • jacksabby.com

Brothers Jack, Eric, and Sam Hendler lead Jack's Abby (named for Jack's wife Abby), which has been brewing wildly popular craft lagers since 2011. With this 67,000-square-foot expansion brewery and restaurant opened in 2015 driving the effort, Jack's Abby canned brews are among the most ubiquitous in the Northeast these days. Stop by for wood-fired pizza, local mussels, and other beer-friendly fare to wash down with well-made brews like the Hoponious Union India Pale Lager.

NEW HAMPSHIRE

Hampton

SMUTTYNOSE BREWING CO.

105 Towle Farm Rd. • Hampton, NH 03842 • (603) 436-4026
smuttynose.com • Established: 1994

SCENE & STORY

Named for Smuttynose Island, the third-largest of the nine islands that form the Isles of Shoals, a small, rugged archipelago offshore, this is one of the Northeast's biggest beer success stories, launched in Portsmouth in 1994 and moved, in 2014, to Towle farm, founded around 1639 and formerly home to nine generations of Towles. Now there's a restaurant and disc golf course amid the orchards, garden plots, and beehives.

Cofounder Peter Egelston, a Spanish Lit grad (who, with his sister, helped to open an earlier pair of pioneering breweries in New Hampshire, in Northampton and Portsmouth), is still in charge. Meanwhile the brewing team has grown and evolved to handle huge packaging projects, like the "Big Beers" and "SmuttLabs" series of large format and experimental beers. Brewery director David Yarrington, a home brewer and chemistry major at Colby College, worked for a number of good breweries before completing the UC Davis Master Brewers Program and joining Smuttynose in 2001 but left at the end of 2002 to pursue other projects.

PHILOSOPHY

All-in. With a farm-based brewery, farm-to-table restaurant, successful IPAs ("Bouncy House" and "Big-A"), and free-wheeling experimental beer series, is there anything these guys won't do well? Don't count on it.

KEY BEER

The English-style Shoal's Pale Ale put Smutty on the map, but it's the new seasonals and experimental Big Beers that are really breaking path these days, like Durty, an engrossing, 8.4% ABV hoppy brown ale, or the 8.2% ABV Smoky Scotch Ale.

Hooksett

WHITE BIRCH BREWING

1368 Hooksett Rd., Unit 6 • Hooksett, NH
03106 • (603) 244-8593
whitebirchbrewing.com • Established: 2009

SCENE & STORY

New Hampshire's first nanobrewery, founded by dedicated home brewer turned-pro Bill Herlicka in a plain industrial space, started with half barrel (about fifteen gallon)–batches that became so popular he was almost immediately planning a 7bbl brewhouse to meet demand. That expansion now complete, Herlicka is still running a small operation dedicated to making excellent beer in unusual styles, many of which are barrel-aged British- and Belgian-style beers. There's a small tasting room area for samples and growler
sales, but no tours of the little brewery.

PHILOSOPHY

White Birch is no-frills but innovative, a classic successful craft brewer combination. It's not that he lacks ideas, he has said, it's that he suffers for a shortage of time and fermenter space—the two most expensive ingredients in brewing.

KEY BEER

Look for the Hooksett Belgian IPA, an intense, spicy, hop-suffused bomb of a beer at 9.5% ABV.

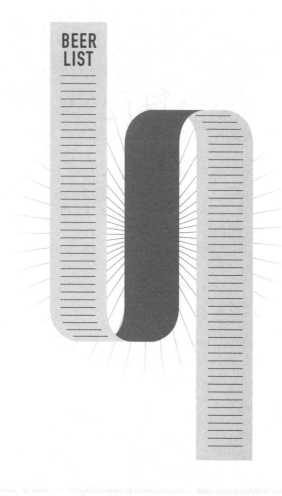

BEER LIST

BEST *of the* REST: NEW HAMPSHIRE

WOODSTOCK STATION INN & BREWERY

135 Main St. • North Woodstock, NH 03262 • (800) 321-3985 • woodstockinnnh.com

The Woodstock Station Inn opened its little copper, wood, and brick-clad seven-barrel brewery in 1996 and soon began booking guests deeply interested in the process of brewing itself. Offered in April and May for $125 (not including room cost), Brewery Weekend guests enjoy a reception Friday night and beer dinner Saturday, breakfast each morning and lunch on Saturday, and the chance to try out some aspects of the process during hands-on sessions in the brewhouse.

7TH SETTLEMENT

47 Washington St. • Dover, NH 03820 • (603) 373-1001 • 7thsettlement.com

A close-knit brew co-op (with One Love Brewing) and farm-to-table restaurant anchor this busy destination in Dover, opened in an historic wool and linen factory in 2013 (and named for Dover, the 7th non-native community settled in the New World). The locavore, nose-to-tail food is super ambitious, with housemade noodles, bread, sausage, bacon, ketchup, and beer-brined chicken, among other offerings, all paired with house beers from a dozen taps, of course.

VERMONT

WITH SOME FORTY BREWERIES AND COUNTING, VERMONT IS ONE OF THE MOST BREWERY-DOTTED states in the U.S. per capita. There are great beer bars and taprooms all over the state and the helpful Vermont Brewers website (vermontbrewers.com) will fill you in on the many options. As of this writing, though, some of the most famous breweries and beers don't have taprooms or tours, like the Alchemist (of Heady Topper fame) and Lawson's Finest Liquids, makers of the beloved Sip of Sunshine IPA. So do some research and ask around in taprooms where your Vermont ale trail should head next.

HILL FARMSTEAD

403 Hill Rd. • Greensboro Bend, VT 05842
(802) 533-7450 hillfarmstead.com
Established: 2010

SCENE & STORY

Eighth-generation Vermonter Shaun Hill recommends you do some Google mapping or consult your onboard GPS before trying to locate his remote brewery down a dirt road in the countryside where he's leading a revolution of the Vermont brewing scene. It is exceedingly tricky to find his award-winning beers anywhere else. Whatever else you hear about Hill Farmstead, understand that a successful visit takes careful prior planning—it's remote and can be very crowded on weekends.

Hill's journey from home to Europe and home again has become northeastern beer geek gospel. First he worked entry-level jobs in a pair of breweries in Vermont after college and then gained increasing responsibilities in three firms in Europe. Among them was Danish craft brewery Nørrebro Bryghus, led at the time by Anders Kissmeyer, a brewer who had taken a revolutionary road of his own by pioneering experimental styles in Carlsberg-saturated Denmark. The partnership was a fruitful one: three beers the still unknown Hill brewed with Kissmeyer earned two golds and a silver at the 2010 World Beer Cup in Chicago, news which filled thousands of attendees with admiration and a question: *Wait, who is this guy?*

Around this time, Hill returned from Europe, and used borrowed equipment and loans from fans and friends to get his own brewery up and running on land not far from the spot where his great-great-grandfather had opened a tavern (on Hill Road).

Shaun Hill is a reluctant prophet, a Jonah of the northeastern kingdom. Even in 2011 the line for growlers could be two hours long, every single weekend. This was not what he signed up for. No one wants to keep customers waiting. And pulling customers' cars out of the mud with his tractor was no fun, either. Patrons selling their purchases on the growing gray and black markets became a growing practice Hill despised. Then in late April of 2013, *Vanity Fair* ran an interview with Hill. Now what had been a semi-underground beer geek conversation was the stuff of glossy checkstand magazines. As any small business owner knows, too much attention can be a very difficult thing. But Hill and Co. managed the chaos well.

Today Hill has built a shiny new brewery next to the original barn and tasting room, and the crowds continue, as do the accolades. In 2015, RateBeer announced Hill Farmstead as its top brewery in Vermont, in the United States, and in the world.

Not that they shouldn't. The beers have been simply outstanding, from Belgian wit beer (Florence) to Black IPA aged in pinot noir barrels and dry-hopped with Simcoe (Jim), a release of a mere twenty-five cases. Ephraim, a 10.3% ABV Imperial IPA, contains five hop varieties and off-the-chart IBUs, but has dazzled the relatively few beer lovers who have been able to taste it. And on the sour spectrum, Hill is just as assured. Prolegomena, a Flanders red collaboration with the Boston-area brewer Will Meyers, of Cambridge Brewing Company, is a great beer, a tart rebuke to the status quo.

PHILOSOPHY

Brewer as Superman? Hill has released beers he says were inspired by Danish philosopher Søren Kierkegaard and Friedrich Nietzsche, and working within the arch-individualistic underpinnings those associations suggest, he aims to please. "All of my decisions, related to the present and future of Hill Farmstead Brewery, are calculated, rational, and existential," Hill says. Make sure your decision to drive up there from Boston or New York is similarly calculated, preferably on a weekday.

KEY BEER

The Ancestor series is an ongoing celebration of Hill's forebears in the area including Edward (an APA that is his best seller). The Collaboration series was launched with a beer Hill called Fear and Trembling (there's the Kierkegaard), a smoked Baltic Porter aged in French oak cabernet barrels. Kissmeyer himself traveled from Denmark to assist his former pupil, hand smoking the malt over maple wood chips outside the barn, resulting in a powerfully smoky 9.3% ABV brew with chocolate- and espresso-like flavors and a vinous finish.

BEST *of the* REST: VERMONT

FIDDLEHEAD BREWING COMPANY

6305 Shelburne Rd. • Shelburne, VT 05482 • (802) 399-2994 • fiddleheadbrewing.com

Opened in 2012 in Shelburne right off Route 7 near Lake Champlain, Fiddlehead has a simple tasting room in a tall, red barnlike building next door to Folino's pizza, which is BYOB and uses a wood-fired oven. With Second Fiddle, an 8.2% ABV canned DIPA, the brewery—led by Matt "Matty O" Cohen—joins the state tradition of great IPAs led by Heady Topper, the canned sensation brewed by the Alchemist Brewery, and Liquid Sunshine, brewed by Lawson's Finest Liquids. Go on a Monday and fill a growler for two dollars off.

THE FARMHOUSE TAP & GRILL

160 Bank St. • Burlington, VT 05401 • (802) 859-0888 • farmhousetg.com

In a beautiful turn of events perhaps indicating some important cultural wind direction, the building that houses this new (2010) gastropub used to be home to a McDonald's—for thirty years. Today, the space is dedicated to a classic farm-to-table eatery with a beer list every bit as curated as its menu of grass-fed beef, free-range poultry, and heritage pork dishes accented by local cheese, charcuterie, and produce. Regional and local producers, including Hill Farmstead, Otter Creek, Trapp, Rock Art, and Wolaver's, are all well represented, as are many of the top American and Belgian small batch and farmhouse-style producers.

THREE PENNY TAPROOM

108 Main St. • Montpelier, VT 05602 • (802) 223-8277 • threepennytaproom.com

A craft beer bar on Montpelier's Main Street, Three Penny Taproom has twenty-four taps and forty-five bottles available, including craft-brewed Belgian, American, and particularly Northeast beers such as Heady Topper, Hill Farmstead, Southern Tier, and Trapp Family, paired with local cheeses.

The Mid-Atlantic ↗

The MID-ATLANTIC

THOUGH THIS REGION WAS ONCE RICH WITH LOCAL AND REGIONAL BREWERIES, NEARLY ALL died off during Prohibition. The comeback, starting in the 1980s and following the lead of West Coast path-breakers, didn't happen overnight. Thanks to their relative nearness to cosmopolitan Europe, cities like New York and D.C. had become hotbeds for pricey imports from England, Germany, and Holland starting in the 1970s. As innovative importers introduced Belgian ales and Eastern European pilsners to choosey, sophisticated northeasterners, their tastes for beer began to wander. At the same time, ambitious British-style brewpubs and microbreweries began to thrive in the suburbs and even in rural towns. These weren't kids in a model U.N. or hippies going back to the land, these were brewers challenging the status quo and marching their fresh creations steadily into the best bars, restaurants, and quarters of town, opening a lot of minds in the process. There is now a tiny artisanal brewery on one Manhattan rooftop (Eataly's La Birreria), and D.C. power players crowd into brewpubs like the Brewer's Art every night of the week. No matter where you start or end up on a tour of the region, it's a beer lover's feast.

NEW YORK CITY

TEN YEARS AGO, NEW YORK CITY WAS A CRAFT BEER BACKWATER. THERE WERE A HANDFUL of bars with ambitious lists, sure, and some true diamonds in the rough (like the original Blind Tiger Alehouse, a gloriously mildewed, Lilliputian tavern in the West Village). But it wasn't enough. A handful of craft breweries had struggled to their feet, some dying soon after, and there was a general sense around the millennium that New York might shrug off the craft beer renaissance and remain the alpha city that it is: expensive and above the fray. It was a place for cocktails, pricey wines, and power lunches, not rare farmhouse ales. New York City habitually ignores trends that do not spring from its culturally superior loins, and the crunchier-than-thou methodology of microbrew culture always seemed out of place.

But good local beer belongs here. New York City has beer in its very foundations: No fewer than three breweries called New Amsterdam home in 1612; in 1913, a man named Jake Ruppert built a $30 million dollar brewery and got himself a baseball team, the Yankees (and Babe Ruth); Brooklyn produced one-fifth of the nation's beer by 1960, according to a recent *New York Times* story. But alas, by 1976, the number of local breweries had dropped to zero, and no one really cared about beer anymore. The best beers in town were standard-issue, mass-produced imports like Bass, Heineken, and Beck's.

All that's changed. It was only a matter of time perhaps, but the Slow Food–obsessed, pickle-your-own-cucumber inclinations (of Brooklynites, in particular) have ignited a new local beer scene. Dozens of reputable small breweries now call the city home, which means beer lovers get to drink far fresher beer, especially unfiltered, unpasteurized beers made in traditional styles, the kind in-the-know beer lovers seek out.

Naturally, the best action for beer travelers is found in the pubs, but for the beer traveler looking to splurge, several of the city's best restaurants have ambitiously scaled up their beer lists recently, too. Where beer was once an afterthought, it's now got its own menus—even beer sommeliers. Now truer than ever: New York, the city where you can get absolutely anything.

ITINERARIES

1-DAY The Blind Tiger; Other Half; Brooklyn Brewery, Spuyten Duyvil; Tørst

3-DAY One-day itinerary plus Carton; Blue Hill at Stone Barns; Defiant Brewing Co.; Captain Lawrence; Sixpoint

7-DAY Three-day itinerary plus Ommegang in Cooperstown

Manhattan

MCSORLEY'S OLD ALE HOUSE

15 E. 7th St. • New York, NY 10003
(212) 473-9148 • mcsorleysnewyork.com
Established: Around 1860

SCENE & STORY

Every New York beer tour should start (and maybe also end) here. Joseph Mitchell's 1943 book *McSorley's Wonderful Saloon* describes this timeless place: "Down the middle of the room is a row of battered tables. Their tops are always sticky with spilled ale. In the centre of the room stands the belly stove, which has an isinglass door and is exactly like the stoves in Elevated stations. All winter Kelly keeps it red hot. "Warmer you get, drunker you get," he says. Some customers prefer mulled ale. They keep their mugs on the hob until the ale gets as hot as coffee. A sluggish cat named Minnie sleeps in a scuttle beside the stove."

Nothing much has changed, and though tourists predictably flock inside, they do so with very good reason. Open since about 1860 and reportedly unchanged inside since 1910, it's New York's oldest continuously operating saloon, and with its sawdust floors and walls packed with ephemera, it's a time machine. To walk in is to follow in the footsteps of Abe Lincoln, Woody Guthrie, and John Lennon, among others. At McSorley's, frankly, it's not about the beer; it's about the place. It's about time spent with good friends, deep (or not so deep) conversations, and conjuring the easy elegance of a simpler time in the city.

PHILOSOPHY

"Be Good or Be Gone" and "We Were Here Before You Were Born" are the two house mottos. Women were not allowed in until 1970, and it can still be a bit of a boy's club (as in modern-day Jersey boys), but on a good quiet afternoon it feels just as it should.

KEY BEER

McSorley's beer, first brewed by a long lost brewing company called Fidelio and later Schmidt, comes in two varieties, both quite light. Hopheads need not apply. Order one beer; two mugs are served. From time to time one hears of plans afoot to remake the recipe, for now it's a pair of Stroh's/Pabst creations, simply one "light" and one "dark" and nothing to write home about.

THE GINGER MAN

11 E. 36th St. • New York, NY 10016
212) 532-3740 • gingerman-ny.com
Established: 1996

SCENE & STORY

A New York standby and offshoot of the original Houston Ginger Man (though only this location is still owned by founder Bob Precious), the beer list is truly incredible here, with some seventy taps and scores of truly obscure beers and a solid menu of upscale pub favorites. The Ginger Man is large and well lit, with varnished wood booths, white tile wall details, framed beer posters, and, perhaps most importantly, the presence of Anne Becerra, one of the only bartending female Cicerones in the United States. Wise imbibers will avoid weekday happy hour, when the bar lines up three deep with Midtown and Murray Hill office workers clamoring for a brew.

But watch the schedule for appearances by brewers and special tappings. On a recent night Jérôme Rebetez, the Swiss founder of cultishly watched Brasserie des Franches-Montagnes, popped in for a bottle release.

PHILOSOPHY

Big and brash yet benign. Around the bar are lovely chalk murals by Julie Gaither, another bartender, attesting that this is a beer bar with its heart in the right place.

KEY BEER

Fluffy White Rabbits from Pretty Things Beer & Ale Project, an 8.5% ABV tripel-style beer. It's hay-hued with funky layers of tropical fruit and spices like thyme and lemon grass.

PONY BAR

637 10th Ave. • New York, NY 10036
(212) 586-2707 • hk.theponybar.com
Established: 2009

1444 1st Ave. at 75th St. • New York, NY 10036 • (212) 288-0090
ues.theponybar.com • Established: 2012

SCENE & STORY

Hell's Kitchen has long been a hellhole of underlit, overpriced sports bars with dirty lines and questionable food—not a craft brew in sight. So the arrival of the Pony Bar was a very welcome change for the countless New Yorkers who live and work nearby. Inspired by an old black-and-white photo of Neil Young, there are exposed brick walls, a handsome bar, and snatches of Americana (wooden oars, a canoe on the ceiling, old wooden beer barrels, parade bunting, and a forty-eight-star Old Glory). The five-dollar, fourteen-ounce pours are quite fair (five dollars for eight ounces on imperials and other big beers) and the vibe is friendly, if a little homogenous. All twenty tap beers are labeled with ABV and brewery; when a new keg comes on tap, the cellarman rings a bell and the patrons cheer "New beer!" In 2012 the Upper East Side location opened, and has been busy ever since, surviving an arson-fire in 2015.

PHILOSOPHY

All of Pony Bar's craft beers are American and on draft (there are only two bottles, in fact—Budweiser and Bud Light, for the uninitiated). There are no dedicated tap lines; the selection continuously changes, with a preponderance of Northeast gems and a happy hour starting at 4:20 p.m. daily (subtle!). It's a bar for both the curious and committed craft beer drinker eager to try every new thing; the owners even organize tours to local area breweries. Regulars who try at least 100 brews earn a cool, Pony Bar short-sleeve button-down; and there have been a good many who've put in that hard work so far.

KEY BEER

There's a strong northeastern regional presence, so look for new releases from Kelso, Sixpoint, Brooklyn, Ithaca, and Captain Lawrence.

RESTO

111 E. 29th St. • New York, NY 10016
(212) 685-5585 • restonyc.com
Established: 2007

SCENE & STORY

The word *resto* is sometimes used as slang in France for a casual restaurant, but the sophisticated Belgian artistry here rises above the fray with sure-handed, nose-to-tail cooking served in a cozy refuge. Moules frites shine here, naturally: try the Dijon, housemade bacon, Parmesan, onion confit, and tarragon combo (the green curry, lemongrass, coconut milk, and kaffir lime combo is also excellent). What's more, there's a bit of bacchanalian sensibility when it comes to both beer and portions, which are available in ultralarge sizes. Fancy a delicious whole roast chicken for two ($60) and a three-liter Jeroboam of luscious St. Feuillen Tripel ($165)? You've come to the right place. The great thing is that you won't feel like an idiot for ordering said jumbo spreads. It's what people do at Resto, and it's worth both the cost and effort. Dining at the bar is a great option if the tables kept open for walk-ins are already spoken for. Sunday dinners are institutional, and recently beer dinners have gotten more frequent. The slightly older crowd consists of well-dressed Manhattanites, but doesn't feel annoyingly business-like. The Cannibal, owner Christian Pappanicholas's beer and butcher shop next door, is also a must-see.

PHILOSOPHY

Elegance and earthiness in equal measure—big measures.

KEY BEER

There are seven good Belgian ales on tap starting with Bavik Pilsner on the lighter side and heading all the way up the scale of liver impact to Koningshoeven's 10% ABV Quadruple, certainly a fine place to stop if you've had the five in between.

JIMMY'S NO. 43

43 E. 7th St. • New York, NY 10003
(212) 982-3006 • jimmysno43.com
Established: 2005

SCENE & STORY

Most nights when you amble down the stairs into this amiable *rathskeller* (a bar below street level) the compact, stocky New York craft beer maven Jimmy Carbone is perched on a stool to greet you, along with the aroma of some very good food cooking—stick-to-your-ribs fare like ribs and gnocchi and recently, even some interesting Filipino comfort food. Jimmy's got a twinkle in his eye and a beer in hand, and he's glad to see you. The bar has a small, cozy dining room area, a narrow bar, and more or less feels like it was transported, inch by inch, out of Germany. There's something wonderfully enveloping about the bar, or maybe that's just the way it feels when you huddle in cheek by jowl to sample beers and rap with Jimmy or and his crew. When an adjacent building collapsed in a fiery gas-leak explosion in 2015, Jimmy's was nearly destroyed, and was forced to close for weeks on end. It was a very, very close call.

PHILOSOPHY

With twelve ever-changing taps of beer and some twenty-six in bottles, Carbone takes things coast-to-coast, and somehow he manages to score a lot of unique kegs other bars never seem to have.

KEY BEER

Jimmy loves his Belgian ales, from the mother country and our American counterparts, sometimes pitting them against one another in taste-offs. Brasserie De Ranke's XX Bitter, a dry, bitter, and peppery Belgian pale ale inspired by Orval is sometimes on tap. It was brewed to be the hoppiest beer in Belgium and is not for the fainthearted, but rewards those who love earthy, intensely flavored brews.

281 Bleecker St. • Ny, NY 10014 • (212) 462-4682 • blindtigeralehouse.com • Established: 1995

Beer, the drink of the people! Few New Yorkers understand this better than the owners of the Blind Tiger, a legendary New York City tavern that was relocated not long ago to the West Village. Dave Brodrick, its co-owner, was forced to close shop in late 2006, weakened by a long-running licensing battle involving the State Liquor Commission and 66th District Councilwoman Deborah J. Glick. His secret weapon? An Internet petition, signed by hundreds of the bar's most fervent fans.

For ten years, the Hudson Street incarnation of the Tiger (as it was often called) had offered a vast selection of artisan-made ales from European and American microbrewers (nary a drop of Bud, Miller, or Coors was served, ever). But the surroundings took some getting used to.

"The Blind Tiger Ale House is Dirty, Unhospitable [sic], Unpleasant, and served Terrible Beer," protested Brian Ó Broin, an assistant professor of linguistics and medieval literature in New Jersey, on a website he created expressly for this complaint. "Ambience: 0 [not a single redeeming quality]," he railed.

To the uninitiated it seemed oppressively small and crabbed, especially on weekends, when regulars shied away. The list could seem by turns eccentric and expensive; there were rare bottles selling for twenty dollars, but if you somehow managed to get to the bar to order one, your feet were sticking to the floor. And a visit to its bathroom, a malevolent place at the bottom of a staircase (itself macabre) was not easily forgotten.

And so the Irishman wasn't much taken in by its charms. Nor was the Tiger's landlord, who hiked the rent in 2005, forcing the tavern to make way for Starbucks no. 374. Brodrick searched eight months for a new venue to house the Blind Tiger, settling on a former bar across from John's Pizzeria, but just before the new location opened, Deborah Glick—councilwoman for the neighborhood—wrote a letter to the State Liquor Commission urging denial of the new Tiger's liquor license on the basis that it would be "a large bar that primarily serves beer." Say it isn't so, Glick! Brodrick launched a charm offensive, opening the new Tiger sans beer—but armed with unusual cheeses, pressed sandwiches, baked goods, espresso drinks, even birch beer (nonalcoholic). No Coyote Ugly, this. Then he invited Glick to come see what the Tiger was all about. A little business trickled in, but no Glick. The stalemate wouldn't break, and eventually, Brodrick shuttered the doors. Fifteen hard months of exile began; New York's beer crowd glowered in their mugs somewhere else, and talked about the Tiger.

Like the Dove, the miniscule Hammersmith, London watering hole once favored by Graham Greene and Ernest Hemingway, or McSorley's Old Alehouse, the original Blind Tiger was dusty and cramped. It was, at its best, old-world squalor exalted. As the stalemate continued, Brodrick and Co. planned their new Tiger, nearly double the size of the original. It would be a beer boutique, a shrine to craft-brewed brews complete with wood-paneled walls and floors, custom bar, temperature-controlled cellar (for aging rare ales), and a selection every bit as byzantine as the menu at Murray's Cheese Shop, just down the block. It wouldn't be easy. But the tigers were restless.

Vive la résistance! Starting in September 2006, a Tiger militia—hailing from the New York area and a handful of foreign countries—began circulating an e-petition aimed at the State Liquor Authority. Thomas Paine, who, more than 230 years ago, cried out for fairness from the Crown on the taxation of beer—"the humblest drink of life"—might have been proud. "[The Blind Tiger] is far removed from those outlets who seek the sort of person that consumes cheap mass-produced drinks associated with binge drinking and uncouth behavior," wrote Alex Hall, of Brooklyn—the document's author and John Hancock. "Good beer is the new wine," wrote David Gould, signer no. 997, adding, a bit unhelpfully, that "drinkers of yellow beer should be drawn and quartered," a reference to both King George III's preferred form of execution and the sort of mass-produced dross unfit for the Tigerian palate. Others struck a more conciliatory tone. The Tiger "will be a nice quiet place where you can bring your mother," assured one. Carry on, men! "Peace and quiet are to be found in the Catskills, not on Bleecker Street! Prohibition is over!" howled one insurrectionary. Another cited Jane Jacobs's 1961 manifesto, *The Death and Life of Great American Cities*, with its endorsement of civilized bars. "As a bouncer in good standing with local law enforcement," wrote Raymond Lopez, signer no. 999, "I can attest to the well-behaved manners of this crowd." One after another cast the closure in patriotic terms. "For a beer enthusiast, the closing of the old BT was as tragic as if they closed the Statue of Liberty," one gloamed. Peter Flanagan—the 1,385th partisan to commit his name—rattled his musket to end the debate: "Enough already; the people have spoken."

Indeed they had. The board eventually relented, and in March 2007, the Tiger reopened with a huge (but civilized!) party that hasn't really stopped. Infinitely cleaner, but no less fun, it's New York's most fiercely defended beer territory.

Here, brewers are rock stars. The Tiger is especially strong in West Coast beers, a good thing for East Coasters looking for beers with aggressive hop character. Cheese samples from Murray's across the street are often on hand for the taking, too. It's all quite civilized, really. Looking back on the battle, Brodrick was circumspect. "A well-dressed woman came in the other day and told me our bathrooms were the nicest she'd ever seen," he said.

The Blind Tiger's menu rotates weekly as brewmasters personally bring in their freshest releases. Simply scan the board, chat with the bartenders (or owners, who are normally on hand), and get busy sampling.

LA BIRRERIA AT EATALY NYC

200 5th Ave. (top floor) • New York, NY
10010 • Entrances on 5th Ave. and 23rd St.
(212) 229-2560 • eatalyny.com
Established: 2011

SCENE & STORY

Set in an 8,000-square-foot aerie soaring above Manhattan with views of the Flatiron and Empire State Buildings, La Birreria serves up the ultimate in Italian-style cask-conditioned ales (brewed on premises) paired with food by Mario Batali. The dream team in charge includes American brewing standout Sam Calagione of Dogfish Head and creative Italian craft beer stars Teo Musso of Birrificio Le Baladin and Leonardo Di Vincenzo of Birra del Borgo. Brewer Brooks Carretta is at the kettles. That's a lot of hands in the brewhouse, but all very able ones indeed.

PHILOSOPHY

Old-world flavors and techniques mingle with unhinged experimentation, both in the kettle and on the plate. "This may well be the craziest and most amazing brewery in the world," says Di Vincenzo.

KEY BEER

All of the Birreria's beers are served on cask, with three cask beer engines featuring two year-round beers and one rotating seasonal. Staples include an English mild made with Italian chestnut powder and American pale ale made with dried thyme from Italy. In addition, there are eight draft taps with beers from Italian and American craft breweries.

ELEVEN MADISON PARK

11 Madison Ave. • New York, NY 10010
(212) 889-0905 • elevenmadisonpark.com
Established: 1998

SCENE & STORY

Only in New York could a restaurant with three *Michelin* stars, four stars from the *New York Times*, and James Beard Awards count as a great beer destination as well. And while it's not exactly the typical beer experience to sample artisanal beers and delicate market-driven cuisine in an elegant, hushed dining room, it's an experience whose time has come. The chef, Daniel Humm, is among the best in the world, and if *he* says beer's acidity, residual sweetness, and sometimes oak barrel-given tannins work just as well with certain foods as the best wines, then who are we to protest? Pick a special occasion. Splurge, guiltlessly. The quieter the room, the louder you can hear your beer.

The beer list here is profound, with just four drafts but over 100 rare and vintage brews that are rarely seen in the

United States. In 2011, Humm developed two unique collaborative beers with Brooklyn Brewery's Garrett Oliver and the Old Rip Van Winkle Distillery. Then to kick things up a notch, Humm and Oliver began to plan a series of dinners for which both the entire menu and the beers were created from scratch to work together for a single meal. When a single beer can take anywhere from ten days to three years to brew, this will be no small effort going forward, and you can be sure spots will be hard to come by.

PHILOSOPHY

Respect, consider, revolutionize. "We have been pushing the presence of beer in our dining room," says Kirk Kelewae, a former server and staff beer guru who worked his way up to GM before age thirty. "I provide beer pairings to guests when they request it, and we've picked up a whole collection of crystal beer glasses from Spiegelau. We're working to redefine how beer is served in a fine-dining restaurant."

KEY BEER

Other than the Brooklyn collaborative beers? It just depends on what you're ordering for lunch—by all means ask for pairings from Kelewae or a member of his staff—but the restaurant's collection of beers from Brasserie Franches-Montagnes, an obscure but highly collectible producer, rivals any in the world.

SCENE & STORY

Vol Du Nuit is a bar in three parts: a dimly lit back room with a back bar made for slurping *moules frites* and Abbey ales, a courtyard in the middle for sitting sort of al fresco, and a tiny bar that most people breeze past as they enter the inner sanctum through a covered tunnel. But it's that one, the street side bar in its diminutive glory, that makes this place worth a stop. And though there are plenty of trendier West Village bars that have better beer lists, and maybe even some that want to transport you to the University district of Brussels, this one succeeds the most convincingly. It's all about the atmosphere, sort of *Ronin* meets *Amélie* minus the gnomes and gunplay. You might suddenly want to bum a smoke from the NYU grad students hanging out, write in a leather-bound journal, and bike around cobblestone streets humming Bjork. It happens.

PHILOSOPHY

This no-frills bar is simply amiable and doesn't pretend to be more nor less than it is, a great place to have a good Belgian beer and some good, restorative food, and catch up with an old friend or two. It's an escape in the busy Village, a hideout from the hustle.

KEY BEER

The Belgian ales Orval and Saison Dupont are both available by the bottle, and they are both world-class, inimitable brews normal college kids can seldom afford, so you probably didn't drink them on your junior year abroad. Belgian ales are often better consumed by the bottle rather than on draft, so simply ask for the list and see what's in the cellar.

Barking Orders

goodbeerseal.com

When in the New York City area, stop and look for a little red sticker on the window or near the door with a red seal hoisting a big stein of beer—"the Good Beer Seal." That means it's one of the beer bars a small but dedicated group of local beer lovers and bar owners (led by Jimmy Carbone of Jimmy's 43 and also including Dave Brodrick of the Blind Tiger) have anointed as a great place to drink craft beer. Jimmy writes, "Good Beer Seal Bars are committed to the presentation, promotion and enjoyment of good craft beer; seeking out the best beers from local, national and international producers. This commitment includes serving these beers the way brewers have intended, including proper glassware and temperature (within reason!). A good portion of a Good Beer Seal Bar's beer should be via a draft beer/cask ale program and draft lines should be properly maintained and cleaned . . . An active community presence is essential for a Good Beer Seal bar." Now you know!

RATTLE N HUM

14 E. 33rd St. (between 5th and Madison)
New York, NY 10016 • (212) 481-1586
rattlenhumbarnyc.com
Established: 2008

SCENE & STORY

Rattle N Hum is the best place to escape the hubbub of Midtown, an ace up the sleeve. Narrow and cozy with a grand, mirrored wood bar and forty beers on tap, the lines are routinely serviced. There are some 100 bottles on the list, and a rotating bevy of cask-conditioned ales (twenty-four on a recent visit). Practice your best New Yorker attitude when sidling up to the bar (it's all in the elbows). And in April—a nice, not too hot time to be in town—RNH hosts a cask ales festival, the back of the bar stacked high with firkins of delicate English-style ales.

PHILOSOPHY

This is a straightforward, narrow, and sometimes crowded bar with a serious beer list and decent pub grub. The menu has a strong Northeast focus, plus specialty Norwegian and Belgian imports, and hard-to-find American releases on cask as well.

KEY BEER

Captain Lawrence Xtra Gold (10% ABV; ten dollars for twenty-five ounces), brewed in nearby Westchester County, is an American interpretation of the traditional "tripel," a hazy golden ale with a spicy backbone and notes of clove and lemon peel. It goes perfectly with the beer-battered fish and chips.

Brooklyn

BROOKLYN BREWERY

No. 1 Brewers Row • 79 N. 11th St.
Brooklyn, NY 11211 • (718) 486-7422
brooklynbrewery.com
Established: 1987

SCENE & STORY

Once, there were some four dozen breweries in Brooklyn, producing a fifth of the nation's brews. Today, there are just a few in operation, and all of them are products of the modern craft beer era. The most famous of them is Brooklyn Brewery, a short ride from Manhattan on the L train into Williamsburg and by all means worth the beer traveler's efforts. Since former Associated Press journalist Steve Hindy and his downstairs neighbor Tom Potter founded the company in 1987 (with a ribbon cutting by Mayor Rudolph Giuliani), and especially with the arrival of brewmaster Garrett Oliver in 1994, the company's fame and acclaim have grown. There's even a brewery in Stockholm now, and Oliver travels there frequently.

The beers are distinctive, especially the small batch brews crafted in Brooklyn (the rest is brewed in Utica, New York). Visitors mingle in a rustic tavern setting (opened in 1996) in view of the shiny tanks in the company's new 50bbl brewhouse. Friday nights have a raucous happy hour vibe and Saturdays and Sundays are for tours; many make the stop en route to other Williamsburg drinking destinations including Brooklyn Bowl, Spuyten Duyvil, Fette Sau, Barcade, the Diamond, and others.

PHILOSOPHY

Brooklyn's beers, under avowed foodie Garrett Oliver's watch, strive for dryness layered over a full malty backbone, and often hint of overt spiciness. Recently the company has released a slew of complex Belgian ales, collaborations, and experimental one-offs including beers made with bacon (!) and barrel-aged whimsies like Cuvée de la Crochet Rouge (his Belgian-style Local 1, a strong Belgian pale ale, aged on botrytis-altered Riesling lees) that continue to spread Oliver's reputation for a steadily creative hand at the kettles.

KEY BEER

Brooklyn Lager, the company's 5.2% ABV flagship, is an unusual brew: it has the spice and fruitiness and body of many ales, but also the creamy but clean and palate-cleansing mouthfeel of German lagers (thanks to a long cold fermentation). Blast, an American-style Double IPA that the brewery has quietly produced for years, is a delicious grapefruity hop bomb.

A BEER WITH
BROOKLYN BREWERY'S GARRETT OLIVER

One of the most accomplished figures in the modern craft brewing world, Queens native Garrett Oliver is also among the most quotable. Over the course of an evening's tasting in Brooklyn on a chilly December night, Oliver, who, at the time, was in the midst of finishing the editing of *The Oxford Companion to Beer* (a tome—not his first—with 1,150 different subjects and 100 contributing editors on board), took time to elucidate his philosophies on being a brewmaster in New York City. And Oliver, as anticipated, was the perfect host.

Getting the Williamsburg operation off the ground, he recalled, was a dicey proposition, even for a seasoned local. "There was nothing. You went outside; it was dark; you were looking over your shoulder the whole time to make sure you didn't get clocked in the head," he said. "Brooklyn was 'Crooklyn' and the cabs wouldn't take you there." But the branding and the move to the budding scene of Williamsburg was incredibly prescient. "It's really only been in the last ten years or something that I would say that the name Brooklyn has become positive to people. It was always positive to us because we're from here, but in other places that we went, it was definitely kind of like, 'Uh, really?'"

But Oliver had very clear ideas about bringing craft beer to internationally experienced New York audiences, starting with their most notoriously decisive organ, the stomach. "Food came before beer," he reminisced. "My father was a serious cook." Oliver's love of food is evident in his book on the synergy of the two, *The Brewmaster's Table: Discovering the Pleasures of Real Beer with Real Food*. Today, Oliver is a regular commentator on the delights of pairing food and beer, and has built a space inside the Williamsburg facility for special beer dinners.

Beyond the culinary aspects of beer that have helped Oliver brew for a New York mindset, he is most outspoken about craft beer's place amid the larger culture of New York, and America beyond. "My original background comes out of filmmaking," he said, "and people often ask me, 'How do you go from being a filmmaker to being a brewer?' In my mind, they are actually almost exactly the same. They are disciplines where you need 50 percent technical ability and 50 percent inspiration and art. Now, you can have a career with only one half or with an imbalance of those two things, but we have all been to movies where all the explosions and car chases are perfect, but you walk out of there and that's just two hours of your life you'll never get back. Basically Anheuser-Busch is Jerry Bruckheimer."

As we moved from the lemon verbena-like Sorachi Ace Saison to the racy, aromatic Blast IPA to the maltier, Belgian Abbey–style Brooklyn Local 2 and Cuvée Noire, a complex, roasty stout, Oliver explained that unlike the nation's truly mass producers, he sees brewing in more writerly terms.

"A beer is like a story. It has a beginning, a middle, and an end, and it should be interesting throughout, and it's supposed to have a structure that beckons to you to say, 'I would love to have a bunch of that'."

To achieve this sort of drinkability, Oliver went on to explain, is to manage a factor that many winemakers also must confront: attenuation. How much residual sugar should remain? "I think dryness is vastly underrated," he says. He's right. What goes for wit in conversation works as well with wheat beer, wild ale, or whatever beer you like: more often than not, less is more.

The genius of restraint is that then you want more of it, achieving perhaps what Oliver calls "the Four Pint Threshold." "That's what I'm always trying to do . . . [the beer] falls into a place on your palate that causes you to say, 'You know what? I could sit down and get really comfortable with this.'" Sounds like a threshold worth putting to the test. His methods have been working out pretty well. Oliver won the James Beard Award in 2014, for Outstanding Beer, Wine, or Spirits Professional in the United States.

SPUYTEN DUYVIL

359 Metropolitan Ave. (between 4th St.
& Havemeyer St.) • Brooklyn, NY 11211
(718) 963-4140 • spuytenduyvilnyc.com
Established: 2003

SCENE & STORY

To many a resident of Gotham, Spuyten Duyvil—by its location in hipster-infested Williamsburg alone—always seemed too precious to be true: a craft beer bar built in a narrow old railroad apartment with a wide, old wood bar, lovingly scripted chalkboards, creaky wooden floors, pressed tin ceilings, and apothecary knickknacks, all completely dedicated to the enjoyment of "rare and obscure" Belgian and other European beers. Ehhh, *fuggheddaboutit.* The upshot is that by leaving the bar alone to the "rare and obscure" sorts of folks—beer geeks and assorted arrivistes equally content with a PBR or rare Flemish geuze in hand, whatever seems tastier at the time—New Yorkers have given the bar a break, and the concept works just about as well as the marriage of chocolate and peanut butter. Which is to say, as New Yorkers sometimes do, it's "freaking awesome."

Today Spuyten Duyvil (loosely, "spitting devil" or "in spite of the devil" in Dutch, depending who you ask) has earned its rightful place among the great craft beer bars of the nation. A round of beers here with the cheese plate and its Brooklyn-made pickles would make the perfect stop before hitting Brooklyn Brewery, Brooklyn Bowl, and local barbecue palace Fette Sau.

PHILOSOPHY

Rare and obscure—what else matters?

KEY BEER

Start with shared bottles of De Ranke's Kriek, then work your way up through a flask of Wostynjte Mustard ale, which is actually made with mustard seeds, giving it a delicious kick. Graduate to a 750-milliliter Cantillon Lou Pepe Framboise, and finish it all off with the world-classic Trappist monastery-brewed Rochefort 10.

THE DIAMOND

43 Franklin St. (between Quay St. & Calyer St.)
Brooklyn, NY 11222 • (718) 383-5030
thediamondbrooklyn.com

SCENE & STORY

A den of ironic glories where craft beer meets pop art and rock and roll, the Diamond is a little out of the way, a little bit kooky, and a lot of awesome. With its bright lighting, pop art in the form of a massive Michael Landon portrait, horseshoe bar, high metal stools, shuffleboard, and back patio equipped with an old ski gondola car, it's a refreshing change of pace from the Ye Olden Days vibe that pervades so many bars and taverns in New York these days. It makes a superb afternoon stop on the way into Williamsburg's other great beer destinations like Spuyten Duyvil and Fette Sau. The bar sponsors a Shuffleboard Biathlon, and "Brew n' Chew," a home-brew and home cooking competition, as well as occasional beer dinners, such as a recent sausage event.

DETOUR ➡ THE BROOKLYN INN

148 Hoyt St. (at Bergen St.) • Brooklyn, NY 11217 • (718) 522-2525 • Established: 1880s

It has no loud lighted sign—it has never needed one, and never will. Regulars and neighbors fretted in 2009 when the Brooklyn Inn, a perfect little jewelbox of a bar on a quiet Cobble Hill street, was rumored to be near closing, then remodeling to expand its seating, then appeared as a set for postadolescent angst in the *Gossip Girl* TV show. It was surely headed for the rocky shoals of history, smashed to bits amid the glare of misguided attentions.

But not so. History has been good to the Brooklyn Inn, open for the last 120 years or so in various incarnations, and with its creamy craftsman light fixtures, high windows, tin ceilings, dark wood walls, massive polished mirror bar (imported from Germany in the 1870s), eclectic jukebox, good local beers, and back room pool table, it's got all the ingredients for perfection for centuries to come.

Perfection, it's true, has its drawbacks. Like many of New York's most vaunted bars, it's to be avoided on Saturday nights, when the crowd seems to have wandered out of New York's most flavorless, résumé-obsessed quadrants and drunk louts are sitting on the pool table instead of running it. It's far better on a quiet afternoon, especially Sunday, ideally when it's snowing and the only sounds in the bar are soft voices and the creaks of a barstool on the old wooden floors.

PHILOSOPHY

The fact is, you're not going to come here for lectures on hop growing—you're coming here to laugh and get a good buzz on. But the beer list is no less worthy, and if you're really lucky, you might get to hear Van Heusen, owner "Diamond Dave" Pollack's Van Halen cover band.

KEY BEER

With seven taps, about thirty-four bottles, and a few cans, the selection is organized into "session beers," "middleweights," "strong," and "extra large." Look for obscurities like Hoppeditz, a big, 7.5% ABV altbier with a long hoppy finish from Sebastian Sauer's Freigeist, a pathbreaking brewery in Cologne, Germany.

MISSION DOLORES

249 4th Ave. (between President St. Carroll St.) • Brooklyn, NY 11215
(718) 399-0099 • missiondolores.com
Established: 2010

SCENE & STORY

From the owners of Bar Great Harry on nearby Smith Street comes an urbanite's shrine to rare and recherché craft beer, classic pinball games, and reclaimed building materials. Owner Mike Wiley says he wanted the interior to look something like a huge Vol du Nuit (see Manhattan entries), with luminous natural light coming through skylights so visitors can luxuriate in all the textures of wood, metal, cement, glass and other materials that were used to form the interior, benches, and bar.

PHILOSOPHY

The owners' own site refers to it as "that weird bar at 4th and Carroll," which is understating how incredibly cool this place looks on the inside, and how pleasant it is to pass some time here among committed beer lovers, or the merely curious. A bar for the adventurous, Mission Dolores has hosted a "Where the Wild Beers Are" festival in the fall, for wild and sour ales.

KEY BEER

There are twenty tap lines, about three-quarters of them American craft beers; the remaining are Belgian or German, and there's usually one cask. Standout offerings include several hard-to-find West Coast brews from Green Flash, Ballast Point, and Firestone Walker. Another recent score: the rare, 9.5% ABV Mikkeller/Brewdog collaboration double IPA, Hardcore You.

TØRST / LUKSUS

615 Manhattan Ave. • Brooklyn, NY 11222
(718) 389-6034 • torstnyc.com
Established: 2013

SCENE & STORY

Tørst, founded by Evil Twin Brewing's Jeppe Jarnit-Bjergsø, is a white marble and pale wood bedecked beer bar in Greenpoint, Brooklyn, that has quickly earned a reputation inversely proportional to its size. Thanks to the deep list of esoteric brews (heavy on Evil Twin, with scores more selected with the help of beersmith Jon Langley), and a crazy tap system called the Flux Capacitor, it's always busy. And it's a terrific place to drink beer and explore all sorts of good tidings from the beer world.

Shoehorned in back, soft spoken ex-Momofuku and Noma chef Daniel Burns presides over Luksus, a twenty-six-seat, Nordic-themed jewel box of a restaurant dedicated to pairing beautiful food and beer. Acclaim has been sustained; even Amelia Lester in the *New Yorker* noted how Luksus conjures a "hushed reverence." It sure does, but it's far from stuffy. Even the *Michelin* star Luksus has earned won't change that.

PHILOSOPHY

Barrels of ambition, kegs of care. On a recent visit to experience the seventy-five-dollar tasting menu (with beer pairings at additional cost), this lucky writer feasted on—among other things—a striking entree of tender duck heart, duck breast, and roasted, sliced, and pureed chioga with red beets and salted plums. This was crazy-delicious on its own, but with the beer pairing this dish really soared: to go with the crimson assembly, Jarnit-Bjergsø selected the luscious Italian sour beer Brugna, from Birrificio Loverbier, in Piedmont, Italy. *Brugna*, which is Piedmontese dialect for "prunes," is fermented for two weeks in stainless steel with a mixed Brettanomyces and lactic acid culture, and then undergoes secondary fermentation for three to four weeks induced by Ramassin (Damaschine) plums, and finally rests for nine to eleven months in 3hl wooden barrels, where the brew's appealing, citric, juicy flavors deepen. We won't even try to make you jealous about what we had for dessert. Pro tip: Reserve early—as in several weeks or more—and when you're there, sit at the bar to watch all the action.

KEY BEER

Well, what's for dinner?

OTHER HALF BREWING

195 Centre St. • Brooklyn, NY 11231
(347) 987-3527 • otherhalfbrewing.com
Established: 2014

SCENE & STORY

From an unlikely basecamp in the shadow

of the Brooklyn Queens Expressway and under the massive, looming Smith-9th Street Subway platform of the F/G Train (it was shown in the movie *Goodfellas*), Other Half has stormed the city. Their timing was perfect. In 2014, after brewing some beers to serve at pop up dinners, the partners (one, Sam Richardson, had studied brewing in Oregon and worked for both Pyramid and Greenpoint Beerworks; the other, Matt Monahan, was working in the NYC food scene) started getting asked to brew for local high-end restaurants and realized their time had come. On the edge of Carroll Gardens and Gowanus they built a tiny tasting room where you can grab cans or fill up growlers, soaking up the adventure of the neighborhood itself.

PHILOSOPHY

Bold and bright. Building a brewery in exorbitant New York is one (crazy) thing, but under a rough-edged subway station near a Superfund site, the canal? The hop-forward beers are really good, and the can designs and company graphics pop with off-kilter style (bright pink keg labels; kelly-green logo-less cans; ironic beer names like "Cool Summer, Bro").

KEY BEER

Try "Doug," an India Black Ale of 7.1% ABV that drinks like an American-style IPA—without any roasty astringency—and comes in a color-etched black can Daft Punk could have come up with.

BAR GREAT HARRY
280 Smith St. • Brooklyn, NY 11231
(718) 222-1103 • bargreatharry.com
Established: 2007

SCENE & STORY

A valid criticism of many of the late-aughts era bars of Brooklyn is that they try too hard—way too hard—to be cool, old, local, artisanal, and gastronomically innovative all at once. The endless iterations of gastropub-meets-speakeasy aesthetic (a Brooklyn epidemic) have become tiresome. Over distilling the past, their suspendered mixologists slinging obscure sloe gin cocktails with house-cured maraschino cherries overreach to the point of absurdity.

Not so at Bar Great Harry. This is a beer bar, period—not a period bar. The tiny, no-frills, dog-friendly Cobble Hill beer lover's hideaway opened without fanfare, then proceeded to cycle through some 450 different tap handles in only two years, hosting brewmasters from across the land, like Carol Stoudt of Pennsylvania's Stoudt's. With low ceilings, a cozy, always-seated-with-regulars bar, and a recent back room addition, it's neighborhood in the extreme, but that's what makes it so worthy. People cram in there, order rarities from Oxbow, Finback, Central Waters, Greenpoint Harbor, and many others, and then repeat the process, as the sounds of Blur and Fugazi echo in the street. Dinner will have to wait.

PHILOSOPHY

Don't judge a beer bar—or a beer—by its size.

KEY BEER

Bear Republic's luscious, hoppy, strong Racer 5 IPA (7% ABV) was on tap, quite literally, for years. It may yet return. Until then, you've got a great range of IPAs from the likes of Other Half and Evil Twin, for example, to choose from.

SUNNY'S

253 Conover St. • Brooklyn, NY 11231
(718) 625-8211• sunnysredhook.com
Established: 1890

SCENE & STORY

There is, at the end of a desolated, cobblestone street in the neighborhood of Red Hook, a bar seemingly cut from pure sail-cloth, burlap, denim, and time. Opened in 1890, Sunny's is one of the last, best, most authentic New York places; to spend some hours there is to understand what makes the unhip, untrendy New York so appealing to a certain sort of drinker. Sunny's grandfather opened up the place, and it doesn't seem like it's changed much, ever. There are electric Christmas light strands and maritime knickknacks left over from its days as a longshoreman's bar. An old green Willy's Jeep sits parked in front; the wooden floors slope, and at night (it's only open Wednesday, Friday, and Saturday, from 8 p.m. to 4 a.m.), you crowd in and listen to really good musicians play western swing, dancing if you feel like it.

Sunny's just might be my favorite bar in the world. It's not for everyone. For starters, Sunny's is not easy to find. There's no subway close by, and the bus service is sporadic. Close to the harbor, you can smell the water, and the piers seem eerie. And even though there are some new bike paths and a fancy Fairway grocery store not too far away, on arrival, one immediately understands the meaning of the term Brooklyn Noir, which was invented for long-shadow streets like this. You can't use a credit card. You bring dollars, and you drink straight out of the bottle or a can. The bartender (Sunny himself, often) does not make old-time cocktails, pretending like he's an extra in *The Great Gatsby*. I spent a birthday there once; strangers bought me oysters. Another night, I found myself with friends in a rousing singalong of the old standard "Dark as the Night, Blue as the Day" by Bill Monroe, as regulars strummed along on old instruments. It gets *late*. It's not a place for the self-conscious, or the critic. It's also not really for cowboys, but the jam session on Saturday nights makes you feel like you might have been one in a past life. You might just want to spend this life there, too.

PHILOSOPHY

Micro-*what*? Hey, in 1844, Pabst Blue Ribbon, named for a German ship captain, was a sort of craft beer, too. This is not beer-geek country, but that's exactly what is so refreshing about coming here.

KEY BEER

The spicy, grainy Brooklyn Lager (5% ABV), if it's on. It's a standby throughout the borough. Truth be told, this is a Budweiser longneck kind of place, and there's nothing wrong with that.

Queens

BOHEMIAN HALL & BEER GARDEN

29-19 24th Ave. • Astoria, NY 11102
(718) 274-4925 • bohemianhall.com
Established: 1910

SCENE & STORY

Founded in 1892 in Astoria, Queens, to support Czech and Slovak immigrants to the area, as well as people of Czech and Slovak ancestry, the Bohemian Citizens' Benevolent Society is housed in "Bohemian Hall" and its tree-shaded beer garden outside is the oldest continuously operated beer garden in New York City, opened in 1910. It can fill up early, so head over early as part of an East New York (i.e., Brooklyn) trek.

PHILOSOPHY

As the Czech proverb says, "a fine beer may be judged with just one sip, but it's better to be thoroughly sure." Come for the traditional Czech and Bohemian food like goulash and dumplings, live music, open-air movies, or just beers in the open air. Sundays bring a small arts-and-crafts market, too.

KEY BEER

You can opt for New York–area craft beers from Blue Point, Ommegang (Hennepin), Chelsea, and Captain Lawrence, but the great, golden-hued Czech import Pilsner Urquell would be the classic choice, and it's fairly priced at five dollars for a half liter (16.5 ounces) or fifteen dollars for a pitcher. It's light and sparkly but packed with malt flavor, and wonderfully quenching from juicy, spicy hops, as well.

DETOUR ➡ CARTON BREWING, NEW JERSEY

6 E. Washington Ave. • Atlantic Highlands, NJ 07716 • (732) 654-2337
cartonbrewing.com • Established: 2011

In 2011 Augie Carton, a finance executive with a serious culinary streak, was treading back and forth on the ferry from Atlantic Highlands (where he grew up) to the piers of Lower Manhattan to work on Wall Street. Fired up on beer (and New York's sudden embrace of it), he and his cousin Chris bought a turn-of-the-century red-brick warehouse near the shore and adapted it for a new fifteen-barrel brewhouse. Success was practically instantaneous. In late 2015, Carton announced a $1 million-plus plan to expand.

Augie is a bon vivant and serious student of flavors and food; he travels with his family frequently to do research on flavors and has overseen some wild projects in the brewhouse, like a sour wasabi ale designed as an intermezzo, a trail-mix beer called GORP, and Rav, a butternut squash/sage/fennel/ hazelnut take on pumpkin beer. He's also what you might call a student of the beer scene. On his podcast "Steal This Beer" he brings on guests and good-naturedly peppers them with well-researched questions about the drink he loves.

Locally the demand for Boat Beer, a crisp, refreshing American Pale Ale of 4.2%, is pegged. The beer is delicious anytime, but tastes the very best when consumed on the upper deck of the ferry that carried you to and from Atlantic Highlands.

BEST *of the* REST:
MANHATTAN AND BROOKLYN

←——————→

PROLETARIAT

102 St. Mark's Pl. • New York, NY 10009 • (212) 777-6707 • proletariatny.com

St. Mark's Place, near the teeming NYU campus, has some terrible bars when it comes to the pursuit of good, fresh beer. This may redeem them all. Opened in 2012, inspired by old tattoo parlors and dedicated to "rare, new, and unusual" beer, Proletariat is a narrow, dimly lit space with copper topped bar, old light fixtures, framed tattoo artwork, and pressed tin ceilings. A recent peek at the menu confirms, with De Struisse, Evil Twin, Hill Farmstead, Grimm (of Brooklyn), and other new-school offerings on draft. Tip: go either early in the evening or very late to get a seat.

THE JEFFREY

311 E. 60th St. • New York, NY 10022 • (212) 355-2337 • thejeffreynyc.com

Opened in 2013, the Jeffrey has high-end coffee, craft cocktails, a deep wine list, and, of course, a killer, ever-evolving tap row. Built across two storefronts in one, under the Queensboro Bridge on East 60th Street, the Jeffrey has a custom-built draft system to keep temperature and pressure on point, and a separate growler bar tasting area with ten taps. *Draft* magazine named the Jeffrey one of America's 100 Best Beer Bars in America in 2014.

TOP HOPS

94 Orchard St. • New York, NY 10002 • (212) 254-4677 • tophops.com

At Top Hops, opened in 2011 between Broome and Delancey by Ted Kenny, a former finance man (and Anheuser-InBev employee—talk about switching teams!), the selection consists of sought-after specialties from 700 breweries, with twenty on meticulously maintained tap lines and the rest organized in twenty-six-foot-long coolers along a polished wood and aluminum bar. Informal, free beer lessons have included a chocolate and beer pairing seminar with the Mast Bros. of Williamsburg, tasting sessions with visiting brewers (like the buzzing Greenport Harbor), and visiting beer writers (present company included).

THREES BREWING

333 Douglass St. • Brooklyn, NY 11217 • (718) 522-2110 • threesbrewing.com

Opened in 2014, Threes Brewing is a thriving brewpub/outdoor beer garden/coffee spot/event space in the gritty Gowanus Canal area between Park Slope and Carroll Gardens in South Brooklyn, easily accessed by several trains. There's a full bar and twenty taplines; the interior is all clean, white-painted bricks, matte-stained hardwoods, and tasteful tile accents—even houseplants!—while the much-loved beers sport deadpan names like "Just Add Water" (a Brett pale ale with mangos) and "Constant Disappointment" (an imperial IPA).

BARCADE

388 Union Ave. • Brooklyn, NY 11211 • (718) 302-6464 • barcadebrooklyn.com

Opened in 2004, Barcade is the original shrine to two things: fresh (mostly local) craft beer and old-school, twenty-five-cent videogames from the '70s, '80s, and '90s. Which makes it cool, if not a place to bring your parents, lest they be reminded of your irrecoverable years spent playing Super Mario Brothers instead of studying.

Westchester County

CAPTAIN LAWRENCE

444 Saw Mill River Rd. • Elmsford,
New York 10523 • (914) 741-2337
captainlawrencebrewing.com
Established: 2005

SCENE & STORY

Captain Lawrence's spacious ta 2proom draws a steady stream of locals and their guests who know that tours and samples are both free. In tony Westchester County, the straight-talking head brewer Scott Vaccaro and his father (often helping out in the taproom) and other crewmembers (many related to the father-son duo) come off as refreshingly down-to-earth. Not so long ago the younger Vaccaro was getting his butt kicked as a freshman in Villanova's accounting track, largely because he spent all his time home brewing with anything he could get his hands on, even plastic gasoline canisters. He transferred to junior college in Cupertino, California, his last step before attending the fermentation science program at U.C. Davis, from which he catapulted into externships in Connecticut and England and finally an actual job at Sierra Nevada. The rest is history, and today Captain Lawrence (named for the street the Vaccaros lived on when Scott was a boy) is among the best-known and most accessible New York area breweries.

PHILOSOPHY

Vaccaro is a pragmatist, and while the beers have been a bit uneven at times, he doesn't seem too concerned. "I just brew beer I like to drink and hope other people like it," he says. "Start with a traditional product and give it your own twist. Extra Gold, for example, is brewed after a Belgian triple, then we dry-hop it like an American IPA."

KEY BEER

The bright, brassy 5.5% ABV Fresh Chester American Pale Ale has a solid New York area presence, but committed beer pilgrims will want to try and get their hands on something rarer like Vaccaro's annual Smoke from the Oak release, generally a porter which undergoes extended aging in port, bourbon, red wine, or even apple brandy barrels.

DETOUR ➡ BLUE HILL AT STONE BARNS

630 Bedford Rd. • Pocantico Hills, NY 10591 • (914) 366-9600 • bluehillfarm.com • Established: 2004

Built amid soaring, remodeled 1930s stone buildings on what was once part of a Rockefeller family estate, the Inn at Stone Barns is more than just a restaurant; it's the apogee of farm-to-table gastronomy in the New York area and maybe the entire United States. Simply put, chef Dan Barber has been called the most important chef in America, and thanks to the hard work of beer sommeliers who have worked under Barber, it's also an absolutely incredible place to indulge in a beer lunch for a special occasion (starting at $148 per person). To get there you simply go to Grand Central, jump on the train to Tarrytown up the Hudson Line, grab a ten-minute cab ride, and step off the face of the known culinary landscape.

At least nine varieties of hops are grown on the property for future collaboration batches of beer. The restaurant fosters a close rapport with the brewers and distributors who are in synch with the overall culinary goals of Stone Barns. One highlight for beer lovers, surely, is the annual Sausage & Beer Dinner; the crew works with an area maltster and local breweries to showcase five malts (rye, spelt, emmer wheat, triticale—a hybrid of wheat and rye—and roasted barley) alongside fresh sausages and cured meats followed by a five-course tasting menu featuring Blue Hill Farm pork, local grass-fed venison, beef, and lamb, and Stone Barns Bourbon Red turkeys.

Farm-to-table cooking meets local Hudson Valley brewing in the name of art, no stone unturned. "It's know your farmer, know your brewer," says former beer director Michael Greenberg. That collaborative relationship extends to diners who come in on a Sunday, as I did, with an interest in beer. Beer is often used in the kitchen as well, from soups and broths to desserts.

Local New York area brewers shine here, obviously, especially Kelso of Brooklyn (also called Greenpoint Beerworks), constantly at work on a number of experiments for the restaurant including brews infused with farm-grown lavender, lemon verbena, farm-fresh honey, housemade apple-mint tea, chocolate mint, fall harvest honey, and roasted beet puree.

There's no way to predict what you'll eat in the elegantly appointed, fifty-five-seat former dairy barn other than by glancing as you walk in at the posted list of what's seasonal, which is going to be a long one, even in early December. One merely indicates any allergies or other restrictions and the rest is up to Barber and his band of thirty or so talented chefs, who interpret vegetables, especially, with a creativity bordering on the gonzo, to do the rest. On the day I visited with a cousin we gazed out the windows at verdant farmland and meandered through at least twelve courses paired carefully with a half-dozen beers, mainly from the immediate area.

Some of the edible and imbibed highlights:

• Tender micro vegetables (including beets, radishes, and carrots) garnished with *ficoides glaciale* (an ornamental edible from the southern hemisphere), and flakes of smoked Tuscan kale
• Cloudy-blonde, 8% ABV saison beer from Brouwerij Hof Ten Dormaal, in Tildonk, Belgium, with wheaty notes of apricot, lemon, and black pepper
• "Vegetable sheets" of liquefied and dried wheat, parsnip, and beet edible stained glass hung from little mini wooden clothesline clips
• Kelso Pilsner of Brooklyn, New York, (infused with lemon verbena and Blue Hill Farm's honey)
• A tiny "burger" of pureed, citrusy beets on a sweet mini brioche with sesame seeds
• A round of tastes of Kelso's cocoa-powdery Chocolate Lager, spicy Christmas Ale
• Defiant Brewing Co., in Pearl River, New York, and Keegan's superbly light and smooth Mother's Milk Stout
• Delicate brook trout with a spicy fall vegetable and Maine crab sauce
• Homemade ricotta from Dan Barber's farm in the Berkshires
• A deliciously herbal 7.4% ABV Saison Deluxe from Southampton Brewery
• Tender pasture-raised venison tenderloin with Brussels sprouts and pistachios
• Bread pudding in a mini cast-iron skillet with housemade vanilla ice cream

Pearl River

DEFIANT BREWING CO.
6 Dexter Plaza • Pearl River, NY 10965
(845) 920-8602 • defiantbrewing.com
Established: 2006

SCENE & STORY

In a narrow old artillery factory built "before electricity" and currently lined with gleaming copper tanks, Bronx native and head brewer Neill Acer holds court over one of the most distinctive and worthwhile little brewpubs in America.

The crowd, a mix of office professionals, firemen, police, and other locals, is loyal and friendly, drawn by the good beers and house-smoked barbecue, which alone is worth a drive from New York. Served heaped on platters, this is some of the best pulled pork, brisket, and dry-rubbed ribs (served with pickles and mac 'n' cheese) you will find in the Northeast.

Perched on a stool behind the bar, Acer stokes a vibe of easygoing misbehavior among patrons. "We work pretty late and we like to brew in front of people. There is a convenience level to being a micro-brewer...just be in a little room with your favorite people and music playing in the background." It's clear he dearly loves his chosen path. "When I discovered how to make beer, it was like someone taught me how to make fire," he laughs.

PHILOSOPHY

Thanks to rigorous training at the Siebel Institute and stints setting up several different brewpubs, Acer has a capable hand with a huge swath of beer styles, from pre-Prohibition-style lagers to 15% ABV Imperial Stouts. And while he can rather effortlessly brew across entire stylistic valleys, he hasn't lost sight of his mission. "There is a level of David and Goliath to doing what we do as brewers," says Acer of the Defiant name. "You are really fighting for huge powers. Right here in the Northeast, this is the jewel in the crown; this is the Manhattan triangle. It is the largest beer market in the world."

KEY BEER

Acer's best beers are also his biggest, so look for the 9% ABV Belgian Tripel, various stouts, and his pièce de résistance, Death, a coal black monster with the complexity of an old vine Bordeaux and heft of a dump truck. Despite its huge profile, it's got an incredibly smooth, decadent palate of chocolate, dark fruits, and vanilla notes.

Cooperstown

BREWERY OMMEGANG

656 County Hwy 33 • Cooperstown, NY 13326 • (607) 544-1800 • ommegang.com • Established: 1997

SCENE & STORY

The roots of Ommegang are tightly intertwined with the history of Belgian beer appreciation in this country. American Don Feinberg headed to Europe after Yale to do his MBA in 1978, ended up in Brussels, and fell in love with Belgian beer. He was also in love with Wendy Littlefield, his college sweetheart; the two of them eloped to Brussels and ended up spending three years there. To make a long story short, when they returned, they started organizing to bring in some cases of Duvel Golden Ale as an import project, and one of the United States' most prestigious beer import companies was born, Vanberg & Dewulf, later responsible for introducing American beer lovers to Affligem, Rodenbach, and Brasserie Dupont's Saison lineup, among many others.

In 1997, the couple collaborated with Affligem, Scaldis, and Moortgat (brewers of Duvel) to launch Ommegang, dedicated to classic Belgian styles of brewing. The brewery itself is incredibly beautiful: an homage to eighteenth-century Wallonian farmstead architecture, the creamy white structures were built on a former hops farm on the banks of the Susquehanna River. With a portfolio of superb, award-winning beers and tours every day, Ommegang has become a true beer lover's destination.

PHILOSOPHY

Ommegang is dedicated to making Belgian beers with superb balance and appropriately decorous packaging. The company stands out in a sea of imitators with its consistent image and beer formulation.

KEY BEER

There are five year-round beers and five seasonals and the occasional one-off or experimental brew, always a hot commodity, like a series of beers pegged to the HBO show *Game of Thrones*. Hennepin, a 7.7% ABV unfiltered golden farmhouse style (saison), is perhaps the most emblematic of Ommegang's year-round brews. It's a delightful melody of grainy toast flavors, mild banana, lemony tartness, and spicy notes of clove and pepper, and a great introductory beer to noncraft beer drinkers. Lately the brewery has been releasing more daring beers with spices and added barrel aging, such as the excellent Zuur, a 6% ABV Flanders oud bruin, or old-style brown ale.

BEST *of the* REST: GREATER NEW YORK STATE

⟷

SOUTHERN TIER BREWING CO.

2072 Stoneman Cir. • Lakewood, NY 14750 • (716) 763-5479 • southerntierbrewing.com

The makers of the excellent, 9.5% ABV Unearthly IPA (a Double or Imperial IPA) offer popular weekend afternoon tours Saturdays at 3 and 5 p.m. and Sundays at 3 p.m. (eight dollars; first come, first served, so arrive early). Tours start and end in the brewery's attached pub, the Empty Pint, which offers fourteen mostly Southern Tier taps and pulled pork sandwiches, a heated patio, and a nice little list of Belgian ales, among other imports.

PENNSYLVANIA

THERE IS NO MORE HISTORICALLY SIGNIFICANT BEER SCENE IN AMERICA THAN IN AND around Philadelphia, Pennsylvania, going all the way back to founder and brewer William Penn himself (who tied up his boat on arrival next to a pub, the Blue Anchor) and the Founding Fathers, many of whom were avid brewers and regulars in the area taverns and public houses, those "nurseries of liberty." By the early twentieth century, Pennsylvania was home to a world-famous beer brewing industry and America's oldest brewery, Yuengling (founded 1829), still in operation. Thanks to the work of a new wave of enterprising small breweries and hardworking tavern, bar, and brewpub owners, it's an absolutely superb place to explore beer, just as it was in America's earliest days.

And there's something else about Philly. The conversations, the approach to bar keeping—it's a no-nonsense town. You ought to discover and drink craft beer and craft-beer cuisine without worrying about it all too much. And getting to know it will take repeated visits, because you will meet more than one tour guide who'd like to show you his or her favorite watering hole, and before you know it, you've discovered ten new, perfect places you never knew existed. That's Philly beer.

Today, there are some ninety breweries in the state, with about twenty in the Philly vicinity, and countless places to enjoy their creations. There are more than 600 beer-friendly bars, including some of the very best in the country, in Philly alone. And then there's that famous Philly "attytood," the bluster and tough talk about the neighborhoods before they cleaned up, giving it soul, authenticity, and depth. In a way—and no disrespect to the excellent breweries—Pennsylvania feels like it is even more of a craft-beer *drinking* state than it is a brewing state, and beer travelers will undoubtedly face many tough choices on a swing through.

Another reason Philly is such a great beer-drinking town is the trifecta of Monk's Café co-owner and Belgian beer guru Tom Peters, the *Philadelphia Daily News* columnist Don Russell, and the late Bruce Nichols of Museum Catering Company. Nichols first brought the late writer Michael Jackson to Philadelphia in 1991 for a tutored beer-tasting dinner at the University of Pennsylvania Museum of Archeology and Anthropology, a smash success followed in years hence by some dozen others, during which time he joined forces with Peters and Russell to create Philly Beer Week, an annual ten-day June bacchanal drawing thousands of visitors to over a thousand events throughout the city and the first such event in the nation, which has spawned scores of similar fetes. The only limit is time. Maybe we should call it the City of Brewery Love?

ITINERARIES

1-DAY The Foodery, Standard Tap, Monk's Café, Local 44, Memphis Taproom (Philadelphia)

3-DAY One-day itinerary plus Victory Brewing Company, Yard's, Teresa's, 700 Club, Jose Pistola's, Bridgid's (Philadelphia)

7-DAY Three-day itinerary plus Capone's (Norristown), the Farmhouse (Emmaus), Grey Lodge Public House, McGillin's Olde Ale House, Yuengling Brewery

Philadelphia

THE STANDARD TAP

901 N. 2nd St. • Philadelphia, PA 19123
(215) 238-0630 • standardtap.com
Established: 1999

SCENE & STORY

In a charming three-and-a-half-story structure dating back to at least 1810, the Standard Tap's headquarters has been a bar many times over, as well as a pharmacy and drugstore. It's also been an apartment, at least on the third floor, when former Samuel Adams brewer Will Reed lived there while working with his partner Paul Kimport to help revitalize Philly's stricken Northern Liberties neighborhood. They'd thought about brewing beer there, too, but the spaces were a bit confining, so they decided to open a beer bar instead. The building had the right bones, and was also just a half block from the site where a brewer named John Wagner became the first American to successfully produce lagers. Reed and Kimport have built a distinctive two-story pub with an ambitious menu (duck confit, anyone?) and solid reputation for taking care of their beer and their customers.

PHILOSOPHY

Good beer and food for locals, by locals. Reed and Kimport felt the area breweries weren't being well represented, and that the city needed to get behind its own residents working hard to remake the area's historic brewing scene. So the beers are exclusively from eighteen local and state breweries and always on draft or cask.

"We looked at places like Portland and Seattle, and we wanted people to be really proud of where their beer came from," Reed recalls. "So we're just going to do all local beer and we're going to do all draft beer. I love the Belgian stuff and everything, but I don't want to be a Belgian or a British pub. I don't want to be an Irish pub. I want to be a Philadelphia pub."

KEY BEER

There are twenty taps, two cask engines, and a single bottle: Lord Chesterfield, an antique recipe still brewed by Yuengling. Avoid it unless you're just one of those irredeemably curious cats. Troëg's is a favorite tap handle; look for the piney, 6% ABV Simcoe dry-hopped Hop Back Amber on cask. It's soft, dry, quenching, faintly sweet, and bitter all at once, just as a good cask-conditioned beer should be.

The Foodery

837 N. 2nd St. • Philadelphia, PA 19123
(215) 238-6077 • fooderybeer.com
Established: 2006

With more than 800 labels of beer available and a vaunted deli, the Foodery also has an especially good selection of large format bottles from U.S. and Belgian craft brewers. The Northern Liberties location is across the street from Standard Tap, so there's no reason not to take a spin through. There are picnic tables inside and the owners sponsor frequent tasting events.

KHYBER PASS

56 S. 2nd St. • Philadelphia, PA 19106
(215) 238-5888 • khyberpasspub.com
Established: late 1970s

SCENE & STORY

The Khyber Pass, which has been a drinking establishment since the 1850s, takes its name from a remarkable story about its Maryland-born owner, Serrill Headley. As the story goes, Headley, daughter of a University of Maryland football star, fled Pakistan and her marriage to a Pakistani diplomat over the Khyber Pass in the early 1970s, moved to Philadelphia, and bought the old bar in a rush of freedom.

In 1987 new owners took over the space, nestled in an unassuming corner of the historic but tourist-clogged zone of Old City, and continued its tradition of live music. Over the next twenty-two years and at least one more change of ownership it would become a venerated indie rock venue featuring the likes of Guided By Voices, Iggy Pop, the White Stripes, Liz Phair, and the Strokes, with locally legendary shows up until 2010. At the same time, the owners were slinging bottles of Chimay, and Philly's young tastemakers were simultaneously sampling some of the best rock music of the era and some world-class beer to boot. Today the Khyber (as it's known) has settled into a quieter groove as an appealingly ramshackle craft beer bar with excellent soul food and a good, deep list of beer served by super-knowledgeable bartenders. There's a gorgeous old wood bar adorned with twinkling Christmas lights and a dining room where the bands once rocked, and a peaceful vibe throughout.

PHILOSOPHY

The Khyber treats its beer list like record collectors treat vinyl, prizing rarities. Look for unusual American Saisons from Pretty Things, St. Somewhere, and Stillwater. At the same time, it's not too stuffy to stock BMC (Bud, Miller, or Coors), though one suspects such options are merely concession to the Jersey Shore-ish crowd that makes Old City (and this bar, sometimes) a no-go on weekends.

KEY BEER

There are twenty taps and two casks; this would be an excellent place to sip a fresh Stoudt's Pils, or something along the lines of a Port Brewing Mongo, a recently on-tap IIPA (a.k.a. DIPA or Double IPA) named for a brewery cat who lived out all its nine lives, not unlike what the Khyber Pass bar seems to be doing.

GRACE TAVERN

2229 Grays Ferry Ave. • Philadelphia, PA 19146 • (215) 893-9580
gracetavern.com • Established: 2004

SCENE & STORY

A beloved local institution, this railroad

apartment–like space is just wide enough for some stools and a rail to line up some beers or throw some dice around and eat some spicy blackened Cajun green beans and remoulade, which is mandatory and only two dollars. It's not a shrine to craft beer with an encyclopedic list, nor an annoying sports bar; it is a tavern for people to relax in, and its layout and architecture encourages conversation. A joint effort by Monk's Café founder Tom Peters and local publican Fergus Carey, it's got battered tin ceilings and a gorgeous built-in 1955 refrigerator called a Bevador and an abiding sense of time well spent. Don't miss it.

PHILOSOPHY

The Grace fosters a sense that a life well lived necessarily involves hours upon hours of sometimes aimless conversation over beers with friends in a local bar. At some point in your life, make this that bar.

KEY BEER

With about nine taps and forty-five well-chosen bottles, there's an ideal blend of funky crafts and everyday sippers from Monk's Flemish Sour to releases from Sly Fox, Nottinghead, Yard's, and Miller Lite for good measure. Start it off with Troëg's crisp and medium-bodied, straw gold 5.3% ABV Sunshine Pils and go from there.

EULOGY

136 Chestnut St. • Philadelphia, PA
19106 • (215) 413-1918 • eulogybar.com
Established: 2002

SCENE & STORY

Built in a narrow, old four-story town-house with a Belgian-flag themed red, black, and yellow paint job, Eulogy has a decent house brew on tap (Busty Blonde, a Belgian pale ale beer brewed by La Binchoise), a decent tap row and 400-bottle list, reputable *moules frites*, burgers, and wings. Because of its location, Eulogy makes a good early afternoon stop after paying respects to the Liberty Bell, but according to the owner himself—an American and former resident of Belgium—it is to be avoided on weekend nights. The bartenders are knowledgeable, but if the place is packed three-deep you won't get to ask any questions or sample the kegs one by one before you make the choice. On any weekend, this is a first beer of the day sort of bar.

PHILOSOPHY

Owner Mike Naessens has channeled the Old World with a cozy but not too cramped "brown bar" feel. In particular, his bar seems to be a manifestation of the quizzical nature of Belgians, who love dark humor as much as they love strong beer. With that in mind, make sure to check the upstairs "coffin room."

KEY BEER

On tap, the tart-sweet Duchesse de Bourgogne, a 6.2% ABV Flanders Red Ale from Brouwerij Verhaeghe is the perfect choice to go with an order of garlic and leek crab cakes.

THE 700 CLUB

700 N. 2nd St. • Philadelphia, PA 19123
(215) 413-3181 • the700.org
Established: 1997

SCENE AND STORY

This Northern Liberties hangout is without a doubt one of the happiest and most cheerful places in Philly to drink craft brews. With its easygoing bar staff, vinyl-spinning DJ, solid tap row and bottle list, and reputation for sweaty late-night weekend dance parties (the Rutger Hauer Power Hour is held on the fourth Wednesday of each month to get you in the mood), it manages to exude good vibes without really trying, and its laid-back clientele is made up of a menagerie of local artists, musicians, and writer types, more often approachable than not.

PHILOSOPHY

Dog-friendly. No bouncer, no attitude, no cover. Just good people, good tunes, and usually a soccer game on the tube.

KEY BEER

There are ten drafts and two casks, plus a

big old vintage refrigerator full of crafts in bottles. Philadelphia Brewing Company's Kenzinger Kölsch will keep the party local and, and at just 4.5% ABV, rolling strong.

THE BELGIAN CAFÉ

601 N. 21st St. • Philadelphia, PA 19130
(215) 235-3500 • thebelgiancafe.com
Established: 2007

SCENE & STORY

Blackboard with an ever-changing tap list. Check. Wooden bar with an armrest lip and a brass pipe foot rail. Check. Elegant back bar and mirrors stacked with glassware. Check. Located in the arty, affluent Fairmont neighborhood, this is one of Monk's Café founder Tom Peters's many establishments (this one a joint venture with fellow Philly publican Fergus Carey), and it has the deep Belgian beer list and nourishing haute-rustic pub menu to match their legendary appetites. But unlike Monk's (most of the time, at least), it lacks constant crowds, and with its amber-hued walls, lustrous dark wood and wainscoting, and classic Victor Horta–style flourishes, the bar possesses an uncanny resemblance to good beer bars in Brussels. Peters even commissioned a local artist to do a series of five art nouveau–style paintings in the main dining room area, and they infuse the space with a color and energy not found in many beer bars

anywhere. The chef is serious about cooking with beer—even tofu dishes are marinated in it—and standout dishes include the vegan barbecue wings, wasabi-dusted sea scallops served with Duvel beure blanc (Duvel is a classic strong Belgian golden ale), and the Monk's Burger, with caramelized leeks and bleu cheese.

PHILOSOPHY

This is a classic, dark, cozy bar, with excellent food and drink on offer, and a serious but not needlessly pedantic approach to beer. It would make a great lunch spot or venue for catching up with an old friend.

KEY BEER

Glazen Toren brewery's Ondineke (on tap) is a yeasty, deeply golden triple from Belgium that tastes of grass, spice, and apricot, deceptively light for a beer of 8.5% ABV, and a great match with mussels.

THE GREY LODGE PUBLIC HOUSE

6235 Frankford Ave. • Philadelphia, PA 19135 • (215) 856-3591 • greylodge.com
Established: 1996

SCENE & STORY

Opened with a distinctive oval bar in the 1950s (under a different name) this Northeast Philly institution has dark red walls and dark-stained wood trim throughout, with an old-school first-floor bar (dart boards and flat-screens) and a more quiet and updated second-floor dining room and whiskey-stocked bar, which also has eight taps of its own. More than familiar pub stylings, though, it possesses a hefty dose of Philly heart, less easily quantifiable but undeniably part of the character. That means that locals rule the roost here but in a good-hearted way for the most part. Events take on a quirky feel, with "Quizzo" on Wednesdays, Friday the Firkinteenth (any Friday the 13th) being dedicated to twenty-five or more firkins on draft, and Groundhog Day, when everyone shows up in Hawaiian shirts and gets well and duly hammered. The food options earn raves, especially the wild boar tacos and cheesesteak.

PHILOSOPHY

This is a beer bar with a bit of edge and off-kilter personality with serious beer cred to boot. Be sure to check out the restrooms, which are elaborately tiled in red, green, and blue mosaics with various bon mots. Beer lists are published online under the rubrics "currently on tap," "on deck," "due in this week," and "barrels being saved for a special night," which helps stoke anticipation for return visits, while tap lines are ceremoniously cleaned on Mondays in front of patrons. Attention all beer bar owners: please follow Grey Lodge's example and do the same.

KEY BEER

There are eleven taps and a cask, plus forty or so bottles and fourteen cans available. Look for nearby New Jersey's Flying Fish, which always has a seasonal release available, or Victory's eminently sessionable Dark Lager.

MEMPHIS TAPROOM

2331 E. Cumberland St. • Philadelphia, PA 19125 • (215) 425-4460
memphistaproom.com • Established: 2008

SCENE & STORY

Four words: beer-battered kosher dills. That's just one of the delicious bites that makes this Kensington area pub shine, along with ten beer-geek-approved taps (always rotating brands) and a beer engine for cask ales. Top rank offerings range from rarities such as De Ranke to Bear Republic and Ridgeway. A co-owner is the outspoken former Khyber Pass barman Brendan "Spanky" Hartranft, who also operates Local 44, making him, like Tom Peters, Will Reed, and Fergus Carey, one of the prime movers in Philly's good beer scene. Starting a craft beer bar in a tough neighborhood wasn't easy. "It was a total renovation; it took four months," recalls Hartranft. "My dad was on the ladder doing some electrical work about three weeks into it one day, and this guy comes over and grabs the bottom of the ladder and goes, 'Drop your wallet or I'm pulling out the ladder.' My dad goes, 'Uh, *no*,' pulls out his hammer, and drops it right on the guy's head. Skull fracture—we called the cops and an ambulance. After that, everyone that had been walking by calling us a yuppie bar beforehand were starting to say, 'Hey, when are you guys opening up?'"

PHILOSOPHY

The bar is "on a mission" to prove that certain dusty, aged bottles of beer deserve equal respect, if not more, than brewery-fresh bottles, and has the deep menu of options to prove it. When the weather cooperates, there's a hearty beer garden scene popping up.

KEY BEER

Oude Beersel Geuze, a lemony-tart, dry geuze with funky notes of unripened fruit.

LOCAL 44
4333 Spruce St. • Philadelphia, PA 19104
(215) 222-2337 • local44beerbar.com
Established: 2009

SCENE & STORY

Ever since Brendan Hartranft and his wife, Leigh, opened this gem of a beer bar in the leafy Port Richmond area of West Philly on New Year's Day in 2009, it has been busy. With its deep-red walls, Edison bulbs, and metal fire door, the space is striking and enveloping. The goal was to create a welcoming, upscale dark bar with twenty taps, each with a distinct style. The well-made fare is "boardwalk cuisine": riffs on comfort food like corndogs, Reuben sandwiches, and mahi-mahi fish tacos. Lately the staff has been doing limited edition collab beers with area breweries as one-offs for the bar.

PHILOSOPHY

No pretense here. Just good beer and a fair shake. "My price structure is based on what my dad would think if he came in here," says Hartranft. In other words, he tries to keep it affordable, and even opened up the bar with the precious Cantillon Lou Pepe kriek on draft for a mere eight dollars (it is often sold for twelve or thirteen dollars).

KEY BEER

The international list of rarities changes daily, but one beer is always available no matter what: Orval, a Belgian Trappist "world classic." It is, in fact, the *only* bottled beer for sale at Local 44. And if you get a chance to ask Hartranft about his passion for this beer, be prepared for some colorful commentary. It's a beer that inspires, to say the least.

MONKS CAFÉ & BELGIAN BEER EMPORIUM

264 S. 16th St. • Philadelphia, PA 19102
(215) 545-7005 • monkscafe.com
Established: 1997

SCENE & STORY

In the religion of *Seinfeld*, Monk's Café—the fictional coffee shop where the main characters gather—is its tabernacle, the cherished brick-and-mortar corner of the universe where Jerry, George, Elaine, and Kramer and some of their most memorable stories unfold and intertwine. In a way, one could say the same thing about the real-life Monk's Café: it's a tabernacle for craft beer lovers—it even has its own "Beer Bible"—but Fergus Carey and Tom Peters's Center City Philadelphia version has far superior food. Among the best-known beer bars in the United States—along with San Francisco's Toronado and Portland's Horse Brass—Monk's Café is more than a tavern where beer is served. It's an institution, and as such, it's to be visited with planning and forethought.

To have the best experience, try Monk's on a weeknight or during the day on weekends, or be prepared for a wait of an hour or two.

But that wait, should you have to endure it, is worthwhile: what beer travelers find when they come here is a narrow, wood-paneled front bar area with fab-ric-covered walls, then an area of a few snug booths and some smaller tables. Assorted breweriana and maps and paintings are carefully displayed throughout; beyond the middle dining area is the darker back bar, with more elegant wood paneling and a different tap list. The crowd is made up of Philly locals, beer pilgrims, and the odd musician in town for a gig. Recent artists to stroll in include Danger Mouse, James Mercer, and members of both Beirut and Broken Bells. It's surely one of the only craft beer bars in the country that can claim Questlove, drummer of the Roots, as a regular.

Beer is the main focus, but not by much. Food options run the gamut from the delicious, wing-style frog legs to mussels steamed in Saison Dupont beer with parsley, caramelized leeks, bacon, bleu cheese, and garlic. Beer options are extensive, naturally, which is where the twenty-page "Beer Bible" comes in: Besides the six taps in the front bar and eight in back, it adds some 200 rarities to your decision-making process.

PHILOSOPHY

La vie Belgique. Any beer traveler knows, as Belgians have proven, that a great beer café can be the lifeblood of local community. With Monk's, Carey and Peters have created a gathering place for lovers of craft beer, and sometimes their causes. When the late, great beer writer Michael Jackson—a regular visitor to Monk's and dear friend of Peters—died in 2007, Peters was among the organizers of a nationwide toast to raise money for Parkinson's (the illness that Jackson battled bravely and privately for ten years before his death).

KEY BEER

In search of the perfect proprietary ale, Peters traveled to Van Steenberge, the last brewery in the Meetjesland (East Flanders) region of Belgium, where Monk's Café Flemish Sour, his superb, ruddy-red house beer, would be born. At 5.5% ABV it's a Flemish Oud Bruin–style ale, aged in oak and fabulously complex, with wild but pleasing blasts of leather, tart fruit, and woody tannins. "I told [Van Steenberg's brewers] the basic parameters I was looking for. I wanted a sour beer with not much sweetness. I wanted a relatively light body, with low to moderate alcohol, a thirst quencher in the summertime," says Peters. He got it. You should, too.

A BEER WITH
MONK'S CAFÉ'S TOM PETERS

In the early 1980s, during the protoplasmic days of Belgian beer appreciation (Merchants du Vin and Vanberg Dewulf had only started bringing in their specialties in 1978, and then only in bottles), Tom Peters began converting one local drinker at a time to Belgian ales. One fateful evening at a bar called Café Nola on South Street, Peters promised a couple of patrons he'd pay for a bottle of Chimay Grand Reserve out of his own pocket if they didn't like it. He'd tried the delicious, tawny brown ale at the recommendation of a barman in Brussels in 1984, and, electrified by its flavors, worked on getting it into his bar, despite the owner's concerns that the brew would fizzle. By the end of the first night he'd sold the whole box, and though he'd failed to keep one for himself ("I'll never make that mistake again," he quipped), a movement was born. Eventually Peters would help bring in a number of Belgian specialties to the United States for the first time ever in kegs, including such iconic brews as Kwak, Houblon Chouffe, Lindeman's, and Corsendonk. When a craft beer lover goes into a bar and sees native Belgian beers actually on tap, Peters is the man to toast.

Peters wasn't always obvious craft beer material, as it were. A dedicated long-distance runner and drummer, he first tried the law, then military life. By the time Philly beer culture came alive in the late 1980s and 1990s—Stoudt's, Penn Brewing, and Dock Street were all ramping up production, as was Home Sweet Homebrew, an incubator of later talents like Bill Covaleski of Victory—Peters was making plans for Monk's, which he opened with his friend and business partner Fergus Carey in 1997. A couple of years before, he'd brought in a pallet of Kwak beer kegs to a bar called Copa Too!, his next managing gig after Café Nola, and they'd sold like hotcakes. The vision for Monk's was vividly apparent. Today their bar sells vast quantities of Belgian beer, and his cellar is easily one of the biggest repositories of rare Belgian ales anywhere in the world. In 2004, he was made a Knight of Honor in *Chevalerie du Fourquet des Brasseurs*, the 400-year-old Belgian brewers' guild, in Brussels, and one of the only *Ambassadeurs d'Orval* in the United States, an honor extended by the famed Belgian Trappist brewery.

Philly, with its blue-collar roots and deep beer history, was the perfect town for Peters to help cultivate the Belgian ale craze, which continues unabated. "The beer culture runs really deep for the whole country, but I think it runs deeper in Philadelphia than anywhere else," says Peters. "There's no other city in the world that has the current beer culture we have here. You can go to any restaurant, new or established. Or to the Phillies stadium, Citizens Bank Park, and you can find good beer at almost every stand." Today he marvels at the new generation of beer drinkers and brewers who started with unusual craft beers right off the bat, and wonders where they'll take the genre—and the market share—for craft brewing. "I think the possibilities are limitless," he says in all seriousness.

With typical humility, the affable Peters is quick to share kudos with others. He points out that bar manager Chris Morris at Khyber Pass was already selling good beers when he had his own aha! moment. "A lot of credit has to go to Craig LaBan, too, our *Philadelphia Inquirer* food reviewer," adds Peters. "He's into beer, and every time he reviews any restaurant he talks about the beer selection, so nobody will dare to open without giving serious consideration to beer."

When you get to Monk's Café, and you have to if you love Belgian beer and food, look for Tom, who may be, if the night is winding down, sipping an Orval or his house beer. He is still enthralled with what has unfolded around him: Belgian beer is more than an oddity now, it's practically a new norm of eating and drinking. "I love my bar," he says. "You have people in New York and all these cities that have the same passion I have and they can't get the culture to take hold. Well, maybe now they can, but twenty-five years ago it wasn't working." But then again, it was never about fashion at Monk's, nor was it about Tom. It was about keeping good company. "I never look at trends. You know, I taste something that I like and then I want to share it with somebody."

SOUTH PHILADELPHIA TAP ROOM

1509 Mifflin St. • Philadelphia, PA 19145
(215) 271-SPTR (7787)
southphiladelphiataproom.com
Established: 2003

SCENE & STORY

Just the words "South Philly Tap Room" have a good ring. With fourteen taps along the lines of California's sought-after Russian River, Founders and Sly Fox, this well-established corner bar deep in South Philly sponsors "Meet the Brewer" nights (Rob Tod, of Allagash, was a recent guest) and earns notice for its upmarket bar food, like a ten-dollar grass-fed bacon cheeseburger.

PHILOSOPHY

Neighborhood hangout with the best possible beer and beloved bar food.

KEY BEER

Stoudt's Karnival Kolsch, a crisp 4.8% ABV beer with a light body and dry finish.

McGILLIN'S OLDE ALE HOUSE

1310 Drury St. • Philadelphia, PA 19107
(215) 735-5562 • mcgillins.com
Established: 1860

SCENE & STORY

Philly's oldest continuously operating pub and one of this country's best Irish pubs, McGillin's opened as the Bell in Hand during the waning days of the Buchanan administration (the only U.S. president from Pennsylvania, alas). Its name came from William McGillin, the publican who ran the place and lived with his thirteen children upstairs. Crammed with dark wood paneling and exposed beams, brewery signs, parade bunting, iron chandeliers, plaques, and bric-a-brac, it's everything you'd hope to see in a 150-year-old pub. Which is exactly why an episode of the hit show *Drunk History* was filmed there recently.

PHILOSOPHY

Hey, where ya from? Friendly and sometimes a bit wild.

KEY BEER

Try a McGillin's IPA, brewed for the pub by Stoudt's, which also brews a real ale and lager for this Philly institution. Other craft standout taps include Yard's, Flying Fish, Victory, Sly Fox, and Dogfish Head.

DOCK STREET BREWING CO.

701 S. 50th St. • Philadelphia, PA 19143
(215) 726-2337 • dockstreetbeer.com
Established: 1985

SCENE & STORY

Built in the historic Cedar Park neighborhood, Dock Street was Philadelphia's first craft brewery and one of the earlier firms to get up and running nationwide. Housed in an historic firehouse, the taproom/pizzeria is known for being a beacon of friendliness in a slightly sketchy neighborhood.

PHILOSOPHY

Unfiltered, unpasteurized, unpretentious. And prone to attention-getting stunts. In the summer of 2015 they attached speakers to a wood barrel of beer and played some choice Wu-Tang Clan (that's hip-hop, in case you didn't know), they said, to see if it affected the outcome of the beer. Utter nonsense, unless the bass was so earth-shakingly loud it could rouse up yeast in a stagnant fermentation . . . no, actually, never mind. For the record, they've also brewed with smoked goat brains.

KEY BEER

The spicy Rye IPA (7.2% ABV) would make a good accompaniment to the brick-oven, wood-fired pizza or calzone, with a snifter of stout for dessert.

BRIDGID'S

726 N. 24th St. • Philadelphia, PA 19130
(215) 232-3232 • bridgids.com
Established: 1989

SCENE & STORY

Even an unassuming neighborhood bar can be memorable, even if just a pit stop on the way to bigger beer lists. Located in the Fairmount area, close to the Philadelphia Art Museum, Bridgid's is small, comfortable café-style bar with an eclectic Euro-Cajun menu and ten taps (plus more than sixty bottles). It also has a unique "gravity tap" stemming from the second-floor ceiling that comes down and hovers over the bar like a too-short fire pole but always has a beer from Yard's brewery. If you're lucky, that beer is Yard's Love Stout, a creamy, light-chocolaty wonder made with actual oysters and quite conducive to conversations at the small, J-shaped bar.

PHILOSOPHY

Where is the love?

KEY BEER

Yard's Love Stout (5% ABV).

JOSE PISTOLA'S

263 S. 15th St. • Philadelphia, PA 19102
(215) 545-4101 • josepistolas.com
Established: 2007

SCENE & STORY

A couple of local bartenders took over a former restaurant in this two-story, Center City space to create a shrine to good Latin/Southwest cooking and American craft beer in 2007. Amid its exposed brick walls, skull-adorned back bar mirror, and wide bar, the patrons are here to drink beer, see friends, and talk among each other, not look at the China patterns—it's a working-class hero bar, boisterous and beery. Expect knowledgeable staff, excellent Mexican fare, and a deep list of unusual American and Belgian micros. They opened a second location in the Fishtown neighborhood in 2013.

PHILOSOPHY

Come one or all. Jose's has a steady crowd of beer pilgrims and industry members gathering for a bit of late night R&D. In the early hours, this is a terrific brunch spot. This is a great fallback plan if Monk's Café is too crowded, or for a nightcap after touring the area's other bars and eateries.

KEY BEER

They recently had a grassy, lemony Taras Boulba on tap from Brasserie de la Senne, the most wished-for, go-to session beer for countless beer geeks (present company included).

YARD'S BREWING CO.

901 N. Delaware Ave. • Philadelphia, PA 19123 • (215) 634-2600
yardsbrewing.com • Established: 1994

SCENE & STORY

The makers of excellent beers like Philly Pale Ale and the silky Love Stout, Yard's also offers shuffleboard and free tours on Saturday afternoons, and perhaps best of all it is walking distance from Northern Liberties (making the Foodery, Standard Tap, and 700 Club easy next stops). Pints are five dollars (a buck or two more than you'll find in many Philly pubs) but it's worth the extra if you take the tour, play some leisurely pool or shuffleboard, and have a grilled cheese.

PHILOSOPHY

Gritty and fun-loving: kind of like the whole city of Philadelphia. Started up by two college wrestling buddies, the Yard's brewery (Philadelphia's largest) is a marvel of DIY spirit: with bar tops made from reclaimed bowling alley lanes and salvaged mahogany trim in the taproom, it's also running 100 percent on wind power, an achievement in itself. They're even doing some bee-keeping.

KEY BEER

Yard's eminently drinkable Extra Special Ale (6.3% ABV) was the favorite of the late British beer writer Michael Jackson when he would visit town.

Outside Philly

TIRED HANDS BREWING COMPANY

16 Ardmore Ave. • Ardmore, PA 19003
(610) 896-7621 • tiredhands.com
Established: 2011

Fermentaria • 35 Cricket Terr.
Ardmore, PA 19003 • (484) 413-2983
tiredhands.com/fermentaria

SCENE & STORY

Having graduated from home brewing and trained at Weyerbacher and Iron Hill, Founder Jean Broillet IV had the experience needed to break out, and in 2011 converted an old brick 1925 doctor's office into the café, where he and his staff bake bread on-site and source cheeses, meats, and seasonal produce from a radius of 100 miles. RateBeer.com named Tired Hands a Best New Brewer in 2013. Then, just a couple of blocks away, he opened the Fermentaria location (and bigger brewery) in an 85-year-old former trolley repair shop. It's got twelve beers on tap, a restaurant, and coffee shop. Both are steps from the Amtrak station in Ardmore, a half hour from the middle of Philly.

PHILOSOPHY

"We are equally inspired by the farmhouse brewers of France and Belgium and the pioneering, heavy handed, brewers of America. We produce our beer in small batches, twelve kegs at a time. We believe that some of the best beer in the world comes from within the confines of an oak barrel."

KEY BEER

Try HopHands (a tangy, citrusy pale ale made with Simcoe, Centennial, and Amarillo; 5.5% ABV) and the rye/oat/wheat/barley SaisonHands, a four-grain saison with Cascade hops of 4.8% ABV.

VICTORY BREWING CO.

420 Acorn Ln. • Downingtown, PA 19335
(610) 873-0881 • victorybeer.com
Established: 1996

SCENE & STORY

Built in a former Pepperidge Farm factory about an hour west of Philly, just east of the rolling Amish countryside, Victory Brewing Company was founded by locals Ron Barchet and Bill Covaleski. The two childhood friends trained in Germany and in other U.S. breweries and searched across the country for a spot to build their own. After nearly picking the Lake Tahoe area, they settled on their home region, which proved a smart move. With little marketing, the company quickly became one of the most powerful players in the craft beer landscape. A visit to Victory affords a chance to try twenty of their current brews on tap in immaculate condition (and a half-dozen more on hand pumps) and to soak up some Philadelphia beer culture in the making: The company is only nineteen years old and certainly feels institutional, part of the fabric of things. This was by design. Covaleski has an eye for populist imagery, and together with the archival WWII photos in a dining room area of the pub and the old copper brewing kettle tops that decorate the main bar space, he's managed to make a space that feels authentically lived-in.

In 2013, inevitably, Victory expanded, more than doubling their overall production capacity to an eye-popping 500,000-plus barrels per year with a new, massive, state-of-the-art production brewery and taproom in Parkesburg. They also opened a location in Kennett Square and launched a beer-infused ice cream project, too. We can hardly keep up.

PHILOSOPHY

The Old World exalted. Using mostly whole flower hops and an "uncommon" number of yeasts, Victory melds traditional brewing methods with new technology in the brewhouse to create distinctive styles of beer. In other words, once-moribund styles sparkle with new depths and dimensions in the able hands of the brewers.

KEY BEER

Victory's Prima Pils, a floral-accented, full-bodied golden sipper, has converted many a skeptic from domestic to craft, but it's the Braumeister series of pilsners exhibiting different hop varieties (including grassy Tettnang and spicy Saaz so far) that truly show what Covaleski and his cohorts are capable of.

TERESA'S NEXT DOOR

124 N. Wayne Ave. • Wayne, PA 19087
(610) 293-9909 • teresas-cafe.com
Established: 2007

SCENE & STORY

With twenty-four taps and several hand pumps (in addition to a vast 200-plus bottle list) this beer geek's hideaway opened in 2007 in the affluent enclave of Wayne (just outside of Philly), drawing immediate acclaim. It's a long, sleek space with stone accents, recessed lighting, brewery-specific glassware, a long bar, and padded booths along the back wall. The bar organizes taps by style, so regulars know that number five, for example, will typically feature Belgian blondes and Belgian pale ales. There are frequent beer events and tastings, including a spring dinner utilizing tangy spring hoop shoots, an asparagus-like delicacy used in Belgian cuisine.

PHILOSOPHY

Beer is treated with the proper respect here, but not pretentious solemnity. There's always a sour beer on, and the bartenders, chefs, and owners are all passionate about craft beer.

KEY BEER

The unofficial house beer is Russian River Damnation, a deliciously spicy-strong Belgian-style pale ale from California (7.75% ABV). Or try Petrus-Aged Pale Ale (7.3% ABV) on tap from Belgium's Brouwerij Bavik, a medium-bodied and not-too-puckering sour with vinous, woody notes and a bracing acidity. It would make a nice complement to the rich kitchen offerings, which include braised rabbit and wood-fired baby back ribs.

YUENGLING

501 Mahantongo St. • Pottsville, PA 17901
(570) 628-4890 • yuengling.com
Established: 1829

SCENE & STORY

Founded in 1829 by German immigrant David G. Yuengling in Pennsylvania coal country, this is America's oldest brewery. It has enjoyed a surge in popularity in recent years, propelled by its easy-drinking flagship brew and nostalgic image. Pronounced "Ying-Ling," the company produces seven beers and is still a privately held, family-run organization, helmed by Dick Yuengling Jr., the fifth generation of Yuenglings to run the show and the father of four daughters, all of whom work for the company.

Touring the Yuengling plant is not remarkable in any technical, beer-making sense; there's no wood or stone fermenters like you'd find in certain old Belgian or British firms. But you're here for the history. Its traditional *rathskeller*, or cellar bar, opened in 1936, and is the end of the line for popular free tours offered on weekdays, after which visitors are treated to a pair of free drafts. The company hit 180 years in 2009, and has surged from producing 127,000 barrels of beer in 1985 to over 2 million in recent years. In 2016, they planned to open a new museum and gift shop for visitors.

PHILOSOPHY

Yuengling's sturdy American image isn't cultivated through marketing or hype. It's the real deal: an old American company getting by with perseverance and hard work, and relatively conservative expansions into new territories.

KEY BEER

A cult beer in the Northeast, Yuengling Premium Lager is an affable amber sipper of 4.4% ABV with a touch of light caramel sweetness and faint citrus from hops on the tail end. Ideally, this beer is consumed while cleaning crab, fishing, or shooting pool.

STOUDT'S BREWING CO.

Rte. 272 • 2800 N. Reading Rd.
Adamstown, PA 19501 • (717) 484-4386
stoudtsbeer.com • Established: 1987

SCENE & STORY

Just off the Pennsylvania Turnpike in Adamstown, the makers of many well-made beers including the 5.4% ABV Stoudt's Pils—an aromatic and flavorful standby session beer in the Northeast for years now—offer free tours (by founder Ed Stoudt) and nourishment in their attached, whimsically painted *gasthaus*-style restaurant, the Black Angus Restaurant & Brewpub.

PHILOSOPHY

Pathbreaking but unpretentious. The affable Carol Stoudt, in 1987, became the first woman to open a brewery since prohibition; she is known in the industry as the "Queen of Hops."

KEY BEER

These days, indie brewers are trying to emulate traditional, German-style lagers left and right, but the unsparing demands of brewing it correctly, and the way it can highlight flaws, make it a real benchmark of brewers' pride. An early breakout is Stoudt's Pils—at 5.4% ABV (and now in cans), it's a crisp, flowery, crushable, German-style pilsner. Delish. It also took Bronze at the 2014 World Beer Cup, beating scores of excellent beers to join the top two winners. Look for it. Locals consider it a sort of standby. When it's fresh, it's hard to resist.

BEST *of the* REST: PENNSYLVANIA

NODDING HEAD

1516 Sansom St., 2nd Floor • Philadelphia, PA 19102 • (215) 569-9525; noddinghead.com

This small brewery and bar up a narrow stairwell in a cozy space on the second floor of an old building has a well-lived in parlor feel. Opened in 1999, the brewery runs a creative gamut from Berliner weisse (which you can order with woodruff syrup, as the Berliners do) to American wild ales, Double IPA and even Scottish Ale.

TRIA CAFÉ

123 S. 18th St. • Philadelphia, PA 19103 • (215) 972-8742 • triacafe.com

This is a sleek Center City café, which opened in 2004 that earns praise for small food and cheese plates complementing a beer list divided by categories: "Invigorating," "Friendly," "Profound," and "Extreme." With standout one-off beers like Victory Braumeister Pils Tettnang on draft and an owner who leads beer appreciation classes, beer is very much on the table. In 2013 they opened a third location, Tria Taproom, with twenty-four taps.

ALLA SPINA

1410 Mt. Vernon St. • Philadelphia, PA 19130 • allaspinaphilly.com • (215) 600-0017

Under the watchful eye of beer maven Steve Wildy, local Italo-American chef Marc Vetri's airy, modern gastropub presents an array of outstanding comfort food and an even more outstanding list of beers ranging from the iconic to aged and esoteric, with a slew of cans, beer cocktails, and large format bottles for good measure. Wildy, beverage director for Vetri's entire restaurant group, curates ambitious draft and bottle lists that constantly evolve, making Alla Spina's popular happy hour that much more fun. What you're eating: cheffed-up but unfussy poutine, fried chicken, raw oysters, and puffy pretzel bites. In your glass? Local Slyfox pils, Tilquin gueuze out of Belgium, and the hard-to-find Loverbeer, out of Piedmont, Italy.

EARTH BREAD & BREWERY

7136 Germantown Ave. • Philadelphia, PA 19119 • (215) 242-6666 • earthbreadbrewery.com

Tom Baker became a craft beer hero when he unleashed a beer called Perkuno's Hammer Imperial Baltic Porter out of his Heavyweight Brewing Co. in New Jersey around the millennium. It was among the first really, *really* big beers available in the region and the Baltic Porter style was rare, not to mention Imperial versions thereof. Despite critical hosannas his little brewery could not stay open in the brutal 2000s. Since 2008 Baker and his wife have been operating this eco-minded flatbread bakery and brewery in the Mt. Airy neighborhood of Philly, with bars and dining areas on two levels. Baker started with session beers but has ably returned to bigger beer styles more recently.

TRÖEGS

800 Paxton St. • Harrisburg, PA 17104 • (717) 232-1297 • troegs.com

Founded in 1996 by brothers Chris and John Trogner, Tröegs has emerged as one of Pennsylvania's most iconic brewing companies on the strength of beers like Nugget Nectar, HopBack Amber Ale, and Mad Elf. The sleek tasting room offers some eleven more, and there are free guided tours every Saturday afternoon (reservations all but required). The brothers broke ground on a new 90,000-square-foot brewery and tasting room location for Hershey in 2011.

MARYLAND

Baltimore

ALEWIFE

21 N. Eutaw St. • Baltimore, MD 21201
(410) 545-5112 • alewifebaltimore.com
Established: 2010

SCENE & STORY

Built in the glorious, old Eutaw bank building in West Baltimore with handsome tile floors, soaring ceilings, art nouveau, leaded glass windows, heavy Craftsman-looking chandeliers, and a spiral staircase leading to a high balcony, the home of Alewife had been sitting empty for a year after housing a tavern when woodworker turned bar manager Bryan Palombo and his business partner took on the challenge of overhauling the much decayed space. The goal was to launch one of the best craft beer spots in the mid-Atlantic. "We walked in and we're like, 'Oh yeah: it's a beer hall. It's perfect. Let's do it.' We got this place ready in five weeks. It was record-breaking. Everything was broken," recalls Palombo. The result? Bulls'-eye. With an ambitious menu of pub grub (try the artery-clogging but oh-so-worth-it Smoked Burger and fries cooked in duck fat; fifteen dollars) and a huge, ever changing list (40 taps, around 100 bottles), it's certainly one of the best things going in Baltimore for the craft beer scene, and a nice, convivial environment for traveling beer lovers.

PHILOSOPHY

Initially, the goal was no compromise ("Find the best beer in the world—done!") Palombo reports, but the reality check of one too many slow-moving beers has prompted a more down-to-earth list, though one that's hardly plebeian.

KEY BEER

Often on tap, the herbal, drying, aromatic Belgian pale ale Zinnebir (Brasserie De La Senne; 6% ABV) would make a great accompaniment to the rich, smoked burger and fries.

THE BREWER'S ART

1106 N. Charles St. • Baltimore, MD 21201
(410) 547-9310 • thebrewersart.com
Established: 1996

SCENE & STORY

Built in an elegant old three-story Mt. Vernon area townhouse, the Brewer's Art is easily one of the most famous brewpubs in the country, thanks to lakes of dedicated ink in the *New York Times*, *Esquire*, and scores of drink magazines. With all its hype, one can be forgiven for worrying about a letdown, but the fact is that it's a true original, well worth a special trip. However, do *not* show up on Friday at 7 p.m. and expect to waltz in— it's extremely popular, and service varies from chipper and friendly to "And you are . . . ?" Upstairs, just above street level, there's a bustling bar crowd in the front window crowded around a black and white Greek Revival bar area, beyond which is a mezzanine and finally a spacious seated dining room area. Downstairs, the vibe is classic *rathskeller*, with a dimly lit horseshoe bar and alcoves for huddling over the well-crafted beers.

PHILOSOPHY

American-style Belgian café, no excuses. "They did not compromise from day one. They did not brew shitty beer just to stay with the masses," says Thor Cheston, of Right Proper Brewing Co. "I mean, with some of their beers like the Green Pep-percorn Tripel—when they first came out—people were like 'What the hell are you thinking?' But you know, it's amazing. Their beers are phenomenal."

KEY BEER

With four house ales, a cast of some twenty rotating seasonals, a strong international bottle list including a few lambics, and other new releases coming on line, there's much to choose from. Resurrection, a sweet, malty Abbey style of 7%, is the most popular beer, but it's the Beazly that stands out. Inspired by the classic Belgian pale ale Duvel, it's a clear golden sipper of 7.25% ABV with a huge rocky head and a yeasty, peppery bite, thanks to a devilish dose of Styrian goldings hops. Fun fact: It was once widely known as Ozzy, but the singer sent the brewery a cease-and-desist order in 2014.

MAX'S TAPHOUSE

737 S. Broadway • Baltimore, MD 21231
(410) 675-6297 • maxs.com
Established: 1986

SCENE & STORY

Fells Point is Baltimore's cobblestoned former colonial seaport boasting over 160 National historic register buildings, a flotilla of historic tall ships tied up along the shore, and alley upon alley of laid-back bars where brothels and old-time boarding houses used to be. It's also home to Max's, one of the best beer bars on the East Coast, if not the entire country. Max's organizes a huge Belgian beer festival, for starters, so the Flemish/Wallonian contingent runs deliriously high. With a long bar lined by 140 rotating taps, 1,200 different beers in coolers, bar top casks, and a wild collection of breweriana, it's absolutely chockablock on weekend nights with a mixed crowd of college kids (and occasionally their parents), hordes of tourists (especially in the summertime), and tourists who end up partying with those college kids and their parents.

PHILOSOPHY

The bigger the beer list, the more fun you're having—right? Or, sometimes, maybe that's "the bigger the *cup*"—Friday is "big-ass draft" night—six dollars for thirty-two ounces of anything on tap (except for big Belgians and other crafts), served in beer pong–ready *plastique*. In other words, avoid Max's on Friday nights, unless your inner collegian wouldn't have it any other way. Tuesdays, on the other hand, are dedicated to the "Beer Social" at 6 p.m. when brewers and members of the local craft crowd mingle upstairs. And you're more likely to get on the pool tables downstairs later, since no one is drunkenly sprawled across it.

KEY BEER

Beers from Baltimore's own Clipper City Brewing Co./Heavy Seas Beer line like Loose Cannon (a 7.25% AIPA) are big favorites, but the chance to drink the even rarer local Stillwater Brewing Company's one-offs (such as "Our Side" saison, a recent 7.5% ABV collaboration with Danish "gypsy brewer" Mikkel Bjergsø) should not be passed up.

THE WHARF RAT

801 S. Ann St. • Baltimore, MD 21231
(410) 276-9034 • thewharfrat.com
Established: 1975

SCENE & STORY

Walking into the late-1700s building that houses the Wharf Rat pub instantly conjures the time when Fells Point was still so teeming with privateers just off a square rigger from some port afar that the British called it a "Nest of Pirates." Low-ceilinged and cluttered with valuable nautical memorabilia, a solid tap row of Northeast and mid-Atlantic craft ales, and several Oliver's English-style ales from Pratt Street Ale House, this is one of Baltimore's most beloved spots, if not for the food then for the massive stone fireplace in the back of the bar and the incredible atmosphere. Legend has it the place is haunted, too, notably by a gentleman who was shot for playing "The

Star-Spangled Banner" far too often (and too loudly) on his gramophone. Ask a bartender or bouncer for the tale.

PHILOSOPHY

Cask-conditioned beers, good friends, and a roaring fireplace is all that matters on a cold winter's night.

KEY BEER

Oliver's Best Bitter, an amber, smooth, gently carbonated traditional sipper of 4.8% ABV.

Washington, D.C.

BIRCH & BARLEY / CHURCHKEY

1337 14th St. NW • Washington, D.C. 20005 • (202) 567-2576
birchandbarley.com • Established: 2009

SCENE & STORY

Located in D.C.'s up and coming Logan Circle area, this is two establishments served by one truly incredible beer selection with the result being one of the United States' top craft beer destinations, hands down. Downstairs, in the chic, low-lit street level space, young chef Kyle Bailey—at thirty, already a veteran of New York power-player restaurants Blue Hill and Allen & Delancey—pre-

pares Birch & Barley's entire New American menu expressly for enjoyment with the place's selection of 550 different beers. There's a nightly seven-course tasting menu, including beers for seventy-seven dollars, which has included such entrées as a strip loin of beef with balsamic-braised cabbage, parsnip gnocchi, and glazed pearl onion, served with Great Divide Grand Cru from Denver. You could do much, much worse.

Upstairs is the more casual, high-ceilinged Churchkey bar, with high brick walls, a long banquette and line of stools, cozy raised booths, and a small section of couch and low padded stools in a sort of chill-out area. But there's not much of that.

Helping usher in something of a D.C. nightlife renaissance, both businesses have been incredibly busy since day one, and . . . well, you know the drill. Arrive early; on weekend nights, the upstairs is a first-come, first-serve, three-deep scrum. If you make it in early, stake out your territory, pounce when you can, and play fair by ordering all night long (not camping out) as the hordes surround. Expect a mixed crowd of beer geeks (lining the bar, having arrived early), K Street lobbyists, and young lawyer types crowding in. The food is fatty and sometimes a bit too clever by half, but there are winners (the tots).

PHILOSOPHY

Both rooms are served by the same beer supply, and here's where things get interesting: beer Director Greg Engert has assembled an upstairs selection of over fifty drafts (organized on menus under categories along flavor lines, i.e., crisp, hop, malt, roast, tart & funky, and fruit & spice) that are stored in a series of temperature-controlled coolers and served according to their ideal temperature: 42, 48, 50–52, and 54 degrees Fahrenheit (in quality house glassware, naturally). All the other bottles, kegs, and casks (about 10 to 15 per week) are organized meticulously as well, likewise stored in their own designated coolers. Even the beer lines themselves run through glycol-cooled lines to keep the beer at the desired temperature before it hits a freshly rinsed (and yes, then re-cooled) glass. Engert leads twice-daily staff meetings to explain what's coming on tap, and longer seminars once a month to drill servers on the nuances of the beers they're serving. It's incredibly (almost insanely) anal, but the fact is that beer does best express itself in the temperature range with which it was created, and Engbert's costly accomplishment is nothing if not admirable. These coolers supply the rocking bar area; downstairs, a gleaming row of copper pipes ("the Beer Organ") descend from the ceiling and into the taps serving the dining room.

KEY BEER

With all the taps turning over regularly and lines meticulously monitored, freshness shouldn't be a problem, and you can order $1.50 taster sizes to sample a variety. On Mondays they bring in a roster of brewers for beer dinners, meaning there's always something very new and interesting on draft from the likes of Victory, Mikkeller, Brooklyn Brewery, Founders, and DC Brau. But the bottle list at your disposal is a thing of beauty. Dive in.

THE MERIDIAN PINT

3400 11th St. NW • Washington, D.C. 20010
(202) 588-1075 • meridianpint.com
Established: 2010

SCENE & STORY

With a clean-lined, garage-doored space, wooden floors, and tin ceilings, this is a two-level beer bar with exclusively American craft beers, some of which are available by the ounce in a pay-as-you-go arrangement from six basement table taps (reservations recommended). It draws a mostly young crowd, especially on weekends and for big games, but there have been a number of events with craft brewing industry rock stars Sam Calagione, Jim Koch of Boston Beer Co., and Ken Grossman of Sierra Nevada. There are now three locations, house beers, and other fun projects coming out.

PHILOSOPHY

The earnest reasoning for the U.S.-only list is that it's better for the environment, as is the wind power, local-dwelling staff (Columbia Heights), and aggressive composting and recycling programs in place. Can't argue with any of that.

KEY BEER

Dogfish Head's neo-Berliner weisse-style Festina Pêche (4.5%) and bottles of the 9% ABV Weyerbacher Double Simcoe IPA ($8) for dessert.

BRASSERIE BECK

1101 K St. NW • Washington, D.C. 20005
(202) 408-1717 • beckdc.com
Established: 2007

SCENE & STORY

Acclaimed Belgian-born chef Robert Wiedmaier opened this airy, marble- and white tile-filled bistro in D.C.'s McPherson Square neighborhood in 2007 to strong reviews. Washington professionals took to the sumptuous dining scene and dramatic open kitchen setting (and its private dining area, for bigwigs and events) while the craft beer and raw seafood-stocked gray marble front bar area quickly became a hot after-work spot. Today it's got a strong Belgian beer list, a superb house-brewed ale from Belgium, and a growing reputation for treating beer like Belgians do—with a deep and joyful respect. To make Belgophiles feel even more at home, there are some plastic woven chairs like you see in Brussels's Grand Place bistros and a large clock displaying the time there, too.

PHILOSOPHY

Proper is the operative word. "It's all about service," the effusive Thor Cheston, Beck's former manager and beer sommelier (who in 2009 was inducted into the Knighthood of the Brewers' Mashtaff, an honorary cadre of Belgian beer supporters coordinated by the Belgian Brewers' Guild). "It's proper service, taking care of the beer, everything from proper temperature for the bottles to proper storage. Everything needs to be held cold and then run through a proper draft system, always running the proper mixture of gas, and the proper amount of pressure on the kegs. I'm an absolute stickler for the proper glassware, a proper pour—the whole presentation. All the servers know how to do a perfect hefeweizen pour, where you dump the bottle in the glass, pour it out and make it really sexy. What I want to do is put the beer into context, really train servers so they know everything about the beer."

KEY BEER

With eleven drafts and a good bottle list (not only Belgian; there are excellent American, German, and French brews as well), beer is an absolute fixture here, with events, tastings, and beer in the kitchen, too. Antigoon, the hazy-golden 6.8% ABV house pale ale, hails from Belgium's Brouwerij De Musketiers and is named for the mythical giant once lording over the town of Wiedmaier's native Antwerp. It's pleasantly bready and yeasty, with a delicate fruity aromas of tulip, pear, and fresh sliced apple, and finishes with a brisk white pepper crack. It's superb with food, and the bottle it's served in has some of the most interesting label art ever created, illustrating the tale of Antigoon's demise.

PIZZERIA PARADISO

3282 M St. NW • Washington, D.C. 20057
(202) 337-1245 • eatyourpizza.com
Established: 2002 (Georgetown location)

SCENE & STORY

This cozy sixteen-tap, ten-stool, twenty-seat beer bar with fireplace is located in the basement of a sunny, bustling wood-oven Georgetown pizza eatery with superb pie (and crowds to show for it). The night to go is Tuesday or Wednesday when the fracas mellows and there are both pizza and draft beer specials from 5 to 7 p.m. Former manager/beer chief Greg Jasgur helped build a massive bottle list as well, and, like his predecessor Thor Cheston, landed the cream of the crop when highly allocated beers became available from brewers with cult followings, a tradition which continues. The Atomica (tomato, salami, black olives, hot pepper flakes, mozzarella) is an excellent choice with beer, and with

such a varied and rotating selection of brews (and pizza specials) it's practically inconceivable to go wrong. Also, there are two more locations, in Old Town and in Dupont Circle. Take your pick.

PHILOSOPHY

The MO here is simple: pizza and beer were made for each other, so why not go for the absolute best of both worlds? The ingredients, food preparation, beers, prices, and service are all exceptional. As usual, go on a quieter night for the best possible experience.

KEY BEER

Del Borgo Re Ale, a nutty, caramelly, citrus-tinged American-style pale ale from central Italy's Birra Del Borgo brewery, if it's available. It's a 6.4% ABV brew absolutely made for pizza.

BLUE JACKET BREWERY

300 Tingey St. SE • Washington, D.C.
20003 • (202) 524-4862
bluejacketdc.com • Established: 2013

SCENE & STORY

Beer luminary Greg Engert, creator of ChurchKey and Birch & Barley, opened Bluejacket with much fanfare in 2013 in a massive, stunning, glass-filled, 7,300-square-foot warehouse, churning out ten new bottled beers a week, from strawberry rhubarb Berliner weisse to Imperial and spiced stouts. In keeping with Engert's MO (friendly, but relentless over-achiever), he had overseen twenty-five collaborations before the doors even opened.

PHILOSOPHY

The best never rest. Ceaseless experimentation, great design—it's all there for this new standard. They also put on a massive beer festival called Snallygaster which is growing in popularity every year.

KEY BEER

Forbidden Planet dry-hopped kölsch is a crisp, 4.2% ABV classic, heavily dry-hopped with Australian-grown galaxy hops, and with aromas of passion fruit, peach, and mango.

RIGHT PROPER

624 T St. NW • Washington, D.C. 20001
(202) 607-2337 • rightproperbrewery.com
Established: 2013

SCENE & STORY

D.C. beer guru Thor Cheston (formerly of Pizzeria Paradiso and Brasserie Beck), along with head brewer Nathan Zeender and John Snedden, founder and owner of Rocklands Barbeque and Grilling Company, built Right Proper to be "a brewery with heart and soul, a neighborhood gathering place that makes and serves fresh beer alongside delicious food that won't break the bank." Built

where Frank Holiday's Pool Hall once stood (and as legend has it, where Duke Ellington learned how to play jazz as a teenager), Right Proper is next to the Howard Theater and stands proud as part of the "real Washington."

PHILOSOPHY

Imaginative. The team takes old styles like wheat beer and porter and, using Belgium-born methods of mixed fermentation, creates new and interesting riffs.

KEY BEER

Ornette, a 3.7% ABV grisette fermented with a mix of yeasts from the crew's favorite traditional farmhouse breweries. It's dry and peppery, with fruity accents, and is named after jazz legend Ornette Coleman.

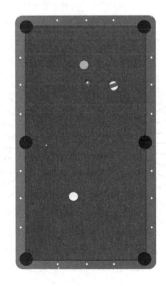

BEST *of the* REST: BALTIMORE & D.C.

OF LOVE & REGRET PUB & PROVISIONS

1028 S. Conkling St. • Baltimore, MD 21224 • (410) 327-0760 • ofloveandregret.com

Ryan Travers and Leigh Philipkosky, working with Brian Strumke from Stillwater (a popular gypsy brewer) opened this Baltimore bar in 2012, focused on craft beer, natural wines, and hand-distilled spirits. The atmosphere is rustic, relaxed, and casual. "We used a lot of found items to decorate the space," says Leigh. "We hand-built several of the large group tables and the draft tower out of a 120-year-old barn in a neighboring town. From the outside, Of Love & Regret looks like classic Baltimore row home, but once inside the restaurant space is candle light, and warm." Choose from a swath of Stillwater brews on draft, like Folklore, an earthy, rich, 8.4% ABV dark Belgian-style ale.

DC BRAU BREWING

3178-B Bladensburg Rd. NE • Washington, D.C. 20018 • (202) 621-8890 • dcbrau.com

In 2010, locals Brandon Skall and Jeff Hancock opened D.C.'s first brewery since the 1950s and have been going from strength to strength ever since, racking up fans and medals by the bucketloads. Go on Friday for half-price pints, or head to the brewery on a Saturday for free tours and a taste of their flagship, the Public, an American-style pale ale.

THE SOVEREIGN

1206 Wisconsin Ave. NW • Washington, DC 20007 • (202) 774-5875 • thesovereigndc.com

From beer maven Greg Engert and Co. (Bluejacket, Birch & Barley/ChurchKey—see pages 339, 342) comes this ambitious, stylishly appointed, all-Belgian style gastropub in Georgetown, opened in 2016 and boasting 50 drafts and nearly 350 bottles. As with ChurchKey, the bar features temperature-controlled taps, high-end Belgian glassware, and of course a deep menu of well-curated beers paired with Franco-

Belgian specialties like coq au vin, burgers, and frites. On draft: rarities from Belgian breweries like De La Senne and Brasserie Blaugies alongside American acolytes like Oxbow, Perennial, and Allagash.

VIRGINIA

MODERN CRAFT BREWING IS RELATIVELY NEW TO THE APPALACHIAN REGION, BUT IT'S MORE than at home already. Five Virginia breweries so far have signed on to the state-sponsored "Brew Ridge Trail" initiative (brewridgetrail.com), to spur interest in and travel through the homegrown scene, which is growing by leaps and bounds. From Blue Mountain Brewery in Afton to Devil's Backbone Brewing Company, there's a groundswell of new brewing afoot that's long overdue.

THE BIRCH

1231 W. Olney Rd. • Norfolk, VA 23507
(757) 962-5400 • thebirchbar.com
Established: 2011

SCENE & STORY

It's fitting that West Ghent, the neighborhood in Norfolk this bar calls home, is named for the Flemish city of Ghent. Belgium looms large here. Since they opened in January of 2011, Malia Paasch and Ben Bublick have graffitied the floor-to-ceiling chalkboard with incredible selections for the twenty-one taps. There's another 100 in the bottle, with Belgian rarities like De Glazen Toren, St. Feuillien, Brasserie de Blaugies, and Picobrouwerij Alvinne (and American-born craft specialties from Allagash, Stillwater, Russian River, and Weyerbacher). Norfolk's first full-fledged craft beer bar has established a lofty tradition in a very short time.

PHILOSOPHY

Generous and informative. Their newsletter is among the best in the entire industry.

KEY BEER

Every few months they do a "forty-three hours festival," committed for one whole week to one style of beer. This is just one of the reasons why Ratebeer.com has dubbed it one of the top fifty beer bars in the world for several years running.

DEVIL'S BACKBONE

200 Mosbys Run • Roseland, VA 22967
(434) 361-1001 • dbbrewingcompany.com
Established: 2008

SCENE & STORY

Devils Backbone is a two-and-a-half-story mountain lodge–style brewpub in a tiny town in the Blue Ridge Mountains of Nelson County. It burst onto the national craft brewing radar at the 2009 Great American Beer Festival and 2010 World Beer Cup in Chicago by racking up no less than twelve medals, including Champion Brewery and Brewmaster at the WBC (in the Small Brewpub category, 2010). Despite having only opened a few years before, the brewery was suddenly Virginia's most award-winning, and the little 8bbl brewpub near the Wintergreen ski area in a town of less than 2,000 was sharing the stage with some truly heavy hitters in the industry. Those 2,000 locals were ecstatic, naturally, and plans to expand with a second location with a 30bbl brewhouse and packaging line near Charlottesville came together rapidly. The original location is a handsome structure made of materials repurposed from a 1900s dairy barn, a horse farm, and a tobacco plantation barn. As of 2015, they're making 67,000 barrels a year, but aim for over 200,000. And in recent years, the medals have started to pile up.

PHILOSOPHY

Brewer Jason Oliver tends to brew and naturally carbonate subtle twists on sessionable old-world styles that might seem tame compared to the fare on draft in some craft beer destinations, but are well made nonetheless—Trojan Horses of craft beer in this neck of Bud country rural American South.

KEY BEER

There are ten beers on tap at all times including four year-round beers and six rotating seasonal beers created by Oliver. Golf Leaf Lager, a 4.5% ABV international-style pilsner, the brewery's flagship, is a good place to start. Lately Oliver has been working on bigger styles, from Wheat Stouts to Black IPAs and Imperial Coffee Stouts.

BLUE MOUNTAIN BREWERY

9519 Critzers Shop Rd. • Afton, VA 22920
(540) 456-8020 • bluemountainbrewery.com
Established: 2007

SCENE & STORY

As the name suggests, this is another brewery with a proud connection to the Blue Ridge Mountains of central Virginia, and resides in a beautiful white building outside of Charlottesville along the Monticello Wine Trail. But the connection to the land here goes even deeper: Starting in 2006, owner and head brewer Taylor Smack began growing his own hops, and is now wrangling 1000 hills of Cascade and Centennial, which are irrigated with brewery runoff and used in the brewing process.

PHILOSOPHY

Innovative brewing with a southern touch—and a green heart. He's keeping an eye on Virginia Tech experiments aiming to develop strains of barley that could flourish locally, and the brewpub is serving beef from cattle raised on his spent grains.

KEY BEER

Start with the light, crisp classic Blue Mountain lager (5.3% ABV) and work your way up to taste more hops from the site. Dark Hollow is an imperial coffee and chocolate stout of 10% ABV you could easily finish your day with.

DETOUR ➡ JEFFERSONIAN ZYMURGY: MONTICELLO

931 Thomas Jefferson Pkwy. • Charlottesville, VA 22902 • (434) 984-9822 • monticello.org

It's a relatively minor point of interest among historians but one enormous point of pride for craft beer aficionados that Thomas Jefferson was highly involved in brewing. Beer was considered one of the "table liquors" traditionally served with meals, and there was a dedicated cellar at Monticello for aging the house ales before they'd be served upstairs. Beer was in the picture early on. According to records from 1772, Jefferson's wife, Martha, was used to brewing fifteen-gallon casks of small beer every two weeks. (Small beers can be made with the spent grain of stronger batches or simply with less grain; either way the technique results in a lower alcohol brew.) By 1794, Jefferson had planted hops, and Monticello, which had been conceived with a brewery in the elevation drawings, was on its way to becoming a full-fledged estate brewery—even a malt house would be added much later, in 1820. In 1815, Jefferson wrote in a letter to Joseph Coppinger (himself a brewer):

"I am lately become a brewer for family use, having had the benefit of instruction to one of my people by an English brewer of the first order."

One man's misfortune is another's gain: Joseph Miller, a British expatriate and trained brewer who had been caught up in the War of 1812, shipwrecked with his daughter in the Delaware River and stranded in Albemarle County, found his way to Monticello to brew with Jefferson. Miller, for his part, is said to have introduced Jefferson to some stronger ales (compared to Martha's style of small beers) which would keep longer in the cellar. Miller also trained one of Jefferson's slaves, Peter Hemings (brother of Sally), how to malt and brew with raw materials grown on the 5,000-acre hilltop estate, which included wheat, corn, and hops (no barley was grown). Hemings was a quick study, and would eventually undertake the brewing of 100 gallons of ale every spring and fall.

By 1814, a sturdy brewhouse was in place, and Hemings and Jefferson began malting estate grains to avoid having to buy them, enough to turn out sixty-gallon batches of brew at a time. Jefferson preferred to bottle condition the ales, decrying local brews from the "public breweries" as "meager and vapid" and was fixated on cork quality. As he served the finished ale to friends, family, and visiting dignitaries, his fame as a brewer spread, and neighbors were soon asking him how they could get into the act, too.

To celebrate Jeffersonian zymurgy (the art and science of brewing), nearby Starr Hill Brewery founder and brewmaster Mark Thompson and brewer Levi Hill collaborated with the Thomas Jefferson Foundation in late 2010 and early 2011 on the launch of Monticello Reserve *Ale*, the official beer of Monticello, inspired by what was produced and consumed by the third president and his guests. Today, Monticello Reserve Ale is sold in 750-milliliter bottles at the brewery and served on tap at local restaurants. It's extremely light in body and bitterness by today's standards, but offers a taste of what Jefferson brewed himself.

BEST *of the* REST: VIRGINIA

RUSTICO

827 Slaters Ln. • Alexandria, VA 22314 • (703) 224-5051 • rusticorestaurant.com

A wood-oven pizzeria with a mean beer selection (thanks to Greg Engbert, who worked at the famous Brickskeller Bar and went on to put Birch & Barley and Church Key on the map), Rustico is a spacious modern eatery with thirty taps and around 250 bottled selections from such incredibly esoteric producers as De Hoevebrouwers and Brouwerij Girardin (Belgium) and Birrificio Troll (Italy). One nice touch: Beers are served in the proper glassware, such as snifters for stronger ales, which help aromas waft out of the glass, and the service and food come highly recommended. Now there are two locations, with one in Arlington called Rustico Ballston.

CAPITAL ALEHOUSE

623 E. Main St. • Richmond, VA 23219 • (804) 780-2537 • capitalalehouse.com

The original of five locations in the area, this well-established beer bar was opened in 2002 in the heart of downtown Richmond within walking distance of Brown's Island, the Richmond Ballet, and the Virginia State Capitol. Constructed with sweat equity by a group of beer fanatics in a 108-year-old building, the bar boasts more than fifty taps, two cask beer engines, more than 200 bottled beers from around the world, and a varied pub grub menu. On a lower level there's a pool table, four dart boards, and a beer garden area with communal seating and a fountain for al fresco beer drinking.

HARDYWOOD PARK

2408-2410 Ownby Ln. • Richmond, VA 23220 • (804) 420-2420 • hardywood.com

Lifelong friends Eric McKay and Patrick Murtaugh, the story goes, discovered craft beer while touring a sheep station called Hardywood Park in Australia back in 2001. Murtaugh, from a long line of family brewers, graduated from the Siebel Institute of Technology in Chicago in 2010, then relocated to Munich, Germany and studied at the vaunted Doemens Academy. Located in the heart of a historic German brewing district in Richmond, Hardywood Park is a two-building affair with a music venue in one and a modern twenty-barrel Newlands brewhouse in the other, but recipes are troubleshot on a twenty-gallon pilot system. They're famous for great service and a wide range of barrel-aged beers, especially a spicy Gingerbread Stout made with local baby ginger, wildflower honey, whole Madagascar bourbon vanilla beans, and Vietnamese cinnamon.

STRANGEWAYS BREWING

2277 Dabney Rd. • Richmond, VA 23230 • (804) 303-4336 • strangewaysbrewing.com

Opened in 2013, Strangeways Brewing is a production brewery with multiple tasting-room spaces pouring over twenty-five unique beers on tap. You've got to go here and see the bar, a shrine of breweriana. Also, there's a terrific *biergarten* where you can nosh from food trucks on site and toss a little cornhole. Take beer to-go by the bottle, growler, or Ball mason jar, and time your visit for some live music, trivia, or even burlesque.

DELAWARE

DOGFISH HEAD BREWINGS & EATS

320 Rehoboth Ave. • Rehoboth Beach, DE
19971 • (302) 226-2739 • dogfish.com
Established: 1995

SCENE & STORY

Named for a spit of land on the craggy Maine coast, Dogfish Head is the brainchild of Sam Calagione, who grew up in a winemaking family in Massachusetts and was once kicked out of prep school for unruly behavior (which, according to Burkhard Bilger's widely-noticed 2008 *New Yorker* profile, included the following: "flipping a truck on campus; breaking into the skating rink and playing naked hockey; "surfing" on the roof of a Winnebago, going sixty miles per hour down I-91." Not to mention selling shoulder-tapped cases of beer he hid in his hockey bag to students for a profit.).

Today, the company he leads (along with his effusive wife, Mariah) has become, along with Sierra Nevada and the Boston Beer Company, one of the best-known craft breweries in the country, widely imitated and envied by competitors. Once touted as the smallest in the nation, it now hovers around #13 out of 4,000 in sales volume—and counting.

The success of Dogfish didn't always seem to be in the cards. After stints in graduate school in New York and a bit of modeling—and having only brewed perhaps ten batches of beer—Calagione headed to Delaware to open that state's first brewery since Prohibition using a tiny pilot system and a bunch of commercially untested and unconventional—even haphazard—recipes. The state laws still forbade brewpubs at the time (a situation he successfully helped lobby to change) and the early years were financially sketchy. But the pub and nanobrewery took off, and Calagione's timing proved impeccable.

Out of the ashes of a nationwide slowdown in the craft beer sector around 1996, Dogfish emerged as a creative juggernaut as the industry regained its composure and the sector returned to double-digit growth, which makes it sound more business-like than it really was. To list the various attention-grabbing (and occasionally award-winning) semistunts released since then—sometimes dubbed "extreme brewing," using such ingredients as African honey, muscat grapes, chrysanthemums, even algae—would be a long and thirst-provoking task involving footnotes. But amid the wacky, sometimes deliberately provocative libations ("Golden Shower" was one ill-advised label) have emerged a few slightly more sober-minded experiments reinterpreting ancient recipes, a track that Calagione and company have spent a great deal of time chasing around the world. Along the way Sam has written a few books, raised a family, and high-fived his way into an ever-brighter spotlight with each new release, making it all look easy. Of course, it's not. Madness, meet method.

Beyond the experiments, Sam's Dogfish crew crafted recipes appealing to wider audiences, too, and it was perhaps inevitable that Calagione and his Dogfish would be ready for a close-up. In 2010, the Discovery Channel created a new show, *Brew Masters*, centered around his globe-trotting recipe hunts and daily business challenges played as life-or-death countdowns to disaster or critical acclaim. While it didn't last, the impact was wide. Every beer geek in America tuned in.

Dogfish offers free tours of the nearby main brewery (reserve ahead by calling); make sure to look out for the bocce courts and treehouse boardroom. A combination brewery tour in Milton and trip to the original two-story pub location in the center of Rehoboth makes for an excellent long afternoon and evening. There are always more than twenty Dogfish brews and a cask (including pub-only drafts). There's also a microdistillery on-site, solid pub grub, and live music on occasion. If Sam's there (and he often is), he'll be rapping with the dishwasher. Despite all his fame and acclaim, he knows everyone who works with him at the company.

Best of all, Dogfish recently built the 16-room Dogfish Inn in Lewes, Delaware, overlooking the harbor in a prime location between Dogfish's brewpub and distillery and the production brewery in nearby Milton. It's a stylish update on the classic American motel, with throwback custom Woolrich blankets, vintage-style tote bags for the beach and breweries, and mini-fridges stocked with locally made snacks. Sweet dreams, beer lovers.

PHILOSOPHY

Dogfish Head is a seamless meld of restless beer-geek thinking plus market savvy and a hearty dose of punk rock attitude, a winning and incredibly unique combo. Its official MO has long been "Off-Centered Ales for Off-Centered People," but "controlled chaos" might be a more succinct description. The beers are designed to make you think, but not at the expense of actually *drinking* them again and again and again.

KEY BEER

The best experimental beer? Take your pick, but the recent Miles Davis–inspired Bitches Brew, made with brown sugar from the island of Mauritius, raw unfiltered Ethiopian honey, and "an a--load of dark, roasty grains to balance the sweetness of the honey," as Calagione explained it to me, is a great example. The company's top seller is 60 Minute IPA, first brewed in 2003 and a graham cracker–like feast Calagione has described as being "super pungent, citrusy, and grassy, without being crushingly bitter."

BEST *of the* REST: DELAWARE

IRON HILL

147 E. Main St. • Newark, DE 19711 • (302) 266-9000 • ironhillbrewery.com

Now the flagship of a mini chain with twelve locations in the area and brewing medals with surprising speed (nine major categories in two prestigious competitions during 2010), the original Iron Hill location is located near the University of Delaware. There are five house standard beers ranging from a light lager to a 5.4% ABV porter, plus an always-on seasonal Belgian ale, several other seasonals, and about seventeen bottled reserves (including some vintage-dated beers). The house beers are fine, but the action for committed craft mavens is in those ever-changing offerings from month to month. The interior is sort of "modern library," with reddish wood paneling and deep green walls beneath a vaulted modern Quonset hut ceiling. The menu reaches for a higher culinary plane than most brewpubs, too, with respectable results.

The South

the SOUTH & SOUTHEAST

SWEET TEA, JAMBALAYA, BARBECUE . . . AND BELGIAN ALE? WITH PROHIBITION-ERA LAWS still on the books in parts of the region, keeping the beer weak and home-brew kettles dry (Alabama and Mississippi only legalized the practice of homebrewing as of 2013), it seemed good beer might never really arrive in the Deep South, much less reweave the social fabric as it has in cities like Philly, Portland, and San Diego. There was— and surely still is, in some dustier corners—a sense that craft beer might not really make sense. There's something about the easygoing South that calls for the finished fermented product of malt, hops, yeast, and water in a red plastic cup, very cold and very light, or, lacking such a distinguished vessel, simply canned and cold on a hot day. The late, great Mississippi writer Larry Brown's imagery (and preferred method) of drinking beer—while blasting Robert Earl Keen with empties clanging around in the back of an old beater and hauling down some country road—seems more apt.

And yet the art of craft beer *has* well and truly arrived in the South. Brewing is nothing if not social, and there's no better match to a spicy pulled pork po'boy than a crisp craft-brewed pilsner. From ambitious new breweries in Asheville and new beer bars in New Orleans, the former "brewing capital of the South," to the anodyne, palm-lined byways of South Florida, it's becoming one of the country's most interesting regions when it comes to craft beer.

Even as government bureaucrats bicker about alcohol strength caps other old laws, the land of fizzy yellow water is going big for the good-beer gumbo—and reviving a proud brewing past.

ITINERARIES

1-DAY	Nola Brewing Co., the Bulldog, Lüke, Avenue Pub, Cooter Brown's, Maple Leaf Bar
3-DAY	One-day itinerary plus Abita Brewing Co., Great Raft, and Bayou Teche
7-DAY	Three-day itinerary plus Creature Comforts, The Brick Store Pub, J. Clyde, Twain's

LOUISIANA

New Orleans

THE AVENUE PUB

1732 St. Charles Ave. • New Orleans, LA
70130 • (504) 586-9243 • avenuepub.com
Established: 1989

SCENE & STORY

It's not necessary to call ahead or plan your visit to New Orleans's best beer bar because it never closes—ever. It has been said that the world-class beer bar in the Lower Garden district, open 24/7 every day of the year, doesn't even have locks on the doors. After her father died, owner Polly Watts took over and rechristened the place in 2006 after her father died and turned this once seedier spot into a real destination for beer lovers everywhere. The charming, slightly ramshackle building overlooking St. Charles dates back to the 1840s and boasts a huge wraparound upstairs porch, making it a coveted spot during Mardi Gras, as the parade passes directly by. On the first level several black chalkboards dense with American craft beers (and some truly wonderful imports) frame a relatively narrow bar area with

seating nearby. A stairwell leads up to a coffeehouse-esque room with antique furniture, framed pictures, and the second bar area with its own menu.

The selection of a few dozen bottles is the most inspired in Louisiana, and there are real finds among the tap list of forty-seven rotating brands. Then there's the friendly, ultra-knowledgeable staff and chilled out locals enjoying a quiet drink at the bar. Last but not least is the excellent—and very affordable—bar food, which is far more advanced than the quotidian menu item names would suggest. The grilled cheese turns out to be a ridiculously gooey-good combo of drunken goat cheese, sharp cheddar, and feta grilled in sourdough with sage, herb pesto, bacon, and tomato. It's hedonism on a plate.

PHILOSOPHY

Enlightened. Watts is an unabashed craft beer maven, but neither she nor her staff will condescend to another's taste. This is New Orleans, after all: Self-serious puffery is ill advised. Knowledge, on the other hand, is power. The bar offers classes for the Cicerone program, a beer expertise certification course, and Watts keeps her tap beers fresh using a costly system that dispenses beers under a mixture of CO_2 and nitrogen that is calibrated according to each beer's ideal mixture. Her staff cleans the lines every two weeks, inhibiting the bacteria growth that can contribute to terribly off flavors in beer. This is a (woefully) rare and yet essential practice.

KEY BEER

Watts recently put the seldom seen Cantillon Lou Pepe Kriek on tap; it's a tart lambic brew from Belgium that is spontaneously fermented with wild yeasts, aged in Bordeaux barrels for up to three years, and refermented with the juice of local cherries before bottling. With its unremittingly tart flavor it would be the perfect foil for the rich artisan cheese board from St. James Cheese Company, a noted Garden District merchant.

NOLA BREWING CO.

3001 Tchoupitoulas St. • New Orleans, LA
70115 • (504) 896-9996
nolabrewing.com • Established: 2008

SCENE & STORY

With its sultry weather and evenings it would seem unlikely that craft beer—with its sometimes intense, attention-demanding flavors and hefty alcoholic punch—would gain much of a foothold in New Orleans. But it has. This is, after all, the city that invented the cocktail, elevating simple spirits to something higher, and, at one time, the former brewing capital of the American South.

Those days may be coming back. It's a short drive from the French Quarter down to Tchoupitoulas Street to get to one of the most remarkable success stories—in beer, or any local business—since Katrina. With the demise of local brand Dixie, the New Orleans Lager & Ale Brewing Company, universally known as Nola Brewing, is poised to become the city's preeminent craft brewery, first by putting superdistinctive batches on draft around town and then by packaging.

Native son and founder Kirk Coco and head brewer Peter Caddoo (a trained chef and former brewmaster of Dixie) have set up shop in a hangar-like former metal shop just south of the Garden District overlooking the Mississippi River. Standing beneath the soaring eaves in view of their compact 20bbl system of kettle and tanks (sure to expand) with the freshest possible brew in hand, it's easy to think the sky's the limit.

Coco, a former lawyer with a wily enthusiasm, was working as a surface warfare officer in the U.S. Navy during Katrina, while Caddoo, a shyer sort but often wearing a contented, slightly wry grin, had been sous chef under Emeril Lagasse at Commander's Palace before working at Dixie—until all the brewers were laid off a few months before Katrina as the company foundered. Both men watched from a safe distance as the storm took its terrible toll on the city and on Dixie, its last proud brewery. Slowly, as the city picked up the pieces in 2007, they began to plan their venture.

Today Nola gets a crowd of fifty or more visitors every Friday at 2 p.m.; samples are offered with the free tours, even though they can't sell six-packs or pints under existing laws (ones Coco hopes to help change). And in 2015, Coco announced a bunch of good news: a new taproom (with local favorite McClure's Barbecue) next door, and a distillery nearby making gin, vodka, and white whiskey.

PHILOSOPHY

Quintessentially local. Coco and Caddoo are experimenting with some local ingredients like watermelon and say they want to stay small (they did about 1,300bbl in 2010, and say they'd top out at 10,000). "More than any other city—except maybe Seattle or San Francisco—New Orleans supports local products so strongly," says Coco. "That's why there are no chain restaurants around. It's very hard to find one. For one, the food's *so, so good*, and for another, most people don't want to support a businesses where the money goes out of the city. Having a brewery located in the city has been great for us. They know we're here in the Irish Channel area, and the people around here, they all drink our beer."

KEY BEER

Too many IPAs on the market are haphazard affairs defined by a long and face-contorting aftertaste. Not Caddoo's 6.5% ABV Hopitoulas IPA, a blend of six malts and six hops, which is then dry-hopped with two different hops beyond that point. It's balanced, with notes of pine, grapefruit, and caramel.

LÜKE

333 St. Charles Ave. • New Orleans, LA 70130 • (504) 378-2840
lukeneworleans.com • Established: 2007

SCENE & STORY

Mid-city native and James Beard Award–winning celebrity chef John Besh's Lüke (one of a half-dozen eateries he owns) has gorgeous tile floors and high, shiny tin-clad ceilings and a mouthwatering menu of dishes like twenty-five-cent oysters, redfish "court-bouillon" (with crab, shrimp, oysters, and rice); and shrimp "en cocotte" (with creamy white-corn grits and andouille). But it's the succulent Lüke burger that sings, with juicy tomatoes, smoky bacon from Madisonville, Tennessee, perfectly caramelized onions, and Emmental cheese with seasoned, thick-cut fries. That gloriously rich ensemble is worth the trip alone. Besh's locally brewed house beers, which have included Lüke Fru (a delicate kölsch),

Lüke Export (a pils with Austrian hops) Lüke Alt (an aged, Düsseldorf-style lager, well matched with meatier fare), and Mardi Gras Festbier, a smooth, potent bock, make the whole package even tastier. Experimental collaborations in 2015 with Great Raft Brewing out of Shreveport, Louisiana, bode well, too, for all the Besh restaurants.

DETOUR ➡ THE MAPLE LEAF

8316 Oak St. • New Orleans, LA 70118 • (504) 866-9359 • mapleleafbar.com

Open since 1974, the old Leaf is the paradigmatic New Orleans music bar, with shows and jam sessions seven nights a week and regular standing gigs for many incredible artists. To walk into its small space and take in its dilapidated floors, red tin walls, and deep-crimson lighting is to become a part of the Crescent City itself. A photo of poet and "Maple Leaf Laureate" Everett Hawthorne Maddox ("in residence 1976–1989") and a bottle of his Famous Grouse bourbon hang on the wall; poetry readings are traditional here, too. Musically speaking, it's pure New Orleans, with nightly performances by the likes of Rebirth Brass Band, Papa Grows Funk, the Radiators, members of the Funky Meters, and surprise appearances by artists of icon status (Springsteen has made an appearance and Beyoncé filmed a video here).

With the famous Jacques-Imo's restaurant next door, one could easily make a night of it. Just get there. Take a good look at the outside, too: The wood speaks volumes. You don't come to the Maple Leaf to drink elaborate cocktails (mixers beyond ice get dicey); you don't come here to analyze Belgian ales. You come here to soak up soul deeper than the roots of a live oak. After the storm, Walter "Wolfman" Jackson played the first (publicized, at least) post-Katrina New Orleans concert on an emotional night. With the famous Jacques-Imo's restaurant next door one could make an easy night of it. Just get there. Take a good look at the outside, too: the wood speaks volumes. As for me, next time I'm in town it will be a Monday, to see the unbelievably talented band Papa Grows Funk. I'll arrive around 10:30, just in time to catch bandleader Jon Gross start trading fat, growly Hammond B3 solos with the Hendrix-like June Yamagishi on guitar, order up some Nola brew and get lost in the music all over again. See you at the Leaf.

PHILOSOPHY

Nostalgic. Besh sought to make Lüke an homage to the grand old Franco-German brasseries that once reigned in New Orleans, and it succeeds beautifully.

KEY BEER

Bok, or bock (German for 'goat') is a strong lager brewed in the winter to drink in early spring. If your timing is right (December to February), go for the medium-bodied Festbier version of this style, which is copper-hued with a smooth malty profile and just enough acidity and bitterness to complement the rich flavors of the burger.

CRESCENT CITY BREWHOUSE

527 Decatur St. • New Orleans, LA 70130
(888) 819-9330 or (504) 522-0571
crescentcitybrewhouse.com
Established: 1991

SCENE & STORY

Overlooking the busy pedestrian area of Decatur Street in the French Quarter, the oldest brewpub in New Orleans features a handsome oval-shaped wooden bar, oyster bar, and musicians' area overshadowed by copper German kettles and a huge sign reading "OYSTERS" and below that "air conditioned," the two main reasons to come here. Dating back to 1794, the building is large, and in addition to the ground and terrace levels there's a small garden terrace and airy patio upstairs overlooking the street. While the food earns good marks, the best way to experience this bar may be by popping in for a look at the copper work, then buying a beer in a plastic cup from the street-level bar and heading on your way uptown in a taxi, having paid your respects.

PHILOSOPHY

Traditional. House brews from the 17bbl system include a pilsner, Vienna-style lager, Munich-style dark, and unfiltered wheat beer, all basic and to some degrees boring; hopefully the brewers will take a look at Nola, Great Raft, Tin Roof, and Bayou Teche and step up the game. Recently they've tackled IPA and American-style brown ales, with some signs of improvement. And they added beer cocktails in 2014.

KEY BEER

Black Forest, a Munich-style dark lager, is a medium- to light-bodied brew with roasty notes of caramel and dark chocolate.

THE BULLDOG

3236 Magazine St. • New Orleans, LA 70115
(504) 891-1516 • bulldog.draftfreak.com
Established: 1994

THE BULLDOG MIDCITY

5135 Canal Blvd. • New Orleans, LA 70124
(504) 488-4191
bulldog-midcity.draftfreak.com
Established: 2004

SCENE & STORY

Magazine Street, in the area generally referred to as uptown (and bordering the Garden District) is lined with cool, old bars, shops, art galleries, and eateries, and makes a nice change from the French Quarter, which varies from magical to insufferably touristy. The original Bulldog on Magazine Street has fifty beers on tap and 100 in bottles, standard pub fare, and a spacious patio out back featuring a fountain made of beer taps. The midcity location is a bit more upscale; both bars offer easygoing environments that make them worth a stop on a pub-crawl. The Bulldog has two other locations as well: Baton Rouge (where you can try the latest brews from Tin Roof, Louisiana's most recent craft brewery to fire up), and Jackson, Mississippi.

PHILOSOPHY

Good fun for good causes. There are generally a lot of Tulane and Loyola students, and it's dog-friendly, and the bar donates often to the local Humane Society and ASPCA. Wednesdays are popular as everyone gets to keep the pint glasses, or, by leaving them, donate to the causes.

KEY BEER

Nola Blonde, an easygoing, light-bodied brew first released in March 2009, is grainy, pale gold, and has an angular hop attack for the style.

COOTER BROWN'S TAVERN, GRILL, & OYSTER BAR

509 S. Carrollton Ave. • New Orleans, LA 70118 • (504) 886-9104
cooterbrowns.com • Established: 1977

SCENE & STORY

The gloriously dive-y Cooter Brown's, in the Riverbend area of uptown New Orleans, is the eccentric granddaddy of New Orleans beer bars, with a vast hoard of beer (over 350 bottles and 42 taps), pool tables, pressed tin walls, wood slatted ceilings, and a gallery of ceramic caricatures of "dead celebrities," clutching beers related somehow to their careers ("Jimmy Dean, an unfulfilled acting career cut short by tragedy, grips a bottle of Golden Promise," explains the website). It's a classic, plain and simple. Recently they added the "Snooty Cooter" bar, a 46-tap homage to the latest and greatest beers.

PHILOSOPHY

No frills. You'll hear it described as a good beer bar and a place to mingle with drunken Tulane students and eccentric locals, and it is indeed both, as well as a decent place to go for oysters and crawfish. And the beer is better than ever.

KEY BEER

A deliciously safe bet is Duvel in a twelve-ounce bottle, the classic 8.5% ABV Belgian strong pale ale. It's a big, refreshing, kicky beer with fine effervescence and Champagne dryness that can stand the extra shelf time that comes for beers in bars with huge lists.

Beyond New Orleans

BAYOU TECHE BREWING CO.

1106 Bushville Hwy. • Arnaudville, LA 70512 • (337) 303-8000
bayoutechebrewing.com • Established: 2010

SCENE & STORY

It's a family affair. Early in 2010 the brothers Knott (Karlos, Byron, and Dorsey) opened the doors on their little train car turned taproom on farmland once used for growing beans, a good-size patch of earth maintained by the Knott family since the 1800s. Karlos and his brothers grew up in a Cajun French-speaking home, and their father Floyd writes about Acadiana, the traditional Cajun name for the area. The only beers around when the boys were growing up in the area were Jax (defunct), Budweiser, and Falstaff, all industrial lagers. Later Karlos served in the military in Germany and then at Fort Lewis in Washington State, and loved the good beers he drank in both locations. On Saint Patrick's Day 2008, they decided to brew professionally. After all, they had a place to do it: the family farm.

To find that farm you drive west and a hair north out of New Orleans for about two and a half hours and wend along LA-31 beside the serpentine Bayou Teche, the 125-mile waterway leading from Arnaudville to the Gulf. As Karlos puts it, the next part involves a T in the road, a Piggly Wiggly store, and "left turn at the twelfth station of the cross." One way or another you'll find their Bayou Teche Brewery, once a nano-size, 1bbl project with modest ambitions, and today a vital presence in southern craft brewing—even a member of the 2016 Sierra Nevada Beer Camp Across America Tour, reserved for cutting edge regional breweries. "The local Budweiser distributor told us locals didn't want craft beer," recalls Karlos, who has a gray-flecked beard, dark eyes, and a

DETOUR ➡ RUINS & RESURRECTION

Not so long ago, of course, all the laughter ended in the Big Easy. When the floodwaters of Katrina breached in August 2005, the area's breweries took a serious hit along with the rest of the beleaguered city. Hardest hit was Dixie Brewing Company, opened in New Orleans in 1907. A familiar landmark in town for ninety-eight grand years, Dixie was inundated with eight or nine feet of water.

Today the wracked shell of a building stands as a grim reminder of what the region suffered in the great storm. Visible from I-90 over on Tulane Avenue, the red brick behemoth stands scarred, its windows blackened and broken out, the interior emptied, the brewing equipment long looted and sold for scrap. After the storm, the owners talked of coming back, but costs were prohibitive, and today the ruins gloam over 3rd Ward streets with an abiding sadness. Once the largest brewery in town and pride of the region, the catastrophic storm reduced it to an empty hulk.

As of mid-2015 there are competing plans to either redevelop or raze the ruins. So if it's still there, be sure to drive past it a few times, perhaps slowing down for a picture or two (it's not currently a safe area to walk around on foot), and apprehend a powerful reminder of what New Orleans once was—the brewing capital of the South. Locals seem resigned to the fact that the wrecking ball can't be far off, but perhaps someone whose heart beats for an old brewery will find a way to make it work.

It's a heavy thing to take in—a real specter of death and destruction—so the best thing you can do next is to head to nearby Mandina's, on Canal Street, for some Italo-Creole comfort food (3800 Canal St.; 504-482-9179). Its quaint pink-with-white trim exterior and front porch conceals thirteen-foot-high ceilings, bow-tied waiters, and a clientele of cheery, well-dressed locals and policemen chatting away. On the day I visited, it felt like a scene from *Back to the Future*.

Refreshingly, there were no tourists whatsoever. I took my seat in the first dining room and ordered a perfect iced tea. Over my left shoulder I spotted a faded old *Times-Picayune* story about how the place was opened in 1932 by the sons of Sebastian Mandina, from Palermo, Sicily. He'd opened it as a shop in 1898, and was briefly jailed for selling home brew, hidden in a false window in the store. It became a neighborhood—and, indeed, citywide—institution, and stayed in the Mandina family.

Katrina tried to silence this place, too, deluging the place up to about six feet.

But because the restaurant is raised up from street level, the water came up to just below the tabletops, which were found eerily still set when Cindy Mandina first ventured back inside about six weeks after the storm. Now restored to its 1930s luster by Cindy and her family, the food is excellent and the portions hearty. The catfish po'boy is one of the best sandwiches I've ever eaten, in any city. And a word to the wise: The "whole loaf" is huge; the "half loaf" could feed two people, and the quarter loaf is just right for one.

genteel manner. "I said 'well, maybe they haven't been offered it,' and sure enough, the beer we'd planned for three months sold out in three days."

It has been a wild ride since then for these bayou brothers, who were hit so hard with demand that Lazy Magnolia Brewery in Kiln, Mississippi agreed to help them meet it by contracting some extra capacity. This is Cajun country, and you'll hear great music in the taproom, perhaps even from the musically talented brothers. In 2011, the Knotts broke ground on a new 8,000-square-foot facility to house their 15bbl brewhouse, and another in 2015, but the train car taproom will stay intact. Since 2010, they've brewed Ragin' Cajun, a kölsch for the University of Louisiana (with added local rice, to lighten it up for tailgaters), and hit both the Food Network and the pages of *Esquire*.

PHILOSOPHY

Call it Low Country craft with a side of southern ease. Karlos and his brothers had been home brewing batches for craw-

fish boils and gumbos for years when the idea took hold to step things up and invest in a pilot brewery. "We thought it would be best to brew beers to complement our low country style of cuisine, and with some hoppier flavors, too, to go with all the pork fat we use," Knott recalls.

KEY BEER

LA 31 Bière Pâle, their Belgian-inflected pale ale named for the state highway, was intended to be the flagship, but Passionné, a wheat beer brewed with passion fruit juice (another local wild fruit) quickly overtook it. The most unique is Boucanée ("smoked"), a lightly smoked wheat beer. As the story goes, there's a local species of wild cherry tree, and when the Knotts were kids, their grandparents would cut one tree down per year. The women would make a liqueur called "cherry bounce" and the men would cut up the branches for smoking andouille and tasso and sausage. This beer is their homage to that tradition. Is your mouth watering yet?

DETOUR → NEW ORLEANS'S BEST COMFORT FOOD

CAFÉ DU MONDE • 800 Decatur St. • New Orleans, LA 70116 • (504) 587-0831
CENTRAL GROCERY • 923 Decatur St. • New Orleans, LA 70116 • (504) 523-1620
STEIN'S DELI • 2207 Magazine St. • New Orleans, LA 70130 • (504) 527-0771 • steinsdeli.net

Unless you have superhuman powers of self-control, exploring the beer bars and eateries of the French Quarter in New Orleans will lead to foggy mornings, your brain, body, and soul crying out for sugar, caffeine, and fatty Italian meats on bread. First, proceed to the wonderfully decayed Café du Monde, a traditional coffee stand open since 1862 (and open every day except Christmas). One order of beignet per person (say "behn-yay") means three puffy, warm dough fritters gloriously dusted with powdered sugar. The joe is strong and not too terrible, though the chicory version is an acquired taste, a blend of coffee and dried endive plant root that was favored during the Civil War.

Just down the block is Central Grocery, an Italian market opened in 1906 and home of the muffaletta, the signature New Orleans sandwich. The concept is simple: It's a circular loaf of soft Italian bread sliced horizontally, layered with top-quality sliced ham, salami, and provolone cheese. That perfect trio is then capped with a layer of olive salad—chopped green and black olives minced with anchovies and garlic. A half feeds two adults handily, and if there's room in the back, you can sit at a little lunch counter and tuck in, or wend your way back outside and try for a bench in front of St. Louis Cathedral in Jackson Square. With the perfect sandwich, the riverboats, and the former home of Jax Brewery (now a shopping area) in view, you're suddenly, completely whole again.

Lastly, make a visit to Stein's Deli, a Jewish-Italian deli opened in the Lower Garden District in 2006. Dan Stein's place is all about life-saving breakfast sandwiches—*sandwich* sandwiches (muffaletta/pastrami/reuben/BLT/New York bagels). The shelves are packed with cured meats, salamis, and a huge selection of domestic and international craft beers, the best of which hidden out of sight in the back (so ask Dan). This is a killer place to refuel and stock up on bottled local specialties if you're staying locally for a while.

ABITA BREWING CO.

21084 Hwy. 36 • Abita Springs, LA 70433
(985) 893-3143 • abita.com
Established: 1986

ABITA BREW PUB

72011 Holly St. • Abita Springs, LA 70420
(985) 892-5837 • Established: 1994

THE ABITA TAP ROOM

166 Barbee Rd. • Covington, LA 70433
(985) 893-3143 • Established: 2015

SCENE & STORY

Abita was the first southeastern craft brewery to emerge and today, with both a modern brewery and the original brewpub (plus a new taproom in Covington, opened in 2015), has an epochal feel, like a shiny new stadium in a town with the old bleachers down the road. To get to the new 49,000-square-foot brewery from New Orleans you drive the straight 30-mile shot across Lake Pontchartrain toward St. Tammany Parrish and Covington and veer right toward Abita Springs. The brewery owners settled on their location due to the presence of the five-million-year-old aquifer of soft artesian water, a celebrated font that happens to have a perfect pH for brewing and requires no spendy chemical adjustment. The local Chocktaw Indians used this water for medicinal purposes, and turn-of-the-century tourists traveled there to recover from yellow fever. You

can—and should!—drink it from water fountains inside the brewery on the tour.

Visitors to the brewery itself (minor hordes actually, with some 20,000 clocked per year at present) convene in a large, porticoed taproom with a wide mahogany bar and watch a surprisingly thorough video before taking a tour amid the brewery's enormous 400bbl tanks the size of school buses. It's a sociable place, and it seems hardly surprising one of the main tour guides is an affable brewer by the name of Sonny Day II, a well-respected veteran of Dixie Brewing Company now helping run the show.

The original brewery location just down the road has, since 1994, housed a 100-seat brewpub where you can sample a few house beers Abita doesn't bottle, like a recent Black IPA. Behind its white picket fence and cypress window frames, it's a nice enough place to spend some time after the tour. Expect above average southeastern pub fare, though the kitchen hasn't done much cooking with Abita beer.

PHILOSOPHY

Abita has grown like a beanstalk since the day it opened in 1986 with a capacity for 1,500bbl, and modernized operations considerably, including the installment of a unique brewing kettle device called the Merlin, a massive steel heating agent more common in Europe and prized for efficiency. Along the way the company has headed north of 130,000 barrels produced annually, but managed to keep a somewhat soulful image. In the aftermath of Hurricane Katrina, Abita launched a beer they dubbed Fleur de Lis Restoration Pale Ale and raised over half a million dollars for hurricane relief, having been spared themselves from major physical damages, and in 2010 released SOS Pilsner to raise funds for the BP Gulf Oil recovery efforts. The brewery is run by David Blossman, a longtime craft beer enthusiast and original shareholder.

"People say there's no beer culture [here], and I just have to disagree," says Blossman. He ties craft beer's success in the Crescent City to the incredible food scene, with its ambitious chefs and a panoply of influences. "We owe a lot of our success to the chefs who took us under their wings," he explains, echoing a point often made in the city's taprooms: The beer scene is intertwined with dining, a central facet of life. Ambitious chefs working from farmers' markets have helped open the city palate wider, expanding on the already wide spectrum of Cajun, Creole, French, North American, and African American traditions. And of course, it's the Big Easy: People like to drink here. "It's a different lifestyle. People like to slow down. We're very social," Blossman adds.

KEY BEER

Abita is best known for its caramel-colored and light-bodied amber (4.5% ABV), but the company has six other year-round beers in all, in addition to five seasonals plus occasional one-offs for the pub brewed on Sonny Day's one-barrel pilot system. The best for daytime drinking is Restoration Ale, a deep gold, lightly dry-hopped ale with Cascade hops, or Purple Haze, a light and cloudy American-style wheat ale (4.2% ABV) blended with raspberry puree postfiltration, giving it a fruity zing.

BEST of the REST: LOUISIANA

COLUMBIA STREET TAP ROOM AND GRILL

434 N. Columbia St. • Covington, LA 70433 • (985) 898-0899 • columbiastreettaproom

Sleepy Covington (population: 9,000) comes alive on occasion, especially when the frequent live bands fire up at "the taproom," as this craft beer bar opened in 1996 is commonly called. It's got classic old-bar appointments, with exposed brick walls and high ceilings, old Dixie Beer signs, and a wide, handsome antique bar. Built in 1906 by the Seilers, a prominent family in town, the building operated for years as a tavern-inn with lodgings on the second floor. Of the thirty taps, about half are Louisiana brews from the likes of Abita, Great Raft, and Bayou Teche, with some great imports such as Blanche de Bruxelles thrown in. The draught lineup is complemented by a smallish but solid bottle list, as well as a selection of burgers and soul food.

THE BARLEY OAK

2101 Lakeshore Dr. • Mandeville, LA 70448 • (985) 727-7420 • thebarleyoak.com

Located at the end of a residential road on the north shore of Lake Pontchartrain, the Barley Oak (established in 2009) is a new British- and German-themed pub with a patio-equipped upstairs bar drawing from a selection of 47 taps and 120 bottles. The service is warm and friendly; the view from the patio on a clear day, looking south toward New Orleans over a Spanish moss–draped live oak and miles of blue water, is unbeatable. Beer prices run high on rarer brews; still, there could be no better place to catch a sunset and an inexpensive bite before heading back into NoLa for the evening. The draught list represents locals with pride, and among the mostly conventional bottle list are some goodies from Blaugies, Brooklyn, Jolly Pumpkin, and Mikkeller.

GREAT RAFT BREWING

1251 Dalzell St. • Shreveport, LA 71104 • (318) 734-9881 • greatraftbrewing.com

Don't rule out a road trip up to Shreveport from NoLa (325 miles). In the fall of 2015, a large panel of reputable local beer experts picked Great Raft, out in Shreveport, as the state's top brewery with the best, most consistent beers—remarkable for a company barely three years old at the time. Opened in 2012, their flagship is Commotion, an American-style pale ale with waves of grapefruit and citrus aromas. Best place to drink it? The air-conditioned taproom on site in the huge brewery, naturally, but the beers are finding wider and wider distribution throughout the state.

PARISH BREWING COMPANY

229 Jared Dr. • Broussard, LA 70518 • (337) 330-8601 • parishbeer.com

Every state seems to have a Double IPA game-changing beer that propelled a newish brewery to stardom (i.e., the Alchemist's Heady Topper). Opened in 2009, Parish is that brewery for Louisiana. Located in sleepy Broussard, south of Lafayette, 165 miles West of NoLa, Parish is the birthplace of Ghost in the Machine, an 8.5% ABV, dank, herbalicious double IPA, a cult beer if there ever was one.

NORTH CAROLINA

Asheville

WHAT MAKES A GREAT BEER CITY COME OF AGE? IT SEEMS THAT WHEN TOWNS OF A SOCIABLE size (say, 50,000 to about 500,000) gain a certain preponderance of outdoorsy young and college folk, a jamming-good music and craft beer scene cannot be far behind. Along with Boulder, Colorado; Portland, Oregon; and San Diego, California, leafy Asheville, North Carolina (and the surrounding area), has become a hotbed of brewing over the past few years—especially since the state legislature raised the limit for beer's alcohol content from 6 percent to 15 percent in 2005 after a campaign led by brewer Sean Lilly Wilson, who went on to found Fullsteam Brewing Company in Durham. The city (nor the craft movement) shows little sign of slowing down, with over 150 breweries in the state—triple the number there were when this book was published (it wasn't easy to narrow down, trust me).

Even the crown of "Beer City, USA" (bestowed by the Brewers Association) has gone to Asheville in multiple years, recently (2009–2012). Then there's the famous southern food and hospitality, which, of course, is wonderful. But it's not just dozens of little guys jumping in the pond: over the last few years, three major U.S. craft breweries picked the area to build their (massive) second, East Coast outposts: Sierra Nevada, Oskar Blues, and New Belgium. Where to begin? Better carve out some time.

ITINERARIES

1-DAY	Wicked Weed Funkatorium, Highland Brewing, Burial
3-DAY	One-day itinerary plus Wedge Brewing, Bruisin' Ales, and The Thirsty Monk in Asheville
7-DAY	Three-day itinerary and The Bier Garden in Asheville; Duck-Rabbit in Farmville; The Raleigh Times Bar (Raleigh); Fullsteam in Durham

HIGHLAND BREWING

12 Old Charlotte Hwy., Ste. H
Asheville, NC 28803 • (828) 299-3370
highlandbrewing.com • Established: 1986

SCENE & STORY

Asheville's original craft brewery launched under the watchful (and patient) eyes of brewer John Lyda and Oscar Wong, a retired engineer, using retrofitted dairy equipment. Located today in a converted warehouse atop a hill just a short drive from the center of town, it's one of Asheville's top craft beer draws and brews some 20,000bbls a year, making it a good-size operation. In the taproom (open Monday through Saturday from 4 p.m. to 8 p.m.), revelers gather for tours amid converted container ship units that serve as offices, a music stage, plenty of seats and tables, and a draft bar with year round-releases and seasonals. The tours and samples are free, but donations of food and cash are accepted for local charities, a nice touch. Visitors gather in the taproom for $3.50 pints afterward and during the blues, bluegrass, and other Americana-inspired shows. In 2012, they built a bigger stage, and added an outdoor bar (in a repurposed shipping container, to match the offices), improvements which have helped their massively popular BaconFest get bigger every year, too, with 2,500 tickets sold in 2015. Food trucks on Fridays and Saturdays keep the weekend crowds well fed.

PHILOSOPHY

Highland's beers broke early ground, but could be maddeningly uneven at first. After some years of trial and error, the outfit began to turn the corner with a lineup of assertive beers. It's a pretty conventional lineup, from light wheat on up to stouts, porters, and other strong ales, but recent brews have shown a more experimental side, with amped up dry-hopping regimes, oak barrel aging, fruit additions, and Belgian styles entering the mix.

KEY BEER

The amber hued Gaelic Ale (5.8% ABV) with its graham cracker sweetness and kiss of Cascade and Willamette hops is something of a flagship, but it's the roasty, mocha-tinged Highland Oatmeal Porter (also 5.8% ABV) that shows off Highland's brewing chops most consistently.

WICKED WEED BREWING

91 Biltmore Ave. • Asheville, NC 28801
(828) 575-9599 • wickedweedbrewing.com

←――――――→

WICKED WEED FUNKATORIUM

147 Coxe Ave. • Asheville, NC 2880
(828) 552-3203 • wickedweedbrewing.com

SCENE & STORY

One of the biggest stories in American craft beer is barely four years old as of 2016. Brothers Luke and Walt Dickinson launched this downtown brewery in late 2012 with full restaurant, downstairs beer bar, bottle shop, and their original brewery. The focus: bold, hoppy beers, rustic farmhouse ales, and some left hook experiments, all coming out of a 15bbl brewery for a local market. Fast-forward to 2016 and they've got a new taproom focused on all wild and sour beers (Funkatorium), a hit beer 100% fermented with *Brettanomyces* (wild yeast), or "brett," (Serenity), a new 50(!)-barrel brewhouse, medal recognition (for Pernicious, an American-style IPA, beating 334 other entries in 2015 in the most competitive category of the GABF), and 18-wheelers full of buzz, it's an exciting time for the brewery named after a phrase King Henry VIII used to describe hops.

PHILOSOPHY

Artfully ambitious. Catching up over beers one night at the Falling Rock Taphouse during the 2015 GABF, Walt Dickinson, Wicked Weed's "Head Blender and Keeper of the Funk" wore the hunted look of a man in the midst of battle. He was having a good time, sure, but things are moving at a breakneck speed. The lines at his booth had been among the longest in the entire hall. Expansions, collaborations, and blueprints were swirling around him like houses in a cartoon twister. "It's pretty crazy right now," he said, going on to declare his love of food pairing with beer, and speak of a deep ambition to continue making his mark in the barrel room. "We want Wicked Weed to be part of the conversation on sour beer worldwide," he told me. I'd say they are already there.

KEY BEER

Serenity, a tart, 100-percent Brettanomyces beer that is barrel-aged for three to five months, has become a touchstone for beer geeks in the region, and increasingly, beyond. The Funkatorium is a separate barrel facility dedicated to wild beers with twelve rotating taps and an upcoming vintage bottle menu. It's open seven days a week, with small plates, sandwiches, and flatbreads meant for pairing with these palate-expanding beers.

BURIAL BEER CO.

40 Collier Ave. • Asheville, NC 28801
(828) 475-2739 • burialbeer.com
Established: 2013

SCENE & STORY

Burial isn't a brewery about death metal or funerals or other such rites. More like: burying seeds and watching them grow . . . and grow. After an inspirational trip to Belgium in 2010, the three founders Tim Gromley and Doug and Jess Reiser moved from Seattle to Asheville around 2012, and, in their first year and a half—working in a drafty, repurposed 1930s warehouse—brewed over 200 batches on a one-barrel system, working out kinks, experimenting, meeting the locals, getting constant feedback. "For the first year . . . we didn't have any employees," Jess told me. "We built basically everything in the taproom, worked the bar, brewed, did it all. It was an amazing experience."

What they ended up with was a raft of solid recipes and a massive local following. The shed-like interior of the barn is a real vision of down-home, with antique farm tools for tap handles, mason jar lights, hanging flags and weathered wood walls (and a velvet Tom Selleck portrait, for good measure). It's a seed, to be sure, of the farmhouse brewery they dream of building someday outside town. For now, they have a terrific little urban getaway with picnic tables on the South Slope, the brewery dotted neighborhood that is home to Wicked Weed's Funkatorium, Hi-Wire Brewing, and Twin Leaf brewing, as well as a great bottle shop called Tasty, among others. In December 2014, Burial expanded to a ten-barrel system and a staff of thirteen, and by 2015, started canning, with expansion plans coming together with each and every new experimental batch.

PHILOSOPHY

Storytelling in beer form. "Several years ago, we fell in love with craft beer realizing that the beers tell a story beyond the style," Jess wrote me. "It is the people behind the beer, the history, the passion and hard work, the dedication to something craft, something local that we truly connected to. We see our brewery as a place that brings the community together over innovative, quality beer."

KEY BEER

Pollination Honey Saison. "This beer truly represents our mission—we are inspired by and place great emphasis on saisons and farmhouse ales, the beer for the farmer," Jess reports. Made with local malt and honey, it's aged on a medley of dried flowers including chamomile, lavender, elderflowers, rose petals, rose hips, passion flower, and hibiscus.

BARLEY'S TAPROOM & PIZZERIA

42 Biltmore • Asheville, NC 28801
(828) 255-0504 • barleystaproom.com
Established: 1994

SCENE & STORY

Every beer bar should have the luxury of this much room. In a renovated, 8,000-square-foot 1920s former appliance store in the heart of Asheville's arts and entertainment district, Barley's is more than a beer bar. It's also a restaurant and music venue, with New York–style sourdough pizza made from the spent grains of local breweries (and other pub fare) to go with all the live Americana music on offer several nights a week. Better yet, there's no cover. The mostly local, twenty-four-tap ground floor section is a deep space of weathered wooden floors and tables, handsome wooden bar with high "captain's chairs," and tinned and carved timber ceilings. For a game of pool, head upstairs to a room of regulation slate billiard tables available by the hour, plus darts and nineteen additional taps.

PHILOSOPHY

This is a shrine for the southern craft beer awakening: Of the approximately 100 total beers available on draught or in bottles, just under half are from the South, while the rest are mostly from American brewers.

KEY BEER

Pisgah's hazy orange organic Pale Ale (5.5% ABV) is the perfect pizza beer: crisp, a touch sweet, and finishing with enough bitter bite to stand up to the zip of the sauce and meats.

THE THIRSTY MONK

92 Patton Ave. • Asheville, NC 28801
(828) 254-5470 • monkpub.com
Established: 2008

Reynolds Village • 51 N. Merrimon Ave., No. 113 • Woodfin, NC 28804 • (828) 424-7807 monkpub.com • Established: 2014

Biltmore Park • 2 Town Square Blvd., No. 170 • Asheville, NC 28803 • (828) 687-3873 monkpub.com • Established: 2013

SCENE & STORY

The first thing you'll notice about the Monk on Patton Avenue is that the outside of the bar is painted a funny color: purple. Then you enter the place by the means of a long ramp, which seems a bit odd, and drop into a long narrow space with cream walls and high ceilings. And there you are: one of the more recent additions to the Asheville scene, the Thirsty Monk happens to be one of the best in the country, with forty-four taps and over 220 bottles of American and Belgian craft specialties. The deep and thoughtful beer list is complemented by innovative beer-friendly foods sourced from local purveyors including farm lamb, bakery breads, cheese, mustard, and trout, which provides for smoked trout sandwiches. It's a happy and bright place with a steady stream of special events, brewer appearances, and other beer-centric gatherings. They now have three locations in Asheville, as well as a cocktail bar, Top of the Monk, and the Belgian-style house beers are getting ever more play.

PHILOSOPHY

Belgian-style beers and hospitality with southern soul.

KEY BEER

If the Monk's house beer is available, order it. Otherwise start with a palate cleansing SweetWater Road Trip, a 5.3% ABV German-style pilsner, then widen your explorations.

WEDGE BREWING CO.

125-B Roberts St. • Asheville, NC 28801
(828) 505-2792 • wedgebrewing.com
Established: 2008

SCENE & STORY

It takes extra effort to find the Wedge taproom, located in the lower level of a dilapidated old warehouse in Asheville's French Broad River Arts district (just keep the number handy and call, should you get lost). Once used for meatpacking

and food storage, the brewery, taproom, and arty patio area overlook a rail yard, and the beer produced there is, like Pisgah's outside of town, fast becoming sought after by beer-savvy locals. And it's right next to New Belgium's new brewery, making this a bona fide brewery district.

PHILOSOPHY

Beer, the best form of art. There are multiple sculptures and artworks on the grounds and inside the pub area, adding to the overall progressive, community-based good vibes here. The latest draw: movies and live bands al fresco.

KEY BEER

Work your way up to the Golem, a 9% ABV strong Belgian Pale Ale with a hazy gold color and rich notes of apricot, wheat, and a lingering spiciness reminiscent of cinnamon and white pepper.

PISGAH BREWING CO.

150 Eastside Dr. • Black Mountain, NC 28711
(828) 669-0190 • pisgahbrewing.com
Established: 2004

SCENE & STORY

Part of the proud American tradition of great brewpubs in downright weird places, Pisgah resides in a nondescript industrial park about twenty minutes outside Asheville with absolutely no pomp and circumstance—the sign is smaller than a spider's eye, with approximately one-inch lettering. All of the energy goes into the organically brewed beers, produced on a small system. There's also an outdoor fire pit, pool table, some picnic benches, and an outdoor stage for blues, rock, and reggae acts as talented as the legendary Steel Pulse. Who needs a spendy taproom in the middle of town?

PHILOSOPHY

Green is the color. Pisgah was the first certified organic brewery in the Southeast.

KEY BEER

Look for the Vortex II Russian Imperial Stout, a devilishly smooth and drinkable 11.7% ABV of roasted black malt flavors.

BRUISIN' ALES

66 Broadway St. • Asheville, NC 28801
(828) 252-8999 • bruisin-ales.com
Established: 2006

SCENE & STORY

The presence of a truly great comprehensive bottle shop can propel a small city to find its craft beer feet and take off running for the good stuff. By making available a wide range of international and domestic craft beers to locals, the store stokes a thirst for homegrown breweries and good beer bars. Bruisin' Ales fills that essential role in Asheville, with over a thousand

beers handsomely presented in a bright, clean space (with two taps as well).

PHILOSOPHY

"Teach a man to fish . . ." It's a real hub of Asheville's craft beer scene, offering events and classes, brewer appearances, meet-ups of the Asheville Brewers Alliance, which is working to promote beer tourism and area festivals.

KEY BEER

The deliciously named (and made) Conduplico Immundus Monachus, from South Carolina's Thomas Creek Brewery (10% ABV). It's a mouthful of dark brown sugar, cocoa, and caramel tastes with a fruity edge.

Raleigh

THE RALEIGH TIMES BAR

14 E. Hargett St. • Raleigh, NC 27601
(919) 833-0999 • raleightimesbar.com
Established: 2006

SCENE & STORY

The hip, nonsmoking bar known as the Raleigh Times goes back to 2006 but the building's history is 100 years older, having housed the august *Raleigh Times*— the newspaper—up until its last edition ran in 1989. Part of a small complex of interconnected businesses with a breakfast counter (Morning Times), eatery (Dining Times), and hipper bar (RTBX), the atmospheric Times Bar has high tinned ceilings, old, exposed brick walls, and hardwood floors next to a wide, burnished wood bar. It's timeless; one half expects Atticus Finch to walk in here clutching a story to take up with the editors in righteous fury. In 2012 they added some good improvements including a takeout window and patio on the roof.

PHILOSOPHY

All the beer that's fit to drink. While there are only eight draft beers at a time (mostly from area producers), the bottle list has more than 100 selections, half of which are American craft releases (especially from North Carolina and the surrounding states), and the other half of which are Belgians.

KEY BEER

The list includes funky sours and other oddities like Drie Fonteinen Kriek, a Belgian sour beer made with cherries and spontaneously fermented Belgian lambics and one of the most acclaimed examples of the style.

Charlotte

GROWLERS POURHOUSE

3120 N. Davidson St. • Charlotte, NC 28205
(704) 910-6566 • growlerspourhouse.com
Established: 2011

SCENE & STORY

The pace of the southern craft beer revolution quickened in 2011 with the arrival of Growlers in Raleigh's arty NoDa area (North of Downtown). With impressive antique Chinese doors, heavy wood tables, hardwood floors and chic track lighting, it strikes a classy pose. But the beer and "beer food" are more than window dressing. Choose from fourteen taps and one rotating cask served from a nineteenth-century hand-pump engine, housemade hot dogs, sausages, and an oyster bar with rotating varieties; treats like peel-and-eat shrimp and tableside marshmallow roasting make this place even more fun. And the "beer-ed" classes on the first Tuesday of each month are a nice touch.

PHILOSOPHY

Housemade or bust. Even the potato chips are fried in the kitchen.

KEY BEER

Foothills Brewing Co. from Winston-Salem should be on tap; look for their Sexual Chocolate (9.75%), a burly (but rare) Russian Imperial Stout.

Durham

SCENE & STORY

Just north of downtown Durham near the corner of Geer and Rigsbee, start looking for a huge backward *F*, the symbol of this upstart brewery in a spacious, beige brick warehouse with a pub inside. Consider it your duty: North Carolina beer travelers owe a lot to the founders of Fullsteam. For one, Sean Lilly Wilson is the man whose "Pop the Cap" campaign successfully raised the state's allowable beer alcohol limit to 15 percent in 2005. In 2010 he joined with former Abita head brewer Brooks Hamaker and über–home brewer Chris Davis to launch one of the South's most ambitious breweries. The trio's R&D Tavern (on-site, enclosed in a boxy red room inside the brewery) is a family-friendly tavern/indoor beer garden featuring Fullsteam beer, guest taps of North Carolina beers, music and events, and dining options via food trucks.

PHILOSOPHY

Originally launched under the banner of "plow-to-pint beer from the beautiful South," Fullsteam is brewing beers that seem unusual not only in said sunny region—they're newfangled for the whole Craft Beer Nation. There are three categories: Workers' Compensation, a group of session beers led by Fullsteam Southern Lager (5.5% ABV); Apothecary, for "radical, farm-focused" beers including Hogwash, a hickory-smoked porter, and Summer Basil; and the Forager series, which utilizes fruit and other fermentables that members of the community are invited to sell to the brewery at a fair market price in exchange for some of the finished beer (and bragging rights, of course). Local persimmons and pears have already made it into the rotation. Other brews either already out or in development make use of parsnip, kudzu, rhubarb, and sweet potato—even grits. One has to wonder, what next? How about nighttime guided canoe trips that are also beer tastings led by Wilson, a James Beard semifinalist in 2012 and 2013? That's just the start of it for these innovative brewers.

KEY BEER

Summer Basil, the first beer brewed on Fullsteam's commercial system, is a 5.5% ABV summer seasonal with fresh local basil added. The idea was born when Wilson plunged a grip of fresh basil leaves into a can of Budweiser while at a house party. The resulting beer is a hazy, peachy gold ale with a bready body and green herb overtones.

BEST *of the* REST: NORTH CAROLINA

FONTA FLORA BREWERY

317 N. Green St. • Morganton, NC 28655 • (828) 475-0153 • fontaflora.com

In search of "a totally unique North Carolina/Appalachian–style of beer," the brewer Todd Steven Boera is one of the pathbreakers shaking up the beer scene in the American South and beyond. By working with the local Riverbend Malt House and foraging for many of his ingredients in the wild, Fonta Flora is part of a wave of American brewers that are taking beer back to premodern flavors and techniques, but thankfully with contemporary "QA-QC"—quality assurance, quality control. Like Scratch Brewing in Illinois, Jester King outside of Austin, Texas, and Arizona Wilderness in suburban Phoenix, it's a brewery where many ingredients hail from truly wild places. A saison, Beets, Rhymes, & Life took a gold at GABF 2015 in the field beer category. That's just the start of it.

JACK OF THE WOOD PUBLIC HOUSE

95 Patton Ave. • Asheville, NC 28801 • (828) 252-5445, ext. 105 • jackofthewood.com

Asheville-go-bragh. A hippified Celtic beer bar in downtown Asheville, Jack of the Wood was the original location of Green Man Brewing and still serves five of its beers, with a small selection brews from beyond town (even Brooklyn!). There are popular jam sessions on Wednesdays (from 6 p.m.), Thursdays (bluegrass, after 9 p.m.) and Sundays (Irish, starting at 5 p.m.), and frequent weekend bands for little or no cover charge.

THE BIER GARDEN

46 Haywood St. • Asheville, NC 28801 • (828) 285-0002 • ashevillebiergarden.com

A family-friendly, casual, and sports-oriented bar established in 1994, the Bier Garden features about 10 North Carolina beers among its 30 taps and some 200 bottles, one of the best selections in all of Asheville. It's not an actual biergarten, though, being housed partly in an atrium-like space in an office building. Still, it's a good place to try a selection of beers, upscale pub grub, and take in a game.

NODA BREWING

2921 N. Tryon St. • Charlotte, NC 28206 • (704) 900-6851 • nodabrewing.com

Opened in 2011, NoDa Brewing in Charlotte won the best IPA in the World Beer Cup in 2014 with Hop, Drop, & Roll, an American-style IPA with Citra and Amarillo hops. This, of course, was some fiercely coveted status—there are hundreds of competitors—and it coincided with their $8 million expansion into a new 32,000-square-foot warehouse at 2921 N. Tryon Street (they're keeping the original as well). The new facility has a sixty-barrel brewhouse, a bigger taproom, and an outdoor patio space. The *modus operandi* is expirimental. Led by former home brewers, the beer list is ever-changing.

THE DUCK-RABBIT CRAFT BREWERY

4519 W. Pine St. • Farmville, NC 27828 • (252) 753-7745 • duckrabbitbrewery.com

Since 2004 "the dark beer specialists" at Duck-Rabbit have grown their business into a small regional brewery, producing around 3,700 barrels annually and steadily rising. Based in the sleepy town of Farmville (which lives up to its name), it's really only a small, packaging-only operation built in a light industrial garage, but there's a small, new taproom for guests to sample brewer Paul Philippon's much lauded creations, like his 9% ABV Baltic Porter and a variety of other stouts and dark beers (he prefers the darker end of the spectrum). Trouble is, it's really far from major cities and the taproom is only open Fridays. But maybe you're up for it? Philippon is a former philosophy teacher, and wanted to honor his past by illustrating labels with a classic Gestalt shift diagram, which appears as either a duck or a rabbit, or something else entirely depending on how many beers you've had. So: is it a duck or a rabbit?

MOTHER EARTH BREWING

311 N. Herritage St. • Kinston, NC 28501 • (252) 208-2437 • motherearthbrewing.com

This is small-town North Carolina at its best. A progressive, family-run brewery in the old tobacco belt named for a Nitty Gritty Dirt Band record and opened in 2008, Mother Earth has transformed the sleepy, little town of Kinston (thirty miles south of Greenville; population 25,000) into a real destination. The brewery is deeply committed to LEED-level conservation ethics and the formulation focus is on Belgian and German styles like witbier and kölsch. Recently the owners also opened a boutique hotel within walking distance, the O'Neil, in an old bank building complete with bar in the gorgeous old vault (the-oneil.com).

SIERRA NEVADA BREWING CO.

100 Sierra Nevada Way • Mills River, NC 28732 • (828) 681-5300 • sierranevada.com

Beer fans raised glasses in respect when Sierra Nevada announced a second production facility and taproom in another town outside of Chico, California, that would
cost a cool *$100 million*. But when it was set for Mills River, nineteen miles outside
one of the best beer towns in America—with bigtime players New Belgium coming
into Asheville and Oskar Blues just outside town—the whole thing turned beerily
surreal. Of course, you should visit them all. At Sierra Nevada, reserve in advance
online and choose from a self-guided tour on catwalks above the brewhouse (no reservations required), the free standard tour inside (90 minutes), the Natural Resources
tour (checking out all the innovative water and solar projects around the property),
the IPA tour (90 minutes; $25), or the Beer Geek Tour (three hours; $30), leading six
lucky sots through the hop cooler, 200 barrel production brewhouse, and the 20-bar-
rel pilot brewery all afternoon. Wrap it all up with beers in the 23-tap bar and beer
garden overlooking a stone terrace and brewery plantings.

HAW RIVER FARMHOUSE ALES

1713 Saxapahaw-Bethlehem Church Rd. • Saxapahaw, NC 27340 • (336) 525-9270 • hawriverales.com

Among the homespun projects these Belgium-inspired brewers have going on is dis-
tributing organic seeds to local fans so they'll raise and donate fruit and vegetables
to be used in future beers. While they're on a farm and the modern-looking taproom
they call home is on the small side, their goals and dreams are big. Make a detour if
you're nearby and try St. Benedict's Breakfast Dubbel.

FOOTHILLS BREWING CO.

638 W. 4th St. • Winston-Salem, NC 27101 • (336) 777-3348 • foothillsbrewing.com

In 2015 Foothills announced it would be adding a tasting room at its new production
brewery. This is a good thing. Up to 70,000 barrels annually since opening in 2005,
they've essentially doubled every year. Why the rampant growth? For one, they entered
a very underserved market at just the right time, with some very good beers. And they
introduced a stout called Sexual Chocolate, which proved irresistible to massive numbers of curious beer drinkers, who snap it up during release days and disappear with
every last bottle. If you're on the way from Raleigh to Asheville, make a pit stop for sure.

SOUTH CAROLINA

Greenville

THE COMMUNITY TAP

217 Wade Hampton Blvd. • Greenville, SC
29609 • (864) 631-2525
thecommunitytap.com • Established: 2010

SCENE & STORY

A top-tier bottle and growler station for beer (and wine, on tap!) that has helped usher in a new era of craft brew appreciation for the city of Greenville, the Community Tap opened in 2010 with ten taps, some 150 breweries in the arsenal, weekly tastings, and occasional food trucks on site. It's helping expose locals to an incredible selection of American and imported beers, all carefully kept and displayed. Unlike a lot of bottle shops, it's clean and well organized, not chaotic and dusty.

PHILOSOPHY

Beer shopping should not be like going to a garage sale, with dusty stacks of boxes. Beer shopping should be *exactly* like this.

KEY BEER

What's freshest? Look for beers from upstart local craft breweries like the Unknown Brewing Co. out of Charlotte, and Coast, from Charleston, South Carolina.

Charleston

HOLY CITY BREWING

4155 Dorchester Rd. • Charleston, SC
29405 • (843) 225-6089
holycitybrewing.com • Established: 2011

SCENE & STORY

Joel Carl and Sean Nemitz were working as pedicab drivers in Charleston and, when business was slow (read: all winter), home brewing fifteen-gallon all-grain batches in the garage on a system "made with welded bicycle parts, elbow grease, and love." They met local businessman Mac Minaudo as his biodiesel project was stalling out—and just as Charleston's craft beer culture was coming alive. Plans took shape, and with Chris Brown, a brewer coming in as a fourth partner, the quartet launched Holy City in the summer of 2011 and has been slammed ever since.

PHILOSOPHY

Laid-back. What else could you expect from a couple of fun-loving guys who started as pedicabbies? The taproom is a spacious, old warehouse tucked behind repair shops and a bike store, with roll-up doors, picnic tables, and lots of space at the bar and a pool table, and groups of locals kicking it and relaxing. The brewing equipment is right inside, and the whole place has a dive bar feel to it . . . but in a good way, of course. There's a core lineup of about a half-dozen Holy City beers, plus another dozen tap handles with experiments like the aforementioned porters.

KEY BEER

Holy City started out with a hoppy German pilsner and a porter. Seasonals range from IPA, to stout, to Belgian Strong Pale Ale, and even experimental bacon- and honey-sriracha porters. Yeast Wrangler, a 10% ABV Double IPA, is becoming one of their best-known beers.

WESTBROOK BREWING COMPANY

510 Ridge Rd. • Mt Pleasant, SC 29464
(843) 654-9114 • westbrookbrewing.com
Established: 2011

SCENE & STORY

Edward Westbrook received his under-grad in Computer Science and then attended Clemson for his MBA; his wife and partner, the ebullient Morgan went to school for Elementary Education and Communication. "We were dating long distance, and when we would get together over the weekends, he would always tease me about beer," Morgan recalls. "I had no money but would splurge on beers with flavor. I have always taken my liquid bread very seriously." Edward, she says, was into cocktails and cooking, so she challenged him to brew. The dare became a hobby, and then, an obsession—and a business opportunity. They built a large, squeaky-clean, modern production brewery ten miles from the center of Charleston, and hooked up with Jeppe Jarnit-Bjergsø, the gypsy brewery of Evil Twin, whose brand has grown by leaps and bounds in recent years. In addition to brewing many Evil Twin beers on contract, Westbrook is expanding their own lineup and operation, especially a huge barrel room.

PHILOSOPHY

Free the beer and your mind will follow? "At the time [we opened], Charleston had two breweries and one brewpub. We wanted to open a brewery, to drink good beer, make America proud, make our parents proud, make my Oma proud. In a way, we wanted to be set free and drink great beer while doing it. We couldn't find what we wanted to drink on shelves and there's only one way to fix that: make it yourself." She avers that they aren't pandering. "We'll never do a crowd-pleaser on purpose, if that makes sense. A lot of our beers come from experiences. We just want to consistently make good, interesting beers."

KEY BEER

Mexican Cake, first brewed for the Westbrooks' wedding, is a super sought-after imperial stout aged on cocoa nibs, vanilla beans, cinnamon sticks and fresh habañero peppers (around 10.5% ABV). New releases aren't even preadvertised, because of the commotion it causes among beer geeks and collectors. Follow #mexicancake on social media when you're in the area and looking for the beer, which always disappears into happy hands, just like the dessert it's named for.

EDMUND'S OAST

1081 Morrison Dr. • Charleston, SC 29403
(843) 727-1145 • edmundsoast.com
Established: 2014

SCENE & STORY

With an open kitchen and chef's counter and house-cured meats hanging overhead in a pale wood and glass window, Edmund's Oast has a total of 130 seats inside, and none too many. This is without of a doubt one of the most talked-about beer-focused restaurants in the entire United States. Inside, there is an expansive bar and communal tables, with warm, wooden ceilings and aged-looking walls that look like something out of a Tuscan villa. Out front there's an ample front patio, (covered) seating, and outdoor seating amid trees and communal tables. In other words, it's all pretty dreamy.

In what was becoming a recurring theme as I wrote this book, during the closing days of reporting, the team announced plans for Edmund's Oast Brewing Co., slated for around 2017. Co-owner Scott Schor talked of a "perfect storm" of factors that propelled what was conceived as a nice, dark, little Belgian-style craft beer bar into a beer bar with a bit of food and then into a remarkable culinary destination with ambitious food, cocktail, and wine programs, and a little brewpub, soon to be a full-on, freestanding production brewery to be opened in 2017. With their local fans and track record, it should be a great move.

PHILOSOPHY

Artful & honest low country cuisine and great craft beer, executed with real taste and care.

KEY BEER

One interesting beer that head brewer Cameron Read has created is Lord Proprietor's, an English-style mild ale brewed with black tea from the Charleston Tea Plantation (4.3% ABV). But they're probably best known for some house blends, like Peanut Butter & Jelly, a 5.5% ABV blended brown ale with none of those actual ingredients, but, remarkably, all the flavors. It won't be coming back with the new production brewery, but the creativity surely will.

TENNESSEE

Nashville

YAZOO BREWING CO.

910 Division St. • Nashville, TN 37203
(615) 891-4649 • yazoobrew.com
Established: 2003

SCENE & STORY

With founders named Linus and Lila and a beer named Sue, Johnny Cash fans and craft beer lovers alike will want to seek out this craft brewery a short drive from the center of Music City. Brewery tours in the warehouse-like space run on Saturdays only, starting at 2:30 p.m. and continuing every hour until 6:30 (six dollars; includes complimentary Yazoo pint glass and beer samples). There's also a cozy taproom open for growler fills only, Wednesdays from 4 to 8 p.m. and Thursday through Saturday from 2 to 8 p.m.

PHILOSOPHY

Linus apprenticed with Garrett Oliver in Brooklyn, knows good beer, and loves to experiment with single-hop varieties and more recently, barrel aging.

Also, they're regulars at the annual Bonnaroo music and arts festival in Manchester, Tennessee, which has an amazing beer garden situation going on, complete with blessed shade and tons of regional craft beers.

KEY BEER

Mexican lagers like Bohemia (the best available) are often descendants of the Vienna-style lager, tending toward a reddish hue, light to medium body, and crackling dry finish. Yazoo's Dos Perros, a superlight American Brown Ale (at just 3.5% ABV) is a great example of the style. And the aforementioned Sue? He's a smoked Imperial Porter on the other end of the intensity spectrum at 9% ABV, a bomber of roasted malt flavor with flavors of nutty caramel and charred bacon fat. In other words, it's a beer that hollers, "My name is Sue! How do you do?"

KENTUCKY

Louisville

SERGIO'S WORLD BEERS

1605 Story Ave. • Louisville, KY 40206
(502) 618-BEER • sergiosworldbeers.com
Established: 2006

SCENE & STORY

Sergio Ribemboim is a globe-trotting Brazilian with an obsessive love for beer, and his man cave–like shop and taproom in Louisville is a cluttered shrine to brew in every imaginable form and from every corner of the planet. With forty-three taps and over 1,300 bottles on offer, the correct phrase to describe this cash-only beer geek destination is "mind-numbing"—there are more than 500 from the United States and 600 from Europe, for starters. Along with the L-shaped bar lined floor to ceiling with coolers, cases, empties, and other ephemera, there's a seating area and kitchen serving an eclectic menu (fajitas, cheesesteak, spaghetti). The food is often very good, but you're really here to wander among the country's oddest, biggest, and best selections of craft beer from around the globe.

PHILOSOPHY

Ribemboim's aim isn't to convert skeptics or please the general consumer, but to delight and awe the aficionado, and he's eager to help when approached.

KEY BEER

There's no itch that cannot be scratched at Sergio's, so take a half hour to peruse the insanity and, if still stumped, ask Sergio for some recommendations. Also ask about the beer dinners he's been doing lately.

THE BEER TRAPPE

811 Euclid Ave. • Lexington, KY 40502
(859) 309-0911 • thebeertrappe.com

Only recently opened (2010), Lexington's top craft beer destination has 8 quickly rotating taps, over 400 bottle selections, leather couches, and walls decked out with brewery signage. The bar also graciously provides tastings, flights, growler fills, and classes, making it a hub for Lexington's growing craft beer community. In late 2015, the owner purchased the next door space with plans to do a restaurant or brewpub.

MISSISSIPPI

UNTIL VERY RECENTLY, THE MAGNOLIA STATE HAS HAD THE LOWEST LEGAL BEER ALCOHOL tolerance in the country at 5 % ABV. Fully half of the counties are still dry. Until the political community sees craft beer for what it is—an enlightened movement toward moderate drinking habits that can bring a state billions in tax dollars when breweries are promoted—craft beer will languish. But for locals, there are a couple of places to gather, sip craft brews, and plot the campaign to get Mississippi at least in line with neighboring states. Recently, beer fanatics worked hard to pass a law increasing the upper limit of beer to 10% ABV, and in 2013, helped legalize home brewing, too. Mississippi, Craft Beer Nation is 100 percent behind you.

Kiln

LAZY MAGNOLIA BREWING CO.

7030 Roscoe-Turner Rd. • Kiln, MS 39556
(228) 467-2727 • lazymagnolia.com
Established: 2005

SCENE & STORY

It's a classic love story, but with a twist (or two). Boy meets girl. Girl buys boy home-brewing kit. Boy brews decent beer; girl falls in love with brewing, takes over, goes to brewing school; couple starts brewing company (and boy designs the label). That's the short version for Leslie and Mark Henderson, who met in college and started Mississippi's first brewery in 2003 and opened for business in 2005 in an industrial facility in tiny Kiln (population: 2,000), a crossroads of a town not too far from the Gulf of Mexico and formerly famous only for the presence of Brett Favre's high school. It's not terribly far from New Orleans (about one hour, without traffic). There are free, no-reservation-required tours every Saturday morning, but state law forbids sampling on-site (post-tour, pick up a list of local bars serving the beer). In other words, it's a pilgrimage. At present (2016), the brewery has at least thirty-five employees, distributes in seventeen states and is on track to chart $5 million in sales a year. Turns out that kit was a very, very good idea.

PHILOSOPHY

Named for the flowers that grow along the banks of the nearby Jordan River (and one malnourished, hence "lazy" specimen on the couple's back porch), Lazy Magnolia uses everything from sweet potatoes to roasted pecans and honey from an uncle's bee-keeping operation in the brewing process.

KEY BEER

Beer nuts are usually on the side, but not in the case of Southern Pecan, a caramel-tinted brown ale flavored with whole roasted pecans. It has a sweet, nutty body and easy-drinking alcohol content of just 4.25% ABV.

Hattiesburg

THE KEG & BARREL BREW PUB

1315 Hardy St. • Hattiesburg, MS 39401
(601) 582-7148 • kegandbarrel.com
Established: 2005

SCENE & STORY

The beating heart of Mississippi's craft beer scene, the Keg & Barrel is a bar in a refurbished 100-year-old house with a wraparound porch, tables in the yard, and a good list for a state that is only recently reforming its beer laws. On draft, sought-after kegs run dry with alacrity. It's just not easy to get beer all the way to Hattiesburg. That is, unless it's made on-site. With about sixty taps and thirty bottles, the selection was the best around for nearly 100 miles, absolutely worth a trip for any beer lover in the area. And you won't go hungry: Choose from southern comfort food staples such as fried chicken and waffles, fried green tomatoes, and chicken-fried steak. (Did someone say fried?)

PHILOSOPHY

Southern-fried and bona fide.

KEY BEER

From Flying Dog to Anchor and Sierra Nevada, there are some familiar and excellent drafts on the list, as well as the whole Lazy Magnolia line.

SOUTHERN PROHIBITION BREWING CO.

301 Mobile St. • Hattiesburg, MS 39401
(601) 584-7877 • soprobrewing.com
Established: 2013

SCENE & STORY

When the first edition of this book came out in 2011, the Keg & Barrel was home to an upstart nanobrewery, Southern Prohibition, a legal resident in a side room (unlike the early days, when one imagines all sorts of interesting excuses for the aromas wafting around Hattiesburg). Now Southern Prohibition (a.k.a. "SoPro") is a full-fledged brand operating out of a 22,0000-square-foot former furniture warehouse, with 20bbl system, on Mobile Street next to a rusted out quonset hut). Currently they're brewing up over 3,000 barrels a year (with a 5,000bbl capacity), releasing barrel-aged and canned beers, and, since 2015, running a busy tasting room of their own. Time your visit for free brewery tours on Thursdays.

PHILOSOPHY

Rise up! This is new-school brewing in the sweet, sunny South with an aim toward improving the community. They even host yoga classes and DIY screen-printing workshops. Times, they are-a-changin', indeed. It's a great thing.

KEY BEER

Start with the Devil's Harvest American Pale Ale (5.8% ABV) and go crazy from there. There's also a seasonal rotation, the Cicada series, named for "Mississippi's favorite invasive species."

OKLAHOMA

Tulsa

PRAIRIE ARTISAN ALES

1803 S. 49th W Ave. • Tulsa, OK 74107
(918) 949-4318 • prairieales.com
Established: 2012

SCENE & STORY

Oklahoma might not seem a likely place for artisanal, barrel-aged, Belgian-inflected beers, but brothers Chase and Colin Healey are quickly changing that. Following the brothers' Kickstarter campaign in 2013 to add some necessary equipment, Prairie started working with the Shelton Bros. importers, who work with a handful of American brands engaging especially committed audiences around the world. Chase Healey's range of saisons, stouts, and hop-driven wild ales (with terrific artwork courtesy of his brother Colin) have earned crowds and acclaim for the Tulsa brewery.

PHILOSOPHY

Belgium comes to Bud country. Launching was no small task, but the Healeys and Co. made it happen. Now the collaborations, expanding *foudre* cellar, and ongoing art and video projects ensure Prairie will be reinventing the Tulsa beer scene for years to come. Best of all, they've got a sense of humor. No custom copper-lined coolship? No problem. Use the bed of a pickup truck. Colin's labels are influenced, he says, by Keith Shore of Mikkeller and Karl Grandin from Omnipollo, two pioneers of artful, deconstructed beer labels. He'll depict himself, his brother, and other brewer they collaborate with in hilarious, sometimes outrageous doodles that rise above mere gags to the level of pop art.

KEY BEER

Funky Gold Mosaic, a 6.55% ABV sour ale flavored with the tropical-noted Mosaic hop, became a much talked-about beer, for good reason—it's delicious. And Bomb!, a 14% ABV imperial stout aged on coffee, cacao nibs, vanilla beans, and ancho chili peppers, has been the talk of many a festival, from the Denver Rare Beer fest during GABF to Vail Big Beers and the annual Shelton Bros. Festival. It's aptly named—and outstandingly made.

JAMES MCNELLIE'S PUBLIC HOUSE

409 E. 1st St. • Tulsa, OK 74120
(918) 382-PINT • mcnellies.com
Established: 2004

SCENE & STORY

Also known for its Scotch selection, this huge, two-story beer bar in Tulsa's booming Blue Dome District was inspired by the owner's travels in Ireland and gleams with a huge brass-clad tap row, copper accents, and other old-world flourishes. Today it boasts three spin-off bars—one in Oklahoma City, one in the town of Norman, and one in South Tulsa—but this is the original and Oklahoma's best beer spot. It has sixty-two beers on tap, two casks on Oklahoma's only beer engines, another 290 bottled brews and great sweet-potato fries from the long and varied pub menu. Lately they've been organizing harvest festival beer bashes.

PHILOSOPHY

Classic Irish. The bar draws a mixed crowd of locals, collegians (upstairs is a more raucous smoking area), beer geeks, and families whose kids perform in fiddle jams. (Present company included! My talented nieces Isabella and Sophia have performed there.)

KEY BEER

Experiment by choosing from flights made up of local and regional favorites as well as beers from further afield (nine to eleven dollars) including "Aromatic & Bitter" (with beers like Tallgrass 16-Bit DPA); "Dark & Roasty" (Warsteiner Dunkel); "Belgian Artistry" (Chimay Tripel); and "Oklahoma breakdown" (Anthem Arjuna, Roughtail Pale Ale, and a Prairie rotating handle).

GEORGIA

Athens

CREATURE COMFORTS BREWING CO.

271 W. Hancock Ave. • Athens, GA 30601
(706) 410-1043 • creaturecomfortsbeer.com
Established: 2014

SCENE & STORY

Athens is a college town with killer barbecue and music, but has almost no local beer, due to restrictive laws that hampered development for years. Undaunted, David Stein, former home brewer turned head brewer at Twain's Billiards & Tap, a well-known brewpub in Decatur, Georgia, (see page 399) was working with the name Creature Comforts for his ambitious line of home brews. He linked up with a brewer friend and former PhD candidate in Genetics, Adam Beauchamp, who was well into his career at Sweetwater in Atlanta, Georgia. Working with a third partner, businessman Derek Imes, Stein and Beauchamp began building Creature Comforts in a huge, old, 13,000-square-foot auto and tire warehouse in downtown Athens.

They salvaged and refinished old wood from the building to form bar tops, tables, wall paneling, and ceilings, winning an award for outstanding rehabilitation by the Athens Heritage Foundation. Nice work, guys. Their $2 million project opened to rapturous welcome in April, 2014 and hasn't slowed down. You pay twelve dollars, get a glass and a wristband (plus, often, some coupons for food in the area), and are allowed to try six beers. There are two tasting bars, with live bands in and out and beanbag/cornhole outside, plus picnic tables. Looking across the street at an old Baptist church, the vibe is idyllic.

PHILOSOPHY

The motto is "crave curiosity." Shouldn't we all? This project has turned into contentment in liquid form. "What started out as curious exploration of what we love, turned into us uncovering our passion, following that passion, and finding happiness," the crew reports.

KEY BEER

They're brewing across the spectrum from a tart Berliner weisse (Athena) to crisp pilsner (Bibo) to an American-style IPA (Tropicalia, lush and fruity).

THE TRAPPEZE PUB

269 N. Hull St. • Athens, GA 30601
(706) 543-8997 • trappezepub.com
Established: 2007

SCENE & STORY

Every beer town worth its salt needs a marquee draw, be it a bar, brewery, bottle shop, or that home-brew store stoking the early sparks. Fortunately for Athens, which has a lively art scene, bike culture, and energetic food-and-drink vibe, the Trappeze Pub pulls off a thirty-three-tap, 200-bottle high-wire routine without breaking a sweat. It can't be easy to maintain such a selection, but in this brightly lit and crisply run bar—all warm terra-cotta-hued walls, big windows, tasteful breweriana and a vast collection of appropriate glassware—but the owners make it seem that way, pulling in vaunted brewers from companies like Belgium's Urthel and Colorado's Left Hand for tasting nights. Inventive pub grub such as spent-grain breads and beef dishes braised in beer round out the bill.

PHILOSOPHY

Good beer is not just something to pull in customers; it's in the foundations—it really matters here. Which is why the place is often slammed, and why you should go, too.

KEY BEER

The tap row runs heavy on regional favorites from Sweetwater, Terrapin, and Wild Heaven Brewing Company, a Decatur upstart for which Trappeze founder Eric Johnson is the brewmaster (the new company is open now and looking to put Decatur on the map as a brewing town). Look for Wild Heaven's Invocation, an 8.5% ABV Belgian Strong Pale Ale, a powerful blend of lush, ripe pear-like fruit flavors from pale malts with spicy noble hops in the background.

Savannah

THE DISTILLERY

416 W. Liberty St. • Savannah, GA 31401
(912) 236-1772 • distillerysavannah.com
Established: 2008

SCENE & STORY

The Volen family honored a colorful bit of local lore when they overhauled this historic former distillery, drugstore, soda fountain, lunch counter, and rumored former bathtub gin dispensary. It's full of atmospheric exposed brick surrounding a glorious mahogany back bar, oak bar, old copper still, and artifacts discovered on-site, from musket balls to old liquor bottles, clay pipes, dishware, and bleached bones. The menu features inspired comfort foods such as fried pickles, wild Georgia shrimp, and a beer-battered cod po'boy sandwich among other goodies, but save room for the Double

Chocolate Deep Fried Moon Pie and Beer Float, made with stout, lambic, or other fresh draft brew.

PHILOSOPHY

Officially: "No crap—just craft." They helped organize and facilitate the first Savannah Craft Brew Fest was in 2008. The staff at the Distillery did a series of events the week leading up to it, which eventually morphed into a legitimate community event called "Savannah Craft Beer Week." So raise a glass: they've helped shape the local beer scene considerably.

KEY BEER

Ode to Mercy, a rich and toffee-ish 8.2% ABV imperial American Brown Ale from Decatur's Wild Heaven Brewing Company, making waves through the Deep South with adventurous, well-crafted beers.

Decatur

THE BRICK STORE PUB

125 E. Court Square • Decatur, GA 30030
(404) 687-0990 • brickstorepub.com
Established: 1997

SCENE & STORY

The Brick Store in downtown Decatur (a short drive from the center of Atlanta) is one of those beer bars you hear about in conversation described as a hallowed place, a sanctuary, the end of the rainbow in humankind's quest for the perfect beer bar. Of course, we all know nothing's perfect (or why keep searching?), but it has got more than a few checks in the win column. The interior downstairs has the paradigmatic blend of exposed brick and creaky wooden floors, cool lighting, 18 rotating taps and about 100 bottles, all superb, centered on local, regional, and nationally acclaimed American craft beers, with a good mix of German and English specialty beers and vintage and reserve bottled beers as well. There's an upstairs bar, too, the Belgian Room, which is as advertised and one of the main reasons to visit, with 8 taps and over 120 bottles laid in.

There's a good and varied food menu, too, with beer snacks (like housemade pretzels and ale-battered chicken fingers), burgers, salads and some beer-friendly entrées such as shepherd's pie and fish and chips, and the prices are very reasonable: There's nothing on the menu over nine dollars.

PHILOSOPHY

Beer appreciation is the focus here. To allow and encourage conversations and cater to the naturally curious drinker, there are "no televisions, no neon, no obnoxious music and no major domestic beers." This is the beer enlightenment in action, but it's not dull or pretentious.

KEY BEER

This is surely one of the only places in the entire American South where you could find a beer like De Proef Signature Ale, a collaboration between Lost Abbey/Port Brewing's Tomme Arthur and Dirk Knaudts of the famed De Proef brewery in Belgium. Their 8.5% ABV golden-colored ale is tart, big, and funky, and as Michael Jackson described it, "Everything promised by the brewers, and more. Aromas fresh as a forest. A hint of green wood. Firm, smooth, rounded, body. Lemongrass, lemon zest, and cedar. A suspicion of sulfur and sweat. A long and distinct finish—you don't want it to end."

Atlanta

THE PORTER BEER BAR

1156 Euclid Ave. • Atlanta, GA 30307
(404) 223-0393 • theporterbeerbar.com
Established: 2008

SCENE & STORY

This diminutive Little Five Points area bar is small in layout but mighty in stature. Along with Decatur's Brick Store, this is one of the premiere beer bars in the South, and the interior is a home run, with long wooden benches, cool metal tables, white-tiled walls, and a collection of retro plastic and vinyl suitcases. With thirty taps and over 800 bottle selections to choose from, the owners go out of their way to print pairing suggestions for the haute-rustic bar bites like pork empanadas with golden raisins, adobo almonds, and cocoa pineapple-jalapeño sauce, hush puppies with applewood smoked bacon, and Fuji apple sauce, and wild Georgia shrimp po'boys.

PHILOSOPHY

Thorough. With both a food and beer blog, a beer list updated "daily by 6 p.m.," beer flights, and other considerations, this bar is going the extra mile.

KEY BEER

Hitachino XH, a Belgian-style brown ale, brewed in Japan and aged for three months in *shochu* (Japanese rice spirit) casks—the kind of beer-world curiosity that is generally far tastier in concept than in execution. But this strong, spicy, frothy oddity is delicious, with a wine like bite that would work well with those bacon and apple-kissed hush puppies (7% ABV).

BEST *of the* REST: GEORGIA

TERRAPIN BEER CO.

265 Newton Bridge Rd. • Athens, GA 30607 • (706) 549-3377 • terrapinbeer.com

Opened in 2002 by friends John Cochran and Brian "Spike" Buckowski, this is a young brewery growing fast with ever more adventurous styles and interpretations. Tours of the 40,000-square-foot space turn festive with live music in the taproom. Look for the Side Project beer series, such as Monk's Revenge, a superstrong (9.6% ABV) Belgian IPA with intense flavors of sweet and ripe citrus with an herbal, hoppy finish, and the Walking Dead Blood Orange IPA, inspired by the hit TV show. Recent upgrades include a new-and-improved tasting room appointed with recovered hardwoods and tap stations (supplied from overhead beer lines), plus a gift shop and a small stage for live music, and cool events like the Hip-Hop Harvest DJ sets on Friday nights.

TWAIN'S BILLIARDS AND TAP

211 E. Trinity Pl. • Decatur, GA 30030 • (404) 373-0063 • twains.net

Brewer Chase Medlin took over in 2012 from David Stein (now at Creature Comforts; see page 395) to craft fresh tap offerings at this superpopular pool hall and brewpub. Criminal Sin India Pale Ale is the house favorite, along with Four Count Pale Ale, River Sunset Amber, and Mississippi Nut Brown. The interior has cool teal-and-blue tile floors, copper pool table lamps, funky art, green wooden chairs, and exposed gray brick. In 2015, the owners announced they were taking over a local bowling alley to create the Comet, with thirty-two lanes, vintage arcade games, shuffleboard, pool tables, and a vast craft beer list. In other words, this is a fun crowd.

ALABAMA

Birmingham

J. CLYDE HOT ROCK TAVERN & ALEHOUSE

1312 Cobb Ln. • Birmingham, AL 35205
(205) 939-1312 • jclyde.com
Established: 2007

SCENE & STORY

Full of classic beer-bar appointments (exposed brick; wooden rafters, beams, and tables), J. Clyde has some sixty taps (with a dozen from Alabama) and another 200 bottles on offer, in addition to a late-night menu and standard pub menu with items like steak au poivre and fried green tomatoes. In 2015 the owners started talking about a brewpub to be constructed nearby.

PHILOSOPHY

Cask and ye shall receive. On most days, and infallibly every Friday at 4 p.m., something notable happens here in the state's best beer bar: A vessel of the only cask-conditioned ale in the state is tapped (and then drained in short order).

Generally, the term "cask conditioned" refers to lighter British-style ales fermented and then "conditioned" or rested for a period of time at temperatures of around 50 to 55 degrees Fahrenheit with some natural fining agents in the beer, resulting in clarity, softness, and a delicate carbonation. (I say "generally" because cask conditioning is migrating into other, not exactly British styles, like the Italo American experiments at Eataly New York's rooftop Birreria.)

KEY BEER

Look for Coffee Oatmeal Stout from Birmingham's Good People Brewing Company on draught (and maybe cask). It's a 6% ABV sipper with deep roasted coffee and cocoa flavors.

FLORIDA

THE SUNSHINE STATE HAS EMBRACED CRAFT BEER WITH THE FORCE OF A TROPICAL STORM.
It seems hard to imagine that in the soporific land of blue-hair retirees, Disney rides, and plastic nightclubs that earthy, funky, DIY craft brewing would take such hold but, in fact, it has, with some seventy-five breweries and brewpubs open and several more in planning stages. The following is but a fraction of what's worth exploring.

Tarpon Springs

SAINT SOMEWHERE BREWING

1441 Savannah Ave., Unit E • Tarpon Springs, FL 34689 • (813) 503-6181
saintsomewherebrewing.com
Established: 2007

SCENE & STORY

Home brewer Bob Sylvester took his tiny Belgian-styles operation pro in 2007 with an ally and imprimatur shared by only a handful of other U.S. brewers: the Shelton Brothers, a distributor of many of the world's most rare and unusual beers from around the world, especially Belgium and Europe. Created in his warehouse and workshop-like brewery, Sylvester's beers have made a deep impression and are now distributed in more than twenty states. Check the location info online; Sylvester announced plans to move in 2015. With collaborations stacking up with great breweries like Jester King, Saint Somewhere is really going places.

PHILOSOPHY

Belgian all the way. With a recent expansion, Sylvester is joining the ranks of the world's top producers of traditional saison beers, which are, loosely, country ales from Belgium that burst with grain-given flavors of ripe pineapple and stone fruits accented by herbs and spices and sugars including (but not limited to) orange peel, clove, honey, and lemongrass.

KEY BEER

Saison Athene, at 7.5% ABV, is Sylvester's contribution to the mustardy-gold style, very popular to brew but rarely mastered.

He's getting it right: fermented at higher temperatures (making Florida a good base) it's got big, interesting layers of fruity complexity with a kiss of honey-like sweetness and a peppery dry finish.

GREEN BENCH BREWING

1133 Baum Ave. N • St. Petersburg, FL 33707 • (727) 800-9836
greenbenchbrewing.com • Established: 2013

SCENE & STORY

At age twenty-one, Green Bench's founder and head brewer Kristopher Johnson was on his second major in college (biochemistry, then literature), and he didn't know what he wanted to do with his life. "I was working two jobs and I really wanted a hobby. I decided to try home brewing—my father was a home brewer," he told me. It wasn't long before he stepped up to try all-grain brewing on a system he put together himself, whipped up an IPA recipe, entered it in a statewide competition and took home second place. "I was hooked," he recalls.

Next came gigs with Wayne Wambles at Cigar City, and then a local home-brew shop who planned to start a small brewery. For two years he helped them set up, taught classes, and started dreaming up Green Bench. "I had a couple of failed projects along the way. Eventually I gathered investors, we decided to become partners, and within a year we opened the doors of Green Bench."

Green Bench would become the first production microbrewery in St. Pete, and stakes were high. What they put together in short order is pretty amazing. Inside the 1,500-square-foot taproom, the front facade of the bar is covered with hexagonal blocks that used to line the streets of Central Avenue in front of the brewery. Outside, there's a huge beer garden with a fire pit and we have a movie screen. The family-friendly space plays host to bands, parties, and food trucks out front. Inside, you can spot the 15bbl brewhouse (with bright green LED lights on the tanks at night), rows of tall steel fermenters, and two custom built *foudres*. Recently they've collaborated with such barnstorming brands as Crooked Stave, Troi Dames (of Switzerland), Jester King, and Prairie Artisan Ales. There's even talk of a coolship, to experiment with the local tropical flora's effect on beer.

PHILOSOPHY

Quality first, then diversity. "Gone are the days in which you could open your doors, make an awesome locally produced IPA, and sell it simply as the 'local option.' Every other brewery in town has that selling point. You have to set yourself apart," says Johnson.

KEY BEERS

Green Bench's range is superambitious and impressive, from 100-percent *fou-*

dre fermented farmhouse ales to barrel-aged and oak-fermented sour blends, hoppy wheats, and Sunshine City IPA, a lip-smacking American-style IPA. The emphasis on wood-aged sours is pretty unusual—this is steamy Florida, not a cool climate in, say, Washington State. But these tart beers are well suited to the climate. "We're the first brewery in the southeast of the country to own a *foudre*," says Johnson. Try the Saison de Banc Vert and Saison de Banc Noir, which are 100-percent oak-fermented with the house Saison yeast culture and Brettanomyces.

Tampa

CIGAR CITY BREWING

3924 W. Spruce St., Ste. A • Tampa, FL
33607 • (813) 648-6363
cigarcitybrewing.com • Established: 2009

SCENE & STORY

Beer writer and Tampa native Joey Redner was immersed in beer—selling it, writing about it, running a bar, and generally loving the entire craft beer scene. He stands apart from his famous father (the elder Joey Redner, a divisive figure in town as the founder of Mons Venus, one of the nation's most notorious strip clubs, said to be the birthplace of the lap dance). Wayne Wambles was a home brewer gone pro; he had discovered the wonders of craft brews during 1996's Hurricane Opal, when a friend shared home brews with him over the course of three days as they waited for the power and water to return. When Redner and Wambles met, the die was cast for Cigar City, a company quickly remaking the entire Florida beer scene with innovative, award-winning beers. There are tours Wednesday through Friday from 11 a.m. to 2 p.m.; reservations are required, so e-mail info@cigarcitybrewing.com to schedule. And if you're already a fan, then you know about Hunahpu Day: Cigar City's largest annual event, celebrating the release of its acclaimed Hunahpu's Imperial Stout, an imperial stout aged on cacao nibs, Madagascar vanilla beans, ancho and pasilla chilis, and cinnamon. *Nine thousand* people showed in in 2013; 2014 was a near riot (counterfeit tickets created a shortage), and 2015 cost $200 a person.

PHILOSOPHY

Brewery-as-melting pot. Redner is an aficionado of Tampa's culinary brew that melds Sicilian, Spanish, Puerto Rican, traditional southern, and especially Cuban traditions. The mission driving Cigar City is to create ales and lagers that pair perfectly with Cuban dishes such as boliche and picadillo, and Wambles is a tireless experimenter, employing everything from additions of apricot, mango, pomegranate, scuppernong grapes, and peppercorn to various sorts of barrel aging with cedar chips, lavender, and heather.

KEY BEER

Wambles's favorite beer, the bombastic 7.5% ABV Jai Alai IPA is a walloping beer with a fat caramel malt backbone and six different hop varietals, including Simcoe, used only in dry-hopping. It's hugely citric and resinous with the waves of tang and fruit in the balance that are required of great IPAs. I've tasted off the canning line, when it's literally never been fresher, and it's worth seeking out.

DeLand

ABBEY WINE & BEER BAR

117 N. Woodland Blvd. • DeLand, FL 32720
(386) 734-4545 • abbeydeland.com
Established: 2006

SCENE & STORY

This upscale beer and wine bar about twenty minutes from Daytona Beach has parchment-colored walls, handsome terra-cotta tile floors, recessed lighting, and eighteen taps with a focus on the rare and hard-to-find Belgian variety. There are 150 beers in bottles including the six Trappist beers available in this country (the seventh, Westvleteren is well-nigh impossible to obtain without traveling to Belgium). Several staffers are Cicerones (the sommeliers of beer) and they've launched a line of meads (Middle Ages–inspired honey wines), but they're not taking things *too* seriously, with retro video game nights and spirited trivia competitions.

PHILOSOPHY

The owners focus on recommending pairings, including vintage ales and other specialties, to go with a rotating menu of sandwiches and other simple fare.

KEY BEER

Where else will you find the extraordinary Dupont Avec Les Bons Voeux? A strong saison from Belgium (9.5% ABV) that is hazy gold in color, fruity and vinous in flavor, with a dry, earthy kick in the finish, it's worth a trip inland from the beach.

FUNKY BUDDHA BREWERY

1201 NE 38th St. • Oakland Park, FL 33334
(954) 440-0046 • funkybuddhabrewery.com
Established: 2010

SCENE & STORY

Built in a former hookah lounge in Boca Raton in 2010, Funky Buddha Brewery launched with a fifty-five-gallon system. In 2014, they added a brand-new production facility in Oakland Park, making it, for the moment, South Florida's biggest craft beer success story. Located in the heart of Oakland Park's Culinary Arts District, the 54,000-square-foot facility is anchored by a thirty-barrel brewhouse and massive taproom with terra-cotta colored walls and polished cement floors. It's open seven days a week, noon to midnight. Note too that the Funky Buddha Brewery & Lounge in Boca Raton (original location) is still open, working as a pilot brewery. In November 2015, Funky Buddha announced its Craft Food Counter & Kitchen, which unfortunately displaced an indoor bocce court, but giant Jenga and cornhole remain.

PHILOSOPHY

Having fun and selling a lot of beer should go hand in hand. Their breakout beer, Maple Bacon Coffee Porter (6.45% ABV), just sounds like a kick. But then it got so popular that RatBeer kicked them up to twenty-sixth place in the world in ratings for a spell. Now *thousands* of people show up for the annual release party of this beer, lining up at 6 a.m., for a taste.

KEY BEER

Floridian hefeweizen and Hop Gun IPA are the well-made flagships, but beer geeks still flock to the taproom for tastes of beer like No Crusts, a jam–and–peanut butter beer.

BEST *of the* REST: FLORIDA

7VENTH SUN

1012 Broadway • Dunedin, FL 34698 • (727) 733-3013 • 7venthsun.com

With a degree in fermentation science from Oregon State, Devon Kreps joined Justin Stange (who brewed with Sweetwater and Cigar City) in 2012 to brew terrific Belgian-style beers, IPAs, and oak-aged sours in Dunedin, twenty-five miles west of Tampa. Working, for the moment, out of a tiny storefront location on a four and a half barrel system, this buzzy brewery is one to watch. Two recent intriguing brews: cucumber gose, and a watermelon/Brettanomyces Berliner weisse.

COPPERTAIL BREWING

2601 E. 2nd Ave. • Tampa, FL, 33605 • (813) 247-1500 • coppertailbrewing.com

In 2014 Tampa got another great brewery with big plans: Coppertail, named for an imaginary sea creature the owner's daughter came up with and built in a spacious, modernized, cinderblock warehouse that was formerly a mayonnaise factory and olive cannery. With head brewer Casey Hughes at the kettles and an impressive brewhouse and wood cellar in action, Coppertail is poised for big things. Formerly head brewer of Flying Fish brewery in New Jersey (which is famous for, among other beers, the hops-forward Exit 4 Tripel), Hughes comes to Coppertail having pulled down medals for his IPA, tripel, dubbel, Belgian strong dark ale, and other projects. Now he's brewing up hop-forward brews of many stripes, from emerging tart and hoppy American to Belgian classics and oceans in between.

J. WAKEFIELD

120 NW 24th St. • Miami, FL 33127 • (786) 254-7779 • jwakefieldbrewing.com

Coming out with a 13% Russian Imperial stout called "Nothing" as your first commercial release takes some *cojones*. The Wakefield crew have proved they have mettle. Armed with the biggest crowdfunding round the craft beer world had seen yet ($110,000), Johnathan Wakefield's brewery sprang onto the beer scene in 2014—a year before their taproom was ready for the public—with a range of rainbow-bright, juicy "Florida weisse" beers that married tart Berliner weisse with tropical fruit juices of Florida. After long (but predictible) delays, as of early 2015, the taproom is open. Don't miss it in Miami.

DUNEDIN HOUSE OF BEER

927-A Broadway • Dunedin, FL 34698 • (727) 216-6318 • dunedinhob.com

Note to aspiring craft-beer bar owners: If you want to stay open, you need a community behind you, especially if your beer bar is found on a faceless stretch of asphalt in a sort of strip mall. The low-key, exposed-brick-walled Dunedin House of Beer is one of those bars, thriving with the support of locals and thanks to a network of the most interconnected beer travelers. The Dunedin's charitable clientele sponsors events and keeps the lines flowing and kegs turning for the right reasons.

REDLIGHT, REDLIGHT

745 Bennett Rd. • Orlando, FL 32803 • (407) 893-9832 • redlightredlightbeerparlour.com

The hometown of Disney World is also home to a world-class but ultra-down-to-earth beer bar with a supercurated beer list comprised of American micros and special European finds. Established in 2005, its location recalls the setting for a 1970s movie car chase, but inside the bar is cozy, with brewery-sign-dotted dark walls and a nicely tiled back bar. The tap row runs to twenty-three taps and two engines, plus another 200 or so in bottles at any given time, like Kulmbacher's roasty Mönchshof Schwarzbier, light but flavorful (4.9% ABV). They started brewing their own beer in 2014. What are you waiting for? Greenlight!

Postscript

←—————→

EVERY DAY I WRITE, OR DRINK A BEER, AND ESPECIALLY WHEN I'M DOING BOTH, I THINK of Michael Jackson. Not "that one," as he would say, but the Yorkshire journalist whose life and career was defined by a glorious world tour of beer. The towering hero of craft beer appreciation since the late 1970s, Jackson—author of sixteen seminal works including *The World Guide to Beer* (1977) and *The New World Guide to Beer* (1988), *The Great Beers of Belgium* (1991), and many others—took me under his wing starting in late 1996. With a seemingly bottomless reserve of graciousness, he helped me get started as a beer writer after I won a postgraduate fellowship that allowed me to delve into beer brewing techniques around the world for a year right out of college.

Those encounters and that year changed my life.

It was August 1996. I was twenty-two, and I had arrived in England just a few days before to start a wandering independent study on brewing for the Watson Foundation. After a needlessly nervous phone call to his office I traveled by train from Shawford, a village outside Winchester, to visit Jackson in his London home, in Hammersmith. We headed to his local, and then the Dove, a gloriously weathered old pub along the Thames, and drank for an entire evening. That day he became a mentor, writing to me (and once, to my amazement, about me, in a story about the Belgian beer Orval, a mutual minor obsession), and even promised me he would write the foreword to my first beer book. Alas, I failed to have this one ready for him in time.

I saw Michael infrequently after my year of research, not entirely by choice. Shortly after we'd met again in Portland, Oregon, at the 1998 American Homebrewers Association's National Conference, I moved to New Mexico for my first national magazine job, then decamped to New York just two days before 9/11 to pursue my luck as a writer. Though we spoke by telephone and corresponded by e-mail intermittently, Michael didn't make many appearances in Gotham, and what's more, I'd drifted away from the craft beer scene a bit in pursuit of New York–based travel writing work, which didn't call for my craft beer expertise nearly enough (yet). It would take five more years in the trenches for me to earn the right to call myself a full-time writer, and I'll never forget how he would always inquire, in the most honestly inquisitive and supportive manner imaginable, if I was getting there. "Keep writing," he wrote to me in a dedication in one of his books he'd given me as a gift. I did.

The last time I saw Michael was at D.B.A., the once-great New York beer bar, on a limpid spring night on March 23, 2007. He was in town for a special tasting at a hotel in Midtown, and the late D.B.A. owner Ray Deter and an assortment of other beer lovers who knew him well had arranged for a late-night session to taste rare Scandinavian ales. By candlelight, around 1 a.m., we watched as Jackson arrived. He was walking with companions including the lovely Carolyn Smagalski, beer importer Dan Shelton (who had called to invite me to join, for which I am eternally grateful), his wife, Tessa, and Monk's Café owner Tom Peters. I was shocked when I looked at my old mentor: he greeted me warmly, but his eyes were weary, his frame hunched. It was not the Michael I once knew. Dan Shelton pulled me aside and told me what was going on; it was then that I learned he had been severely weakened by a decade-long battle with Parkinson's, a closely held secret for years, but something Jackson had begun to discuss bravely.

This was devastating news for me—and as Deter opened up his back patio area for the gathering, I struggled to find words, to feel at ease. We piled in shoulder to shoulder at a picnic table as sam-

ples made the rounds, and soon Jackson was bantering like his old self. Though his eyes were glassy and his head swayed gently from side to side, he was in his element. I felt both profoundly sad and grateful all at once.

There we stayed into the early morning, candles flickering and oozing all over the tables, sampling the beers Dan Shelton had discovered during his journeys. As glasses and bottles crisscrossed the table for inspection, Jackson—ever the journalist—spoke of the Norse tradition of home brewing a beer for your own approaching death, so that your loved ones may send you off in proper style. There was no pathos in his tone, but I detected a glint in his eye as he broached the topic—that of death, and his own, by extension—as he looked around at the brood over his wire-frame glasses perched at the end of his nose. The words ached; I was a little bit afraid of his state. But I didn't need to be. He had been writing about beer for as long as I'd been alive, and though the eeriness of the moment hovered in the air like smoke—this part, we heard in echoing silence—he wasn't being maudlin; he was doing what he always loved to do the most: talk about beer, drink, and laugh among old friends.

It's a bitter irony that in his final years, like the beverage he loved, Jackson was often misunderstood. Many mistook the effects of his illness for excess. He joked that his next book was going to be about Parkinson's: "I'm Not Drunk," he thought of calling it.

It was the last time I ever saw him; Jackson died five months later, on August 30, 2007, in his home. Shelton called me to tell me the news while I was out in New Mexico visiting old friends and colleagues at *Outside* magazine. It was a teary phone call for us both: Dan was one of the lucky people who was able to spend a lot of time with "the Bard of Beer," and even filmed a set of extraordinary interviews with him in England. In September, as shock surrendered to sorrow, beer lovers, including at D.B.A., participated in organized tributes worldwide. It's an annual tradition for me on his birthday (March 27) to salute the man and what his efforts have inspired in me and in so many others. As a beer lover, writer, and friend, I will always owe him the world.

Acknowledgments

The gratitude I feel for all the people who helped me craft volume one of this book will never fade, especially for Jonathan Miles and John Rasmus, my literary agent Alia Habib of McCormick & Williams, first editor Jennifer Kasius, original designer Ryan Hayes, Garrett Oliver of Brooklyn Brewery, assistant friends Georgia Perry and Avery Houser, as well as many dear family and other assorted friends and supporters including beer industry role models Charlie Papazian and Sam Calagione. In publishing, I am grateful to a huge cast of supporters from Amelia Lester, Michael Agger, Daniel Fromson, and Burkhard Bilger to Joshua Wesson, Will Bostwick, Hampton Sides, Liesl Schillinger, Anne Zimmerman, Lynne Rosetto Kasper, Dave Miller, Ryan Krogh, Gabrielle Langholtz, Pauline Frommer, Jen Murphy, Mike Thelin and Carrie Welch of Feast Portland, Talia Baiocchi, and Margo True, all of whom have helped realize my dreams of releasing a successful first book. The release party at Hopworks Urban Brewery in Portland, Oregon was one for the ages, and I'm profoundly grateful to the many friends and strangers who helped organize dozens of signings, dinners, and other book-related gatherings over the past five years. I'm also deeply honored that the Society of American Travel Writers awarded the book the 2012 Lowell Thomas Award for Best Guidebook.

For their careful work on this expanded, revised edition, I heartily thank Jessica Fromm, Jennifer Kasius, Amanda Richmond, and the whole team at Running Press. Thank you to Susan Hom and Ruoxi Chen for their eagle-eyed reads, and to Dan Cantada for the new cover design. Georgia Perry again supported the project from afar with reams of ace fact-checking and research skills. And Lila Martin was, as always, my dearest source of balance, inspiration, and optimism from beginning to end.

I'm deeply grateful for the suggestions of many beer brewers, experts, and fans across the country on the new edition. It's surely an incomplete list, but I would like to recognize the support of Margo Knight Metzger, Campbell Levy, Justin Bresler, Andra and Kyle Zeppelin, Kate Lacroix, Debbie Rizzo, Brian Yaeger, Christopher Solomon, Michael Moser, Sarah Bart, Mark Hampton, Lee Jones, George Stevens, Hannah Wallace, Meredith Klinger, Justin Kennedy, Chris O'Leary, Joseph Alton, Erika Rietz, Matt Dinges, Tara Nurin, Joanne Jordan, Karen Wong, Lisa Allen of

Heater Allen Brewery, and Julie Wartell for their long lists of ideas. On Twitter and Facebook, many friends and anonymous users alike were supportive to queries. Thanks @JodieVero, @CodyHaskell, @DanielGNYC; thanks also to Reddit users DropBearHug, Rockheart_Ridgerunner, GenderChangers, IkariWarrior, JGrogr, ProudTyrant, DeFroach84, PatsPints, Broham13, and PatEvansMSU.

Thank you all! I could never have finished this book without your help.

Glossary

3.2 laws: Laws in certain states that only permit beer to be sold when it has an alcohol by weight of 3.2%, equivalent to 4% ABV. Famously applied in Utah, though laws are changing.

22 oz.: aka "bomber." A U.S. standard size for large bottles of beer sold individually.

750ml: aka "wine bottle size." The European standard size for a large bottle of beer, as opposed to 22 oz., which is also becoming more popular in U.S. craft brewing. The "750" is popular with Belgian and Belgian-style brews, and may be closed with a traditional crown cap, cork-and-cap, or cork-and-wire cage combination.

Abbey-style: Refers to malt-forward, typically fruitier beers made with traditional methods of brewing first used by the breweries of Belgian monks, including the Trappist monasteries. Something of a catch-all phrase. See also:Tripel.

Acidity: Level of acid in beer; proportional to the degree of sour/vinegar/lemony taste. A by-product of fermentation adds dimensions of flavor beyond sweet, bitter, and estery notes. See also: Esters.

Ale: Formerly, beer without hops; today, beer fermented with ale yeast at warmer temperatures than lagers (which are made with lager yeast), imparting fruitier and more aromatic notes.

Altbier: A style of robust German pale ale that is typically aged, or "conditioned," for longer than standard periods of time, resulting in a smooth brew.

American wild ale: Beer fermented with ambient, naturally-occurring yeast in the United States that is allowed to settle in the beer naturally and begins the fermention spontaneously rather than with the intentional addition of brewers' yeasts. See also: Lambic.

American Pale Ale (APA): Distinguishable by an elevated but still balanced presence of malt and hops, with fruity, floral, and citrus-like flavors.

Attenuation: The degree to which a beer's fermentable sugars have been consumed by yeast or yeasts. See also: Dryness.

Barley wine: Traditionally sweet, nutty, sherry or whiskey-ish beers named for their high alcohol content, which approaches that of wine; often aged in oak barrels.

Barrel-age/aging/aged: Beers aged in wood barrels, resulting in intentional flavors from the wood, of the alcohol formerly aged in the wood (i.e. red wine, Bourbon, Scotch, sherry, rum), or of microorganisms living in the wood.

Bbl (abbrev.): aka "Barrels;" a barrel of beer is 31 gallons and the standard size for a keg is a half-barrel.

Beer engine: A traditionally English device for pumping beer from a cask in a pub's cellar into the drinker's glass.

Belgian-style: A style of brewing that tends to produce beers that are spicier due to the use of certain yeast strains, more intensely flavored and higher in alcohol content than their American counterparts, and often bear the tannins and acids from wood barrels and wild yeasts.

Bière de Garde (France): Literally, "beer to store," which ranges in color from golden to light brown, characterized by a light to medium body, with a slight malt sweetness and slight hop character.

Bierstube (German): A large pub that specializes in beer. Found throughout Germany.

Bitter/Bitterness: The perception of a bitter flavor imparted to beer by hops or malt husks; determined by a sensation on the back of the tongue; measured in International Bitterness Units (IBUs).

BMC: Budweiser, Miller, Coors (casual phrase for major industrial breweries making light lagers on a mass scale).

Body: The heft of a beer, related to its grain content and dryness, or degree of attenuation.

Brettanomyces: A genus of yeast; called "Brett" for short and viewed as a contaminant by most brewers but sometimes used on purpose to create a sour or "barnyard" taste in beer, especially Belgian and Belgian-style beers. Its taste is also described as leathery, funky, and horse-blanket.

Brewhouse: A brewery; a place that houses the equipment used to make beer. Interchangeable with the core equipment itself, which is often clustered.

Brewpub: A pub that makes its own beer and sells it on site.

Cask: A barrel-shaped container for beer, usually made of metal.

Cask-conditioned: Beer that undergoes a secondary fermentation and maturation in the cask; results in light carbonation.

Cicerone: Like a sommelier for beer—a trained expert in selecting and serving beer. The levels are Certified Cicerone and Master Cicerone; both require certification.

Collaboration beers: Beers made when two or more breweries get together to produce one beer.

Craft brewery: A brewery producing six million barrels per year or less using more or less traditional methods of making beer from malted barley, primarily.

Cream ale: Offshoot from the American light lager style; ale that has corn or rice added to it to lighten the body.

Czech-style: Coppery-hued lager heavily hopped with earthy, spicy noble hops from Europe, especially Southeastern Germany and the Czech Republic.

Diacetyl: A natural by-product of fermentation that can give beer unpleasant, butterscotch-like or artificial butter flavors. A common flaw eliminated through careful brewing and sanitation.

Dry, Dryness: Degree to which fermentable sugars have been consumed, or "dried out" from the beer during fermentation and aging.

Dry-hopped: Beer with an addition of dry hops to fermenters and/or aging tanks to punctuate hop aroma without adding high levels of bitterness.

ESB: Extra Special/Strong Bitter; Originally a British style of bitter beers with more aggressive alcohol and hop character and ample malt body.

Esters/Estery: Fruity-smelling, harmless chemical compounds created as a by-product of high-temperature fermentations.

Extreme beer: Catch-all phrase for aggressively hopped ales fermented to a high alcohol percentage, usually around 7% but sometimes nearly double that (most beer hovers between 4% and 6% alcohol, while craft beers average 6%.) Sometimes interchangeable with "Imperial" and "Double." May contain herbs, spices, and fermentable starches other than barley or wheat, fruit, coffee, or other natural additions.

Farmhouse ale: Ale made in a farm setting; a tradition originating in Belgium and northern France and now made on a very small scale in the United States. See also: Saison

Fermenter: Tanks for fermenting beer; can be steel cylindro-conical vessels (CCVs), open stone vessels, or wooden vats.

Filter/Unfiltered: To remove harmless sediments from the brewing and fermentation process from beer; generally unfiltered beer is hazy with yeast cells or grain matter.

Flanders-style: Reddish, sour ales with winelike qualities brewed in Belgium and aged a year or longer in oak barrels, often with Lactobacillus yeast.

Gastropub: A bar or pub that also serves high-quality food.

Geuze (Belgian-style): A type of Belgian beer made from blends of young and old wild yeast beers (aged from three months to three years) that is then bottled with additions of yeast and a small amount of sugar for a second fermentation.

Growler: A half-gallon glass jug (64 oz.), often sold at breweries and brewpubs for beer to go.

Hallertau: The original German lager hop, named after an area in Bavaria that is the largest hop-planting area in the world.

Hefeweizen: Wheat beers that are bottled with the yeast in suspension, creating a cloudy, frothy, and refreshing effect.

Hop/Hops: A perennial vine that produces resinous flowers that impart bitterness and aromas to beer.

IIPA/Double IPA/Imperial IPA: Like an extra-strong IPA; robust and malty with a high hop content; originated in the western United States.

IPA: India Pale Ale; Has a strong bitter taste and a higher hop content than most ales.

Izakaya (Japanese): A Japanese bar that also serves food.

Kellerbier: Literally "cellar beer;" usually German-style lager, served directly from conditioning tanks with a bready, yeasty flavor at the peak of freshness.

Kettle: Meaning brew kettle, in which the brewer boils the ingredients of beer. Often made of stainless steel; occasionally copper-plated.

Kölsch, or Koelsch: A straw-gold, clear, light-bodied beer with a prominent hoppiness locally brewed in Cologne, Germany.

Lager: The beer that results from yeast working at colder fermentation temperatures than ales; typically results in breadier, crisper-tasting beer than ales.

Lambic (Belgian): A typically dry, sour beer created through spontaneous fermentation in a small number of rural breweries in and just outside of Brussels, aged in oak barrels up to three years.

Lupulin: The pollen-like, resinous powdery substance in hop flowers which impart bitterness and aroma to beer.

Macrobrewery: A large industrial brewery making beer on a massive, profit-driven scale.

Malt (ingredient): Barley which has been harvested, wetted, germinated, and dried (or kilned). "Malting" modifies the internal structure of barley to make it ready for brewing.

Malty (descriptor): Tasting like malt sugar, or maltose, which is present in malted barley and other grains that are prominent players in the fermentation of beer.

Märzen-style or Maerzen-style: A style of German lager beer characterized by a reddish brown color, medium to full body, a malty flavor and a clean, dry finish. Traditionally German "Oktoberfest" beer was made in the maerzen-style, but in recent years Oktoberfest beers have gotten more pale.

Mash: (Verb) To release malt sugars by soaking the grains in hot water. (Noun) The liquid that results is called wort, and that is brewed with hops in the brewing kettle.

Michael Jackson, writer: (March 27, 1942 – August 30, 2007). Yorkshire-born journalist whose 1977 book *The World Guide to Beer* and 16 later titles on beer and whiskey firmly established him as the world's foremost authority on both. Known for his gentlemanly demeanor, dry wit, and warmth, he was also the host of "The Beer Hunter," a two season beer and travel program shown on the U.K.'s Channel 4 and Discovery Channel. A massive image of his face hangs on a banner over the Great American Beer Festival, held in Denver each fall.

Microbrewery: A brewery that produces less than 15,000 barrels per year.

Munich-style: A dark lager with a distinctive taste of malt, produced in Munich since the tenth century.

Nanobrewery: A brewery operating with a system no larger than seven barrels—many have just one or two barrels.

Orval: The beer and company name of one of the most storied breweries in Belgium is in the Notre Dame d'Orval monastery in Villers-devant-Orval, near Florenville in the Belgian province of Luxembourg (not to be confused with the independent duchy of Luxembourg to the east). It is one of the world's six remaining Trappist abbey breweries, owned and occupied by cloistered Trappist monks. The Orval abbey is more than 850 years old.

Oud bruin: Also known as Flanders Brown, a sour tasting beer originating from the Flemish region of Belgium with long aging process that can take up to a year, including secondary fermentation and bottle aging. Often has some residual balancing sweetness.

Pasteurize: To heat beer to a certain degree in order to sterilize it, increasing shelf life.

pH (for brewing): The ideal number is 5.2, which facilitates perfect starch to sugar conversion during the brewing process and before fermentation.

Pils, Pilsner: A pale lager with a strong hoppiness; first brewed in the Bohemian town of Pilsen (Czech: Plzeň).

Porter: A dark-colored ale originated in London brewed with dark malts, possibly named for the street and river porters who popularized it.

Rathskeller (German): A beer hall or restaurant in a basement or underground.

Reinheitsgebot: Also known as the German Purity Law of 1516, which limits beer ingredients in Germany to water, hops, malt and yeast. Though no longer a binding law, it is voluntarily observed in many German breweries, especially in the southern state of Bavaria, and by many German-style breweries outside the country.

Russian Imperial Stout: A stout with high alcohol by volume and a high malt character; tastes like chocolate and burnt or roasted malt.

Saison: Means "season" in French; earthy, unfiltered, low-alcohol pale ales meant to refresh farm workers during the summer; also called "farmhouse ales" and originated in the French-speaking part of Belgium known as Wallonia. Generally 6–8% ABV.

Session beer: An easy-drinking, mild beer with an alcohol content typically less than 4%, intended to be consumed several to a sitting.

Smoky/Smokiness: A taste in beer with a smoke flavor created by using malted barley dried or smoked over wood such as alder, beech, or over peat.

Sour beer: Beers fermented with wild yeasts and bacteria, sometimes but not always utilizing wood. Styles include Flanders Red, Oud Bruin, Lambic (known as American wild ale in the US) with varying degrees of acidity and little or no hop character.

Spontaneous fermentation: Beers made with natural, ambient yeasts in the air ("wild" strains of yeast), rather than yeast being added by the brewer.

Steam beer: A beer made with lager yeasts at the warmer temperatures of ale fermentation; uniquely linked to the Anchor Steam brewery in California. Also called "California Common."
Stout: A dark beer made using roasted malt or barley, hops, water, and yeast; traditionally meant extra strong porter beer.

Tannins: In beer, organic compounds derived from grain husks, non-lupulin hop flower parts, and oak (as in oak barrels) which pucker and dry the mouth, balancing malty sweetness.

Trappist: Refers to beer made by Orval or one of the other six officially authorized Trappist abbeys: Rochefort, Westmalle, Westvleteren, Chimay, and Achel (Belgium); Schaapskooi lies just over the Dutch border at the Koningshoeven monastery. Monks take a vow of silence and live austerely, focused on the contemplative life and some agrarian pursuits such as farming, baking, and brewing.

Tripel: A lighter bodied Belgian-style or Belgian beer with a bright yellow color and a sweet finish; deceivingly alcoholic and good for sipping; named for the brewing process of this type of beer, in which brewers use two to three times the standard amount of malt.

Vienna-style: A lager named for the city in which it originated, brewed using a three-step decoction boiling process; subtle hop taste with residual sweetness.

Wild yeasts/wild ale: Beers fermented with yeast or bacteria strains including Brettanomyces, Lactobacillus, and Pediococcus, microorganisms considered taints in most beers and wine that can have appealing earthy and acidic flavors in beer when wrangled with care.

Yeast: A microorganism added into the raw ingredients of beer in order to facilitate the conversion of malt sugars into alcohol and CO_2.

Zwickelbier: See "Kellerbier".

Zymurgy: The art and science of brewing beer.

Index

MICHIGAN

Arcadia Brewing	Battle Creek	249
Ashley's Restaurant & Pub	Ann Arbor	249
Bell's Brewery Eccentric Café	Kalamazoo	248
Blackrocks Brewery	Marquette	249
Brewery Vivant	Grand Rapids	250
Founders Brewing Co.	Grand Rapids	246
Hopcat	Grand Rapids	247
Jolly Pumpkin Café & Brewery	Ann Arbor	245

MINNESOTA

The Happy Gnome	St. Paul	254
Indeed Brewing Company and Taproom	Minneapolis	256
The Muddy Pig	St. Paul	256
Surly Brewing	Minneapolis	254

MISSISSIPPI

Lazy Magnolia Brewing Co.	Kiln	390
The Keg & Barrel Brew Pub	Hattiesburg	391
Southern Prohibition Brewing Co.	Hattiesburg	392

MISSOURI

Boulevard Brewing Co.	Kansas City	225
Schlafly Bottleworks	St. Louis	226
Perennial Artisan Ales	St. Louis	227
The Side Project Cellar	Maplewood	227
International Tap House	St. Louis	227
Bridge Tap House & Wine Bar	St. Louis	228

MONTANA

Bayern Brewing	Missoula	189
Big Dipper Ice Cream	Missoula	191
Big Sky Brewing Co.	Missoula	188
Bitter Root Brewing Co.	Hamilton	187
Bozeman Brewing Co.	Bozeman	184
Carter's Brewing Co.	Billings	180
Flathead Lake Brewing Co.	Bigfork	196
Glacier Brewing Co.	Polson	192
The Great Northern Bar & Grill	Whitefish	194
The Great Northern Brewing Co. & Black Star Draught House	Whitefish	194
Kalispell Brewing Co.	Kalispell	197
Kettlehouse Myrtle St.	Missoula	190
Kettlehouse North Side	Missoula	190
Lolo Peak Brewing Co.	Lolo	196
Madison River Brewing Co.	Belgrade	183

NEW YORK CITY

Bar Great Harry	Brooklyn	304
Barcade	Brooklyn	309
The Blind Tiger Alehouse	New York	292
Bohemian Hall & Beer Garden	Astoria	306
Brooklyn Brewery	Brooklyn	297
The Brooklyn Inn	Brooklyn	301
The Diamond	Brooklyn	301
Eleven Madison Park	New York	294
Fette Sau	Brooklyn	300
The Ginger Man	New York	289
The Jeffrey	New York	308
Jimmy's No. 43	New York	291
La Birreria at Eataly NYC	New York	294
McSorley's Old Ale House	New York	288
Mission Dolores	Brooklyn	302
Other Half Brewing	Brooklyn	303
Pony Bar	New York	289
Proletariat	New York	308
Rattle N Hum	New York	296
Resto	New York	290
Spuyten Duyvil	Brooklyn	300
Sunny's	Brooklyn	305
Threes Brewing	Brooklyn	309
Top Hops	New York	308
Tørst/Luksus	Brooklyn	303
Vol Du Nuit	New York	295

NORTH CAROLINA

Barley's Taproom & Pizzeria	Asheville	376
The Bier Garden	Asheville	381
Bruisin' Ales	Asheville	378
Burial Beer Co.	Asheville	375
The Duck-Rabbit Craft Brewery	Farmville	382
Fonta Flora Brewery	Morganton	381
Foothills Brewing Co.	Winston-Salem	383
Fullsteam	Durham	380
Growlers Pourhouse	Charlotte	379
Haw River Farmhouse Ales	Saxapahaw	383
Highland Brewing	Asheville	373
Jack of the Wood Public House	Asheville	381
Mother Earth Brewing	Kinston	382
Noda Brewing	Charlotte	382
Pisgah Brewing Co.	Black Mountain	377
The Raleigh Times Bar	Raleigh	378
Sierra Nevada Brewing Co.	Mills River	383

Logsdon Barrel House & Taproom	Hood River	39
McMenamin's Edgefield	Troutdale	35
Ninkasi Brewing Co.	Eugene	33
Occidental Brewing Co.	Portland	48
Oregon Brewers Festival	Portland	17
Pelican Pub & Brewery	Pacific City	46
Pfriem Family Brewers	Hood River	36
Saraveza Bottle Shop & Pasty Tavern	Portland	25
Terminal Gravity Brewing Co.	Enterprise	32
Three Creeks Brewing Co.	Sisters	49
Upright Brewing Co.	Portland	20
The Victory Bar	Portland	48
Wolves & People Farmhouse Brewery	Newberg	28

PENNSYLVANIA

The 700 Club	Philadelphia	320
Alla Spina	Philadelphia	334
The Belgian Café	Philadelphia	321
Bridgid's	Philadelphia	328
Dock Street Brewing Co.	Philadelphia	328
Earth Bread & Brewery	Philadelphia	334
Eulogy	Philadelphia	320
The Foodery	Philadelphia	318
Grace Tavern	Philadelphia	319
The Grey Lodge Public House	Philadelphia	321
Jose Pistola's	Philadelphia	329
Khyber Pass	Philadelphia	318
Local 44	Philadelphia	323
McGillin's Olde Ale House	Philadelphia	327
Memphis Taproom	Philadelphia	322
Monks Café & Belgian Beer Emporium	Philadelphia	324
Nodding Head	Philadelphia	334
South Philadelphia Tap Room	Philadelphia	327
The Standard Tap	Philadelphia	317
Stoudt's Brewing Co.	Adamstown	333
Teresa's Next Door	Wayne	331
Tired Hands Brewing Company	Ardmore	330
Tria Café	Philadelphia	334
Tröegs	Harrisburg	335
Victory Brewing Co.	Downington	330
Yard's Brewing Co.	Philadelphia	329
Yuengling	Pottsville	332

SOUTH CAROLINA

The Community Tap	Greenville	384
Edmund's Oast	Charleston	386

Big Time Brewery & Alehouse	Seattle	52
Black Raven Brewing Co.	Redmond	63
Boundary Bay Brewing & Bistro	Bellingham	65
Brouwer's Café	Seattle	53
The Burgundian	Seattle	64
Chuckanut Brewery & Kitchen	Bellingham	60
Collins Pub	Seattle	53
Diamond Knot	Mukilteo	61
Elysian Brewing Co.	Seattle	54
Everybody's Brewing	White Salmon	66
Fremont Brewing	Seattle	64
Hale's Ales	Seattle	55
Holy Mountain	Seattle	51
Latona Pub	Seattle	56
The Masonry	Seattle	63
Naked City Brewery & Taphouse	Seattle	56
The North Fork Brewery, Pizzeria, Beer Shrine & Wedding Chapel	Deming	66
Parkway Tavern	Tacoma	59
The Pike Pub & Brewery	Seattle	57
The Pine Box	Seattle	63
Red Hook Brewery & Forecasters Public House	Woodinville	58
Reuben's Brews	Seattle	64
Schooner Zodiac	Bellingham	61
Stoup Brewing	Seattle	65
The Stumbling Monk	Seattle	65
Über Tavern	Seattle	65
Walking Man Brewing Co.	Stevenson	62

WASHINGTON, D.C.

Birch & Barley/ChurchKey	Washington, D.C.	339
Blue Jacket Brewery	Washington, D.C.	342
Brasserie Beck	Washington, D.C.	341
DC Brau Brewing	Washington, D.C.	344
The Meridian Pint	Washington, D.C.	340
Pizzeria Paradiso	Washington, D.C.	342
Right Proper	Washington, D.C.	343
The Sovereign	Washington, D.C.	344

WISCONSIN

Ale Asylum	Madison	259
New Glarus Brewing Co.	New Glarus	257
The Old Fashioned	Madison	258
Tyranena Brewing Co.	Lake Mills	259

WYOMING

Snake River Brewing Co.	Jackson	176
Q Roadhouse and Roadhouse Brewing Company	Jackson	177